高等院校"十二五"规划精品教材

International Trade Practices

国际贸易实务

（英文版·第二版）

主　编　邢学杰
副主编　刘韩云 周记顺

西南财经大学出版社
Southwestern University of Finance & Economics Press
中国·成都

图书在版编目(CIP)数据

国际贸易实务:英文/邢学杰主编.—2版.—成都:西南财经大学出版社,2016.9

ISBN 978-7-5504-2334-3

Ⅰ.①国… Ⅱ.①邢… Ⅲ.①国际贸易—贸易实务—高等学校—教材—英文 Ⅳ.①F740.4

中国版本图书馆CIP数据核字(2016)第042500号

国际贸易实务(英文版·第二版)

GUOJI MAOYI SHIWU

主　编:邢学杰
副主编:刘韩云　周记顺

责任编辑:张明星
助理编辑:周晓琬
封面设计:杨红鹰　张姗姗
责任印制:封俊川

出版发行	西南财经大学出版社(四川省成都市光华村街55号)
网　　址	http://www.bookcj.com
电子邮件	bookcj@foxmail.com
邮政编码	610074
电　　话	028-87353785　87352368
照　　排	四川胜翔数码印务设计有限公司
印　　刷	四川森林印务有限责任公司
成品尺寸	185mm×260mm
印　　张	20.5
字　　数	445千字
版　　次	2016年9月第2版
印　　次	2016年9月第1次印刷
书　　号	ISBN 978-7-5504-2334-3
定　　价	38.00元

第二版前言

本书是在2012年出版的《国际贸易实务》的基础上，根据国家大力发展现代职业教育，提升人才培养质量，培养高等应用型人才的要求，修改并出版的《国际贸易实务》第二版。本书根据有关国际贸易的最新法规和国际惯例，优化了课程内容，以国际贸易交易的环节为主线，系统介绍了国际贸易各环节的基本知识，并结合国际贸易过程中的各个环节展开了详细阐述。主要内容包括：国际贸易理论与政策的基本知识；国际商务谈判的步骤；国际货物买卖合同的基本条款、国际贸易惯例和国际贸易术语；国际贸易商品条款；出口价格；国际货物运输；国际货物运输保险；国际支付；出口单证及不可抗力、检验和索赔等，内容涵盖了国际贸易的所有交易环节。为适应国际贸易术语的新变化，本书在附录中介绍了最新修订的《2010年国际贸易术语解释通则》。

全书用英文编写，分十章，环环相扣，通俗易懂。修订内容增加了每章的关键词及贸易流程的票据。本书不仅能让使用者学习国际贸易的相关理论知识，而且更重要的是能让使用者在学习国际贸易实务的过程中熟练掌握国际贸易实务的实用技能。

全书结构安排合理，语言通俗易懂，各章配有修订后的习题，适合于国际贸易专业及商务英语专业的本科学生和外贸专业人员使用。

本书共分十章，由邢学杰编写大纲。第一章、第二章、第三章、第四章、第八章、附录、索引由邢学杰编写；第五章、第六章、第十章由刘韩云编写；第七章、第九章由周记顺编写。全书由邢学杰和刘韩云负责统稿和定稿。

本书在编写和修订过程中参考了大量国内外的论著和文献资料，以及国际贸易研究领域的专家、学者前辈们的最新成果，不胜感激，在此一并致谢。

由于编者水平有限，书中难免出现疏漏和错误，敬请国内外专家、学者、同行和广大读者批评指正，以便再版时予以修订，使其不断完善。

编者

2016年4月

目 录

Chapter 1 Introduction

Learning Objectives

1. To master the definition of international trade and other terms concerned
2. To understand reasons for international trade
3. To understand the instruments of trade policy
4. To understand the classification of international trade

Key Words

International trade; Theory of absolute advantage; Comparative advantage theory; New trade theory; Transit trade; Indirect trade; Trade barrier

International trade has a long history. Dated back as far as the Middle Ages, merchants shipped canoes overseas, and sold the goods directly to foreign buyers. With the development of transportation and communication technologies developed especially during the industrial revolution, international trade grew rapidly, which in turn stimulated an upsurge of insurance industry and banking operations oriented toward international payments and settlement. Recently, thanks to the unprecedented development of techniques and services in all trade - related fields as well as the great improvement in trade - related laws, regulations and conventions, international trade is growing even faster and involving even more countries. As one of the most important economic activities in the world today, international trade plays a more and more important role in the development of a nation's economy and in the acceleration of globalization worldwide.

1.1 Instruction of International Trade

1.1.1 International Trade

International trade is the exchange of capital, goods, and services across international borders or territories. In most countries, such trade represents a significant share of gross domestic product (GDP). While international trade has been present throughout much of history (see Silk Road, Amber Road), its economic, social, and political importance has been on the rise in recent centuries.

Industrialization, advanced transportation, globalization, multinational corporations, and outsourcing are all having a major impact on the international trade system. Increasing international trade is crucial to the continuance of globalization. Without international trade, nations would be limited to the goods and services produced within their own borders.

Instead of importing a factor of production, a country can import goods that make intensive use of that factor of production and thus embody it. An example is the import of labor-intensive goods by the United States from China. Instead of importing Chinese labor, the United States imports goods that were produced with Chinese labor. One report in 2010 suggested that international trade was increased when a country hosted a network of immigrants, but the trade effect was weakened when the immigrants became assimilated into their new country.

International trade is also a branch of economics, which, together with international finance, forms the larger branch of international economics.

1.1.2 Characteristic of International Trade

The fundamental characteristic that makes international trade different from domestic trade is that international trade involves activities across national boundaries. Special problems may arise in international trade that are not normally experienced when trading at home. In particular:

(1) Deals might have to be transacted in foreign languages and under foreign laws, customs (cultural shocks) and regulations.

(2) Information on foreign countries needed by a particular firm may be difficult to obtain.

(3) Foreign currency transaction will be necessary e. g. USD, GBP, EURO, JPY.

Exchange rate variations can be very wide and create many problems for international trade.

(4) Risk level might be higher in foreign markets. The risks include political risks (of the imposition of restrictions on imports etc); commercial risks (market failure, products not appealing to foreign customers, etc); financial risks (of adverse movement in exchange rates, high rates of inflation reducing the real value of a company's working capital, and so on); and transportation risks.

(5) International managers need a broader range of management skills than do managers who are only concerned with domestic problems.

(6) Large amount of important work might have to be left to intermediaries, consultants and advisers.

(7) It is more difficult to observe and monitor trends and activities (including competitor's activities in foreign countries).

1.1.3 Risk in International Trade

Companies doing business across international borders face many of the same risks as would normally be evident in strictly domestic transactions. For example,

(1) Buyer insolvency (purchaser cannot pay);

(2) Non-acceptance (buyer rejects goods as different from the agreed upon specifications);

(3) Credit risk (allowing the buyer to take possession of goods prior to payment);

(4) Regulatory risk (e. g. a change in rules that prevents the transaction);

(5) Intervention (governmental action to prevent a transaction being completed);

(6) Political risk (change in leadership interfering with transactions or prices);

(7) War, piracy and civil unrest or turmoil;

(8) Natural catastrophes, freak weather and other uncontrollable and unpredictable events.

In addition, international trade also faces the risk of unfavorable exchange rate movements and the potential benefit of favorable movements.

1.1.4 Domestic Trade

Domestic trade is the exchange of domestic goods within the boundaries of a country. This may be sub-divided into two categories, wholesale and retail. wholesale trade is concerned with buying goods from manufacturers or dealers in large quantities and selling them in smaller quantities to others who may retailers or even consumers. Wholesale trade is undertaken by wholesale merchants or wholesale commission agents. Retail trade is concerned with the sale of goods in small quantities to consumers. This type of trade is taken care of by retailers. In actual practice, however, manufacturers and wholesalers may also undertake retail distribution of goods to bypass the intermediary retailer, by which they earn higher profits.

The importance of domestic trade in a country is that it facilitates exchange of goods within the country. By doing this it also makes sure that factors of production reach to the right places so that the economy of the country can grow. By allowing all different types of goods and services to reach to all parts of the country it improves the standard of living of the residents of the country as well as the employment rate of the country. And it helps the growth of an industry by ensuring the availability of raw materials. It even facilitates foreign trade. Traders from outside the country will have to come in contact with internal traders, because it is not easy to come directly into another country and get the required products.

Wholesalers play a major role in working of domestic trade. One could even say that it is the backbone of the domestic market. A wholesaler is one that is directly in contact with the manufacturers but in indirect contact with the consumers. A wholesaler generally deals with one type of industry. e. g. machinery, textile, stationery. A wholesaler is not only into selling of products as its also involved in packaging, advertising, grading, and market research. They have their own go downs which saves the manufacturers from bothering about storage. They normally make cash payments from retailers and sometimes consumers themselves and give advance payments which benefits the manufacturers. They sell in smaller quantities to retailers, which refrains the retailers from requiring storage space. They do allow credit facilities to retailers at times.

A retailer is normally the final seller of a product. It makes its purchases made from wholesalers and sales are made to the customers directly. Retailers do not have particularly have to be from one industry i. e. they can trade in a variety of products at the same time. It generally has purchases made by credit and sales made in cash. Sales as compared to wholesalers are made in small quantities.

1.2 Reasons for International Trade

1.2.1 The Origin of International Trade

In today's complex economic world, neither individuals nor nations are self-sufficient. Nations have utilized different economic resources; people have developed different skills. This is the foundation of international trade and economic activities.

1.2.2 Resources Reasons

International trade take place for many reasons. Basic reason of it is the uneven distribution of resources around the world.

① Natural resources. The distribution of natural resources around the world is somewhat haphazard, which includes land resources, water resources, forest resources, mineral resources, biological resources and energy (oil, wind, power).

② Favorable climate conditions and terrain. This is the main reason of agricultural trade. e. g. Peru and Zair's copper; South Africa's diamonds; the Middle East's petroleum; the US Great Plains' wheat; Brazil and Colombia's coffee.

③ Skilled workers. US, Japan, western European country have rich skilled workers.

④ Favorable geographic location and transportation costs. For example, Sino-Japan, US and Canada, EU trade relationship is to some degree determined by geographic proximity and low transport cost.

⑤Capital Resources. Developing countries need to modernize their industry and economy with advanced machinery, equipment and plant. However, they are lack of capital.

1.2.3 Economic Reasons

① Absolute advantage—by Adam Smith in the *Wealth of Nations An Inquiry into the Nature and Causes of the Wealth of Nations*. In the case of Zambia, the country has an absolute advantage over many countries in the production of copper. This occurs because of the existence of reserves of copper ore or bauxite. We can see that in terms of the production of goods, there are obvious gains from specialisation and trade, if Zambia produces copper and exports it to those countries that specialise in the production of other goods or services.

② Comparative advantage—by David Ricardo in *Principles of Political Economy* (1871). For example, the United States imports lots of oil from countries in other continents. Resources do not have to be material goods, but can also be labor related as well. Lots of companies take their factories overseas because labor tends to be much cheaper over there. Because of this, they are able to produce their products for a much lower cost, increasing their profitability. This helps both the company producing the products as it lowers their cost, but also helps the people doing the labor, as it provides a place of employment for them.

③ Strong domestic demand. For example, after the financial turmoil in 2008, the global economy has begun to recover, especially for the China market which recorded continual booming trade figures. According to the National Bureau of Statistics, in Jan-Aug 2010, the total import-export value of textile machinery was USD 3.726 billion, showing year-on-year rise of 59.84% while the import value was USD 2.642 billion, witnessing a year-on-year rise of 63.13% and with a growth rate of 108.08%. The huge increase in growth rate proves that China has become one of the prominent markets for foreign enterprises.

④ Preference reasons, innovation of style. For example, Unites States is the No. 1 car-producer, it still import large quantities of autos from Germany, Japan and Sweden, because of market needs.

1.2.4 Political Reasons

Political objectives are another factor in promoting trade between nations. One nation might trade with another to support a government which upholds the same political doctrine. Or it might do so for the purpose of the supports in political affairs.

Countries may wish to get closer bonds culturally and politically and this can be done through trade. By the way of foreign trade, countries can defend their national interests and its social economy system, and build an international and regional economic; countries can increase the strength of international and economic struggles, and improve the country's political and diplomatic relations as well as the international economic environment, and create good external conditions for its economic development.

1.2.5 Other Reasons

Other reasons mainly refer to invisible trade such as transportation, insurance and tourism. In addition to visible trade, which involves of the importing and exporting of tangible goods, there is also invisible trade, which involves the exchange services between nations. For instance, Brazilian coffee is often transported by ocean vessels because these steamships are the cheapest method of transportation. Nations such as Greece and Norway have large maritime fleets and provide transportation service. When an exporter arranges for this kind of transportation, he rents space in the cargo compartment of a ship for one voyage.

The prudent exporter buys insurance for his cargo's voyage. While at sea, every shipment has to run the risk of a long list of dangers: fire, storm, collision, theft, leakage, explosion, etc. To prevent these risks, the marine cargo insurance is provided to protect the exporter or importer from the financial loss. Thus, insurance is another service in which some nations specialize. Britain, because of the development of Lloyd's of London, is a leading exporter of this service, earning fees for insuring other nations' foreign trade.

For example, China's Tourism services play a decisive role in the trade in service. In recent years, along with the China's opening to the outside world, the growing tourist industry has become important source of the surplus in the China's international trade. In view of the import and export of this sector, From 2002 to 2006, China's Tourism services, was in the surplus in international trade. the trade balance of the 5 years were 4. 987 billion US dollars, 2. 219 billion US dollars, 6. 59 billion US dollars, 7. 537 billion US dollars and 9. 627 billion US dollars, respectively. And from 2003 to 2006, the annual growth rates were -55. 51%, 197. 00%, 14. 37%, 27. 73%, respectively; but from 2008 to 2011, China's Tourism services, was in the deficit in international trade.

1. 3 Theory of International Trade

International trade volume has been expanding with the industrialization of the western countries.

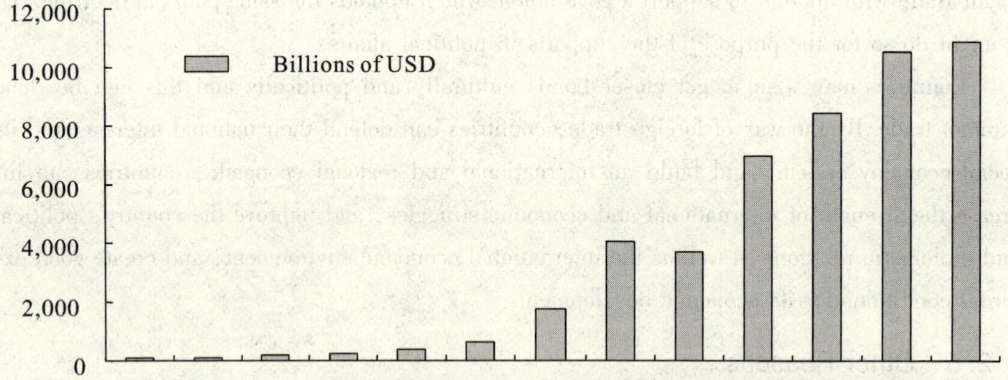

Figure 1 - 1 the development of world trade since the end of WW Ⅱ

The trade volume increased over 100 times since 1947. But why do countries trade with each other? Briefly, countries trade for two reasons. First, counties trade because they are different from each other. Nations, like individuals, can benefit from their differences by reaching an arrangement in which each does the things it does relatively well. Second, countries trade to achieve economies of scale in production. That is, if each country produces only a limited Range of goods, it can produce each of these goods at a larger scale and hence more efficiently than if it tried to produce everything. In this light, the theory of trade can be divided into two groups: traditional trade theory and new trade theory.

(1) Traditional trade theory

Assumptions: constant returns to scale/perfect competition

The theory of absolute advantage　　2 ×2 ×1

This theory was developed by Adam Smith. He observed that when one nation is more efficient than (or has absolute advantage over) another in the production of one commodity but is less efficient than (or has an absolute disadvantage with respect to) the other nation in producing a second commodity, then both nations can gain by each specializing in the production of the commodity of its absolute advantage and exchanging part of its output with the other nation for the commodity of its absolute disadvantage.

Absolute Advantage

	US	UK
Wheat (bushels/man-hour)	6	1
Cloth (yards/man-hour)	4	5

The law of Comparative Advantage: David Ricardo 2 ×2 ×1

According to the law of comparative advantage, even if one nation is less efficient than (has an absolute disadvantage with respect to) the other Nation in the production of both commodities, there is still a basis for mutually beneficial trade. The first nation should specialize in the production and export. The commodity in which is absolute disadvantage is smaller (this is the commodity of its comparative advantage) and import the commodity in which its absolute disadvantage is greater (this is the commodity of its comparative disadvantage).

Comparative Advantage

	US	UK
Wheat (bushels/man-hour)	6	1
Cloth (yards/man-hour)	4	2

Heckscher-Ohlin theory (Factor—proportions theory), developed by two Swedish economists, Eli Hecksher and Bertil Ohlin (Ohlin received the Nobel Prize in economics in 1977).

If labor were the only factor of production, comparative advantage could arise only because of international differences in labor productivity. In the real world, however, while trade is partly explained by differences in labor productivity, it also reflects differences in countries' resources. Canada exports forest products to the US not because its lumberjacks are more productive relative to their US counterparts, but because sparsely populated Canada has more forested land per capita than the US. A realistic view of trade must allow for the importance not just of labor, but of other factors of production such as land, capital, and mineral resources.

Countries tend to export goods that are intensive in the factors with which they are abundantly supplied.

(2) New trade theory

Assumptions: increasing returns to scale, imperfect competition

Increasing returns to scale refers to the production situation where output grows proportionately more than the increase in inputs or factors of production. Many industries are characterized by increasing returns to scale, or economies of scale. Because of economies of scale, neither country is able to produce the full range of manufactured products by itself; thus, although both countries may produce some manufactures, they will be producing different things.

In a world without economies of scale, there would be a simple exchange of manufactures for food.

If manufactures is a monopolistically competitive industry, Home and Foreign Will produce differentiated products. As a result, even if Home is a net export of manufactured goods, it will import as well as export manufactures, giving rise to intra-industry trade.

Intra-industry trade (manufactures for manufactures) does not reflect comparative advantage. It is economies of scale that keep each country from producing the full range of products for itself. The relative importance of inter-industry and intra-industry Trade depends on how similar countries are. If Home and Foreign are similar in their Capital—labor ratios, then there will be little inter-industry trade, and intra-industry trade, based on economies of scale, will be dominant. On the other hand if the capital—labor ratios are different, so that, for example, Foreign specializes completely in food production, there will be no intra-industry trade based on economies of scale. All trade will be based on comparative advantage.

1.4 The Instruments of Trade Policy

1.4.1 Tariff

A tariff may be either tax onimports or exports (trade tariff), or a list or schedule of prices for such things as rail service, bus routes, and electrical usage (electrical tariff, etc.).

Tariffs have played different roles in trade policy and the nation's economic history. Tariffs (often called customs) were by far the largest source of federal revenue from the 1790s to the eve of World War I, until they were surpassed by income taxes. Tariffs are import tax rates and the collected income is called customs or custom duties or Ad valorem taxes. A protective Tariff is often used by governments to attempt to control trade between nations to protect and encourage their noncompetitive or undeveloped local industries, businesses, unions etc. giving them time to become competitive. In addition it was thought under the theory of mercantilism generally believed by many countries in this era that exclusive trade with the colonies should be nearly all on ships of the parent country and all advanced industries etc. should be restricted to the mother country. Raw materials should be exported to the parent country and finished goods exported to the colonies.

The reasons for an industry or business being noncompetitive are basically four: Their average wages may be higher than is typical in the competitor's country. They do not have the innovations or inventions that their competitors have. They do not have the skill sets or organization their competitors have. They lack raw materials needed to make some product.

① A specific tariff is an import duty that assigns a fixed monetary (dollar) tax per physical unit of the goods imported. Thus, a specific duty might be $ 25 per M/T imported or 2 cents per pound. The total import tax bill is levied in accordance with the number of units coming into the importing country and not according to the price or value of the imports. Tax authorities can collect specific tariffs with ease because they need to know only the physical quantity of imports coming into the country, not their monetary value. The specific tariff has a fundamental disadvantage as an instrument of protection for domestic producers because its protective value varies inversely with the price of the import.

② The ad valorem tariff makes it possible for domestic producers to overcome the loss of protective value that the specific tariff was subject to during inflation. The ad valorem tariff is levied as a constant percentage of the monetary value of 1unit of the imported good.

③ Preferential duties are tariff rates applied to an import according to its geographical source; a country that is given preferential treatment pays a lower tariff.

④ Ad valorem tariffs are taxes that are levied as a fraction of the value of the imported goods .

⑤ Compound Tariff: specific tariff, ad valorem tariff (but only one is the main part, the other is a plus).

⑥ Alternative Tariff: select the higher one.

1.4.2 Other Instruments of Trade Policy

① Export Subsidies: a payment to a firm or individual that ships a good abroad. Like tariff, an export subsidy can be either specific (a fixed sum per unit) or ad valorem (a proportion of the value exported).

② Import Quota: a direct restriction on the quantity of some good that may be imported. The restriction is usually enforced by issuing to some group or individuals or firms. An import quota always raises the domestic price of the imported good. The difference between a quota and a tariff is that with a quota the government receives no revenue. When a quota instead of a tariff is used to restrict imports, the sum of money that would appear as government revenue with a tariff is collected by whomever receives the import license. License holders are able to buy imports and resell them at a higher price in the domestic market. The profits received by the holders of import license are also known as quota rents.

③ Voluntary Export Restrains (VER). VER are generally imposed at the request of the importer and are agreed by the exporter to forestall other trade restrictions.

④ Local Content Requirements is a regulation that requires that some specific fraction of a final good be produced domestically. From the point of view of the domestic producers of parts, a local content regulation provides protection in the same way an import quota does. From the point of view of the firms that must buy locally, however, the effects are somewhat different. Local content does not place a strict limit on imports. It allows firms to import more, provided that they also buy more domestically.

⑤ Export credit subsidies. This is like an export subsidy except that it takes the form of a subsidized loan to the buyer. The US, like the most countries, has a government institution, the Export-Import Bank, that is devoted to providing subsidized loans to aid exports.

⑥ National procurement. Purchases by the government or strongly regulated firms can be directed toward domestically produced goods when these goods are more expensive than imports.

⑦ Red-tape barriers. Sometimes a government wants to restrict imports without doing so formally. e. g. in 1982 French government ordered that all Japanese videocassette recorders must pass through the tiny customs house at a small town—effectively limiting the actual imports to a handful.

1.5 Classification of International Trade

While learning the differences between international trade and domestic trade may get traders better prepared for a future trade, knowing which type of trade they are entering into will help them shape the particular steps they need to follow in order to fulfill a trade activity. There are various forms of international trade and they can be classified into various categories according to a number of different criteria.

1.5.1 Export Trade, Import Trade and Transit Trade

From the direction of cargo flow, international trade can be classified into export trade, import trade and transit trade.

Export trade means to transport the goods which are produced and processed in domestic market to international market for sale. On the other hand import trade is made in the reverse direction; it refers to the transaction to transport the goods from foreign countries to domestic markets for sale or use.

If goods are transported from the producing country to the consuming country via a third country's border, this is known as transit trade. Transit trade can be further divided into direct transit trade and indirect transit trade. Direct transit trade means the goods are not placed in the bonded warehouse of the third country, but further transported toward outside along the domestic transportation line under supervision of the customs of the third country. In this sense, the third country earns its profit mainly by imposing import and export duties on the goods when they enter into or leave the boundary of the third country.

In contrast, indirect transit trade refers to the fact that goods are first placed in the bonded warehouse of the third country and then transported further to the importing country without any additional processing. Under this situation, the third country is able to earn the warehouse charges besides the above mentioned customs duties. However, under neither case shall the third country obtain profits from goods processing or assembling.

1.5.2 Direct Trade, Indirect Trade and Entrepot Trade

From the number of participants involved, international trade can be classified into direct trade, indirect trade and entrepot trade.

Direct trade means that goods are transported directly from the production country to the consuming country. In this case, only two parties are involved in the transaction, namely the exporter and the importer.

Indirect trade, or trade through intermediate countries, on the other hand occurs when goods pass through an intermediate country other than the producing or consuming country, remaining in that country for some length of time before shipment to the destination. Three parties are involved in indirect trade: the exporter, the importer and the intermediate party.

Entrepot trade refers to the transaction which involves importing goods from overseas for further processing or assembling and then re-exporting the goods abroad. Entrepot trade involves only one party, who is the importer, the processor and at the same time also the exporter.

1.5.3 Visible Goods Trade and Invisible Goods Trade

According to the form of the goods, international trade can be classified into visible goods trade and invisible goods trade.

Visible goods trade, also known as tangible goods trade, refers to the exchange of physically tangible goods such as cars, wines, shoes between countries, involving the export, import, and re-export of goods at various stages of production. It is distinguished from Invisible goods trade, also known as intangible goods trade, which involves the export and import of intangible items (those that are not visible) such as services and technology (e. g. shipping and education).

As most of the trade in the world today refers to the exchange of visible goods rather than invisible goods and many rules, regulations and conventions concerning trade in the world such as Incoterms, United Nations Convention on Contracts for International Sale of Goods (CISG), Uniform Customs and Practice for Documentary Credits (UCP), etc. are all made to deal with visible goods trade, the focus of this book therefore is on trade where only visible goods are concerned.

1.5.4 Barter Trade and Free-liquidation Trade

According to the settlement instrument involved, international trade can be classified into barter trade and free-liquidation trade.

Barter trade means the direct exchange of goods or services without an intervening medium of exchange or money—either according to established rates of exchange or by bargaining. It is considered the oldest form of trade.

Free-liquidation trade refers to the exchange of goods or services with an intervening medium of exchange or money according to rates of exchange. Cash trade is one form of free-liquidation trade.

In addition to the above mentioned forms of international trade, there are also some other types of international trade that are classified under other norms or criteria. For example, according to the mode of transportation, international trade can be classified into Trade by Roadway, Trade by Seaway, Trade by Airway and Trade by Mail Order.

1.6 Summary

International trade is the process of fair and deliberate exchange of goods or services between two or more countries, involving the use of two or more currencies. It concerns trade operations of both import and export and includes the purchase and sale of both visible and invisible goods. Nations engage in international trade for many reasons, including the uneven distribution of natural resources and human resources, the different development of technological skills and productivity, the economic state and potential of certain countries, the political needs to be met, the variety in the taste of the consumers around the world to be satisfied, etc. The means of classification used in international trade vary greatly. Based on different classification method, international trade can be generally classified into export trade, import trade and transit trade; direct trade, indirect trade and entrepot trade; visible trade and invisible trade; barter trade and free-liquidation trade; etc.

Exercises

Ⅰ. short questions.

1. What is international trade?
2. Explain the differences between international trade and domestic trade.
3. Why do nations conduct trade with one another?

4. What are the major benefits that result through international trading?
5. What are the instruments of trade policy?
6. How many forms are adopted in the process of negotiation?

Chapter 2 Business Communication

Learning Objectives

1. To master the four links of negotiation
2. To understand the main contents of contract
3. To understand export and import procedure

Key Words

Offer; Enquiry; Counter-offer; Acceptance; Cancel; Contract; Sales confirmation

2.1 Business Negotiation

2.1.1 Preparation of a Transaction

Suppose you want to start your business by selling your color TV sets to the world market. You may wonder which market is profitable to enter into and who is a potential partner in that particular market. Even if you have already found the right market and the potential partner, you will still have to evaluate the target market and make credit enquires of the potential partner. So there are a lot of steps to take before you can start to do business.

(1) Selecting the right market

To select the right market, one needs to do some market research. Market research is vital to win the trade game. Even if you have some experience in international trade, it's unwise for you to jump into an un-researched market. In fact, it's not unusual to spend several weeks learning about the product, market and its profit potential before getting serious. Then what do you need to know to evaluate the target market?

The evaluation of the target market is the first step in implementing a successful trade plan. Factors related to the country, its cultural background and economic situation, infrastructure, political climate, current import and export statistics, information on trade barriers and restrictions may well worth investigating before deciding to enter the target market.

The above information can be obtained from both domestic sources and overseas sources. Domestic organizations in China such as MOFCOM (Ministry of Commerce) of the People's Republic of China and its provincial committees provide you accesses to the information needed.

Foreign organizations such as Chinese Embassy, local banks, agents, etc. are also available to you. You can also get the information from local newspaper or journal articles both in the domestic country or foreign countries.

(2) Finding the potential partners

After finding the right market, the next step involved is to find the potential partners. There are various channels through which one can make contacts with the potential foreign partners: radefairs, directsales, directmail, manufacturer's representatives, wholesalers, distributors, personal contacts, etc.

There are also other sources available for international traders to find the potential business partners, for example, the nearest consulate office, ICC (International Chamber of Commerce), consulting firm; local chamber of commerce, foreign exchange banks, trade directors and publications such as *Economist*, *Financial Times*, *Wall Street Journal*, etc.

(3) Studying creditability of the partners

Your potential partners might speak too high of themselves. Don't be baffled by foreign business partners. In order to ensure your rights and benefits, you need to know the following information about your potential partners: credit reference from local bank or correspondent bank; business range and annual sales volume; sales literature and pricelist; major customers; business culture.

The relevant information can be obtained by contacting the references provided by the partner or by employing a consulting firm to investigate the market. A financial study is essential and helps you minimize any future loss arising from financial problems with the partner.

(4) Applying for export or import license

When the right customer has been determined, you may think it's time for you to start a business negotiation with him. However, it's still bit early. You have to make sure whether the products you intend to sell are within some certain export controls. If so, you have to deal with them before negotiation.

A lot of areas and countries around the world exercise export controls over certain merchandise. Even in economic free zones such as Hong Kong, export control is not viewed as unusual. Therefore, in some business, the exporter may be required to apply for an exporting license or a quota according to the regulations. It is the exporter's duty to obtain the exporting license or the quota before the negotiation of trade terms and conditions of the transaction. If the exporter is unable to obtain export license from the government, he needs to negotiate business under proper trade terms, for example, the price term under EXW in Incoterms 2010.

This is also applicable to importers. Normally, countries have more import controls than export controls on commodities in international trade. An importer also must make sure whether a license is needed and can be obtained before he starts the transaction with an exporter. If the importer is unable to obtain import license from the government, he is advised to arrange a contract under trade terms such as DDP in Incoterms 2010.

2.1.2 Business Negotiation

International business negotiation is an important part of conducting a foreign trade. A negotiation is a process of communication between parties to manage conflicts in order for them to come to an agreement, solve a problem or make arrangements. It is the dealing between supplier and customer in order to reach agreement on the price, quantity, payment and other terms and conditions of a sale. Obviously, the conclusion of sales contract results from the business negotiation to the satisfaction of both sides.

To reach to an agreement of the various terms mentioned above international business negotiation, generally, needs going through five links: enquiry, offer, counter-offer, acceptance and conclusion of a contract. Of course, it is not necessary to have all five links taken for every transaction, sometimes, only offer and acceptance will do.

2.1.2.1 Enquiry

An enquiry is a request for business information, such as price lists, catalogue, samples, and details about the goods or trade terms. It can be made by either the importer or the exporter. On receiving the enquiry, it is a regular practice that the exporter should reply to it without delay. The seller and the buyer both can make an Enquiry. Usually, the Enquiry made by the buyer is also called bid, and the Enquiry made by the seller is also called selling Enquiry. Enquiry will not bind upon both parties, but usually when you receive an Enquiry, you should reply it as soon as possible.

e. g. , One of our clients in Odense is in the market for a parcel of 50 metric tons Bitter Apricot Kernels of 2002 crop and we, therefore, would ask you to make us your best possible firm offer on CIFC 2% Odense basis, stating terms of payment and the earliest date of shipment.

2.1.2.2 Offer

(1) The meaning of an offer

An offer is a proposal made by sellers to buyers in order to enter into a contract. In other words, it refers to trading terms put forward by offerers to offerees, on which the offerers are willing to conclude business with the offerers. There are two kinds of offers, one is the firm offer, the other, non-firm offer.

The party who makes an offer is called an offerer, in the case of the seller, the offer is called a selling offer, while in the case of the buyer, and it is called a buying offer.

(2) The basic conditions of an offer

A. The offer shall be made to one or more specific persons

The offer shall be the definite representation in which the offerer expresses that he shall conclude transaction on the terms and conditions stipulated therein.

B. Contents of the offer shall be sufficiently definite, i. e. trade terms of the offer shall be complete, clear and final. The "Convention" stipulates that a sufficiently definite offer should include three basic elements: name, quantity and price . In our foreign trade practice, a complete offer shall include the quality, quantity, packing, price, terms of delivery of the goods and terms of payment.

C. The offer shall indicate the intention of the offerer to be bound in case of acceptance. This intention may be indicated by terms as "firm" offer, "offer with engagement", etc.

If the offer has a restrictive condition, i. e. "subject to our final confirmation", then it's a non-firm offer regarded as an invitation for offer.

(3) Time of Validity or Duration of Offer

Stipulate the term of validity clearly.

The term of validity is not an indispensable condition of an offer.

A. Stipulate the latest date for acceptance

For example:

Offer subject to reply here Fifteenth, June.

B. Stipulate a period of time for acceptance

As to this method, there is a question of computing validity time.

See article 20 of "Convention".

If an offer doesn't clearly stipulate the time of validity, it will be valid within a reasonable time. An oral offer, unless otherwise agreed, must be accepted immediately unless the circumstances indicate otherwise.

(4) Time that an offer becomes effective

Different views of the time that a written form offer becomes effective:

A. Despatch Theory

B. Arrival Theory

Both "convention" and our "contract law" adopt arrival theory.

(5) Withdrawal or revocation of an offer

A. Withdrawal

The British laws and the American laws have different explanations to withdrawal.

The spirit of " Convention "

Suitable occasion for withdrawal: The offer is sent by mail or telegram.

B. Revocation

As to whether an offer can be revoked or not, different laws have different explanations.

The "Convention" adopts a compromise regulation.

(6) Termination of an offer

In the following cases, an offer is terminated: The time validity stipulated in the offer becomes due; The offeree rejects or makes a counter offer; The offerer revokes the offer before acceptance.

(7) Offer with engagement and offer without engagement

A. Offer with Engagement

The kind of offer in which the offerer's intention of making a contract is definitely indicated, and under which the offerer cannot revoke or amend when he has offered during the validity of the offer. Once unconditionally accepted by the offeree within its validity, it is binding upon both parties. Also called "firm offer", "irrevocable offer", an offer with engagement must be clear, complete and final.

It should include:

A detailed description of the item

Price, currency

Packaging

Minimum or maximum quantity

Quality

Shipping date, mode

Terms of payment

A timeframe during which the offer is available.

B. Offer without Engagement

An offer which is unclear, incomplete or with reservations. It is not binding upon both parities.

Indicative expressions: "reference price", "subject to our final confirmation", "subject to being unsold", "subject to change without notice", etc.

2. 1. 2. 3 Counter-offer

A reply to an offer which purports to be an acceptance but contains additions, limitations or other modifications is a rejection of the offer and constitutes a counter offer.

① A reply to an offer which alter the terms of the offer materially constitutes a counter-offer.

② An acceptance with restrictive conditions is another form of counter-offer, such as "subject to our final confirmation".

③ If offeree accepts the original offer after he made a counter-offer, the contract is invalid.

2. 1. 2. 4 Acceptance

An acceptance is the unqualified agreement to the terms of the offer.

Once an acceptance takes effect, a contract comes into existence. The parties are bound by the contract.

An acceptance must be unpualified/unconditional, that is to say it should exactly match the terms of an offer. It must be a mirror image. A reply to the offer, which varies the terms of the offer or adds new conditions to the offer, is not an acceptance but a counter-offer.

An agreeing either expressly or by conduct to the act or offer of another so that a contract is concluded and the parties become legally bound.

2.2 Contents of Contract

A contract is an agreement between two or more competent parties in which an offer is made and accepted, and each party benefits. It is an agreement which sets forth binding obligations of the relevant parties. An International Sale Contracts is a legal document which is signed by two international companies or individuals for selling products or services. This type of contract mentions the details of both the companies and the details of the product or services which are to be sold. The agreement can be formal, informal, written, oral or just plain understood. Some contracts are required to be in writing in order to be enforced.

In international trade, contracts vary in both names and forms. A contract is also named confirmation and can be drafted by either seller or buyer. A contract/confirmation drafted by the seller is called a sales contract/confirmation, while that drafted by the buyer is a purchase contract/confirmation. A contract is more formal and contains more details than a confirmation. However, they are equally binding on the parties concerned. The choice of either a contract or confirmation depends largely on the goods you are selling, your relationship with the buyer and your personal preferences, etc. Also, in different jurisdictions, there may be different requirements that must be met for a contract to be effective.

A contract proper includes: the full name and address of the buyer and the seller; the commodities involved; all the terms and conditions agreed upon; indication of the number of original copies of the contract, the language used, the term of validity and possible extension of the contract.

In international trade practice today, when a sales or purchase contract is formed, it is normally subject to United Nations Convention on Contracts for International Sale of Goods (CISG). According to it, a business contract need not be evidenced by writing and is not subject to any form.

terms of contract:

Parties

Clauses

1. Products
2. Price
3. Delivery conditions
4. Packaging
5. Means of payment
6. Date of payment

7. Delivery period
8. Delivery delays
9. Contractual responsibility
10. Patents, trade marks and industrial property rights
11. Certification of product quality
12. Certification of product origin
13. Fulfilment of contract
14. Termination due to breach of contract
15. Insolvency
16. Subsistence of obligations
17. Granting rights and obligations
18. Term of contract
19. Ownership
20. Force Majeure
21. Applicable law
22. Resolution of disputes
23. Taxation
24. Language Signatures

Sample:

International Sale Contract

This International sale contact is entered on 16th July 2010 by and between Mr. Alexander Smith residing in London, United Kingdom, hereinafter referred to seller, and Mr. David Kutcher residing New York, USA, hereinafter referred to as the buyer who agrees to purchase from seller the designated product with approved terms and condition.

Identities of the Parties

Seller, Mr. Alexander Smith whose business address is 1 – 1304 Drummond Street in the city of London, United Kingdom, is in the business with Mr. David Kutcher, Buyer, whose business address is 120 Pit Kin Park Road, Montpelier, New York, USA – 98776.

Description of the Goods

Seller agrees to transfer and deliver to Buyer, on or before 12th October 2010, the XYZ Products.

Buyer's terms and condition:

Buyer approves to receive the goods and pay for them through online bank transfer.

Goods are considered received by Buyer upon delivery at stated address as mentioned.

Buyer has the right to inspect the commodity upon delivery and has 7 days to notify seller to claim for reimbursements, grading, and quality of the commodities. Such notification must lay down in detail of the claim. Failure in delivering such communication within the perquisite time found immutable acceptance of a commodity.

Seller's terms and condition:

In anticipation of commodities from Buyer, all possibility of loss to the above-stated commodity is abided by Seller.

Seller warranties that the commodities are open from any and all sanctuary interests, hindrances, and impediments.

Attestation

Mr. David Kutcher Sign ________________

Mr. Alexander Smith Sign ________________

2.3 Performance of the Contract

After preparation and signing of the contract, the orders shall be processed. It is important to note that the complex procedures of all sectors shall be followed correctly and in accordance with the terms stipulated in the contract and/or letter of credit.

Business contracts are an important part of conducting business and even more important if your business operates online. This vile piece of paper describes the job duties in detail, delivery time, payment terms, and legal terms of conducting business between the client and you. Without a business contract that addresses expectations, procedures, and policies, it's likely you'll find yourself in a dispute at one time or another.

The business contract keeps the work legitimate and protects both parties. It's essential that both parties agree to the terms outlined in the contract and acknowledge their agreement with an authentic signature. For every transaction that requires you to conduct a different task for your client, you need a business contract. Some clients may not like this idea, but then again, this is a procedure that ensures both parties keep to their end of the deal.

At one time, a handshake or someone's word was all a business deal needed. Today, transactions are a lot more complex and it is helpful to come to an agreement in writing regarding the responsibilities of both the virtual assistant and the client.

A business contract also provides a sense of security to both parties to knowing they are on "common ground" in regards to the business relationship. A well thought out contract helps alleviate potential problems by addressing them before they actually take form.

2.4 Export and Import Procedures

Among the various forms of international trade, export trade and import trade are the two most frequently referred trade forms in the world. They are actually two sides of the same transaction. Considering its significance, this section devotes to the procedures involved in both the export and import. Generally speaking, from the beginning to the end of a transaction, the whole operation undergoes four stages, namely the preparation of a transaction, the negotiation of the contract, the performance of the contract and finally the settlement of disputes (if any).

2.4.1 Export Procedure

Even though it is recognized that there are many variations in progressing an export contract, there is a general way of doing transactions that could be sought after. As contracts for export in China are mostly concluded under CIF on L/C (Letter of Credit), we will use this type to illustrate the export procedure.

(1) Examining L/C

Under CIF contract with L/C as its payment term, the importer is required to open the L/C on time, but he may delay for various reasons. With a view to make collection of payment safe, the exporter should urge the importer to expedite the opening of L/C. Upon receipt of the relevant L/C, the exporter then must check the L/C against the sales contract carefully to ensure all terms and conditions in L/C are in strict conformity with those in the sales contract. If any discrepancies are found, the exporter should urge the importer to amend the L/C as quickly as possible.

(2) Getting goods ready

If the exporter is supposed to produce the goods for shipment, this stage may take place well before the examination of the letter of credit. However, if the exporter is to purchase the goods for shipment, he will normally start the preparation of the goods after or slightly before the L/C is ready, depending on the time involved to prepare the goods and the shipping schedule stipulated in the contract. The exporter shall prepare the goods in line with the name, quality, quantity, packing and marking required in the contract. If any certificate (e.g. Certificate of Origin) is required in the contract, the exporter also has to get them ready as stipulated.

(3) Applying for mandatory inspection

If required by the stipulations of the governments or the contract that goods need to be inspected, the exporter should obtain the mandatory inspection certificates from the authorized institutions before shipping. The exporter should fill out an application form for the inspection of exports and submit it for inspection.

At submission, he will be asked to present the following documents: commercial invoice, the copy of sales contract, letter of credit, samples if the goods are sold by sample, as well as the inspection report supplied by the manufacture. If the goods inspected are up to the standard required, the inspection institutions concerned will issue relevant inspection certificates.

(4) Receiving importer's inspection

Although not an obligation of the buyer in the contract, it is almost always the case in international trade that the importer will inspect the goods at the port of shipment. This is usually conducted after the necessary mandatory inspection has been completed or after the goods are ready if no such mandatory inspection is required.

(5) Booking shipping space

After receiving the relevant L/C, at the time when goods are being prepared, the exporter should contact the shipping company or its agents for the chartering or booking of shipping space. Chartering is required for goods of large quantity which needs full shipload, while for goods in relatively small quantity, booking shipping space would do.

(6) Clearing goods for export

After having the goods inspected, before the goods are loaded, the exporters should complete certain customs formalities. He should declare the export goods to the Customs by filling in certain customs forms and submitting appropriate documents such as commercial invoice, export license, copy of sales contract, inspection certificates, shipping order, etc. The Customs will inspect the export goods and decide if the shipment can be cleared through.

(7) Getting goods loaded

After that, the exporter may start to prepare for the loading of the goods. Generally speaking, goods can be loaded for shipment only after they are cleared for export. After the completion of the shipment, the exporter will receive the Bill of Lading from the carrier. It is important to note that the date of issuance of bill of lading shall fall within the period allowed in the letter of credit, otherwise it will be refused by the bank for the negotiation of payment.

(8) Obtaining insurance

Under CIF contract, the exporter should also obtain cargo insurance at his own expense as agreed upon in the contract. Therefore, after loading, he can contact insurance company or his agents to arrange for insurance. According to Incoterms 2000, the coverage on CIF term is the minimum coverage. However, if the importer asks for additional insurance coverage, the exporter is expected to effect insurance as required but the expense shall be for the importer's account. This should be made clear in the sales contract.

(9) Presenting documents for bank negotiation

After shipment is made and insurance is obtained, the exporter should then present all necessary documents specified in L/C for the negotiation of payment within the presentation period required in the contract or the letter of credit. All documents must be made out in accordance with the requirement in the L/C. The documents generally include the following: commercial invoice, packing list, bill of lading, insurance policy, inspection certificates, etc. Some importing countries may also require such documents as the Certificate of Origin, the Consular Invoice, etc. to issue import license or to calculate import customs duty.

Under such circumstances, the exporter is expected to obtain these documents as required and present them together with other documents to the bank for negotiation of payment. If the details in the documents presented are in strict conformity with those in the L/C, the exporter will receive payments from the bank as expected.

2.4.2 Import Procedure

Import procedure is closely related to export procedure. Most of the import transactions in our country are under FOB term with payment on L/C. The general procedure for import is:

(1) Opening the letter of credit

If the payment in the sales contract is to be made by L/C, after signing a contract, the importer should apply for the issuance of an L/C at the issuing bank in time and then forward it to the exporter. The importer has to make sure that the opening of the L/C should be made in time and the terms in the L/C should fit that in the sales contract to avoid future amendments which are costly and time consuming to both parties and may delay shipment. Special attention should be paid to the total sum, description of the goods, validity, documents required, etc.

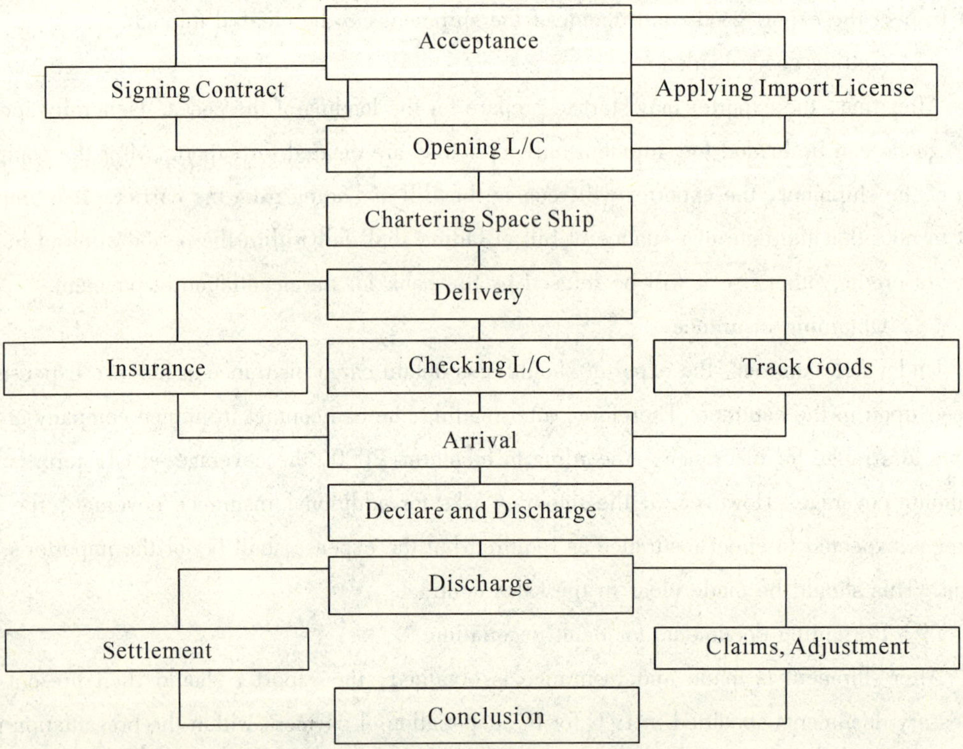

Figure 2 - 1 Export and Import Procedures

(2) Booking shipping space

Under FOB, it is the importer who must contact at his own expense for the carriage of the goods from the named port of shipment. After receiving notice from the exporter and knowing that the exporter has got the goods ready for shipment, the importer should charter or book shipping space with the carrier and give the exporter sufficient notice of the information such as the name of the vessel, the name of the loading point and the required delivery time so as to enable the exporter to deliver the goods to the carrier smoothly and without delay.

Inspecting and supervising at the port of shipment.

Before shipment, the importer or his agent will inspect the goods at the port of shipment before loading. If necessary, the importer may also want to supervise the shipment at the loading port.

(3) Obtaining insurance

Although under FOB in incoterms 2010 the importer has no obligation for the contract of insurance, considering the fact that the potential risks threatening the goods in transit are great and the importer is the party who is exposed to these risks, the importer will normally be expected to effect insurance on his own.

(4) Examining documents and making payment

If payment is made by L/C in the sales contract, the importer will be asked to make payment to the issuing bank upon receiving the relevant documents. Even though both the negotiating bank and issuing bank have examined the documents before they make payment to the exporter, it is important for the importer to exam the documents on his own carefully before making payments. If no problem is found with the documents, the importer has to make the payment as has been stipulated in the contract.

(5) Clearing goods for import

Upon arrival, imported goods from other countries have to be cleared through the Customs. So the importer should prepare the necessary documents such as the commercial invoice and inspection certificate while clearing the goods for import. If necessary, the importer also needs to carry out all customs formalities for the transit of his goods through any other country.

(6) Taking delivery and inspecting

After making the payment and getting the shipping documents, the importer can take delivery of the goods from the carrier after the arrival of the goods at the destination. However, it should be noted that the importer should inspect the goods to ensure that the goods delivered conform to the description of the goods in the sales contract. Should there be any inconformity, the importer will lodge claims against parties concerned for compensation.

2.4.3 Settlement of Disputes

Sometimes complaints or claims inevitably arise in spite of the careful performance of contract by the exporter and the importer. In international trade, most of the claims are made by the importer. Therefore, upon inspection of the goods at the destination, should any problem arise, the importer would reserve the right to reject the goods totally or lodge a claim against the relevant party, if problems concerning weight shortage, inferior quality or wrong shipment are found and attributed to the exporter, the importer should lodge claims against the exporter. However, if the loss of or damage to the goods is found to be caused by the negligence of the carrier, the importer should make claims against the carrier. If the loss or damage is due to the risks in transit and has been covered by the insurance, the claim should be made against the insurance company.

It should be noted that claims should be filed within the time limit stipulated in the relevant contracts and the importer has to present all documents necessary for the claims. If a claim cannot be settled between the parties involved through negotiation or mediation, the dispute should be submitted to arbitration if that has been agreed upon before hand in the contract. Otherwise litigation will be necessary.

2.5 Summary

This chapter has mainly introduced the general procedures of business negotiation, the basic contents and establishment of contract, etc.

International business negotiation is an important part of conducting a foreign trade. A negotiation is a process of communication between parties to manage conflicts in order for them to come to an agreement, solve a problem or make arrangements.

International trade procedure usually consists of four stages: the preparation of a trade transaction, the negotiation of the contract, the performance of the contract and the settlement of disputes if applicable.

An exporter procedure for a CIF contract on L/C term involved in the performance stage embraces the following steps: examining L/C, preparing goods, arranging mandatory inspection and buyer inspection, booking shipping space, clearing goods for export, loading goods in exchange for bill of lading, obtaining insurance and presenting documents for payment.

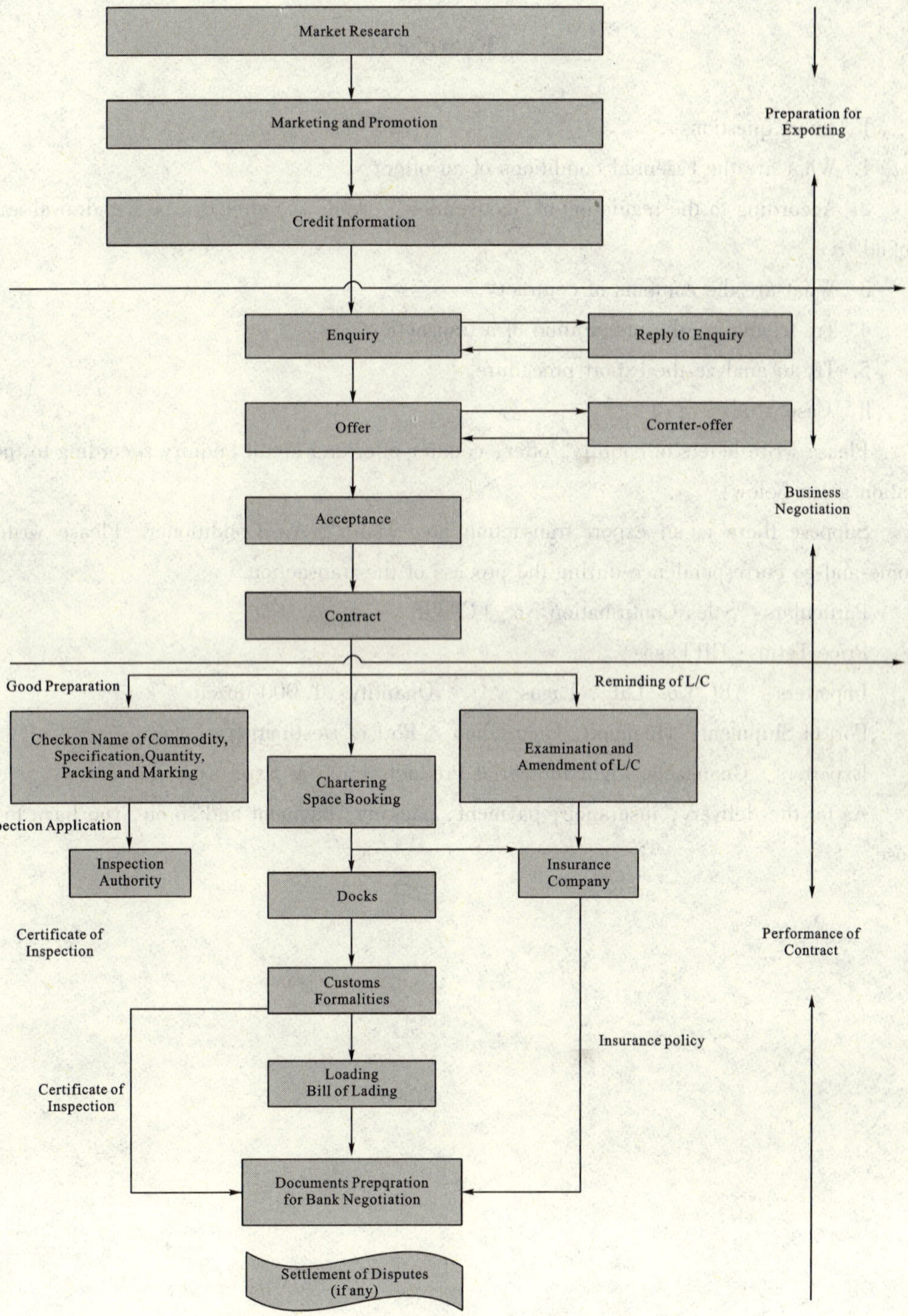

Figure 2－2 Establishment of Contract procedure

Exercises

Ⅰ. Short questions

1. What are the essential conditions of an offer?

2. According to the regulation of "convention", when the offer can be withdrawal and revoked?

3. What are the contents of contract?

4. Try to analyze the preparation of a transaction.

5. Try to analyze the export procedure.

Ⅱ. Case Study

Please write letters of enquiry, offer, counter-offer and credit enquiry according to the situation given below:

Suppose there is an export transaction on "Haier" Air Conditioner. Please write the come-and-go correspondence during the process of the transaction.

Particulars: Sales Confirmation No. FC9998

Price Terms: CIFLagos

Importers: ABC Co. Ltd., Lagos Quantity: 1,000 dozen

Port of Shipment: Huangpu, Guangzhou Port of Destination: Lagos

Exporters: Guangzhou Light Industrial Products Imp. & Exp. Corp.

As for the delivery, insurance, payment, packing, payment and so on, you have to suppose.

Chapter 3 International Trade Terms

Learning Objectives

1. To understand three sets of rules
2. To master rules for any mode of transport: EXW, FCA, CPT, CIP, DAT, DAP, DDP
3. To master rules for sea and inland waterway transport: FAS, FOB, CFR, CIF
4. To understand how to use trade terms

Key Words

Port of destination; Port of discharge; Port of shipment; Price terms; Symbolic delivery; Trade terms; FOB; CFR; CIF; Transfer of risk

This simple real life example illustrates the reality and complexities of doing business: the prices quoted in international trade are not just about a simple price quotation but cover other areas of the service, in international trade a transaction of goods will probably involve getting goods across the borders of different countries, long distance transportation with considerable risks, and incurring various other costs. Who will take the responsibility of handling and paying for particular expenses? Who will bear the risk of the goods at a particular time? Detailed issues like these always need to be settled when the traders agree on the prices. It also adds to traders' time and expense if they have to go over this ground every time they set an order price.

What is Trade Terms? The trade terms are the short terms or abbreviations or brief English concept to indicate/explain the composition/formation of the unit price and determine the responsibilities/rights and obligations, expenses and risks borne by two parties as well as the time of the passing of the property in the goods.

The primary goal of this chapter is to introduce the trade terms, the special "language" used in international trade, and illustrate how these terms in their simplest form are used to facilitate international trade.

3.1 Three Sets of Rules

The history of international trade shows that prior to development of modern communications (before the early part of the nineteenth century) the form of international trade remained relatively homogeneous. Merchants shipped goods overseas and sold the goods directly to foreign buyers. In other cases the buyer would have chartered, or perhaps taken personally, a vessel to the exporting port and purchased the goods there. Transactions under these circumstances were face to face and therefore simple.

As communications improved and the insurance and banking industries developed, accompanied by the gradual establishment and perfection of relevant legislation, international trade grew at an unprecedented speed and started to take various forms. Complexity was twinned with the rapid growth of trade.

These do not have any legal binding force unless they have been listed in the relevant contract as an integral part and are protected by relevant legal instruments.

3.1.1 Warsaw-Oxford Rules 1932

During the 1928 convention of the International Law Association held in the capital of Poland, Warsaw, a set of uniform rules were established— "Warsaw Rules, 1928". There were altogether twenty-two provisions and they governed the rights and obligations of the parties to a sale of goods on CIF (Cost, Insurance and Freight) contract terms.

In 1930 and 1931 the Association held conventions in New York and Paris discussing further amendment to the Rules. In the 1932 convention in Oxford, England, the rules were combined into twenty-one provisions and these became the "Warsaw-Oxford Rules 1932".

3.1.2 Revised American Foreign Trade Definition 1990

3.1.2.1 foreword

Since the issuance of American Foreign Trade Definitions in 1919 many changes in practice have occurred. The 1919 Definitions did much to clarify and simplify foreign trade practice, and received wide recognition and use by buyers and sellers throughout the world. At the Twenty Seventh National Foreign Trade Convention, 1940, further revision and clarification of these Definitions was urged as necessary to assist the foreign trader in the handling of his transactions.

The following Revised American Foreign Trade Definitions 1990 are recommended for general use by both exporters and importers. These revised definitions have no status at law unless there is specific legislation providing for them, or unless they are confirmed by court decisions. Hence, it is suggested that seller and buyers agree to their acceptance as part of the contract of sale. These revised definitions will then become legally binding upon all parties.

In view of changes in practice and procedure since 1941, certain new responsibilities for sellers and buyers are included in these revised definitions. Also, in many instances, the old responsibilities are more clearly defined than in the 1941 Definitions, and the changes should be beneficial both to sellers and buyers. Widespread acceptance will lead to a greater standardization of foreign trade procedure, and to the avoidance of much misunderstanding.

Adoption by exporters and importers of these revised terms will impress on all parties concerned their respective responsibilities and rights.

General Notes of Caution

① As foreign trade definitions have been issued by organizations in various parts of the world, and as the courts of countries have interpreted these definitions in different ways, it is important that sellers and buyers agree that their contracts are subject to the Revised American Foreign Trade Definitions 1990 and that the various points listed are accepted by both parties.

② In addition to the foreign trade terms listed herein, there are terms that are at times used, such as Free Harbor, C. I. F. &C. (Cost, Insurance, Freight, and Commission), C. I. F. C. &I. (Cost, Insurance, Freight, Commission, and Interest), C. I. F. (Cost, Insurance, Freight), and others. None of these should be used unless there has first been a definite understanding as to the exact meaning thereof, It is unwise to attempt to interpret other terms in the light of the terms given herein. Hence, whenever possible, one of the terms defined herein should be used.

③ It is unwise to use abbreviations in quotations or in contracts which might be subject to misunderstanding.

④ When making quotations, the familiar terms "hundredweight" or "ton" should be avoided. A hundredweight can be 100 pounds of the short ton, or 112 pounds of the long ton. A ton can be a short ton of 2, 000 pounds, or a metric ton of 2, 204. 6 pounds, or a long ton of 2, 240 pounds. Hence, the type of hundredweight or ton should be clearly stated in quotations and in sales confirmations. Also, all terms referring to quantity, weight, volume, length, or surface should be clearly defined and agreed upon.

⑤ If inspection, or certificate of inspection, is required, it should be agreed, in advance, whether the cost thereof is for account of seller or buyer.

⑥ Unless otherwise agreed upon, all expenses are for the account of seller up to the point at which the Buyer must handle the subsequent movement of goods.

⑦ There are a number of elements in a contract that do not fall within the scope of these foreign trade definitions. Hence, no mention of these is made herein. Seller and buyer should agree to these separately when negotiating contracts. This particularly applies to so - called "customary" practices.

3. 1. 2. 2 definitions of quotations

(1) EXW (Ex Works-named place)

"Ex Factory", "Ex Mill", "Ex Mine", "Ex Plantation", "Ex Warehouse", etc. (named point of origin)

Under this term, the price quoted applies only at the point of origin, and the seller agrees to place the goods at the disposal of the buyer at the agreed place on the date or within the period fixed.

Under this quotation:

Seller must ① bear all costs and risks of the goods until such time as the buyer is obliged to take delivery; ② render the buyer, at the buyer's request and expense, assistance in obtaining the documents issued in the country of origin, or of shipment, or of both, which the buyer may require either for purposes of exportation, or of importation at destination.

Buyer must ① take delivery of the goods as soon as they have been placed at his disposal at the agreed place on the date or within the period fixed; ② pay export taxes, or other fees or changes, if any, levied because of exportation; ③ bear all costs and risks of the goods from the time when he is obligated to take delivery whereof; ④ pay all costs and charges incurred in obtaining the documents issued in the country of origin, or of shipment, or of both, which may be required either for purposes of exportation or of importation at destination.

(2) F. O. B. (Free on Board)

Note: Seller and buyer should consider not only the definitions but also the "Comments on all F. O. B. Terms" given at the end of this section, in order to understand fully their respective responsibilities and rights under the several classes of "F. O. B. " terms.

a. F. O. B. (named inland carrier at named inland point of departure)

Under this terms, the price quoted applies only at inland applies only at inland shipping point, and the seller arranges for loading of the goods on, or in, railway cars, trucks, lighters, barges, aircraft, or other conveyance furnished for transportation.

Under this quotation:

Seller must ① place goods on, or in, conveyance, or deliver to inland carrier for loading; ② provide clean bill of lading or other transportation receipt, freight collect; ③ be responsible for any loss or damage, or both, until goods have been placed in, or on, conveyance at loading point, and clean bill of lading other transportation receipt has been furnished by the carrier; ④ render the buyer, at the buyer's request and expense, assistance in obtaining the documents issued in the country of origin, or of shipments, or of both, which the buyer may require either for purposes of exportation, or of importation at destination.

Buyer must ① be responsible for all movement of the goods from inland point of loading and pay all transportation costs; ② pay export taxes, or other fees or charges, if any, levied because of exportation; ③ be responsible for any loss or damage, or both, incurred after loading at named inland point of departure; ④ pay all costs and charges incurred in obtaining the documents issued in the country of origin, or of shipment, or of both, which may be required either for purposes of exportation, or of importation at destination.

b. F. O. B. (named inland carrier at named inland point of departure), Freight Prepaid To (named point of exportation)

Under this term, the seller quotes a price including transportation charges to the named point of exportation and prepays freight to named point of exportation, without assuming responsibility for the goods after obtaining a clean bill of lading or other transportation receipt at named inland point of departure.

Under this quotation:

Seller must ① assume the seller's obligations as under a. except that under ② he must provide clean bill of lading or other transportation receipt, freight prepaid to named point of exportation.

Buyer must assume the same buyer's obligation as under a., except that he does not pay freight from loading point to named point of exportation.

c. F. O. B. (named inland carrier at named inland point of departure) Freight Allowed To (named point)

Under this term, the seller quotes a price including the transportation charges to the named point, shipping freight collect and deducting the cost of transportation, without assuming responsibility for the goods after obtaining a clean bill of lading or other transportation receipt at named inland point of departure.

Under this quotation:

Seller must assume the same seller's obligations as under a., but deducts from his invoice the transportation cost to named point.

Buyer must assume the same buyer's obligations as under a., including payment of freight from inland loading point to named point, for which seller has made deduction.

d. F. O. B. (named inland carrier at named point of exportation)

Under this term, the seller quotes a price including the costs of transportation of the goods to named point of exportation, bearing any loss or damage, or both, incurred up to that point.

Under this quotation:

Seller must ① place goods on, or in, conveyance, or deliver to inland carrier for loading; ② provide clean bill of lading or other transportation receipt, paying all transportation costs from loading point to named point of exportation; ③ be responsible for any loss or damage, or both, until goods have arrived in, or on, inland conveyance at the named point of exportation; ④ render the buyer, at the buyer's request and expense, assistance in obtaining the documents issued in the country of origin, or of shipment, or of both, which the buyer may require either for purposes of exportation, or of importation at destination.

Buyer must ① be responsible for all movement of the goods from inland conveyance at named point of exportation; ② pay export taxes, or other fees or charges, if any, levied because of exportation; ③ be responsible for any loss or damage, or both, incurred after goods have arrived in, or on, inland conveyance at the named point of exportation; ④ pay all costs and charges incurred in obtaining the documents issued in the country of origin, or of shipment, or of both, which may be required either for purposes of exportation, or of importation at destination.

e. F. O. B. Vessel (named port of shipment)

Under this term, the seller quotes a price covering all expenses up to, and including, delivery of the goods upon the overseas vessel provided by, or for, the buyer at the named port of shipment.

Under this quotation:

Seller must ① pay all charges incurred in placing goods actually on board the vessel designated and provided by, or for, the buyer on the date or within the period fixed; ② provide clean ship's receipt or on-board bill of lading; ③ be responsible for any loss or damage, or both, until goods have been placed on board the vessel on the date or within the period fixed; ④ render the buyer, at the buyer's request and expense, assistance in obtaining the documents issued in the country of origin, or of shipment, or of both, which the buyer may require either for purposes of exportation, or of importation at destination.

Buyer must ① give seller adequate notice of name, sailing date, loading berth of, and delivery time to, the vessel; ② bear the additional costs incurred and all risks of the good from the time when the seller has placed them at his disposal if the vessel named by him fails to arrive or to load within the designated time; ③ handle all subsequent movement of the goods to destination; (a) provide and pay for insurance; (b) provide and pay for ocean and other transportation; (4) pay export taxes, or other fees or charges, if any, levied because of exportation; (5) be responsible for any loss or damage, or both, after goods have been loaded on board the vessel; (6) pay all costs and charges incurred in obtaining the documents, other than ocean ship's receipt or bill of lading, issued in the country of origin, or of shipment, or of both, which may be required either for purposes of exportation, or of importation at destination.

f. F. O. B. (named inland pointing country of importation)

Under this term, the seller quotes a price including the cost of the merchandise and all costs of transportation to the named inland point in the country of importation.

Under this quotation:

Seller must ① provide and pay for all transportation to the named inland point in the country of importation; ② pay export taxes, or other fees or charges, if any, levied because of exportation; ③ provide and pay for marine insurance; ④ provide and pay for war risk insurance, unless otherwise agreed upon between the seller and buyer; ⑤ be responsible for any loss or damage, or both, until arrival of goods on conveyance at the named inland point in the country of importation; ⑥ pay the costs of certificates of origin, consular invoices, or any other documents issued in the country of origin, or of shipment, or of both, which the buyer may require for the importation of goods into the country of destination and, where necessary, for their passage in transit through another country; ⑦ pay all costs of landing, including wharfage, landing charges, and taxes, if any; ⑧ pay all costs of customs entry in the country of importation; ⑨ pay customs duties and all taxes applicable to imports, if any, in the country of importation.

Note: The seller under this quotation must realize that he is accepting important responsibilities, costs, and risks, and should therefore be certain to obtain adequate insurance. On the other hand, the importer or buyer may desire such quotations to relieve him of the risks of the voyage and to assure him of his landed costs at inland point in country of importation. When competition is keen, or the buyer is accustomed to such quotations from other sellers, seller may quote such terms, being careful to protect himself in an appropriate manner.

Buyer must ① take prompt delivery of goods from conveyance upon arrival at destination. ② bear any costs and be responsible for all loss or damage, or both, after arrival at destination.

Comments on All F. O. B. Terms

In connection with F. O. B. terms, the following points of caution are recommended:

① The method of inland transportation, such as trucks, railroad cars, lighters, barges, or aircraft should be specified.

② If any switching charges are involved during the inland transportation, it should be agreed, in advance, whether these charges are for account of the seller or the buyer.

③ The term "F. O. B. (named port)", without designating the exact point at which the liability of the seller terminates and the liability of the buyer begins, should be avoided. The use of this term gives rise to disputes as to the liability of the seller or the buyer in the event of loss or damage arising while the goods are in port, and before delivery to or on board the ocean carrier. Misunderstandings may be avoided by naming the specific point of delivery.

④ If lighterage or trucking is required in the transfer of goods from the inland conveyance to ship's side, and there is a cost therefor, it should be understood, in advance, whether this cost is for account of the seller or the buyer.

⑤ The seller should be certain to notify the buyer of the minimum quantity required to obtain a carload, a truck-load, or a barge-load freight rate.

⑥ Under F. O. B. terms, excepting "F. O. B. (named inland point in country of importation)", the obligation to obtain ocean freight space, and marine and war risk insurance, rests with the buyer. Despite this obligation on the part of the buyer, in many trades the seller obtains the ocean freight space, and marine and war risk insurance, and provides for shipment on behalf of the buyer. Hence, seller and buyer must have an understanding as to whether the buyer will obtain the ocean freight space, marine and war risk insurance, as is his obligation, or whether the seller agrees to do this for the buyer.

⑦ For the seller's protection, he should provide in his contract of sale that marine insurance obtained by the buyer include standard warehouse to warehouse coverage.

(3) F. A. S. (Free Along Side)

Note: Seller and buyer should consider not only the definitions but also the "Comments" given of the end of this section, in order to understand fully their respective responsibilities and rights under "F. A. S." terms.

a. F. A. S. Vessel (named port of shipment)

Under this term, the seller quotes a price including delivery of the goods along side overseas vessel and within reach of its loading tackle.

Under this quotation:

Seller must ① place goods along side vessel or on dock designated and provided by, or for, buyer on the date or within the period fixed; pay any heavy lift charges, where necessary, up to this point; ② provide clean dock or ship's receipt; ③ be responsible for any loss or damage, or both, until goods have been delivered along side the vessel or on the dock; ④ render the buyer, at the buyer's request and expense, assistance in obtaining the documents issued in the country of origin, or of shipment, or of both, which the buyer may require either for purposes of exportation, or of importation at destination.

Buyer must ① give seller adequate notice of name, sailing date, loading berth of, and delivery time to, the vessel; ② handle all subsequent movement of the goods from along side the vessel: (a) arrange and pay for demurrage or storage charges, or both, in warehouse or on wharf, where necessary; (b) provide and pay for insurance; (c) provide and pay for ocean and other transportation; ③ pay export taxes, or other fees or charges, if any, levied because of exportation; ④ be responsible for any loss or damage, or both, while the goods are on a lighter or other conveyance along side vessel within reach of its loading tackle, or on the dock awaiting loading, or until actually loaded on board the vessel, and subsequent thereto; ⑤ pay all costs and charges incurred in obtaining the documents, other than clean dock or ship's receipt, issued in the country of origin, or of shipment, or of both, which may be required either for purposes of exportation, or of importation at destination.

b. F. A. S. Comments

① Under F. A. S. terms, the obligation to obtain ocean freight space, and marine and war risk insurance, rests with the buyer. Despite this obligation on the part of the buyer, in many trades the seller obtains ocean freight space, and marine and war risk insurance, and provides for shipment on behalf of the buyer. In others, the buyer notifies the seller to make delivery along side a vessel designated by the buyer and the buyer provided his own marine and war risk insurance. Hence, seller and buyer must have an understanding as to whether the buyer will obtain the ocean freight space, and marine and war risk insurance, as is his obligation, or whether the seller agrees to do this for the buyer.

② For the seller's protection, he should provide in his contract of sale that marine insurance obtained by the buyer include standard warehouse to warehouse coverage.

(4) CFR (Cost and Freight)

Note: Seller and buyer should consider not only the definitions but also the "CFR Comments" and the "CFR and C. I. F. Comments", in order to understand fully their respective responsibilities and rights under CFR terms.

a. CFR (named point of destination)

Under this term, the seller quotes a price including the cost of transportation to the named point of destination.

Under this quotation:

Seller must ① provide and pay for transportation to named point of destination; ② pay export taxes, or other fees or charges, if any, levied because of exportation; ③ obtain and dispatch promptly to buyer, or agent, clean bill of lading to named point of destination; ④ where received-for-shipment ocean bill of lading may be tendered, be responsible for any loss or damage, or both, until the goods have been delivered into the custody of the ocean carrier; ⑤ where on-board ocean bill of lading is required, be responsible for any loss or damage, or both, until the goods have been delivered on board the vessel; ⑥ provide, at the buyer's request and expense, certificates of origin, consular invoice, or any other documents issued in the country of origin or of shipment, or of both, which the buyer may require for importation of goods into country of destination and, where necessary, for their passage in transit through another country.

Buyer must ① accept the documents when presented; ② receive goods upon arrival, handle and pay for all subsequent movement of the goods, including taking delivery from vessel in accordance with bill of lading clauses and terms; pay all costs of landing, including duties, taxes, and other expenses at named point of destination; ③ provide and pay for insurance; ④ be responsible for loss of or damage to goods, or both, from time and place at which seller's obligations under ④ or ⑤ above have ceased; ⑤ pay the costs of certificates of origin, consular invoices, or any other documents issued in the country of origin, or of shipment, or of both, which may be required for the importation of goods into the country of destination and, where necessary, for their passage in transit through another country.

b. CFR Comments

① For the seller's protection, he should provide in his contract of sale that marine insurance obtained by the buyer include standard warehouse to warehouse coverage.

② The comments listed under the following C. I. F. terms in many cases apply to CFR terms as well, and should be read and understood by the CFR seller and buyer.

(5) C. I. F. (Cost, Insurance, Freight)

Note: Seller and buyer should consider not only the definitions but also the "Comments", at the end of this section, in order to understand fully their respective responsibilities and rights under "C. I. F." terms.

a. C. I. F. (named point of destination)

Under this term, the seller quotes a price including the cost of the goods, the marine insurance, and all transportation charges to the named point of destination.

Under this quotation:

Seller must ① provide and pay for transportation to named point of destination; ② pay export taxes, or other fees or charges, if any, levied because of exportation; ③ provide and pay for marine insurance; ④ provide war risk insurance as obtainable in seller's market at time of shipment at buyer's expense, unless seller has agreed that buyer provide for war risk coverage [see comment 10 (c)]; ⑤ obtain and dispatch promptly to buyer, or his agent, clean bill of lading to named point of destination, and also insurance policy or negotiable insurance certificate; ⑥ where received-for-shipment ocean bill of lading may be tendered, be responsible for any loss or damage, or both, until the goods have been delivered into the custody of the ocean carrier; ⑦ where on-board ocean bill of lading is required, be responsible for any loss or damage, or both, until the goods have been delivered on board the vessel; ⑧ provide, at the buyer's request and expense, certificates of origin, consular invoices, or any other documents issued in the country of origin, or of shipment, or both, which the buyer may require for importation of goods into country of destination and, where necessary, for their passage in transit through another country.

Buyer must ① accept the documents when presented; ② receive the goods upon arrival, handle and pay for all subsequent movements of the goods, including taking delivery from vessel in accordance with bill of lading clauses and terms; pay all costs of landing, including any duties, taxes, and other expenses at named point of destination; ③ pay for war risk insurance provided by seller; ④ be responsible for loss of or damage to goods, or both, from time and place at which seller's obligations under ⑥ or ⑦ above have ceased; ⑤ pay the cost of certificates of origin, consular invoices, or any other documents issued in the country of origin, or of shipment, or both, which may be required for importation of the goods into the country of destination and, where necessary, for their passage in transit through another country.

b. CFR and C. I. F. Comments

Under CFR and C. I. F. contracts there are the following points on which the seller and the buyer should be in complete agreement at the time that the contract is concluded:

① It should be agreed upon, in advance, who is to for miscellaneous expenses, such as weighing or inspection charges.

② The quantity to be shipped on any one vessel should be agreed upon, in advance, with a view to the buyer's capacity to take delivery upon arrival and discharge of the vessel; within the free time allowed at the port of importation.

③ Although the terms CFR and C. I. F. are generally interpreted to provide that charges for consular invoices and certificates of origin are for the account of the buyer, and are charged separately, in many trades these charges are included by the seller in his price. Hence, seller and buyer should agree, in advance, whether these charges are part of the selling price, or will be invoiced separately.

④ The point of final destination should be definitely known in the event the vessel discharges at a port other than the actual destination of the goods.

⑤ When ocean freight space is difficult to obtain, or forward freight contracts cannot be made at firm rates, it is advisable that sales contracts, as an exception to regular CFR or C. I. F. terms, should provide that shipment within the contract period be subject to ocean freight space being available to the seller, and should also provide that changes in the cost of ocean transportation between the time of sale and the time of shipment be for account of the buyer.

⑥ Normally, the seller is obligated to prepay the ocean freight. In some instances, shipments are made freight collect and the amount of the freight is deducted from the invoice rendered by the seller. It is necessary to be in agreement on this, in advance, in order to avoid misunderstanding which arises from foreign exchange fluctuations which might affect the actual cost of transportation, and from interest charges which might accrue under letter of credit financing. Hence, the seller should always prepay the ocean freight unless he has a specific agreement with the buyer, in advance, that goods can be shipped freight collect.

⑦ The buyer should recognize that he does not have the right to insist on inspection of goods prior to accepting the documents. The buyer should not refuse to take delivery of goods on account of delay in the receipt of documents, provided the seller has used due diligence in their dispatch through the regular channels.

⑧ Seller and buyers are advised against including in a C. I. F. contract any indefinite clause at variance with the obligations of a C. I. F. contract as specified in these Definitions. There have been numerous court decisions in the United States and other countries invalidating C. I. F. contracts because of the inclusion of indefinite clauses.

⑨ Interest charges should be included in cost computations and should not be charged as a separate item in C. I. F. contracts, unless otherwise agreed upon, in advance, between the seller and buyer; in which case, however, the term C. I. F. and C. I. F. I. (Cost, Insurance, Freight, and Interest) should be used.

⑩ In connection with insurance under C. I. F. sales, it is necessary that seller and buyer be definitely in accord upon the following points: (a) The character of the marine insurance should be agreed upon so far as being W. A. (With Average) or F. P. A. (Free of Particular Average), as well as any other special risks that are covered in specific trades, of against which the buyer may wish individual protection. Among the special risks that should be considered and agreed upon between seller and buyer are theft, pilferage, leakage, breakage, sweat, contract with other cargoes, and others peculiar to any particular trade. It is important that contingent or collect freight and customs duty should be insured to cover Particular Average losses, as well as total loss after arrival and entry but before delivery. (b) The seller is obligated to exercise ordinary care and diligence in selecting an underwriter that is in good financial standing. However, the risk of obtaining settlement of insurance claims rests with the buyer. (c) War risk insurance under this term is to be obtained by the seller at the expense and risk of the buyer. It is important that the seller be in definite accord with the buyer on this point, particularly as to the cost. It is desirable that the goods be insured against both marine and war risk with the same underwriter, so that there can be no difficulty arising from the determination of the cause of the loss. (d) Seller should make certain that in his marine or war risk insurance, there be included the standard protection against strikes, riots and civil commotions. (e) Seller and buyer should be in accord as to the insured valuation, bearing in mind that merchandise contributes in General Average on certain bases of valuation which differ in various trades. It is desirable that a competent insurance broker be consulted, in order that full value be covered and trouble avoided.

(6) DEQ Delivered

Ex Quay (Duty Paid)

Note: Seller and buyer should consider not only the definitions but also the "DEQ Comments" at the end of this section, in order to understand fully their respective responsibilities and rights under "DEQ" terms.

Under this term, seller quotes a price including the cost of the goods and all additional costs necessary to place the goods on the dock at the named port of importation, duty paid, if any.

Under this quotation:

Seller must ① provide and pay for transportation to named port of importation; ② pay export taxes, or other fees or charges, if any, levied because of exportation; ③ provide and pay for marine insurance; ④ provide and pay for war risk insurance, unless otherwise agreed upon between the buyer and seller; ⑤ be responsible for any loss or damage, or both, until the expiration of the free time allowed on the dock at the named port of importation; ⑥ pay the costs of certificates of origin, consular invoices, legalization of bill of lading, or any other documents issued in the country of origin, or of shipment, or of both, which the buyer may require for the importation of goods into the country of destination and, where necessary, for their passage in transit through another country; ⑦ pay all costs of landing, including wharfage, landing charges and taxes, if any; ⑧ pay all costs of customs entry in the country of importation; ⑨ pay customs duties and all taxes applicable to imports, if any, in the country of importation, unless otherwise agreed upon.

Buyer must ① take delivery of the goods on the dock at the named port of importation within the free time allowed; ② bear the cost and risk of the goods if delivery is not taken within the free time allowed.

DEQ Comments

This term is used principally in United States import trade. It has various modifications, such as "Ex Quay", "Ex Pier", etc. but it is seldom, if ever, used in American export practice. Its use in quotations for export is not recommended.

3.1.3 International Rules for the Interpretation of Trade Terms 2010 (Incoterms 2010)

Incoterms or International Commercial terms are a series of sales terms. They are published by the International Chamber of Commerce (ICC) and are widely used in international commercial transactions. The purpose of Incoterms is to provide a set of international rules for the interpretation of commonly used trade terms in international transactions. They closely correspond to the U. N. Convention on Contracts for the International Sale of Goods. The first Incoterms were issued in 1936. The most recent Incoterms were updated in 2010 and became effective January 1, 2011.

Incoterms assist trade practitioners in interpreting the most commonly used international trade terms. Using correct Incoterms in an international transaction reduces considerably uncertainties arising from the different interpretation of such terms in different countries. They apportion international trade transaction costs and responsibilities between buyers (importers) and sellers (exporters) and reflect modern - day transportation practices. Incoterms assist in significantly reducing misunderstandings among traders and thereby minimizing trade disputes and litigation. However, their scope is limited to matters related to the international rights and obligations of the parties involved in the contract of sale with respect to the delivery of the goods sold. Thus, they apply to the contract of carriage, not the contract of sale.

What are the main changes in Incoterms 2010 that you should be aware of?

① Removal of four terms (DAF, DES, DEQ and DDU) and introduction of two new terms (DAP—Delivered at Place and DAT—Delivered at Terminal).

② Creation of two classes of INCOTERMS: (a) rules for any mode or modes of transport and (b) rules for sea and inland waterway (INCOTERMS 2000 had four categories).

③ Rules which are able to serve both domestic and international trade.

④ Express reference to the use of "equivalent electronic records", if the parties agree or it is customary.

⑤ Amended insurance cover to reflect the alterations made to the Institute Cargo Clauses.

⑥ Allocation of parties' respective obligations to obtain or to provide information in order to obtain security-related clearances.

⑦ Responsibility for Terminal handling charges expressly allocated.

⑧ Including an obligation to "procure" goods to reflect current practices in string sales.

The Detail:

(1) Removal of four terms from Incoterms 2000

The onward march of containerization and point-to-point deliveries appear to have persuaded the ICC to introduce two new "Delivered" terms:

Delivered At Place (DAP) which should be used in place of DAF, DES and DDU; and Delivered At Terminal (DAT) which replaces DEQ.

These terms may be used irrespective of the agreed mode of transport.

Part of the reasoning for fewer terms/simplification was that traders often chose the "wrong" term or muddled terms, leading to contradictory or unclear contracts.

(2) Creation of two, rather than four categories of terms

The 11 terms have been categorized under two categories:

Deliveries can use any mode of transport (sea, road, air, rail) - EXW, FCA, CPT, CIP, DAP, DAT and DDP. These may all be used where there is no maritime transport at all; and deliveries by sea/inland waterway - FAS, FOB, CFR and CIF.

This, again, is to make the new INCOTERMS easier to use.

(3) Adapted Rules

The new INCOTERMS are expressly stated to be for "both domestic and international trade". In fact, this is stated on the front page! This is achieved by statements within the rules that the obligation to comply with export/import formalities only exists where applicable.

For trade blocs (eg the EU) where "border" formalities have largely disappeared and in the US, where there has been an increasing willingness to use INCOTERMS rather than the former Uniform Commercial Code shipment and delivery, the new terms are now easier to apply.

Why were the INCOTERMS® 2000 revised?

INCOTERMS® 2010 are the updated version of INCOTERMS® 2000. INCOTERMS® 2010 have been developed as a result of an extensive review of current shipping practices and trends in an effort to keep up with the rapid expansion of world trade. The key drivers for this update include: a need for improved cargo security, changes to the Uniform Commercial Code in 2004 that resulted in a deletion of U. S. shipment and delivery terms, and new trends in global transportation.

How do INCOTERMS® 2010 differ from INCOTERMS® 2000?

In addition to providing a set of rules for the interpretation of commonly used trade terms, INCOTERMS® 2010 significantly revise Group D listed in INCOTERMS® 2000.

The five INCOTERMS® 2000 listed in Group D included the following:

DAF Delivered At Frontier

DES Delivered Ex Ship

DEQ Delivered Ex Quay

DDU Delivered Duty Unpaid

DDP Delivered Duty Paid

INCOTERMS® 2010 contain the following categories:

DAT Delivered At Terminal

DAP Delivered At Place

DDP Delivered Duty Paid

Moreover, INCOTERMS® 2010 reduces the number of Incoterms groupings from four to two, allowing trade experts to choose the most suitable rule related to the mode of transport.

The 13 INCOTERMS® 2000 contained four essential categories of Incoterms. They were:

Group E—Departure

Group F—Main carriage unpaid

Group C—Main carriage paid

Group D—Arrival

The two main categories of INCOTERMS® 2010 are now organized by modes of transport. Used in international as well as in domestic contracts for the first time, the new groups aim to simplify the drafting of contracts and help avoid misunderstandings by clearly stipulating certain obligations of buyers and sellers.

Group 1. Incoterms that apply to any mode of transport are:

EXW Ex Works

FCA Free Carrier

CPT Carriage Paid To

CIP Carriage And Insurance Paid To

DAT Delivered At Terminal

DAP Delivered At Place

DDP Delivered Duty Paid

Group 2. Incoterms that apply to sea and inland waterway transport only:

FAS Free Alongside Ship

FOB Free On Board

CFR Cost And Freight

CIF Cost, Insurance, and Freight

Further, the two new groupings listed above note a reduction of the number of Incoterms from 13 to 11.

Finally, INCOTERMS® 2010 provide additional helpful guidance and clarify obligations. For instance, the revised terms also spell out rules regarding the use of electronic procedures; detail information on security-related clearances for shipments; and offer advice with respect to domestic trade.

(1) Main features of the Incoterms® 2010 rules

Two new Incoterms rules—DAT and DAP—have replaced the Incoterms 2000 rules DAF, DES, DEQ and DDU.

The number of Incoterms® rules has been reduced from 13 to 11. This has been achieved by substituting two new rules that may be used irrespective of the agreed mode of transport—DAT, Delivered at Terminal, and DAP, Delivered at Place—for the Incoterms® 2000 rules DAF, DES, DEQ and DDU.

Under both new rules, delivery occurs at a named destination: in DAT, at the buyer's disposal unloaded from the arriving vehicle (as under the former DEQ rule); in DAP, likewise at the buyer's disposal, but ready for unloading (as under the former DAF, DES and DDU rules).

The new rules make the Incoterms® 2000 rules DES and DEQ superfluous. The named terminal in DAT may well be in a port, and DAT can therefore safely be used in cases where the Incoterms® 2000 rule DEQ once was. Likewise, the arriving "vehicle" under DAP may well be a ship and the named place of destination may well be a port: consequently, DAP can safely be used in cases where the Incoterms® 2000 rule DES once was. These new rules, like their predecessors, are "delivered", with the seller bearing all the costs (other than those related to import clearance, where applicable) and risks involved in bringing the goods to the named place of destination.

(2) Classification of the 11 Incoterms® 2010 rules

The 11 Incoterms® 2010 rules are presented in two distinct classes:

RULES FOR ANY MODE OR MODES OF TRANSPORT

EXW EX WORKS

FCA FREE CARRIER

CPT CARRIAGE PAID TO

CIP CARRIAGE AND INSURANCE PAID TO

DAT DELIVERED AT TERMINAL

DAP DELIVEREDAT PLACE

DDP DELIVERED DUTY PAID

RULES FOR SEA AND INLAND WATERWAY TRANSPORT

FAS FREE ALONGSIDE SHIP

FOB FREE ON BOARD

CFR COST AND FREIGHT

CIF COST INSURANCE AND FREIGHT

The first class includes the seven Incoterms® 2010 rules that can be used irrespective of the mode of transport selected and irrespective of whether one or more than one mode of transport is employed. EXW, FCA, CPT, CIP, DAT, DAP and DDP belong to this class. They can be used even when there is no maritime transport at all. It is important to remember, however, that these rules can be used in cases where a ship is used for part of the carriage.

In the second class of Incoterms® 2010 rules, the point of delivery and the place to which the goods are carried to the buyer are both ports, hence the label "sea and inland waterway" rules. FAS, FOB, CFR and CIF belong to this class. Under the last three Incoterms rules, all mention of the ship's rail as the point of delivery has been omitted in preference for the goods being delivered when they are "on board" the vessel. This more closely reflects modern commercial reality and avoids the rather dated image of the risk swinging to and fro across an imaginary perpendicular line.

(3) Rules for domestic and international trade

Incoterms® rules have traditionally been used in international sale contracts where goods pass across national borders. In various areas of the world, however, trade blocs, like the European Union, have made border formalities between different countries less significant. Consequently, the subtitle of the Incoterms® 2010 rules formally recognizes that they are available for application to both international and domestic sale contracts. As a result, the Incoterms® 2010 rules clearly state in a number of places that the obligation to comply with export/import formalities exists only where applicable.

Two developments have persuaded the ICC that a movement in this direction is timely. Firstly, traders commonly use Incoterms® rules for purely domestic sale contracts. The second reason is the greater willingness in the United States to use Incoterms® rules in domestic trade rather than the former Uniform Commercial Code shipment and delivery terms.

(4) Guidance Notes

Before each Incoterms® 2010 rule you will find a Guidance Note. The Guidance Notes explain the fundamentals of each Incoterms® rule, such as when it should be used, when risk passes, and how costs are allocated between seller and buyer. The Guidance Notes are not part of the actual Incoterms® 2010 rules, but are intended to help the user accurately and efficiently steer towards the appropriate Incoterms® rule for a particular transaction.

(5) Electronic communication

Previous versions of Incoterms® rules have specified those documents that could be replaced by EDI messages. Articles A1/B1 of the Incoterms® 2010 rules, however, now give electronic means of communication the same effect as paper communication, as long as the parties so agree or where customary. This formulation facilitates the evolution of new electronic procedures throughout the lifetime of the Incoterms® 2010 rules.

(6) Insurance cover

The Incoterms® 2010 rules are the first version of the Incoterms® rules since the revision of the Institute Cargo Clauses and take account of alterations made to those clauses. The Incoterms® 2010 rules place information duties relating to insurance in articles A3/B3, which deal with contracts of carriage and insurance. These provisions have been moved from the more generic articles found in articles A10/B10 of the Incoterms® 2000 rules. The language in articles A3/B3 relating to insurance has also been altered with a view to clarifying the parties' obligations in this regard.

(7) Security-related clearances and information required for such clearances

There is heightened concern nowadays about security in the movement of goods, requiring verification that the goods do not pose a threat to life or property for reasons other than their inherent nature. Therefore, the Incoterms® 2010 rules have allocated obligations between the buyer and seller to obtain or to render assistance in obtaining security-related clearances, such as chain-of-custody information, in articles A2/B2 and A10/B10 of various Incoterms® rules.

(8) Terminal handling charges

Under Incoterms® 2010 rules CPT, CIP, CFR, CIF, DAT, DAP, and DDP, the seller must make arrangements for the carriage of the goods to the agreed destination. While the freight is paid by the seller, it is actually paid for by the buyer as freight costs are normally included by the seller in the total selling price. The carriage costs will sometimes include the costs of handling and moving the goods within port or container terminal facilities and the carrier or terminal operator may well charge these costs to the buyer who receives the goods. In these circumstances, the buyer will want to avoid paying for the same service twice: once to the seller as part of the total selling price and once independently to the carrier or the terminal operator. The Incoterms® 2010 rules seek to avoid this happening by clearly allocating such costs in articles A6/B6 of the relevant Incoterms rules.

(9) String sales

In the sale of commodities, as opposed to the sale of manufactured goods, cargo is frequently sold several times during transit "down a string". When this happens, a seller in the middle of the string does not "ship" the goods because these have already been shipped by the first seller in the string. The seller in the middle of the string therefore performs its obligations towards its buyer not by shipping the goods, but by "procuring" goods that have been shipped. For clarification purposes, Incoterms® 2010 rules include the obligation to "procure goods shipped" as an alternative to the obligation to ship goods in the relevant Incoterms rules.

International Rules for the Interpretation of Trade Terms 2010 (Incoterms 2010)

ICC rules for the use of domestic and international trade terms

Entry into force: 1 January 2011

Obligations of both parties

A. The Seller's Obligations

A1. General obligations of the seller

A2. Licences, authorizations, security clearances and other formalities

A3. Contract of carriage and insurance

A4. Delivery

A5. Transfer of risks

A6. Allocation of costs

A7. Notices to the buyer

A8. Delivery document

A9. Checking - packaging - marking

A10. Assistance with information and related costs

B. The Buyer's Obligations

B1. General obligations of the buyer

B2. Licences, authorizations, security clearances and other formalities

B3. Contract of carriage and insurance

B4. Taking delivery

B5. Transfer of risks

B6. Allocation of costs

B7. Notices to the seller

B8. Proof of delivery

B9. Inspection of goods

B10. Assistance with information and related costs

Table 3 - 1　**INCOTERMS** 2010 **Analysis**

Trade Terms	Place of Delivery	Division of Risks	Ex. clearance	Contract of		Im. clearance	Mode of transport
				carriage	insurance		
EXW	Seller's premises	Goods at the disposal of buyer	B	B	B	B	Any mode
FCA	Inland place or port of shipment	Goods at the disposal of carrier	S	B	B	B	Any mode
CPT	Inland place or port of shipment	Goods at the disposal of carrier	S	S	B	B	Any mode
CIP	Inland place or port of shipment	Goods at the disposal of carrier	S	S	S	B	Any mode
DAT	Terminal at port or place of destination in the importing country	Goods at the disposal of buyer	S	S	S	B	Any mode
DAP	Inland place in the importing country	Goods at the disposal of buyer	S	S	S	B	Any mode
DDP	Inland place in the importing country	Goods at the disposal of buyer	S	S	S	S	Any mode
FAS	Port of shipment	Goods placed alongside the vessel	S	B	B	B	Sea or inland waterway
FOB	Port of shipment	Delivering goods on board the vessel	S	B	B	B	Sea or inland waterway
CFR	Port of shipment	Delivering goods on board the vessel	S	S	B	B	Sea or inland waterway
CIF	Port of shipment	Delivering goods on board the vessel	S	S	S	B	Sea or inland waterway

3.2 Rules for any Mode of Transport

3.2.1 Ex Works EXW (named place of delivery) Incoterms® 2010

This rule may be used irrespective of the mode of transport selected and may also be used where more than one mode of transport is employed.

It is suitable for domestic trade, while FCA is usually more appropriate for international trade.

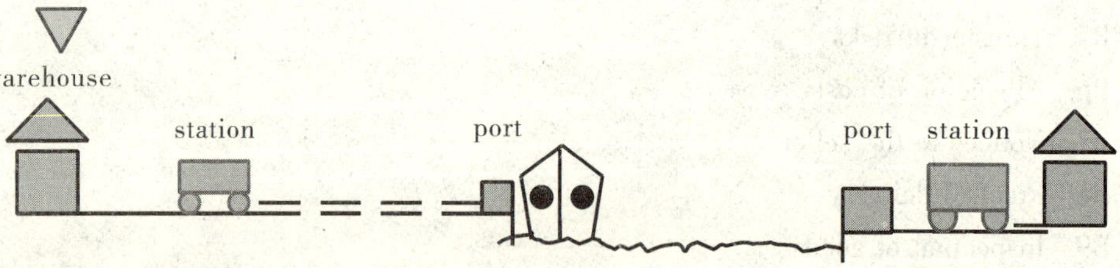

Figure 3-1 The Goods' Delivery Under EXW

"Ex Works" means that the seller delivers when it places the goods at the disposal of the buyer at the seller's premises or at another named place (i. e. works, factory, warehouse, etc.). The seller does not need to load the goods on any collecting vehicle, nor does it need to clear the goods for export, where such clearance is applicable.

The parties are well advised to specify as clearly as possible the point within the named place of delivery, as the costs and risks to that point are for the account of the seller. The buyer bears all costs and risks involved in taking the goods from the agreed point, if any, at the named place of delivery.

EXW represents the minimum obligation for the seller. The rule should be used with care as:

① The seller has no obligation to the buyer to load the goods, even though in practice the seller may be in a better position to do so. If the seller does load the goods, it does so at the buyer's risk and expense. In cases where the seller is in a better position to load the goods, FCA, which obliges the seller to do so at its own risk and expense, is usually more appropriate.

② A buyer who buys from a seller on an EXW basis for export needs to be aware that the seller has an obligation to provide only such assistance as the buyer may require to effect that export: the seller is not bound to organize the export clearance. Buyers are therefore well advised not to use EXW if they cannot directly or indirectly obtain export clearance.

③ The buyer has limited obligations to provide to the seller any information regarding the export of the goods. However, the seller may need this information for, e. g. taxation or reporting purposes.

3.2.2 Free Carrier FCA (named place of delivery) Incoterms® 2010

This rule may be used irrespective of the mode of transport selected and may also be used where more than one mode of transport is employed.

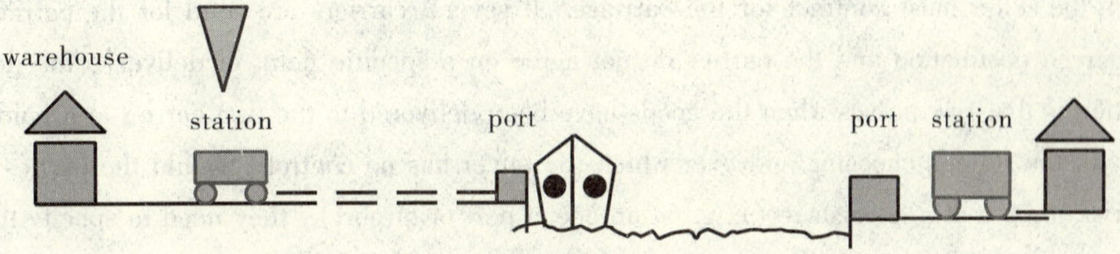

Figure 3 - 2 **The Goods' Delivery Under FCA**

"Free Carrier" means that the seller delivers the goods to the carrier or another person nominated by the buyer at the seller's premises or another named place. The parties are well advised to specify as clearly as possible the point within the named place of delivery, as the risk passes to the buyer at that point. If the parties intend to deliver the goods at the seller's premises, they should identify the address of those premises as the named place of delivery. If, on the other hand, the parties intend the goods to be delivered at another place, they must identify a different specific place of delivery.

FCA requires the seller to clear the goods for export, where applicable. However, the seller has no obligation to clear the goods for import, pay any import duty or carry out any import customs formalities.

3.2.3 Carriage Paid To CPT (named place of destination) Incoterms® 2010

This rule may be used irrespective of the mode of transport selected and may also be used where more than one mode of transport is employed.

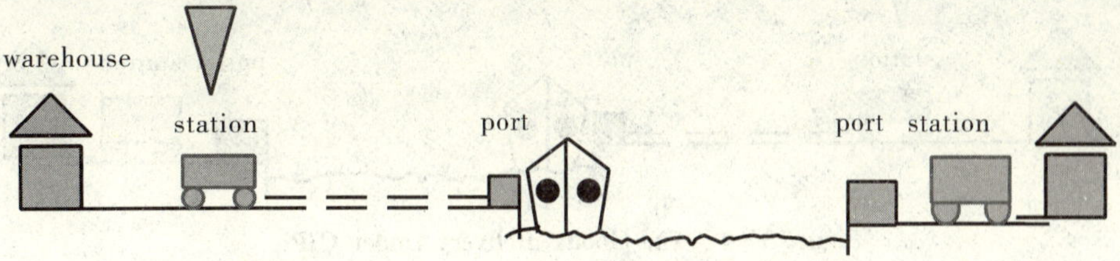

Figure 3 - 3 **The Goods' Delivery Under CPT**

"Carriage Paid To" means that the seller delivers the goods to the carrier or another person nominated by the seller at an agreed place (if any such place is agreed between the parties) and that the seller must contract for and pay the costs of carriage necessary to bring the goods to the named place of destination.

When CPT, CIP, CFR or CIF are used, the seller fulfils its obligation to deliver when it hands the goods over to the carrier and not when the goods reach the place of destination.

This rule has two critical points, because risk passes and costs are transferred at different places. The parties are well advised to identify as precisely as possible in the contract both the place of delivery, where the risk passes to the buyer, and the named place of destination to which the seller must contract for the carriage. If several carriers are used for the carriage to the agreed destination and the parties do not agree on a specific point of delivery, the default position is that risk passes when the goods have been delivered to the first carrier at a point entirely of the seller's choosing and over which the buyer has no control. Should the parties wish the risk to pass at a later stage (e. g. at an ocean port or airport), they need to specify this in their contract of sale.

The parties are also well advised to identify as precisely as possible the point within the agreed place of destination, as the costs to that point are for the account of the seller. The seller is advised to procure contracts of carriage that match this choice precisely. If the seller incurs costs under its contract of carriage related to unloading at the named place of destination, the seller is not entitled to recover such costs from the buyer unless otherwise agreed between the parties.

CPT requires the seller to clear the goods for export, where applicable. However, the seller has no obligation to clear the goods for import, pay any import duty or carry out any import customs formalities.

3.2.4 Carriage and Insurance Paid To CIP (named place of destination) Incoterms® 2010

This rule may be used irrespective of the mode of transport selected and may also be used where more than one mode of transport is employed.

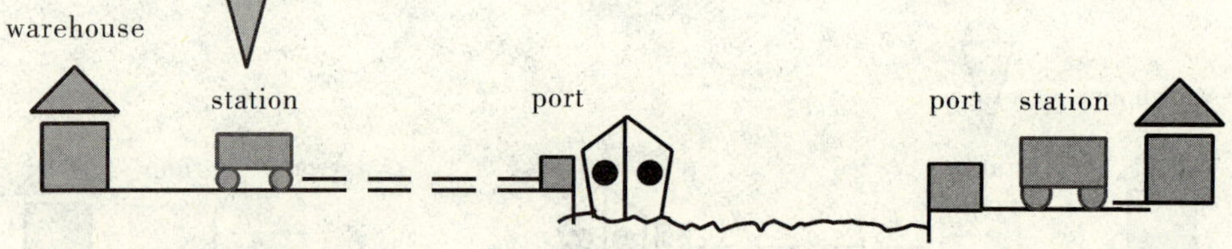

Figure 3 - 4 The Goods' Delivery Under CIP

"Carriage and Insurance Paid to" means that the seller delivers the goods to the carrier or another person nominated by the seller at an agreed place (if any such place is agreed between the parties) and that the seller must contract for and pay the costs of carriage necessary to bring the goods to the named place of destination.

The seller also contracts for insurance cover against the buyer's risk of loss of or damage to the goods during the carriage. The buyer should note that under CIP the seller is required to obtain insurance only on minimum cover. Should the buyer wish to have more insurance protection, it will need either to agree as much expressly with the seller or to make its own extra insurance arrangements.

When CPT, CIP, CFR or CIF are used, the seller fulfils its obligation to deliver when it hands the goods over to the carrier and not when the goods reach the place of destination.

This rule has two critical points, because risk passes and costs are transferred at different places. The parties are well advised to identify as precisely as possible in the contract both the place of delivery, where the risk passes to the buyer, and the named place of destination to which the seller must contract for carriage. If several carriers are used for the carriage to the agreed destination and the parties do not agree on a specific point of delivery, the default position is that risk passes when the goods have been delivered to the first carrier at a point entirely of the seller's choosing and over which the buyer has no control. Should the parties wish the risk to pass at a later stage (e. g. at an ocean port or an airport), they need to specify this in their contract of sale.

The parties are also well advised to identify as precisely as possible the point within the agreed place of destination, as the costs to that point are for the account of the seller. The seller is advised to procure contracts of carriage that match this choice precisely. If the seller incurs costs under its contract of carriage related to unloading at the named place of destination, the seller is not entitled to recover such costs from the buyer unless otherwise agreed between the parties.

CIP requires the seller to clear the goods for export, where applicable. However, the seller has no obligation to clear the goods for import, pay any import duty or carry out any import customs formalities.

3. 2. 5 Delivered At Terminal DAT (named terminal at port or place of destination) Incoterms® 2010

This rule may be used irrespective of the mode of transport selected and may also be used where port more than one mode of transport is employed.

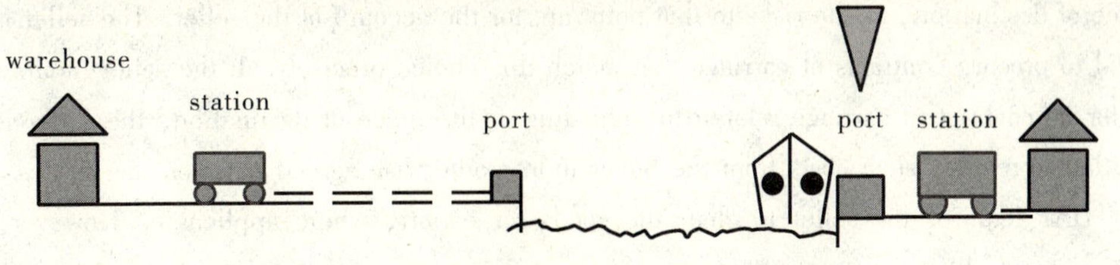

Figure 3 - 5 **The Goods' Delivery Under DAT**

"Delivered at Terminal" means that the seller delivers when the goods, once unloaded from the arriving means of transport, are placed at the disposal of the buyer at a named terminal at the named port or place of destination. "Terminal" includes any place, whether covered or not, such as a quay, warehouse, container yard or road, rail or air cargo terminal.

The seller bears all risks involved in bringing the goods to and unloading them at the terminal at the named port or place of destination. The parties are well advised to specify as clearly as possible the terminal and, if possible, a specific point within the terminal at the agreed port or place of destination, as the risks to that point are for the account of the seller. The seller is advised to procure a contract of carriage that matches this choice precisely.

Moreover, if the parties intend the seller to bear the risks and costs involved in transporting and handling the goods from the terminal to another place, then the DAP or DDP rules should be used.

DAT requires the seller to clear the goods for export, where applicable. However, the seller has no obligation to clear the goods for import, pay any import duty or carry out any import customs formalities.

3. 2. 6 Delivered At Place DAP (named place of destination) Incoterms® 2010

This rule may be used irrespective of the mode of transport selected and may also be used where more than one mode of transport is employed.

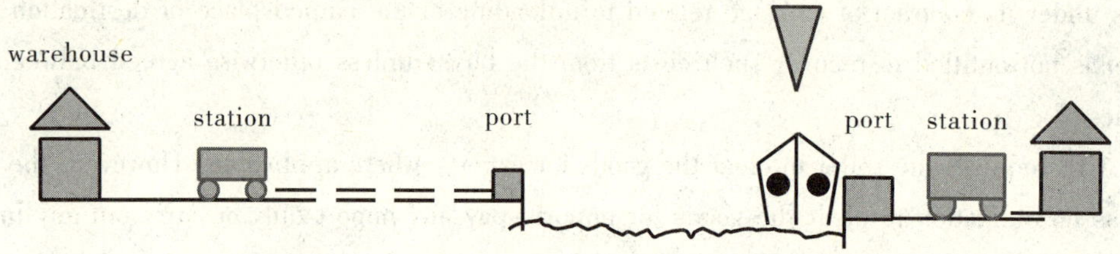

Figure 3 - 6 **The Goods' Delivery Under DAP**

"Delivered at Place" means that the seller delivers when the goods are placed at the disposal of the buyer on the arriving means of transport ready for unloading at the named place of destination. The seller bears all risks involved in bringing the goods to the named place.

The parties are well advised to specify as clearly as possible the point within the agreed place of destination, as the risks to that point are for the account of the seller. The seller is advised to procure contracts of carriage that match this choice precisely. If the seller incurs costs under its contract of carriage related to unloading at the place of destination, the seller is not entitled to recover such costs from the buyer unless otherwise agreed between the parties.

DAP requires the seller to clear the goods for export, where applicable. However, the seller has no obligation to clear the goods for import, pay any import duty or carry out any import customs formalities. If the parties wish the seller to clear the goods for import, pay any import duty and carry out any import customs formalities, the DDP term should be used.

3. 2. 7 Delivered Duty Paid DDP (named place of destination) Incoterms® 2010

This rule may be used irrespective of the mode of transport selected and may also be used where more than one mode of transport is employed.

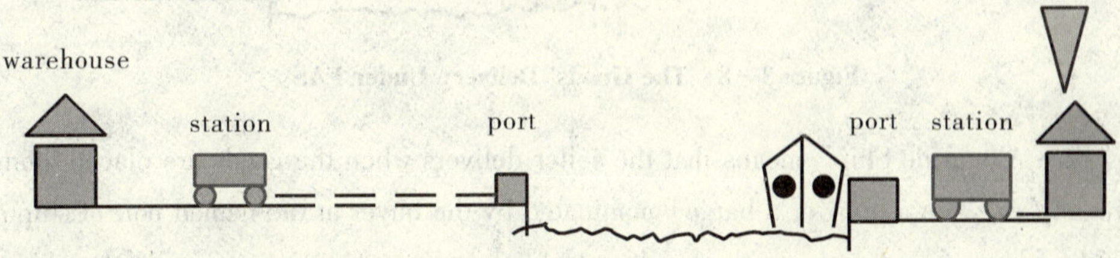

Figure 3 - 7 The Goods' Delivery Under DDP

"Delivered Duty Paid" means that the seller delivers the goods when the goods are placed at the disposal of the buyer, cleared for import on the arriving means of transport ready for unloading at the named place of destination. The seller bears all the costs and risks involved in bringing the goods to the place of destination and has an obligation to clear the goods not only for export but also for import, to pay any duty for both export and import and to carry out all customs formalities.

DDP represents the maximum obligation for the seller. The parties are well advised to specify as clearly as possible the point within the agreed place of destination, as the costs and risks to that point are for the account of the seller. The seller is advised to procure contracts of carriage that match this choice precisely. If the seller incurs costs under its contract of carriage related to unloading at the place of destination, the seller is not entitled to recover such costs from the buyer unless otherwise agreed between the parties.

The parties are well advised not to use DDP if the seller is unable directly or indirectly to obtain import clearance.

If the parties wish the buyer to bear all risks and costs of import clearance, the DAP rule should be used.

Any VAT or other taxes payable upon import are for the seller's account unless expressly agreed otherwise in the sales contract.

3. 3 Rules for Sea and Inland Waterway Transport

3. 3. 1 Free Alongside Ship FAS (named port of shipment) Incoterms® 2010

This rule is to be used only for sea or inland waterway transport.

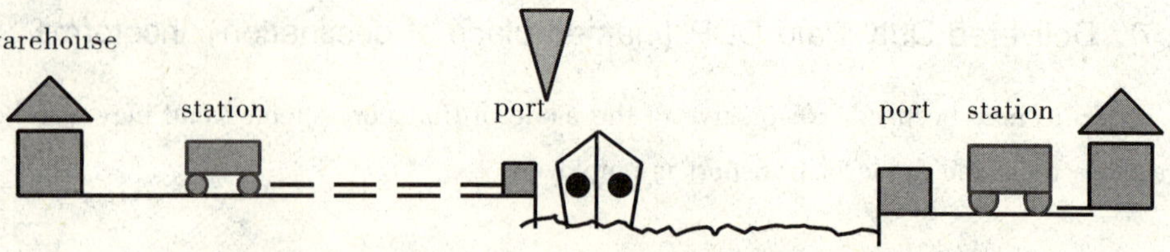

Figure 3 - 8 **The Goods' Delivery Under FAS**

"Free Alongside Ship" means that the seller delivers when the goods are placed alongside the vessel (e. g. on a quay or a barge) nominated by the buyer at the named port of shipment. The risk of loss of or damage to the goods passes when the goods are alongside the ship, and the buyer bears all costs from that moment onwards. The parties are well advised to specify as clearly as possible the loading point at the named port of shipment, as the costs and risks to that point are for the account of the seller and these costs and associated handling charges may vary according to the practice of the port. The seller is required either to deliver the goods alongside the ship or to procure goods already so delivered for shipment. The reference to "procure" here caters for multiple sales down a chain ('string sales'), particularly common in the commodity trades.

Where the goods are in containers, it is typical for the seller to hand the goods over to the carrier at a terminal and not alongside the vessel. In such situations, the FAS rule would be inappropriate, and the FCA rule should be used. FAS requires the seller to clear the goods for export, where applicable. However, the seller has no obligation to clear the goods for import, pay any import duty or carry out any import customs formalities.

3. 3. 2 Free On Board FOB (named port of shipment) Incoterms® 2010

This rule is to be used only for sea or inland waterway transport.

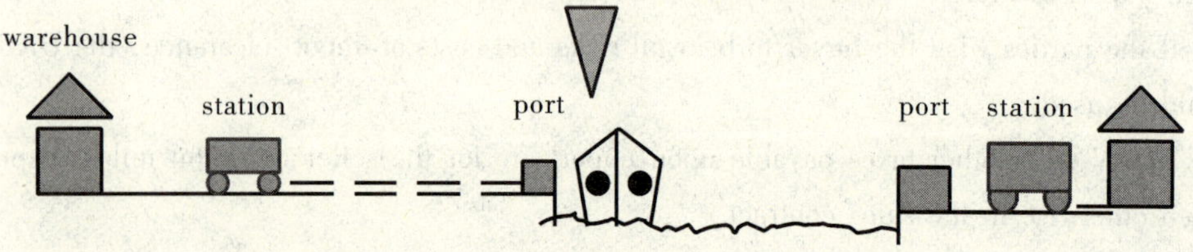

Figure 3 - 9 **The Goods' Delivery Under FOB**

"Free on Board" means that the seller delivers the goods on board the vessel nominated by the buyer at the named port of shipment or procures the goods already so delivered. The risk of loss of or damage to the goods passes when the goods are on board the vessel, and the buyer bears all costs from that moment onwards.

The seller is required either to deliver the goods on board the vessel or to procure goods already so delivered for shipment. The reference to "procure" here caters for multiple sales down a chain ('string sales'), particularly common in the commodity trades.

FOB may not be appropriate where goods are handed over to the carrier before they are on board the vessel, for example goods in containers, which are typically delivered at a terminal. In such situations, the FCA rule should be used.

FOB requires the seller to clear the goods for export, where applicable. However, the seller has no obligation to clear the goods for import, pay any import duty or carry out any import customs formalities.

3.3.3 Cost And Freight CFR (named port of destination) Incoterms® 2010

This rule is to be used only for sea or inland waterway transport. "Cost and Freight" means that the seller delivers the goods on board the vessel or procures the goods already so delivered. The risk of loss of or damage to the goods passes when the goods are on board the vessel.

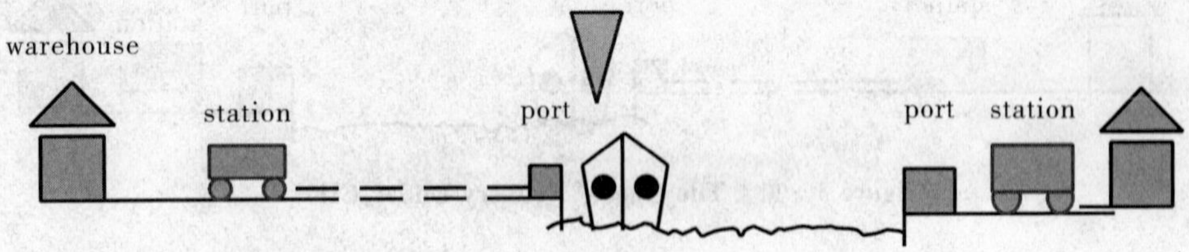

Figure 3-10 The Goods' Delivery Under CFR

The seller must contract for and pay the costs and freight necessary to bring the goods to the named port of destination. When CPT, CIP, CFR or CIF are used, the seller fulfils its obligation to deliver when it hands the goods over to the carrier in the manner specified in the chosen rule and not when the goods reach the place of destination.

This rule has two critical points, because risk passes and costs are transferred at different places. While the contract will always specify a destination port, it might not specify the port of shipment, which is where risk passes to the buyer. If the shipment port is of particular interest to the buyer, the parties are well advised to identify it as precisely as possible in the contract.

The parties are well advised to identify as precisely as possible the point at the agreed port of destination, as the costs to that point are for the account of the seller. The seller is advised to procure contracts of carriage that match this choice precisely. If the seller incurs costs under its contract of carriage related to unloading at the specified point at the port of destination, the seller is not entitled to recover such costs from the buyer unless otherwise agreed between the parties.

The seller is required either to deliver the goods on board the vessel or to procure goods already so delivered for shipment to the destination.

In addition, the seller is required either to make a contract of carriage or to procure such a contract. The reference to "procure" here caters for multiple sales down a chain ('string sales'), particularly common in the commodity trades.

CFR may not be appropriate where goods are handed over to the carrier before they are on board the vessel, for example goods in containers, which are typically delivered at a terminal. In such circumstances, the CPT rule should be used.

CFR requires the seller to clear the goods for export, where applicable. However, the seller has no obligation to clear the goods for import, pay any import duty or carry out any import customs formalities.

3.3.4 Cost Insurance And Freight CIF (named port of destination) Incoterms® 2010

This rule is to be used only for sea or inland waterway transport.

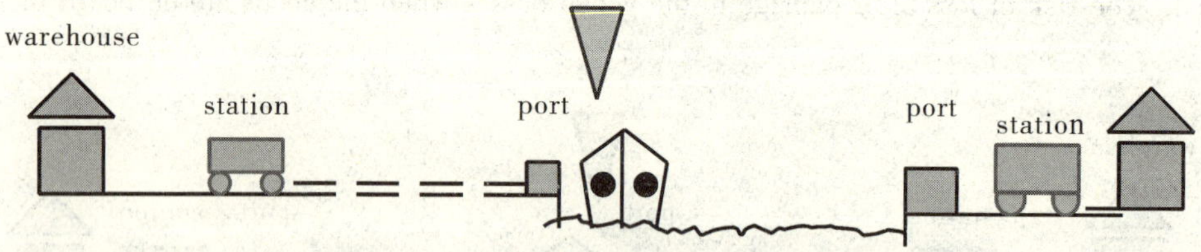

Figure 3 - 11 **The Goods' Delivery Under CIF**

"Cost, Insurance and Freight" means that the seller delivers the goods on board the vessel or procures the goods already so delivered. The risk of loss of or damage to the goods passes when the goods are on board the vessel. The seller must contract for and pay the costs and freight necessary to bring the goods to the named port of destination.

The seller also contracts for insurance cover against the buyer's risk of loss of or damage to the goods during the carriage. The buyer should note that under CIF the seller is required to obtain insurance only on minimum cover. Should the buyer wish to have more insurance protection, it will need either to agree as much expressly with the seller or to make its own extra insurance arrangements.

When CPT, CIP, CFR or CIF are used, the seller fulfils its obligation to deliver when it hands the goods over to the carrier in the manner specified in the chosen rule and not when the goods reach the place of destination.

This rule has two critical points, because risk passes and costs are transferred at different places. While the contract will always specify a destination port, it might not specify the port of shipment, which is where risk passes to the buyer. If the shipment port is of particular interest to the buyer, the parties are well advised to identify it as precisely as possible in the contract.

The parties are well advised to identify as precisely as possible the point at the agreed port of destination, as the costs to that point are for the account of the seller. The seller is advised to procure contracts of carriage that match this choice precisely. If the seller incurs costs under its contract of carriage related to unloading at the specified point at the port of destination, the seller is not entitled to recover such costs from the buyer unless otherwise agreed between the parties.

The seller is required either to deliver the goods on board the vessel or to procure goods already so delivered for shipment to the destination. In addition the seller is required either to make a contract of carriage or to procure such a contract. The reference to "procure" here caters for multiple sales down a chain ('string sales'), particularly common in the commodity trades.

CIF may not be appropriate where goods are handed over to the carrier before they are on board the vessel, for example goods in containers, which are typically delivered at a terminal. In such circumstances, the CIP rule should be used. CIF requires the seller to clear the goods for export, where applicable. However, the seller has no obligation to clear the goods for import, pay any import duty or carry out any import customs formalities.

3. 4 Important notes

In trade negotiation, contracts or documentation, all Incoterms must be expressed by the three-letter code with the naming of a physical place of handover. Since there are other rules existing for the interpretation of trade terms, it is important to clearly indicate Incoterms 2000 as the source of reference for definition. Just as the Incoterms 2010 publication states, "Incoterms will not apply unless incorporated into the trade contract by clearly specifying that the contract is governed by incoterms 2010. "

There are some other issues worth mentioning when the Incoterms are applied. The next section examines these key issues and provides some general guidelines in using the terms.

3. 4. 1 Customs Clearance

The customs clearance is an important issue in international trade. According to the Incoterms 2000, the obligation in connection with "passing the goods through customs refers to not only the payment of duty and other charges, but also the performance and payment of whatever administrative matters are connected with the customs clearance. " It is obviously desirable that the customs formalities are handled in a convenient manner. Therefore the Incoterms 2010 makes some revisions to the 1990 version and provides clear and reasonable regulations on these matters. Except EXW and DDP, all the other terms divide the obligations by country. The exporter is responsible for the export customs clearance and the importer is responsible for the import customs formalities. EXW allows the seller to bear minimum obligation and risk, so minimum that he does not even handle the export customs clearance. On the other hand, DDP imposes the maximum obligation and risk to the seller, obligation so onerous that the seller has to cover the import customs formalities and relevant risk and costs as well.

3.4.2 Quality Confirmation

While fulfilling a contract, it is the concern of both sides that the quality of the goods traded is guaranteed to be in conformity with the specifications contracted. Both the seller and the buyer may take different approaches to achieving the same goal. The Incoterms 2010 defines that it should be the seller's expense to cover checking operations which are necessary for the purpose of delivering the goods. These may include the quality control (QC) during the production stage, and measuring, weighing and counting at the time of delivery. For the interest of the buyer, it is normally necessary to inspect the goods before he agrees to take the delivery. Hence the buyer must pay the costs of any pre-shipment inspection.

In addition to the quality checking conducted by the traders, some inspections are required by the authorities of the exporting or importing country. This kind of inspection normally constitutes an integral part of the customs formalities. As a result, the Incoterms 2010 stipulates that the party which is responsible for handling the local customs clearance will also cover the costs of any inspections mandated by the local authorities.

3.4.3 Appropriation

The word "appropriate" originates from Late Latin "appropriates", meaning "to set aside". In modern law and government documents, appropriation refers to the act of setting apart something for its application to a particular usage, to the exclusion of all other uses.

Under Incoterms 2010, appropriation of the goods has become one of the conditions for realizing the transfer of risks from the seller to the buyer. That is to say, the seller has to use a certain way to clearly identify the goods as the goods assigned for that particular contract.

Failure to do so will result in the risk unable to be transferred even the specified point of transfer has been reached.

In practice the way of appropriation varies. The most common one is to identify the goods by using the unique shipping marks provided by the buyer. Bearing the logo or similar pictographic of a particular buyer the goods in question will be easily distinguished from the goods of other contracts.

3.4.4 Shipment Notice

Whenever the buyer is responsible for arranging the carriage of the cargo, he has the obligation to provide his counterpart with sufficient notice related to the transportation. Information necessary for that purpose may include the name of the carrier, the mode of transport, the date or period for delivery and if applicable, the point within the place where the goods should be delivered. Similarly, whenever the seller makes the shipment, he must give the buyer full details of the transport. Inability to provide sufficient and prompt shipment notice to the counterpart may lead to the failure of transfer or advanced transfer of risk.

A CFR contract may well demonstrate the significance of providing shipment notice. Under CFR the seller is responsible for arranging the ocean transport. If he fails to provide shipment details to the buyer after the shipment is made, the buyer will not be able to obtain insurance against his risk of loss of or damage to the goods during the ocean transport. In this case even though the goods cross the ship's rail, if loss or damage happens, the seller still has to bear the risk since he has not fulfilled his obligation of providing shipment notice to the buyer. Under an FOB contract, however, if the buyer provides false information about the time, place or any other arrangement for shipping the goods and causes extra costs to the seller or damage to the goods, the buyer has to bear all the loss even though actually delivery has not been realized.

3.4.5 Shipment Contract Term vs. Arrival Contract Term

If an Incoterms indicates that the delivery will happen at the time or before the time of shipment, this term is a shipment contract term. If the term specifies the seller to deliver at the time of arrival, it is an arrival contract term. This classification further highlights the importance of identifying the risk bearing issue. Traders must be clear about the nature of each Incoterms in the sense of risk bearing. For example, if a shipment contract is established, there should not be any provision or clause guaranteeing the arrival time of the shipment. And if it is an arrival contract, it is not necessary to stipulate a time of shipment. Previous lawsuit cases prove that if there is any contract clauses contrasting to the definition of the Incoterms employed, the court may support the contractual clauses rather than the implication of the terms. It is imperative therefore for the traders to be aware of the classification.

3.4.6 Symbolic Delivery vs. Actual Delivery

It often happens that when the seller delivers, the buyer does not physically receive the goods. The delivery is proved by the submission of transport document by the seller to the buyer. Such delivery is called a symbolic delivery. In a situation of symbolic delivery, it is especially important to mention when the buyer accepts the delivery by taking the transport document, it only means that the buyer agrees to the fact that the seller has performed his obligation to hand the goods over for carriage accordingly. This, however, does not mean that the buyer accepts the goods as conforming to the contract of sale. In case the buyer finds that the goods do not comply with the specifications on the contract upon receipt of the goods, he would be entitled to take any remedies against the seller, which has already been outside the scope of Incoterms.

On the other hand, if the buyer physically receives the goods upon the time of delivery, it is called an actual delivery. In reality sometimes the buyer may nominates a third party, a carrier typically, to take the delivery on his behalf. In this case the third party will be seen as the buyer himself and the delivery is still an actual one. The EXW term is a good example of this type. It is different from those terms under which a carrier has been explicitly defined asthe party for receiving the cargo.

3.5 Determinants of Choice of Trade Terms

The main objective of the lncoterms is to give the two trading parties a guideline of the obligations they need to fulfill. In an actual transaction, which term to choose is eventually determined by the traders' degree of acceptance of cost, obligation and risk. It is very important to consider all the possible aspects while choosing the lncoterms. Traders should not accept any term which requires a performance beyond his ability. Other criteria for selecting terms may include:

exporting and importing possibilities,

pricing purpose,

availability of transport,

competitive position on the transport market,

ability of risk control.

It is a noticeable fact that in spite of its detailed definition about relevant issues, the lncoterms 2010 has a very restricted scope of governance. It cannot replace any provisions in a sales contract which regulates an aspect other than those governed by it. The familiarity with the Incoterms enables the traders to communicate more easily, but other skills obtained through long time of practice and experience will be indispensable.

3.6 Summary

The trade terms are the short terms or abbreviations or brief English concept to indicate/explain the composition/formation of the unit price and determine the responsibilities/rights and obligations, expenses and risks borne by two parties as well as the time of the passing of the property in the goods. The two main categories of INCOTERMS® 2010 are now organized by modes of transport. Used in international as well as in domestic contracts for the first time, the new groups aim to simplify the drafting of contracts and help avoid misunderstandings by clearly stipulating certain obligations of buyers and sellers.

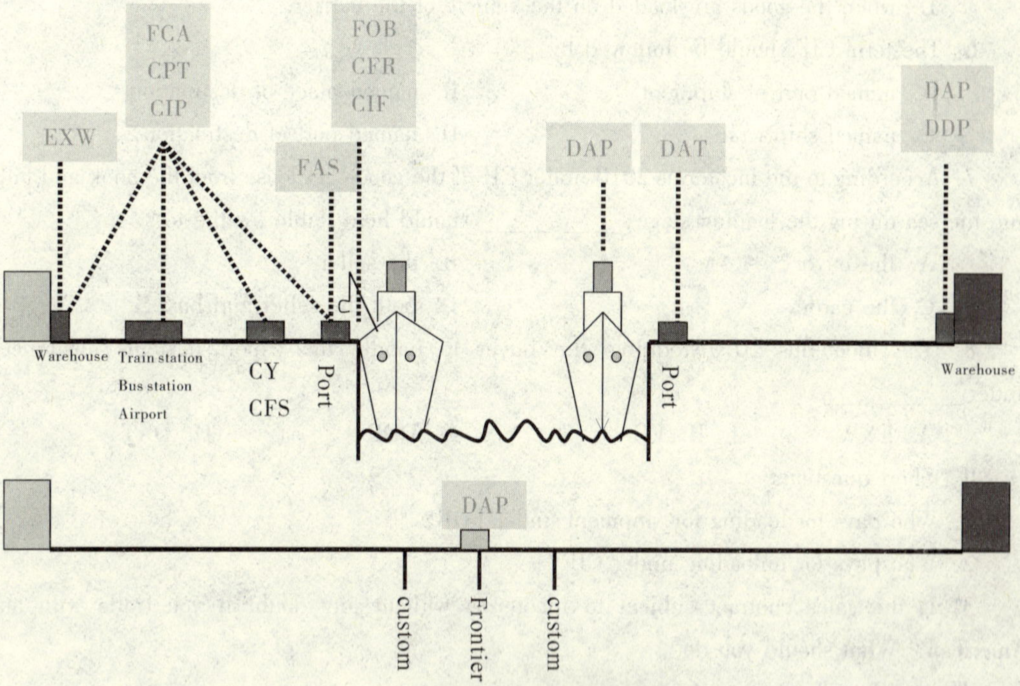

Figure 3 - 12 Risk of Transfer and Delivery

Exercises

Ⅰ. Choices

1. There are mainly __________ sets of international rules related to the interpretation of trade terms.

A. two B. three C. four D. five

2. There are altogether __________ terms defined by the Incoterms 2010.

A. 1 B. 6 C. 11 D. 13

3. In the Incoterms 2010, __________ imposes the minimum obligation and cost to the seller.

A. EXW B. CIF C. DAP D. DDP

4. In the Incoterms 2010, __________ imposes the minimum obligation and cost to the buyer.

A. CIF B. FOB C. DDP D. EXW

5. According to the lncoterms 2010 under FCA the risk of goods will be transferred from the seller to the buyer

A. when the goods are placed at the disposal of the buyer.

B. when the goods are delivered to the named place in the exporting country.

C. when the goods are given to the nominated carrier.

D. when the goods are loaded on the vehicle of the carrier.

6. The term CIF should be followed by

A. named port of shipment　　B. named place of destination

C. named ship's rail　　D. named port of destination

7. According to the incoterms 2010 under CIF if the goods get loose from the hook and fall into the sea during the loading stage, __________ should hold liable for the loss.

A. the buyer　　B. the seller

C. the carder　　D. both the seller and buyer

8. The lncoterms 2010 requires the buyer to handle the export customs clearance under __________.

A. EXW　　B. FCA　　C. DDP　　D. DAT

Ⅱ. Short questions

1. Who pays for loading for shipment under FOB?

2. Who pays for unloading under CIF?

3. Is the sales contract subject to Incoterms without any doubt if you trade with an American'? What should you do?

Ⅲ. Case study

A Chinese import and export company concluded a Sale Contract with a Holland firm on August 5, 2013, selling a batch of certain commodity. The contract was based on CIF Rotterdam at USD 2500 per metric ton. The Chinese company delivered the goods in compliance with the contract and obtained a clean on board Bill of Lading. During transportation, however, 100 metric tons of goods got lost because of rough sea. Upon arrival of the good, the price of the contracted goods went down quickly. The buyer refused to take delivery of the goods and effect payment and claimed damages from the seller. How would you deal with the case?

Question:

1. Is the buyer's refusal reasonable? Why?

2. How should the buyer to deal with the loss?

Chapter 4 Terms of Commodity

Learning Objectives

1. To master how to name a Commodity
2. To master the methods of specifying Quality and measuring Quantity
3. To understand the function and methods of Packing and Marking

Key Words

Name of commodity; Sale by seller's sample; Sale by buyer's sample; Original sample; Duplicate sample; Counter sample; Return sample; Sale by grade; Fair Average Quality; Quality tolerance; Gross weight; Gross for net; Net weight; Legal weight; More or less clause; Transport packing; Shipping mark; Indicative mark; Neutral packing

A sales contract is a transfer of title to the subject matter of the contract. In international trade, the subject matters of trade are various. Different subject matter have their specific names and certain quality. Subject matters in every transaction include certain quantity and packing. Therefore, both parties in the process of trade negotiation and signing contract must settle on the main trade terms of subject matter in the contract such as specific name, quality, quantity and packing and so on. Therefore, terms and conditions concerning commodity must be explicitly stipulated in the sales contract to avoid subsequent disputes between the seller and the buyer.

4.1 Name of Commodity

4.1.1 Significance of Definite Name of Subject Matter

Sales contract concerns subject transmission. Delivery of goods is important element of sales. The important characteristic of sale contract is that seller transfers title of subject matter to buyer. As we know, in international trade, cash on delivery is very rare and it needs long time from signing contract to delivery of goods. In addition, in the process of negotiating and signing contract both parties of trade usually seldom see specific goods, generally communicate subject matter by necessary description of commodity. So it becomes an imperative term to stipulate name of commodity.

In accordance with the relevant laws and regulations, the description of the subject matter for the deal is a major component of commodity explanation and a basis of the handover commodity of both parties. It concerns the rights and obligations of both parties. If the seller's delivery of the goods are not in conformity with the agreed the name or description, the buyer shall have the right to make a damage compensation claims, until the rejection of the goods or cancel of the contract. Therefore, specific name of commodity has the important legal and practical significance.

4.1.2 Content of Name of Commodity

There is no unified format to request the name term of commodity in international trade contract, so both parties can determine the name of commodity by negotiation. The name terms of Commodity in contract is simple, usually under the title of the "product Name" or "Commodity" (Name of Commodity), detailing the Name of the Commodity. Sometimes for the sake of omission, it just stipulate trading some commodity of both parties at the beginning of the contract.

The terms of the name of commodity, also depend on the varieties and characteristics of goods. About the general commodities, sometimes it is enough to give the name of the commodity. But some commodities often have different varieties, levels and types. Therefore, for the purpose of unambiguous interpretation, description of commodity also include relevant specific varieties, levels or types and so on for further limit. In addition, some even include quality and specification of goods. In this case, it is not only the terms of commodity, but includes commodity terms and quality terms.

4.1.3 Announcements of Formulating Name of Commodity

The name of commodity in international trade contract is main term. Therefore, to avoid subsequent disputes, the following four issues need to be considered:

(1) be clear and specific

The methods of naming the commodity are various, such as named by main application, main raw materials or main ingredients, exterior modelling or manufacturing process, name of person or place, commendatory term and so on. Therefore, when stipulating name of commodity, it is to make specific and clear name of subject matter to avoid the argue, general or ambiguous provisions, which facilitate the implementation of the contract.

The name of a commodity is an indispensable part of a sales contract. In most cases, it may be simply put under the contract item "Name of Commodity" (e. g. Name of Commodity: China Sesame Seed). However, many goods under the same name are of different kinds. It is necessary to provide further description such as specifications, grade, etc. Hence, the name and the quality description are often merged into one (e. g. Description of Commodity: China

Black Tea, Grade One). In such a case, the name of commodity may constitute part of the "Description of Commodity" or "Description of Goods" in the contract.

(2) realistic provisions

The name of commodity stipulated in the clause must be the goods that seller can supply and buyer need. All unnecessary descriptive phrases shall not be employed to avoid to perform the contract difficultly.

(3) use common international name

Sometimes a product is named differently in different countries and regions. As a result, different names may refer to the same commodity or the same name may mean different products. For example, "Coke" may refer to the soft drink Coca-Cola, or coke. To protect the interests of both parties, commodity names used on contracts should bear common interpretation by the seller and the buyer. Possible disputes can be further avoided by adopting internationally standardized and widely accepted names such as those listed in the H. S.

(4) choose the right names

In some cases, the appropriate choice of commodity names may facilitate the flow of import and export and reduce costs of transaction in terms of reducing customs tariff, avoiding non-tariff trade barriers and lowering transportation costs. It happens that when the same product is imported or exported under different names or categories of commodities, differential tariff rates or freight rates and trade policies may apply. Traders, therefore, should give some consideration to the tactical employment of the commodity names so as to benefit the most.

Case: Sino-German quality dispute of marijuana

Some export company exports a batch of marijuana to German trader, the following of the quality term of commodity:

moisture (Max): 15%

impurities Contain (Max): 3%

In the process of negotiation, we sent the samples to the buyer. After contracting, we advise counterparty to deal with goods similar to samples by fax.

As result, the arrival of goods to Germany, by inspection counterpart found that the quality of goods meet the specifications of contract stipulated, but 7% lower than the specifications of sample. The buyer took the certificate of inspection to require us to pay compensation for the losses of 600 pounds.

Our company stated the delivered goods were carefully selected, but impossible for the full conformity with the sample owing to the specialty of agricultural products. Also we thought it was impossible that the specification was 7% lower than the sample.

Because of our company losing retained samples, we could not prove our statement. Finally we had to pay the surcharge of quality difference to close this case.

4.2 Specifying Quality

The quality of the goods refers to complex of the internal quality and appearance shape of goods. The former includes natural attributes of the goods, such as the physical properties, the mechanical properties, chemical composition and biological characteristics and so on. The latter include the appearance of goods, color, style and transparency, etc.

It is very important significance to improve the quality of the commodity, because quality of commodity directly affect value and price of commodity, which is important factor to determine using efficiency of goods and market price. When the competition of international market become more and more fierce, many countries take improving quality of commodity into consideration as an important component of non - price competition. It has been necessary approach to strengthen competition and international trade. Hence, in export trade constantly improving and enhancing the quality of the export products, not only can enhance export competition ability, expand market, increase the price to create more foreign exchange income for the country and enterprise, but also can improve reputation of the export goods in international market.

Owing to the fact that large portions of international commodity transactions are conducted for goods normally unavailable at the time of contracting, two major ways have been developed to describe the quality of goods in a contract: sale by description and sale by sample. In some rare cases, a third way may also be adopted for the deal of ready goods—sale by actual commodity or sale by actual quality. In the following section, we will introduce the details of the methods and discuss some issues concerning quality clauses in the contract.

4.2.1 Sale by Description

Sale by description is a way to specify the quality of most commodities in international trade. Sale by description may take the form of sale by specification, sale by grade, sale by standard, sale by brand name or trade mark, sale by origin and sale by descriptions or illustrations. Different forms may be chosen depending on the attributes, nature, and characteristics of a commodity. Generally speaking, sale by description is applicable to commodities of which quality can be expressed by some scientific indices.

4.2.1.1 Sale by Specification

Commodity Specifications refer to some leading indicator to reflect commodity quality, such as chemical composition, content, purity, performance, capacity, length, size, etc. In international trade, when both parties negotiate trade terms, if the products are for Sale by specifications, both parties shall provide specifications to illustrate the basic quality goods condition, and specified in the contract. When sale by specifications, different goods employ different indicator to illustrate quality of commodity. Even, due to different application, the requirement of specification of the same goods is different. For example, if trade of soybean suits for oil expression, the indicator of specification must include oil content in contract. But if trade of soybean suits for edible oil, the indicator of oil content is unnecessary, but protein content necessary in specification. Sale by specifications is simple, easy, pacific, and flexible adjustment according to specific quality. So this method is widely applied in the international trade.

Example 1:

Chinese Ground-nut, FAQ Moisture (max.) 13%

Admixture (max.) 5%

Oil Content (min.) 44%

Bleached Cotton Shirting 30s × 30s, 72 × 69, 38inch × 121.5yd

4.2.1.2 Sale by Grade

Owing to goods of different grade with different specification, when stipulating grade in quality terms, it is necessary to provide every grade specific specification to avoid further disputes. If traders are familiar with specific specification of every grade, it is unnecessary to provide definite specification. According to the knowledge of long-term production and experience, manufacturers or exporters formulate the grade of commodity based on the the master its quality specification. The grade of commodity helps to meet all kinds of needs, helpful for arranging production and processing according to various needs. This method is useful to simplify procedures and promote transaction.

Example 2:

Fresh Hen Eggs, shell light brown and clean, even in size

Grade AA: 60—65gm per egg

Grade A: 55—60gm per egg

Grade B: 50—55gm per egg

Grade C: 45—50gm per egg

Tungsten Classification

Special Grade

Tungsten Trioxide (min) 70%, Tin (max) 0.2%, Arsenic (max) 0.2%, Sulphur (max) 0.8%

1st Grade

Tungsten Trioxide (min) 65%, Tin (max) 0.2%, Arsenic (max) 0.2%, Sulphur (max) 0.8%

2nd Grade

Tungsten Trioxide (min) 65%, Tin (max) 1.5%, Arsenic (max) 0.2%, Sulphur (max) 0.8%

4. 2. 1. 3 Sale by Standard

When specifications or grades are laid down and proclaimed in a unified way, they become standards. Standards are formulated either by governments or by commercial organizations. Some apply to individual country; others are used internationally. Many countries have their own standards, for example, BS in Britain, ANSI in the USA, JIS in Japan and GB in China. The typical international standard is ISO Standard.

As standards of commodities are subject to changes or amendments over time, it is important to mark the year in which the standard is created to avoid ambiguities.

Different categories of products have different standards. Some special standards are designed for particular reasons. Fair Average Quality (F. A. Q.) and Good Merchantable Quality (G. M. Q.) are good examples of this type. Generally speaking, it is difficult to establish fixed quality standards for agricultural products since they can be easily affected by all sorts of external factors. Thus F. A. Q. is used to indicate that the quality of the product offered is about equal to the average quality level of the same crop within a certain period of time (e. g. a year). G. M. Q. on the other hand, means that the goods offered are of a quality sufficiently good to satisfy the purpose of use or consumption which are mutually understood by both the buyer and the seller. It is used sometimes as the bottom-line of quality requirement.

Similar as using sale by grade, standards are usually supplemented by some detailed specifications for clearer presentation of information.

Example 3:

Tetracycline HCL Tablets (Sugar Coated) 250mg. B. P. 1973 (Note: B. P. refers to British Pharmacopoeia).

China Northeast Soybean 2006 New Crop, F. A. Q:

Moisture (max.) 15 %

Admixture (max.) 1%

Imperfect granules (max.) 7%

Oil content (min.) 17%

4. 2. 1. 4 Sale by Brand Name or Trade Mark

It is possible to define the quality of some products by simply referring to their brand names or trademarks. Many consumption products adopt this approach. Typical examples include Sony Televisions, Haier Refrigerators, Tigerhead Batteries and Triangle Tires. Brand is the name, term, symbol, or design or a combination of these to identify a product. It has a narrower meaning in which an enterprise means to distinguish its products from the products of other enterprises. There are so many brands that we take them for granted. In the grocery product area alone, there are more than 40, 000 brands. Brands are of great importance to their owners because they help identify the company's marketing mix and help consumers recognize the firm's products and advertising. Trade mark is a legal term. It includes all those words, symbols, or marks that are legally registered for use by a single company. It is a symbol or ornamental printed on a commodity or its packing. The word Buick can be used to explain these differences. The Buick car is branded under the brand name "Buich". When "Buick" is printed in a certain kind of script, however, it becomes a trademark. A trademark need not be attached to the product. It can be a word or a symbol. These differences may seem technical. But they are very important to business firms that spend a lot of money to protect and promote their brands.

Some reputed products have well-known trade marks and brands, hence the trade marks and brands can represent the quality of the products. And such products can sell well their brands and trade marks. Sometimes firms use individual brands to encourage competition within the company. Each brand is managed by a different group within the firm. Management feels that internal competition keeps everyone alter. This kind of competition is found among General Motor's brand. Chevrolet, Pontiac, Oldsmobile, Buick, and even Cadillac compete with each other in some markets.

Sales by brand or trade marks are conducted mostly for goods with fixed quality. It is unnecessary to inquire much about the quality of these products in business negotiation. But you should state the type and specifications of the products you want.

4. 2. 1. 5 Sale by Origin

Sale by origin refers to the sale of goods by using the name of the place of origin as the indication of quality. This is more suitable for agricultural products or by - products. Owing to the unique and favorable natural conditions or traditional production techniques in some areas, the native products are renowned for their specially and excellence in quality. Sale by origin is usually used in company with other necessary quality indices such as specifications, grade or brands. The way to specify the tea as "West - lake Longjing Tea, Grade 1, Zhejiang Origin" is a typical example.

4. 2. 1. 6 Sale by Descriptions or Illustrations

Sale by descriptions or illustrations is especially applicable to full sets of equipment or instruments. These commodities are usually complicated in property and structure. It is difficult to use simple indicator such as data or parameters to describe the quality. In addition, the installation, usage and maintenance of such equipment or instruments shall follow certain procedures. Therefore specific descriptions, sometimes with illustrations, are necessary for specifying the quality.

In the case of sale by descriptions or illustrations, clauses such as "quality and technical data to be in conformity with the description submitted by the seller" are to be stipulated in the contract and relevant technical manuals, booklets of directions, drawings or diagrams will be attached as well to serve the purpose.

Example 4:

Panasonic Television, TH42PV65C. quality and data to be strictly in conformity with the instructions attached.

Haier Refrigerator, Model XXX, quality and technical data to be strictly in conformity with the descriptions submitted by the seller.

4.2.2 Sale by Sample

A sample refers to a single item of a consignment of goods or a part of a whole product, possibly selected from a whole consignment or specially designed or processed. It is a usual practice that a sample can be regarded as the representative of the whole shipment to be delivered. In trading, samples are frequently offered to potential buyers as the evidence of quality.

A sale is made by sample when the seller and buyer agree that samples are used as reference of quality and condition of the goods to be delivered. This method is used when it is difficult to describe quality of the commodity by words. Some products contain some properties or features that are far beyond the scope of any scientific or technical description. When words are futile, the product can talk. A lot of light industrial products, agricultural native produce, arts and crafts, and garments rely on samples for quality confirmation. In the case of a sale by sample, the reference number and the date of sampling should be indicated. Typical expression on the contract may read as "Teddy Bear Size 15, Quality as per Sample X07111SA".

Samples can be provided by either the seller or buyer. According to the supplier of the sample, there are three cases under sale by sample: sale by seller's sample, sale by buyer's sample and sale by counter sample.

4.2.2.1 Sale by Seller's Sample

When a sale is made based on the sample provided by the seller, it is a sale by seller's sample. In international trade it often happens that the seller presents collection of samples and the buyer makes his selection. Since the buyer's purchasing decision is based on the samples presented by the seller, it is rather natural to stick to the same samples for the purpose of quality specification. This is the most common one among the three.

If this method is used, it should be clearly stipulated in the contract that quality is "as per Seller's Sample" and the quality of the actual goods should conform to that of the sample.

4.2.2.2 Sale by Buyer's Sample

Sometimes buyers may provide samples to sellers, requesting supply of the same goods. In this case, samples from buyers are referred to as the benchmark of quality requirement. This is a sale by buyer's sample.

Under such circumstances, wording like "quality as per Buyer's Sample" should be clearly stipulated in the contract and the seller should provide goods of the same quality as that of the buyer's sample.

In case of sale by buyer's sample, the seller has to study the samples thoroughly, ensuring that all details are covered. A frequent mistake sellers may make is that they are able to identify the external features, but ignore the intrinsic characteristics of the sample. In addition, he might need to pay special attention to factors such as raw material supply, processing techniques and equipment available, managing to achieve the equivalent quality of the samples. Considering the probability of miscomprehension of product properties and the limitation of local conditions sometimes, sellers are not encouraged to use this approach.

4. 2. 2. 3 Sale by Counter Sample

A counter sample is a replica made by the seller of the sample provided, normally by the buyer. As the buyer is usually required to return the sample back to the seller with his confirmation if he approves of the sample, a counter sample is also called a returned sample or a confirmed sample.

This method is a good substitute to sale by buyer's sample because it removes the risk sellers have to bear under other approaches. By sending a replica to the buyer, the seller is free from the uncertainty of getting the right picture of the product. If the counter sample is not in conformity with the original one, it will be disapproved by the buyer. The seller hence will not have the chance to provide the wrong mass products due to his misunderstanding. On the other hand, once the counter sample is confirmed by the buyer, it will replace the original sample. and become the final standard of quality of the transaction. The seller would be more comfortable to prepare the mass products according to a sample provided by himself. Even in the worst scenario that the buyer later finds the counter sample does not match with the original, the seller will not carry any responsibility as the counter sample has been confirmed by the buyer.

When a transaction is made by sample, the seller should keep one or more equivalent samples for file when sending a sample to the buyer. This is called a duplicate sample. If necessary, the seller may also, before sending samples or delivering the goods to the buyer, have one additional sealed sample. The sample is sealed by sealing wax in the presence of the buyer or a notary party or a local commercial inspection institution. Both the seller and buyer will sign or stamp on the sample. The duplicate sample and sealed sample can serve as the proof of quality in case there is a dispute about the quality of the goods to be delivered in the future.

In addition, when sale is made by description sometimes, either the seller or the buyer may send a sample to his counterpart as a material reference. Samples provided for this purpose should carry marks clearly showing "For Reference Only". A reference sample is not considered as the basis of delivery and a transaction using reference sample does not belong to sale by sample.

4. 2. 3 Sale by Actual Commodity or Sale by Actual Quality

In some occasions, traders may also deal with goods already available at the time of contracting. The quality of the actual goods will then form the condition of transaction. This is called sale by actual commodity or sale by actual quality.

Trading under this term, buyers normally inspect the goods before their purchase is made and once the sale is finalized sellers do not provide any guarantee on the quality or condition of the goods sold, nor hold any liability of compensation in case of defects. Sale by actual commodity or sale by actual quality applies to items such as jewelry, paintings, arts and crafts and most products in stock. They mainly take place in some special forms like sale by consignment, sale by auction, exhibition sale, etc.

It should be noted that all approaches discussed above are not independent of each other. If necessary, two or more ways can be used simultaneously in order to specify the quality with clarity. In the meantime, traders, especially sellers, should also be aware of the problem of "double standard". When one specifying method is sufficient to serve the purpose, it is advisable not to employ any others because sellers are obliged to provide goods in strict conformity with the requirements contracted. As CISG Article 35 states, if a transaction is made both by description and by sample, the seller must deliver goods not only conforming to quality descriptions in the contract, but also possessing the equivalent quality of the sample. The more criteria are set, the greater the difficulties would be for the sellers to fulfill their obligation.

4. 2. 4 Other Quality Clauses

Apart from defining the basic quality criteria, quality clauses in a sales contract usually include some other elements as well, which constitute the condition to apply the quality standards formerly identified. One of them is the statement of quality latitude or quality tolerance. If it is a sale by buyer's sample or a sale by counter sample, a safeguard clause is also inserted.

4. 2. 4. 1 Quality Latitude or Quality Tolerance

Absolute equivalence of quality is not practically feasible in most cases. Therefore, the quality latitude or quality tolerance clause is introduced to address the issue.

Quality latitude means the permissible range within which the quality of the goods delivered by the seller may be flexibly controlled. Quality tolerance refers to the quality deviation recognized, which allows the quality of the goods delivered to have certain difference within a range. According to international practice, quality with some deviation within a certain range is still considered to meet the quality stipulation in a contract.

Evidently a quality latitude or tolerance clause is necessary in the contract. It is normally set by stating the flexible quality range or scope, the maximum or minimum requirements, or a deviation allowance for certain quality indexes.

Example 5:

To stipulate a certain scope e. g. The width of the cotton cloth is 47/48 inches.

To stipulate "max" or "min" e. g. Moisture (max): 8%

Admixture (max) 2%

To stipulate more or less allowance e. g. Duck's down content 18% ±1%

When a sale is made by sample, it is also impossible for the seller to deliver goods of quality identical to that of the sample. Therefore, wording such as "about" should be added to the quality clause to allow quality flexibility.

Example 6:

"Quality shall be about equal to the sample."

"Quality is nearly the same as the sample."

"The quality of the goods shipped to be about equal to the sample."

"Shipment shall be similar to the sample."

In most cases, prices of the commodities remain unchanged when the quality varies within the tolerance or latitude unless otherwise specified in the contract. However, when the difference in quality is big enough to constitute fundamental change to the quality of goods, prices are to be adjusted accordingly and it should be explicitly stipulated in the contract.

Example 7:

"Soybean, if the oil content of the goods shipped is 1% higher, the price will bc accordingly increased by 2 %."

Chinese Sesame seed F. A. Q. 2008 Crop, Moisture (max.) 8%; Admixture (max.) 2%; Oil Content 52% basis. Should the oil content of the goods actually shipped be 1% higher or lower, the price will be accordingly increased or decreased by 1%, and any fraction will be proportionally calculated.

4. 2. 4. 2 Safeguard Clause

According to CISG Article 42, the seller must deliver goods that are free from any right or claim of a third party based on industrial property or other intellectual property. In the case of sale by buyer's sample or sale by counter sample、however, there exists the possibility that the seller might provide goods alleged to have infringed the copy right of a third party without his privities. Therefore, a safeguard clause is usually stipulated in the contract. It can protect the seller from any undeserved liabilities.

Example 8:

"It is the buyer rather than the seller who shall be responsible for any disputes arising from the infringement of the third party's intellectual properties."

For any cotton piece goods produced with the design, trade marks, brands, and/or stampings provided by the buyer, should there be any disputes arising from the infringement upon the third party's industrial property rights, it is the buyer to be held responsible for it.

In case the buyer's sample results in any disputes of infringement of industrial property, the seller will have nothing to do with it.

4. 3 Measuring Quantity

Quantity is one of the essential conditions in a business contract in international trade. It is obligatory for sellers to deliver the quantity of goods that is identical to that called for in the contract.

According to CISG, if the quantity delivered is more than agreed upon, the buyer is entitled to reject delivery of the excess quantity, or he may take delivery of all or part of the excess quantity, he must pay for it at the contract rate. If the quantity delivered is less than that agreed upon, sellers should make up for the shortage within the time limit without rendering buyers any unreasonable inconvenience and cost. However, buyers are still entitled to lodge a claim for compensation.

4. 3. 1 Use of Unit

In international trade, the quantity of commodities is always shown as a specific amount in different measurement units such as weight, number, length, area and volume. Since different commodities have different natures and characteristics, the adoption of measurement units varies. The commonly used measurement units are as follows:

(1) Weight

Kilogram (kg.); ton (t); metric ton (m/t); quintal (q.); gram (gm.); pound (lb.); ounce (oz.); long ton (l/t); and short ton (s/t.) are units of weight. These are widely used for the measurement of raw materials and agricultural products such as minerals, raw chemicals, coal, oil, wool, cotton, corns and medicine.

(2) Capacity

Units of capacity are liter (l.); gallon (gal.); bushel (bu.), etc. They are applicable to products such as wheat, corn, gas, gasoline and beer.

(3) Number

There are various measurement units by means of number such as piece (pc.); package (pkg.); pair; set; dozen (doz.); gross (gr.); great gross (g. gr.); ream (rm.); roll or coil; unit; head; case; bale; barrel or drum; bag, etc. They are lot daily industrial and general products, such as stationery, paper, toys, ready-made clothes, vehicles and live animals.

(4) Length

Yard (yd.); meter (m.); foot (ft.); centimeter (cm.), etc. are measurement units of length. They are often used for textiles, roves and wires and so on.

(5) Area

Square yard (yd^2); square meter (m^2); square toot (ft^2) and square inch, etc. are measurement units of area. These units are for leatherwear and plastic products such as plastic sheet and floor, leather, and wire meshes.

(6) Volume

Measurement units of volume are cubic yard (yd.); cubic meter (m.); cubic foot (ft.); cubic inch, etc. They are for chemical gas, wood, etc.

When adopting a particular measurement unit to define the quantity, traders need to be aware of the consistency of system. Currently, the measurement systems in use include the Metric System, the U. S. System, the British System and the International System of Units (S. I.), among which the metric system and S. I. Units are universally accepted and adopted in all countries. A notable fact is that some units in different systems carry the same name though; they are indicating standards of measurement with significant difference. In addition, it is true that due to the local background and customary practice, different countries adopt different systems of measurement. As a result, traders, while having their business communications, need to clarify the use of unit and measurement system to avoid unnecessary disputes. ame measurement unit indicating different quantity

Ton may be interpreted as 1 metric ton, 1 long ton or 1 short torn: 1 metric ton = 1 000KG; 1 short ton =907. 18KG; 1 long ton =1 016. 05KG.

4. 3. 2 Interpretation of Weight

In international trade, weight is a very important concept. Besides serving as the most frequently used unit for defining quantity of commodity in transaction, it constitutes an indispensable part of information about each consignment, frequently demanded by different parties with different intentions. Moreover, when used in various occasions, the data would be treated differently, resulting in a series of different names. Being able to interpret the concepts properly will add value to the operational proficiency of the practioners. The next part will focus on explaining the application of weight data in different scenarios.

(1) Gross Weight

Gross weight refers to the weight of the commodity plus the weight of the packing. Gross weight is applicable to commodities of comparatively low value.

(2) Net weight

Net weight means the actual weight of a commodity itself excluding the weight of the packing. According to CISG Article 56, the weight of a commodity is calculated by its net weight unless otherwise stated in the contract.

However, some products can be weighted only when they are packed. If net weight is used, the weight of packing, i. e. the tare, must be deducted. Thus the relationship between net weight and gross weight is as follows:

Net weight = Gross weight − Tare.

(3) Tare Calculation

In international trade, tare can be calculated by actual/real tare, by average tare, by customary tare or by computed tare.

Actual/real tare refers to the actual weight of the packing of the commodities. In order to get the actual tare of the goods, each packing of a good has to be weighed in order to get a total.

By average tare the weight of the packing is calculated on the basis of the average. The average tare can be calculated by weighing a part of the packing of the commodities and working out the average when the packing materials are uniform and the specifications of goods are standardized. The packing of some commodities are unified and standardized and the weight of the packing is known and accepted by everyone. In this case, the recognized weight of the packing, which is called the customary tare, can be used in calculating the net weight.

Computed tare is the weight of the packing agreed upon by the parties concerned. In this case, the net weight is calculated by deducting the tare previously agreed upon from the gross weight of the commodity.

Sometimes the packing may become an indivisible part of the product, such as tobacco flakes; or the packing material is almost of the same value as that of the goods, like grain and fodder. If it is inconvenient to measure the net weight of the commodity, the "gross for net" practice will be adopted. In the case of "gross for net", the goods are priced by their gross weight instead of the net.

(4) Conditioned Weight

This refers to the weight of the goods derived from such a process with which the moisture content of the commodity is removed and standardized moisture content is added by scientific means. Conditioned weight is chiefly applicable in the calculation of the weight of such commodities like raw silk, wool, etc., which are of high value and with unsteady moisture content. This is done by first measuring the actual moisture weight from the total weight of the commodity and then adding the standard moisture weight. The formula of calculating the conditioned weight is explained as below:

Conditioned weight = Actual weigh × (1 + Standard regain rate) / (1 + Actual regaining rate)

Understanding the formula of calculating conditioned weight:

Dried net weight: the weight of the goods when all the water content is abstracted by a scientific method from the goods;

Regain rate: the ratio between the water content and the dry weight of the goods;

Standard regain rate: the ratio between the water content and the dry weight of the goods, which is accepted in the world market or agreed upon by the seller and the buyer;

Actual regain rate: the ratio between the actual regaining water content in the goods and the actual dry weight.

In international trade, tare can be calculated by actual/real tare, by average tare, by customary tare or by computed tare.

Illustration: An exporter has signed a contract to export 10 metric tons (5% more or less) of raw silk to Spain. It is stipulated in the contract that conditioned weight is used and the standard regain rate is 10%. If the actual regain rate is 21% when shipment is made, how many metric tons of raw silk should the exporter deliver in order to fulfill the contract?

Calculation:

Actual weight = Conditioned weight × (1 + Actual regaining rate) / (1 + Standard regain rate)

Actual weight = 10 M/T × (1 + 21%) / (1 + 10%) = 11 MT

Answer: In order to fulfill the contract, the exporter should deliver 11 metric tons of raw silk, 5% more or less.

(5) Theoretical Weight

The weight is a theoretical weight when the total weight of the product is calculated by multiplying the total quantity and the unit weight, rather than measured actually. Theoretical weight is applicable to commodities such as galvanized iron, tin plate and steel plate. These commodities are of identical or standardized sizes and specifications; the weight of each unit is almost the same, thus the total can be obtained by means of theoretical calculation.

(6) Legal Weight

Legal weight is the weight of the goods including the immediate, inner, or direct packing of the goods. According to the customs laws and regulations in some countries, legal weight is usually used as the basis for tariff calculation.

4.3.3 More or Loss Clause

At the time of the conclusion of contract, the quantity clause should be clearly and definitely stipulated so as not to give rise to disputes thereafter. So, such expressions as "about/approximate 10 000metric tons" had better be avoided because "about/approximate" may be given several ambiguous interpretations: some refer to 2.5% more or less, and some 5%, and some 10%. However, it is very difficult to measure accurately some agricultural and mineral products like corn, soybean, wheat, coal etc. What's more, influenced by natural conditions, packing patterns, loading and unloading methods, the quantity of goods delivered by the seller usually does not conform to the quantity definitely stipulated in the contract. In order to facilitate the processing of the contract, the seller and the buyer, generally, agree to use "more or less clause". It means over-load and under-load are permitted but should not surprise a certain percentage of the stipulated quantity. For example, "2000 metric ton, 5% more or less at seller's option". "Plus or minus" or the sign "±" may also be used to take the place of "more or less". Under the "more or less" clause, the payment for the over-load or under-load will be made according to the contract price or at the market price at the time of shipment.

There is no fixed rule to decide how much the range of quantity difference should be.

Traders normally make their decisions based on customs or result of negotiation. The ratio also varies among different lines of products. Most traders prefer to express the flexible portion by percentage: and the common range for the ratio is between 3% and 10%. An example may read as "1 000 metric tons, with 5% more or less". Other traders, on the other hand, would like to set an absolute number as the tolerable quantity disparity. Whatever way chosen, the stipulation should be clear and specific. Ambiguous terms like "about", "circa", or "approximately" should be avoided, as they are easy to be interpreted differently.

To reduce disputes, UCP600 Article 30 stipulates that the words "about" or "approximately" used in connection with the amount or the quantity or the unit price are interpreted as allowing a tolerance not exceeding 10% more or 10% less. In absence of any more or less specifying the quantity, a tolerance not exceeding 5% more or 5% less is allowed, provided the quantity is not stipulated by number (of packing units or individual items) and provided that the total amount of the goods does not exceed the amount of the credit.

Which party is to make the decision?

Who should determine how much more or less would be allowed? This should also be legibly stipulated in the contract to avoid possible disputes. In practice, as the quantity of goods delivered may be influenced by the natural condition of goods, the packing patterns, and the actual handling of shipment, it is practical to allow the party in charge of shipment to decide the quantity.

Under a "more or less" clause, the payment for the over-load or under-load portion will be made either according to contract price or at the market price at the time of shipment. According to CISG, unless otherwise stipulated in the contract, the payment for the more or less portion of the goods shall be calculated at the contract rate.

However, if the parties are concerned about the possible great change in price at the time of delivery, they may further include statements in the contract that settlement for this more or less part is based on the market price at the time when the goods are shipped on board the vessel. In doing so, the method of calculation should also be set forth in the contract in full detail.

Examples of More or Less Clause:

△800 metric tons, 5% more or less at seller's option

△20 000 metric tons, the sellers are allowed to load 5% more or less, the price shall be calculated according to the unit price in the contract

△1 000 metric tons 5% more or less, at Buyer's option with more or less portion priced at the market price at the time of shipment

The quantity clause in a sales contract is the legal basis for the seller to effect shipment and for the buyer to take delivery and make payment later on. Considering the various measurement units and systems, it is crucial to stipulate the quantity clause in a manner, which is clear, specific, and reasonable at the same time, to make the fulfillment of the contract flexible and smooth.

4.4 Packing and Marking

Most internationally traded goods typically have to travel long distance. In the course of transit, goods are vulnerable to all sorts of unexpected events. To protect the safety of cargo to the fullest extent possible, usually exporters have to take every necessary step from the design of packaging to the choice of transport.

However, some exceptions do exist. For a special category of products, packing is neither necessary nor viable. These kinds of goods normally have a primitive and stable nature, hence not apt to be easily damaged, unless accidents out of the ordinary range happen. Raw material or industry products like rolled steel, lead ingots, rubber and timber fall into this category. According to the extent of encapsulation, they are called nude cargo. Some finished products like complete automobiles are also considered nude cargo. There is another type of goods which shares the similar features of not easily being influenced by outside circumstances and hereby bearing no packing. These goods are addressed as bulk cargo. The differences are only that while nude cargo usually are in a solid state, bulk cargo are more of a liquid-like existence and normally of low value. Ore, coal, grain, and liquid chemicals not sold with individual container all belong to this category.

Appropriate packing nevertheless remains important for the majority of export goods. This part will discuss some basic knowledge and relevant operations related to the packing of export cargo.

4.4.1 Functions and Determinants of Packing

Packing has become more and more important in competing for overseas markets. One of its basic purposes is to protect the product. This is important because the product may have to withstand a lot of handling during transportation between the factory and the consumer. The second purpose of packing is to make the product look appealing to the buyer. Products that are packed in such way as to catch the consumer's eye will help to sell. Other common purposes of packaging are to provide information about the product inside, make it easy to carry the product, and provide convenience in using the product. Therefore, more and more people, not only manufacturers, have come to realize the importance of packaging. The major ones can be briefly summarized as follows:

Protecting goods: Packing can be used to protect the goods and keep them good and complete in the circulation field. Usually, strong packing can prevent the goods from being stolen or damaged.

Facilitating delivery: Packing makes it convenient to store, transport, load, unload and count the goods.

Reducing cost: Reasonable packing can optimize the use of shipping space and thus lower transportation costs.

Promoting sales: Packaging provides retailers easier distribution and end customers convenient purchase and delivery. In addition, unique and attractive packaging can help create product image, build up brand, and ultimately promote sales.

In order to maximize the function of packing, decision has to be made with careful consideration for different factors. Some variables are key to the choice of packing.

(1) Properties of Cargo

Cargoes of different properties may require different methods of packing. Typical characteristics such as nature, value and fragility have great impact on packing of goods. For example, apples can be consigned in cases, boxes, cartons or pallet boxes while cement may be shipped in five-ply or six-ply paper bags, in containers or in bulk. Generally speaking, consignment of high value normally requires more expensive packing than low value commodities; and the more fragile the cargo is, the higher the packing requirement would be.

(2) Mode of Transport

The use of various transportation may have some implication for the packing of cargo. For instance, air transport encourages palletized consignments with cargo strapped to it throughout the transit, and packing materials light in weight such as fiberboard cartons will be preferred. For ocean freight, however, strong and durable packing are always the first choice.

(3) Customs or Statutory Requirements

Customs or statutory requirements are another affecting factor for packing. While using certain kind of packing, exporters must be sure that the material and pattern of packing used strictly comply with the regulatory requirements of the importing country. For example, in some countries, straw, rice husks and wood products are unacceptable packing materials due to the risk of insects being imported.

(4) Weather

Packing must take the weather condition in transit into account. For instance, if great variation in temperature is expected during the course of the transit, packing must be designed to permit the cargo to breathe and avoid excessive sweating.

(5) Ease of Handling and Stowage

Awkwardly shaped cargoes are usually packed in regular shape containers such as cartons, cases to facilitate cargo stowage and handling.

(6) Insurance

When cargoes are to be covered by insurance, there are likely to be some conditions imposed on the packing. For example, cargoes which are particularly fragile or which are more likely to be subject to damage or pilferage may have to conform to a prescribed packing specification.

(7) Transportation Cost

To minimize transportation cost, size, shape and strength are the three main considerations in proper packing. In addition, a shipper need consult his shipping agent in order to ascertain the mode of packing in order to secure a favorable rate of freight.

It can be noted from the above discussion that proper packing is important for most of the goods traded internationally; and packing may serve different purposes. With a closer look at those functions covered in previous sections of this chapter, We can conclude that packing in general can be put into two categories: the one used for transportation purpose, and the other designed for marketing intention. They are named as transport packing and sales packaging respectively. In the following section, transport packing is the focus of discussion, and only some typical issues related to sales packaging in international trade will be touched on.

4.4.2 Transport Packing

Transport packing, also called shipping packing, outer packing or big packing, is mainly to keep the goods safe and sound during transportation. It must not only be solid enough to prevent the packed goods from damage, but also be pilferaged – proof, easy to store, convenient to load and unload. On the basis of packing materials and packing methods, transport packing includes the following types. (see Table 4 – 1)

Table 4 – 1 **types of packing containers**

Bags	May be made of strong paper, linen, canvas, rubber, etc
Sack	A large bag usually made of jute.
Carton	Made of light but strong cardboard, or fiberboard with double lids and bottoms, fixed by glue, adhesive tapes, metal bands or wire staples. Sometimes a bundle of several cartons is made up into one package, held by metal bands.
Case	A strong container made of wood. For extra strength it may have "battens". Sometimes thinner wood may be used with metal bands or wires passed around the case. The inside of the case may be "lined" with various materials, eg damp resisting paper, tin foil, etc, to prevent damage by water, air or insects.
Box	A small case, which may be of wood, cardboard or metal, and may have a folding (hinged) lid.
Crate	This is a case, but one not fully enclosed. It has a bottom and a frame, sometimes open at the top. Crates are often built for the particular things they have to carry machinery packed in crates needs a special bottom to facilitate handling.
Drum	A cylinder – shaped container for carrying liquids, chemicals, paint, etc. It is usually made of metal. Certain dry chemicals or powder are sometimes packed in wood or cardboard drums.
Bale	A package of soft goods tightly pressed together and wrapped in a protective material. Usually size 30 × 15 × 15 inches. May be strengthened by metal bands.

Table 4－1(续)

Can/tin	A small metal container in which small quantities of paint, oil or certain foodstuffs are packed.
Carboy	A large glass container protected in a metal or wicker cage with soft packing between glass and cage. It is used for chemicals.
Bundle	Miscellaneous goods packed without a container. A number of small carton fixed together could be called a bundle.
Container	A very large metal box for transport of goods by road, rail, sea or air. Packing goods in a large container facilitates loading and unloading by mechanical handling; thus time is saved.
Pallet	A large tray or platform for moving loads (by means of slings) e. g from a lorry into a train or onto a ship, and so save time for handling of seperate items.

Figure 4－1 Pallets

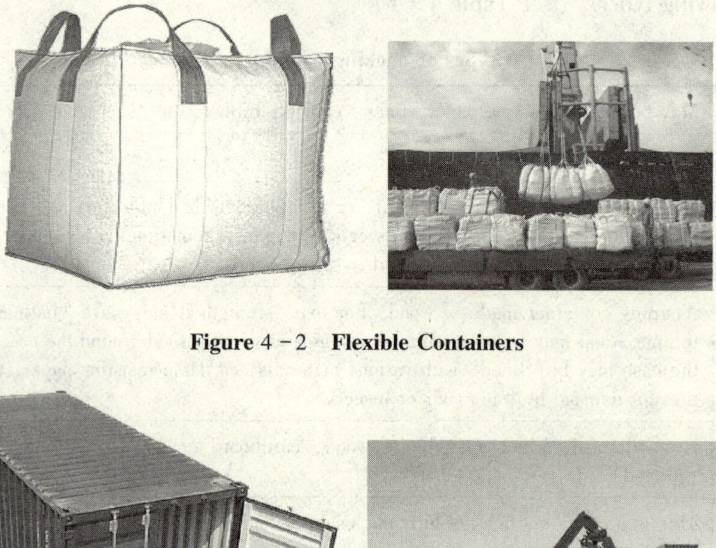

Figure 4－2 Flexible Containers

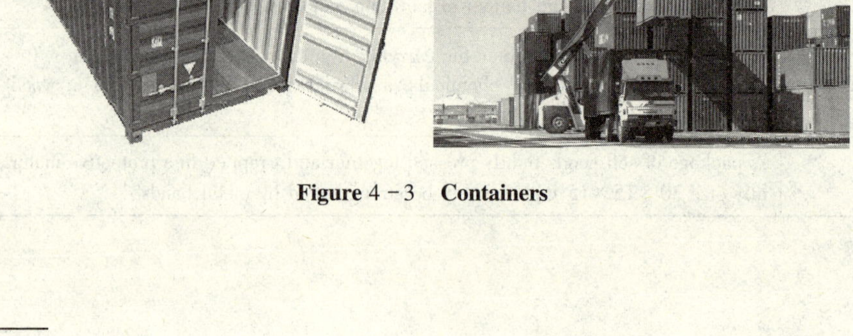

Figure 4－3 Containers

Apart from protecting the cargoes, collective packing also facilitates and speeds up the loading and unloading operation. At present, in order to improve the speed of operation and utility of ports and docks, some countries enforce regulations stipulating that cargoes shall be transported in collective packing.

4.5.3 Marking

Marking refers to different diagrams, words and figures which are written, printed, or brushed on the outside of the shipping packing. When goods are well enwrapped by the packing, there is no clue to the identification of them. People need certain kind of indicator to guide their handling of the cargo along the flow of logistics. Making plays on important role in the use of transport packing. According to its function, marking can be classified into four types: shipping marks, indicative marks, warning marks, and supplementary marks.

(1) Shipping Marks

Shipping marks are a type of marking on the shipping packing. It quickens the identification and transportation of the goods and helps avoid shipping errors.

Therefore, the design of shipping marks should be simple, clear and easily identifiable. For instance, the position of the shipping marks should be proper; the color of the marks should be durable. Besides, no advertising words and pictures are allowed to insert into the shipping marks.

International standard shipping marks recommended by The International Standard Organization are made up of the following four parts:

Consignee's Code: usually the initial or abbreviation of a consignee;

Destination: the name of the port or place of destination;

Reference No: the number of the relevant contract, order, invoice, etc;

Number of Package: the consecutive number of each package.

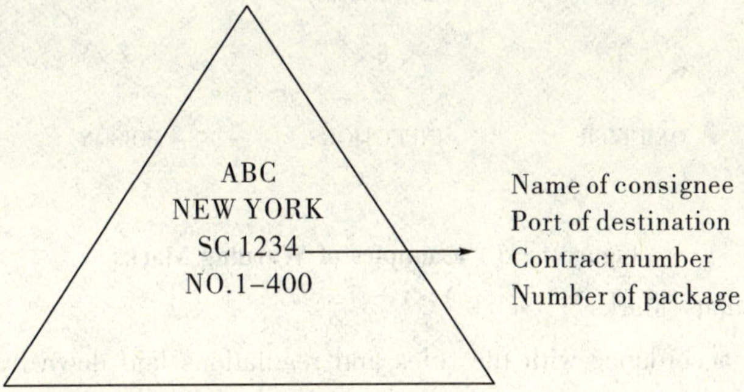

Adopting standard shipping marks can not only make it easy to identify and transport the goods, but also simplify the process of checking the relative documents and certificates.

(2) Indicative Marks

Indicative marks are diagrams and simple words used to remind the relevant people for attention when they handle the goods in the process of loading, unloading, carrying and storing. Indicative marks, when necessary, are also painted or stenciled on the outer packing of the commodities.

Figure 4 - 4　Examples of Indicative Marks

(3) Warning Marks

To ensure safe carriage of dangerous goods in international transportation, warning marks, also called dangerous marks, are used to indicate dangerous cargoes such as explosive, corrosive, inflammable and radioactive products.

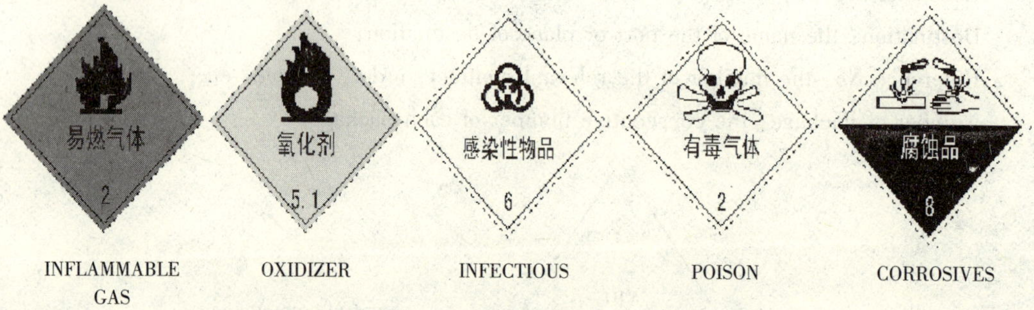

Figure 4 - 5　Examples of Warning Marks

(4) Supplementary Marks

Sometimes, in accordance with the rules and regulations laid down by the importing and exporting countries, or the agreement entered into by the parties concerned, some supplementary marks are inserted such as the mark of weight or volume and the mark of origin.

(5) Mark of Weight or Volume

Weight or volume marks are marks indicating the volume or the gross/net weight of the package to facilitate loading/unloading or booking shipping space.

(6) Mark of Origin

Marks of origin are required by many exporting or importing countries for customs statistics and taxation. In some countries, mark of origin is compulsory for imported goods. While some other countries may require marks of origin to avoid confusion over the real origin of the goods.

The mark of origin must be legible, indelible and clearly visible. In addition, each country has relevant regulations governing the way of marking for imported goods, including language and marks to be used and even the size of the letters of marking. Therefore, the way of marking depends on the requirements of the particular country.

Usually, exporters, who put on the mark of origin, should look into the importing country's marking regulations before packing and marking their goods for export shipment.

4. 4. 4 Sales Packaging

Sales packaging is also called inner packaging, small packaging, immediate packaging or marketing packaging. The main purpose of such packaging is for sales promotion. To facilitate sales, different packagings are designed to match with various kinds of goods: carrying packaging, hang-up packaging, easy-open packaging, spraying packaging, pilling-up packaging, gift packaging, and so on.

Instead of exploring the variety and novelty of the design of sales packaging, a topic probably more appropriate in the field of marketing, we will address several issues that are related to the sales packaging and relevant to the practice of international trade at the same time.

(1) Neutral Packing

Neutral packing is a special type of marking rather than a type of packing as its name may indicate. While neutral packing is required, no marking of origin or name of the manufacturer should appear on the product, on the shipping packing or sales packaging.

There are two cases for neutral packing: neutral packing with designated brand and neutral packing without designated brand. In the case of neutral packing without designated brand, neither brand or mark nor the country of origin is indicated on the packing. There are cases when the exporter is required to use a specified brand or trade designated by their importer, it becomes neutral packing with designated brand.

Neutral packing is generally adopted as a means to promote export sales. By means of neutral packing, exporters may break down the high customs duties or unreasonable import quota levied on the imports by the importing countries. However, in recent years, neutral packing has been restricted by many countries. For instance, as mentioned in the previous section, mark of origin is compulsory for imported goods in some countries. Goods packed in neutral packing, in absence of marking of origin, are not allowed to enter into these countries. Therefore, cautions must be taken while exporters agree to adopt neutral packing.

(2) OEM

OEM is the short form of Original Equipment Manufacturer. It refers to a kind of international trade practice that sellers use the brand name or trademark designated by buyers on their manufactured goods.

OEM is popular internationally. Supermarkets, large department stores and monopolized-commodity stores in many countries adopt OEM for the goods sold to secure a rise both in their reputation and price. To large and regular orders, exporters are also willing to accept OEM. By means of OEM, sellers can make good use of buyers' well established brand names or trade marks, good reputations and status to expand sales and increase competitiveness in the world market.

In case of neutral marking with trade marks or brands designated by the buyer, or OEM, close attention should be paid to issues concerning infringement on a third party. Usually, the buyers are required to produce certificate evidencing their right in using the brand name or trademark they designate. Still, it is advisable for sellers to insert a safeguard clause or similar stipulations in the contract to that effect.

Examples:

As to the trade marks designated by the buyer, if the seller is charged with the infringement by any third party, the buyer shall take up the matter with the plaintiff and it has nothing to do with the seller. Any losses thus sustained shall be compensated by the buyer.

Labeling

Labels refer to the tags on the sales packaging of goods, which usually consist of words, diagrams and figures. There are special requirements for labeling goods such as prepared goods, beverages, pharmaceuticals and toys.

Usually, regulations require that the label shows the name and address of the manufacturer, a list of ingredients, the weight or volume of the contents, and all other relevant information in the language and weight and measuring systems of the importing country. Thus exporters should ensure that their export goods comply with the labeling requirements of the importing country.

Bar Code

Bar code, composed of bars and spaces of varying width, provides a means of expression for human-readable characters in a form (bars and spaces) readable by a laser scanner. It contains such information as the name, specifications, origin and price of the product in international trade.

6 927425 500417

Figure 4 - 6 Bar Code

Several bar code systems exist at the same time. The Universal Product Code (UPC), compiled by the Universal Code Council (UCC), is the universal bar coding system. There are five versions of UCP from A to E, among which Version A, the basic version, is most common and usually seen on store items and UCP Version E is next common and used on packaging. Another universally used coding system is the European Article Numbering System (EAN) compiled by European Article Number Association (EANA). There are two principal EAN versions. One is the Standard EAN (also called EAN-13) which has tell numeric characters, two or three characters, and a check digit. The other is the EAN-8. EAN-8 consists of eight digits, which is actually the short form of EAN-13, only used if the article is too small for a EAN-13 when a EAN-13 may use more than 25% of the front space of the article.

International Article Number Association (IANA) later replaced European Article Number Association (EANA). The International Article Numbering System (IAN) is a world-recognized system as many countries and regions adopt this system. In 1988, the Chinese Article Code. Center was set up, responsible for the promotion and management of the bar code technology in China. In April 1991, China took part in the International Article Number Association (IANA) and was assigned the use of digits "690", "691" and "692". Since then any product beginning with any of these digits indicates that it is of Chinese origin.

4.4.5 Packing Clause in the Sales Contract

A sales contract should expressly indicate the packing method (e. g. the material, dimensions, weight of every single piece, filling material used and reinforcement conditions, etc.), the packing cost and the shipping marks.

Details of the packing methods must be clear in the packing clause and shall include such details as shape, size, material used, etc. For example, 30cm×40cm×50cm cartons, new iron drums containing 190kg net weight, or 4 ply kraft paper bags containing 25kg. In addition, reinforcement conditions or filling material, if applicable, must also be properly stipulated. For instance, "packed in wooden drums reinforced with iron band"; "packed in cartons, 10 cartons to a plastic pallet"; "packed in iron drums, 80 drums to a container". Ambiguous expressions such as "seaworthy packing", "customary packing" should be avoided in the contract. When the buyer is required to supply the packing material, wholly or partly, the seller should also stipulate in the contract the time limit within which the packing material shall arrive.

Examples of Packing Clause

Packing: In new iron drums of 175 kg each, net.

Packing: Each piece in a polybag, halt' dozen in a box and 10 dozen in a carton.

Packing: In new single jute bags, 100 kg net each.

Shipping Marks: At seller's option.

Shipping Marks: At buyer's option, the relevant shipping marks should reach the seller x x days before the time of shipment.

Shipping cost division must be specified in the packing clause. Packing expense can be included in the price of the commodity; in this case, it is the seller who bears the packing cost. However, it can also be excluded from the price with packing cost borne wholly or partly by the buyer. In the latter case, the seller should specify in the contract the expense to be paid by the buyer and the method of payment as well.

Shipping marks are usually to be supplied by the buyer. Occasionally they are at the seller's option. When the buyer designates the shipping marks, it is advisable for the seller to stipulate the arrival time of the marks.

In trade practice, unless otherwise stipulated in the contract, the cost of packing is included in the contract price and the design of the shipping marks is at a seller's option.

4.5 Summary

Description of commodity comprises two components: name of commodity and quality of commodity.

Goods in international trade are normally sold by description or by sample. Sale by description may take different forms which may be used simultaneously to supplement each other. Sale by sample is not suggested to use if the quality can be specified by description.

There are four basic measurement systems in the world, among which metric system and SI are the most widely adopted in international trade practice.

Quantity of commodity can be measured in terms of weight, length, number, area, volume and capacity, among which weight is most frequently adopted. Weight of commodities may be calculated by gross weight, net weight, conditioned weight, theoretical weight or legal weight.

As strict conformity in terms of quality and quantity sometimes is impossible in international trade, clauses such as quality latitude or tolerance and quantity latitude such as more or less clause are necessary to be included in contract.

Packing marks can be classified into different types: shipping marks, indicative marks and warning marks and supplementary marks. Standard shipping marks are simple and effective, and therefore are popular in trade practice. They are generally made up of four parts: consignee's code; reference no. ; destination and the number of packages.

Issues concerning neutral packing, OEM, labeling and bar code are closely associated with packing and marking in international trade. A shipper, when deciding shipping marks and packing methods, needs to take them into consideration.

When specifying the name, quality, quantity and packing of commodities in the sales contract, both parties in question should ensure that the relevant clauses are complete, simple, clear and specific.

Exercises

Ⅰ. Choices

1. If parties enter into business according to actual quality of goods, this trade is called ________.

A. Sales by sample B. Sales by actual quality

C. Sales by specification D. sales by name of origin

2. According to the sample of buyer, if the seller produces a sample and sends buyer to confirm, the confirmed sample is called ________.

A. Duplicate sample B. Return sample

C. Reference sample D. Seller's sample

3. In international trade, it is difficult to stipulate unified standard to agricultural and subsidiary products, because the quality of these products don't fix. So, the provision of these products' quality often is ________.

A. Fair Average Quality B. Sales by actual quality

C. Good merchantable quality D. Sales by brand

4. In international trade, about strong hygroscopicity goods such as raw silk, wool, cotton and so on, the measurement of weight often employs ________.

A. Gross weight B. Net weight

C. Conditioned weight D. Theoretical weight

5. To industrial products, the practice often employ ________ to design quality indicator in quality term.

A. quality tolerance

B. Quality latitude

C. Quality to be about equal to the sample

D. Stipulation of approximate

6. According to UCP600, "about" allows the quantity to be ________ more or less.

A. 3% B. 5% C. 10% D. 15%

7. ________ is NOT frequently used in international trade.

A. Metric System B. British System C. U. S. System D. French System

8. A credit stipulates that the quantity of the bulk cargo is 2 000M/T and total amount is USD 1. 9 million. It shows no "more or less clause" and partial shipment is not allowed. According to the UPC600, ________

A. the quantity and total amount of the goods delivered should not increase or decrease.

B. the quantity and total amount of the goods delivered can be 10% more or less.

C. the quantity and total amount of the goods delivered can be 5 % more or less.

D. the quantity of the goods delivered can be 5 % more or less, while the total amount cannot exceed USD 1. 9million.

Ⅱ. Explain the following terms

1. Sale by specification

2. Counter sample

3. Shipping mark

4. Net weight

5. Neutral packing

Ⅲ. Short questions

1. Why is the quantity of goods one of main conditions of trade?

2. How many methods are there to express the quality of goods?

3. What do the marks of package include?

Ⅳ. Case studies

1. Some company exported aquatic product 10 M/T. In contract, the term stipulate: packed by case, net weight 40 pounds/ case, 5% more or less of quantity allowance. If the L/C allows 5% more or less, how many to load maximum and minimum respectively?

2. Some company in our country exported 20 M/T frozen mutton to Egypt, FOB USD400/ MT. The contract allowed 10% more or less of quantity. The issuing bank opened L/C in time, which stipulated amount USD8000 and about 20M/T. In result, seller delivered 22M/T, but were dishonoured when handling negotiation. Why?

Chapter 5 Export Price

Learning Objectives

1. To understand pricing consideration and expression of export price
2. To master calculation of export price
3. To understand and master the procedure of price communication

Key Words

Commission; Discount; Price including commission; Net price; Money of account; Money of payment; Export cost for foreign exchange; Export profit rate

In international trade, it is an important issue of common concern of both parties to determine export commodity prices and stipulate the contract price terms. Therefore, bargaining often becomes the focus of trade negotiations and price terms in the contract becomes core terms in business. The interest of other terms in the contract are reflected generally in commodity prices. Because, the price terms in the contract have the close relation with other terms. In practice of business, it has very important sense of grasping export commodity prices, employing reasonable pricing, choosing favorable currency valuation, applying proper policy of commission and discount.

5.1 Expression of Export Price

The clear presentation of an export price involves a proper expression. The standard format of a price in international trade has four components: a code of currency, a number indicating the price, a unit for measuring quantity and a certain trade term. They typically look like the following expression.

USD250.30/piece CIF New York or FOB Guangzhou EUR120.80/set

It is up to the exporter if they put the trade term at the beginning or the end of the price. But all terms should be followed by the name of an appropriate place as defined by the Incoterms 2010.

5. 2 Pricing Considerations

Pricing for foreign markets is usually quite different from that for the domestic market. Without adequate research into the build-up of an export price and unforeseen cost components and contingencies, transactions that initially appear attractive may prove unprofitable or unexpectedly resource-intensive. The next section will provide you with details of the major components determining the export price. Some of these may be the same as domestic pricing, but an analysis of each component from an export perspective may result in export prices that are quite different from domestic prices.

5. 2. 1 Cost

The cost of export price mainly refers to purchasing cost. It is commodity prices about trader purchasing from supplier, also called the purchase cost. It takes the biggest proportion of export price, which is the main component of the price.

5. 2. 2 Expenses/Charges

The expenses or charges of export goods price mainly refer to the circulation of commodities expenses. It takes smaller proportion in export goods price, but it concerns various information and there is not the complete same calculating method. Therefore, charges becomes the complicated factors in price structure. The following charges frequently happen.

□Packing charges: commonly included in purchasing cost. If client request specially packing, charges happen.

□Warehousing charges: charges of purchasing in advance or storage in addition.

□Inland transport charges: charges before loading in inland transport, such as truck, charges of inland water transport, toll charges, transit fee, handling charges.

□Certification charges: charges when exporter handles export license, quota, certificate of origin, other certificates.

□Port charges: all kinds of charges before loading in port.

□Inspection charges: charges when Export commodity inspection authorities check the goods at the request of national provision or exporter.

□Duties and taxes: concerned taxes and dues levied or returned, such as customs, value-added tax.

□Interest: concerned interest of advance expenditure in the process of exporting.

□Operating charges: concerned charges in the process of business, also called management fee, such as communication fee, car fee, allowance for entertainment. According to particular cases of goods, operation and market, exporter ascertains a charge rate. Generally, the rate of charge, between 5% and 15%, is calculated based on purchasing cost. Operating charges = purchasing cost × rate of charge.

□Banking charges: handling charges when exporter entrusts bank to collect payments or credit information.

□Freight charges: transport charges

□Insurance charges: charges when exporter covers cargo insurance or credit insurance.

□Commission

□Discount

5.2.3 Anticipated Profit

Another essential part of the export price is the anticipated profit. How much an exporter wants to make out of a particular transaction directly impacts on the price level of the product. This has a direct relationship with the company's marketing objective in the foreign market. For example, some companies may attempt to launch into a new market; some may look for long-term market growth; some just want to set up an outlet for surplus production or outmoded products; and many firms view the foreign market as a secondary market and consequently have lower expectations regarding market share and sales volume. All these different objectives naturally affect pricing decisions.

5.2.4 Capability of Target Market

Market capability here refers to the consumption power, income level, supply and demand relationship in the target market. Pricing strategy may be tailored to particular foreign markets. For most consumer goods, per capita income is a good reflection of a market's ability to pay. Simplifying the product to reduce its selling price may be an answer for the exporter to most lower per capita income markets. Products of higher quality, with more ornaments and charged premium prices may be targeted at developed countries. The firm should also anticipate the specific segment of potential customers. For example, if the firm's primary customers in a developing country are expatriates or belong to the upper class, a higher price might be feasible even if the average per capita income is low. In addition, the supply and demand relation in the foreign market is well worth measuring. Some products may create such a strong demand such as popular goods like Levis garments, that even low per capita income will not affect their selling price. Thus, traders should try to be aware of the consumption variety in target markets in export pricing.

5.2.5 Other Factors

Other factors like competition and relationship between the exporter and the importer all have implications on companies' pricing strategy. Pricing is a complex activity always subject to many contingencies. There is no set rule to follow, but only unexpected factors to consider.

Exporters have to be aware of the dynamics in the market environment so that they will not miss any significant factor which might influence their pricing decision.

(1) The quality and class of the goods

In the international market, it is a common principle of fixing price on quality, namely, the good product good price, inferior goods cheap price. Many factors affect the prices of goods, such as quality, class, packing, design, trademark, brand.

(2) Transportation distance

The international sale of goods generally need a long-distance transportation. Transportation distance affects freight and insurance costs, which affect the prices of goods. Therefore, it is necessary to account carefully transportation cost.

(3) Delivery place and delivery terms

In international trade, owing to different delivery place and delivery terms, both parties will take various responsibility charge and risk. When both parties stipulate commodity prices, these factors must be considered. For example, the price of commodities within the same distance, if the trade bases on CIF terms or DES terms, should be different.

(4) Seasonal changes of demand

In the international market, if some seasonal products enter into market before season, they will sell a good price. But when season passes, these products will sell at a lower price. Therefore, we should make full use of seasonal demand change and master the seasonal price difference to fight for the favor price in business.

(5) The amount of deal

According to international trade practices, the trading volume affects the last price. When there is a big trading volume, the dealing price should give proper privilege, such as quantity discount, otherwise, lower than the minimum order, it can be an appropriate increase in price.

(6) The terms of payment and the exchange

The terms of payment and the exchange change affect price of commodity. For example, if the same goods in the same conditions of other trading terms respectively take payment in advance and payment by credit, the price of commodity should be different. Meanwhile, when confirming the price, trader should fight for deal by favorable currency. In addition, the delivery time, market sales habits and consumer preference also affect the price.

5.3 Calculation of Price

Once the determining factors have been taken into consideration, the choice of a particular calculation method depends on the priority of the company as to which factor ranks first.

(1) Cost-plus Pricing

In the cost-plus calculation the exporter starts with the domestic manufacturing costs or factory purchasing cost if he is not the manufacturer. Then he adds overhead costs covering administration, research and development, and marketing. In addition, freight charges, distributor margins, customs handling fees and profit would also be added. This is probably the most basic approach, but the effect of this kind of pricing may be that the export price becomes uncompetitive.

(2) Marginal Cost Pricing

This method considers the expenses of producing and selling products for export as a floor beneath which prices cannot be set without incurring a loss. It establishes the base price using the direct costs of production and sales, with fixed costs apportioned to the volume of the sale. This would include any product modifications plus economy of scale savings as the incremental costs of producing additional products for export should be lower than the earlier average production costs for the domestic market.

When using this method, it is important to find out the break-even point—the minimum quantity required by which the exporter can sell at a particular price without a loss.

It can be done by using the formula as:

Break-even point = Total fixed cost/Unit selling price-Unit variable cost

Suppose the fixed cost of a plant is USD2 500, if the unit selling price and variable cost of its product is USD5.0 and USD2.5 respectively, then the break-even point will be:

2 500/ (5 − 2.5) = 1 000 Units

By adjusting the quantity of production, the manufacturer can understand the price implication to his profitability. This approach is particularly useful where the company has excess production capacity and needs to reduce its export prices to be competitive.

(3) Buyer Based Approach

This is a more psychological method. Prices are set according to the perceived value in the target market. It needs a good understanding of the marketplace if this approach is to be adopted.

(4) Competition Based Approach

If competition is fierce, the exporter has to provide prices benchmarked to competitors or market average so as to stay in business. In this case profit margins could be lowered.

Generally speaking, no matter what technique is used, an export price must cover costs and contribute a certain portion of profit. Otherwise it is meaningless to export. Based on this assumption, we take the cost-plus approach as the basic tool for pricing. The calculation requires one to analyse in detail costs incurred. Using a worksheet can make the process easier and clear to understand.

Focus needs to be on the calculation of the most commonly used trade terms: FOB, CFR and CIF. The following part will explore details related to the price conversion of the three terms.

5.3.1 FOB

As shown in Table 4.1, if the exporter is supposed to be an agent rather than a manufacturer, then his FOB price will typically include items listed below.

FOB (named port of shipment) = Factory purchasing cost

+ Profit margin

+ Transport cost from plant to shipping port

+ Transport insurance to shipping port (optional)

+ Storage costs, terminal handling charge (THC), loading onto ship charge

+ Export customs clearance cost

Normally the price will be calculated in the exporter's local currency. If he decides to quote the price in a foreign currency, at the end of the calculation he then has to apply a valid exchange rate to the result and convert it into foreign currency. The whole calculation can be expressed as:

FOB = (Total Cost + Profit) /Exchange Rate

Apart from those direct costs, exporters also need to always bear in mind the indirect costs as discussed in the previous section of the chapter. The temptation to accept an order can result in overlooking or the underestimation of some cost items which lead to a loss on the transaction.

5.3.2 CFR

If an FOB price is available, it is much easier to calculate the CFR price. According to the definition in the Incoterms 2000, the difference between FOB and CFR, in the sense of cost, is the ocean freight for sending the goods from the port of shipment to the port of destination.

CFR = FOB + Ocean Freight

Ocean freight quotations can be provided by shipping lines or shipping forwarders. Sometimes they are quoted as packaged prices; hence no additional charges may occur later beyond the quoted ones. But sometimes the quotation for ocean freight is strictly referred to the basic charge of using a vessel. There is another list of costs under the title of "additionals" or "surcharges". Exporters have to double check before a freight charge is confirmed.

5.3.3 CIF

In a similar pattern the CIF price can be calculated given the FOB or CFR price.

CIF = FOB + Ocean Freight + Insurance Premium or

CIF = CFR + Insurance Premium

The key here is to find out the insurance premium charge. It is the normal practice of the insurance company to calculate the insurance premium based on the face value of a contract. In addition, it is also a standard industry norm that a markup, which is normally 10%, will be added on top of the contract value covering the incidental costs like processing the claim, survey costs, and the possibly inflated costs of replacements. Consequently, the formula for calculating the insurance premium will be:

Insurance Premium (I) = CIF × (1 + 10%) × Premium Rate (R)

You may find that the calculation falls into a loop. If you desire a CIF price, the insurance premium charge must be given; but if you want to calculate the insurance premium, the CIF price must be known. The solution is simple. If the two formulas are combined, the result will be:

CIF = CFR + CIF × (1 + 10%) × Premium Rate (R) or CIF = CFR/ (1 − 110% × R)

The premium rate for a product can be obtained from any insurance company. When CFR price is available, the formula can help calculate the CIF price directly.

5.3.4 Price Including Commission

If a price shown in the contract directly comes from the calculation of basic costs and profit, it is called a "net price". But occasionally traders have to make some adjustments to the net prices to achieve the goal of promoting sales. These adjustments include commission and discount.

Commission is an incentive payment made to the middle-persons or brokers for their intermediary service. Modern international trade has been getting more and more specialized. Therefore any party who might be involved in facilitating the transaction can be a commission, receiver.

A price which contains a proportion as commission payment is called a "price including commission". It is normally expressed by mentioning a percentage as commission rate at lilt end of the net price. For example:

CIF Hamburg USD100 per metric ton including 3% commission

A more frequently adopted way of quoting price including commission is to use a capitalized "C" to indicate commission behind the trade terms. For example:

CIFC 3 Hamburg USD100/set or CIFC 3% Hamburg USDl00/set

The calculation of commission is comparatively easy. It is internationally customary to conduct the multiply calculation based on the invoice value or contract value of a transaction, which is:

Commission = contract value × commission rate

For example, if the contract value of a transaction is USD10 000, the commission rate is 2%, the commission value will then be 10 000 × 2% = 200.

Another practice of calculating commission is using FOB or FCA prices as the basis of calculation irrespectively. This means that if the deal is finalized by CIF, CIP or any other terms, costs like ocean freight and insurance should be deducted before the commission is calculated. This approach seems more reasonable since the end buyer or seller does not need to pay commission for the freight charges, insurance or any costs of the same nature, but only for the value of the goods itself. The downside of this, however, is that it incurs a lot more trouble in calculating. Which way to adopt purely depends on the agreement between the parties concerned.

Sometimes it occurs that during negotiation one needs to calculate the price including commission from a net price. If the net profit is not to be eroded, the formula will be:

Price including commission = net price/ (1 - commission rate)

For example, if the net price is USD100 per piece, the commission rate is 5%; the price including commission will be USD105. 26.

An easy mistake to make is to use the net price as the basis and add the commission percentage on top straightaway by doing like this in the example question 100 × (1 + 5%) = 105. A note to remember is that the price including commission consists of both the net price and the commission. The net price is only a portion of the price including commission and it should remain constant when the commission has been taken away.

In most cases commission payment will be made openly. It is indicated in the sales contract and normally paid after the transaction is completed. Either when the importer makes payment to the exporter through the middleman it is deducted directly, or after the exporter receives the full payment from the importer it is returned to the middleman from the exporter's account. Sometimes, however, commission can also be made implicitly, especially when the middle party does not want either of the end traders, normally the buyer to know about this payment. Under these circumstances the commission will not be mentioned in the contract, but mutually agreed upon by the parties in question.

5. 3. 5 Price with Discount

Similar to commission in the sense that it is also used to promote the transaction, discount, however, has a rather different nature. It is a deduction from the net price rather than a mark - up. The reasons for providing discount can be multifold. The most common one is to increase the competitiveness of the product in the market. Providing a price, with discount can be considered as lowering a product price, which is a frequently used approach to increasing sales. Another reason for using discount is as a motivator for importers to introduce products into the market. In some cases discount is useful for enterprises to get rid of their stocked goods and speed up cash flow. More often than not discount is used as compensation for settling some disputes of previous orders between the traders.

If discount is applied it should be clearly expressed in the contract as a percentage of the total value or a fixed amount. For example:

FOB Guangzhou EUR2000/ M/T less 2% discount

The calculation of discount is simple.

Discount = contract price × discount rate

Then the actual price of the product will be:

Actual price = contract price − discount

= contract price × (1 − discount rate)

It is normally deducted before the buyer pays.

5.3.6 Price Adjustment Clause

The majority of international trade contracts are fixed price contracts. When goods are delivered, importers will pay the exact amount shown on the contract. Prices of goods sold stay constant between the contracting time and the payment date. However, there are still a number of transactions which are handled by flexible price contracts, especially for resource-intensive commodity transactions, and project-oriented transactions which may take over six months to complete. When the macro economic environment is highly volatile, the market price of resource type of goods like oil, steel, rubber and so on may experience dramatic upward and downward movements. If the prices of products traded are fixed, when market prices change greatly, either the seller or the buyer may suffer a loss. In order to protect the interest of both sellers and buyers and promote fairness, a contract can leave the prices unfixed and subject to adjustment according to the market prices of certain variables. The provision of such nature in a contract is normally called a price adjustment clause. A simple version of the price adjustment clause can be expressed by a formula in the following way:

$$P = P_0 (A + B \times M/M_0 + CW \times /W_0)$$

Here, P stands for the final paying price of the commodity at the time of delivery and P_0 stands for the initial price agreed when the contract is first established. A, B and C represent the operation cost and profit, the major material cost and the wage cost as a percentage of the price respectively. M is the material price index at the time of delivery and M_0 at the time of contracting. Similarly W is the wage index at the time of delivery and W_0 at the time of contracting. The assumptions are that the ratios indicating the price structure remain constant and that M and W are set as the benchmark of comparison. As far as the referencing indexes are available, the final paying price P will be easily calculated.

Of course when a price adjustment clause is used, both sides should agree on the use of the ratios and confirm the authority of the sources providing the referencing indexes. These should all be formally included in the contracts.

5.4 Understanding the Price

Being able to calculate the prices under different trade terms is not good enough. If one wants to be a competent international trader he must understand the implication of each price, especially from the point of profitability. Some financial ratios can serve this purpose.

5.4.1 Export Profit Margin

Profit margin is probably the best known and most widely used ratio for measuring the profitability of a company or a particular transaction. By considering the relationship between the net profit and the sales volume, profit margin tells, in an accounting sense, how much profit can be generated for every unit of currency in sales. This ratio can also apply in export transaction with some currency adjustment.

Export Profit Margin = [Export revenue in RMB (FOB) - Export cost in RMB (FOB)] /Export cost in RMB (FOB)

Note: All the figures normally would be calculated in the exporter's local currency.

If an American exporter has a transaction resulting in a 15% profit margin, it can be interpreted as that the exporter is making 15 cents in profit for every dollar in sales. One thing needs to be noted that the calculation of both export revenue and cost must exclude any overseas transportation charge and insurance cost since exports are not supposed to make profit from the transportation charge and insurance payment. We only consider the real revenue and cost.

5.4.2 Export Cost for Foreign Exchange

Another more direct way to interpret the profitability of an international transaction is to use the export cost for foreign exchange ratio (ECFFE). It is a measure bringing the foreign currency factor into the calculation. The fact that a large amount of orders are transacted in foreign currencies highlights the value of this ratio. It is defined as:

Export Cost for Foreign Exchange = Export cost in RMB / Export Revenue in Foreign Currency

Because the ratio investigates the relationship between the cost in local currency and revenue in foreign currency, it tells us how many units of local currency the exporter should pay so as to make one unit of foreign currency. Let us look at one example. Suppose the ECFFE ratio of a deal for a Chinese company in March 2008 was 6.5, and the exchange rate at that time was USD1: RMB7.05. From the ratio it is clear that in order to earn 1 U.S. dollar, the exporter had to pay 6.5 Yuan, the local currency. To put it in another way, from each U.S. dollar earned, the Chinese exporter could make 0.55 Yuan as profit. It is obvious that the less the ratio is, the more profit the exporter can make.

Is the profit margin 10% a good one? Does an ECFFE ratio of 7 always indicate a loss? It is very hard to tell. No matter which ratio is used, they will not make any sense until they are used in comparison and with good consideration of prevailing conditions. One can always use historical records and industry norms to set the benchmark for analysis.

5.5 Summary

The standard form of a price quoted in international trade includes four elements: a certain kind of currency, a number indicating the value, a unit and a term of delivery or a trade term. Typical example can be CIF Hamburg USD100/piece.

While making pricing decision, exporters need to consider major factors like cost, anticipated profit, capability of target market, and terms of payment. Other factors like competition, relationship with the trading partner should also be kept in mind.

The calculation of the most commonly used price terms are handled by applying the formulas listed below.

1. Export Cost for Foreign Exchange
   = Export cost in RMB / Export Revenue in Foreign Currency
2. Export Profit Margin
   = [Export revenue in RMB (FOB) − Export cost in RMB (FOB)] /Export cost in RMB (FOB)
3. FOB = (All Cost + Profit) / Exchange Rate
4. FOBC% = FOB/ (1 − Commission)
5. CFR = FOB + Freight
6. CIF = CFR + I (where I is insurance premium)
7. I = CIF × 110% × R (R is premium rate)
8. CIF = CFR / (1 − 110% × R)
9. Price Adjustment Clause $P = P_0 (A + B\ M/M_0 + C\ W/W_0)$

It is important to understand the profit implication of a price calculated. Two ratios can serve this purpose: export profit margin and export cost for foreign exchange. The export profit margin tells us the relative relationship between the profit earned and the total cost incurred by percentage. The export cost for foreign exchange directly illustrates the local currency cost for making one unit of foreign currency income. Both ratios are meaningful only when they are used in comparison.

Communication of price typically involves four stages. An inquiry is the act of a potential client asking for information from the counter party to his intention of buying or selling of a certain commodity. An offer refers to a sufficiently definite proposal addressed to one or more specific persons for concluding a contract. While a counter-offer is a reply to an offer containing additions, limitations or other modifications. An acceptance is a token made to present the willingness of the offeree to conclude a transaction. Offer and acceptance are the two compulsory stages in the process of communication.

Exercises

Ⅰ. Choices

1. Export total cost refers to ________.

A. Purchase cost

B. Selling price

C. Purchase cost + all expenses before export

D. Purchase cost + all expense before export + all taxes before export

2. Which one of the following price is correctly expressed?

A. CIF ROTTERDAM US $ 1010/MT

B. CIF ROTTERDAM $ 1,010. 00/MT

C. CIF ROTTERDAM US $ 1,010. 00/MT

D. CIF ROTTERDAM US $ 1,010. 00/TON

3. The seller takes off some percent of original price to buyer, namely appropriate preferential treatment in price. This is ________.

A. Commission B. Discount C. Advance payment D. Subscription

4. In international trade, the calculation of commission is ________.

A. Net price × commission rate

B. price including commission × commission rate

C. Net price/ (1 − commission rate)

D. unit price × commission rate

5. Who does take the commission in international trade? ________

A. seller B. buyer C. shipper D. middle man

6. Which one of the following price does include commission? ________

A. FOBS B. FOBT C. FOBST D. FOBC

7. In international trade business, if net income of export sale exceeds export total cost, then it means that this trade is ________.

A. profitable B. even

C. loss D. possible of the above choices

8. In international trade, when trader choose currency of settlement, he should obey the following rules: ________.

A. employing strong currency to settle

B. employing weak currency to settle

C. employing strong currency to settle in export, employing weak currency to settle in import

D. employing strong currency to settle in import, employing weak currency to settle in export

Ⅱ. Short questions

1. While making pricing decision, what major factors should be considered?

2. What are the differences and similarities between commission and discount?

Ⅲ. Calculations

1. An original export offer by a Chinese company (let's say "company A") is USD 30 per dozen CIFC2 London, now the other party requests company A to quote CIFC5. By how much shall the income for Company A be reduced if the offer remains unchanged? And how much should Company A quote if it wants to keep the original income?

2. A Chinese seller exports commodity X to Japan. The price is USD 500 CIF Osaka per unit, including USD50 of freight and USD7 of insurance premium. If the domestic purchase price is RMB 1 600 per M/T, and domestic direct and indirect expenses are 17% of the purchase price, calculate the RMB cost in return for foreign exchange.

Chapter 6 International Cargo Transport

Learning Objectives

1. To understand the procedure of ocean transportation and the function of different B/L of ocean transportation
2. To understand the procedure of other modes of transportation
3. To master to stipulate the shipment clause in the sales contract

Key Words

Shipment by installments; Transshipment; Liner transport; Charter transport; Bare boat charter; Weight ton; Measurement ton; A. V. ; W/M; Gross terms; F. O. ; F. I. ; F. I. O. ; Working days; Weather working days; On board B/L; Clean B/L; Through B/L; Original B/L; Full container load; Less than container load; Container yard; Container freight station

Transportation is one of the most important factors in export process. Without transportation, goods are not able to be carried from the exporting country to the importing country. With the development of modern technology in transportation, speed and capacity for shipment has been largely improved and modes of transportation have been greatly varied, which, of course, contribute a lot to the expansion of international trade. The commonly used modes of transporting export goods are ocean transportation, rail transportation, road transportation, air transportation, international multimodal transportation and container transportation.

6.1 Ocean Transportation

Ocean transportation is mostly preferred in cargo transportation due to its low freight cost and large capacity. However, it is comparatively slow (as compared with air), vulnerable to bad weather and inefficient in punctuality. To understand marine transport, we should first of all understand the types of ships used in international trade. There are oil tankers and dry cargo ships. In dry cargo ships, there are general cargo vessels, bulk vessels, refrigerated cargo vessels, container ships, lighter aboard ships, roll-on/roll-off ships, etc.

There are two main types of ocean transportation: liner transportation and charter transportation, of which liner transportation is more commonly used in international trade.

6.1.1 Liner Transportation

A liner is a vessel with regular sailings and arrivals and sails on a fixed (regular) sailing route and calls at fixed (regular) base ports. It adopts a comparatively fixed timetable and charges at comparatively fixed freight rates.

(1) Types of Liners

Liners can normally be classified into two types: conference liners and non-conference liners. Conference liners are provided by shipping conferences which is composed of a group of members. Any member of a shipping conference shall provide scheduled sailing service on particular routes at standardized freight rates established by the conference. By establishing common freight rates, conference members are likely to alleviate competition and obtain stable profits. Generally speaking, stable freight rates and regular services are the main advantages of conference liners.

Non-conference liner service, however, is provided by independent carriers or vessel operators who are not a member of a freight conference. Non-conference liners may or may not have regular sailing schedules between ports. The freight rates are quoted independently, varying from one carrier to another. Although non-conference liner service is perceived as less dependable, its flexibility in freight and service is still preferred by many shippers.

(2) Liner Freight

Freight is the remuneration payable to the carrier for the carriage of goods. Liner freight is usually inclusive of the loading and unloading cost and other costs such as demurrage or dispatch money. Normally, the freight of liner service is made up of two parts. One is the basic freight; the other is the surcharges and additionals.

Basic freight is charged for carriage of goods from the port of shipment to port of destination. Basic freight constitutes the main cost of liner transportation. The main criteria used in the tariff for calculating basic freight of liners are W, M, W/M, A. V., W/M or A. V., unit/head, minimum rate and open rate.

For items marked with "W" in the tariff, freight is to be calculated on the basis of weight ton (WT). Internationally, one weight ton equals to one metric ton (1 000kg), or one long ton (1 016kg) or one short ton (907.18kg), depending on the measurement system adopted by the shipping company. Freight for heavy cargo is usually charged on this basis.

For items marked with "M" in the tariff, freight is to be calculated according to the measurement ton (MT) of the goods, i. e. the volume. One measurement ton is one cubic meter or 40 cubic feet. Freight for light cargo is often charged on this basis. Weight ton and measurement ton both fall under the name of freight ton.

For items marked with "W/M", the freight is to be calculated on the basis of either weight ton or measurement ton, subject to the higher one. When making a comparison between W and M, one has to follow the notion that 1 WT is equal to 1 MT.

For items marked with "Ad Val. ", the freight is charged according to the value of the cargo. This is normally expressed by a certain percentage (ranging from 1% to 5 %) of the FOB price or value of the goods carded. This is more suitable for goods that are of high value such as gold, silver, precious stones, expensive furs and valuable drawings and paintings.

For items marked "W/M or Ad val. ", the freight is to be calculated on the basis of weight ton, measurement ton or the value of the goods, subject to the highest rate.

Unit/Head For items marked "Unit" in the tariff, freight is calculated according to the number of the cargo carded, e. g. USD60 per Unit of truck, USD15 per Head of live animal.

For carriage of cargo in extremely small quantities, a minimum freight is adopted for the obtainment of freight.

For items marked "Open" in the freight tariff, freight is to be calculated according to the temporary or special agreement entered into between the carrier and the consignor. Usually, shipment of cargo in extremely large quantity such as grains, ores, and coal is subject to open rate.

In addition to the basic freight which is calculated on the above basis, payment of surcharges and additional fees may be required on some special occasions or for some cargo that needs special care in handling. There are a great multitude of surcharges and additionals in freight calculation. The following are some examples:

Total freight can be calculated using the following formula:

Total freight = Total Quantity × Basic Rate × (1 + Surcharge/Additionals Rate)

6.1.2 Charter Transportation

Unlike the liners, a charter (tramp) does not sail on a fixed route and a fixed schedule, but goes all over the world in search of cargoes, primarily bulk shipments, like coal, grain, timber, steel, ores, fertilizers, etc. , which are carried in complete shiploads. Charter vessels are engaged under chartering on a time and voyage basis, and sometimes are chartered to supplement existing liner services to meet peak cargo shipment demands. Chartering might be voyage charter, time charter, or demise charter.

(1) Voyage charter or trip charter

It is for the carriage of goods from one special port to another. It might be for one single or consecutive single voyage or for one return or consecutive return voyage.

(2) Time charter

As the name signifies, it is on the time basis. The chartering might be a year or many years. During which the business of the boat is under the management of the charter.

(3) Demise charter or bare boat charter

It is a form of time charter. Under demise charter, the ship owner only rents the charter the boat, while the charter will supply by himself the crew and the boat is under complete control of the charter.

(4) Charter party

The contract signed between the ship owner and the charter is called the charter party. Given in the charter party are the charter and the shipowner, the name of the boat, flag, the cargoes to be carried, the time of the charter, freight, loading and unloading charges, demurrage and the dispatch money, etc.

Freight can be prepaid or be paid after the arrival of the goods at the destination. Before the freight is paid by the charterer, the shipowner has the right over the cargoes, that is, he is entitled to refuse delivering the cargo before the freight is paid.

Division of loading and unloading cost

Four methods are usually used to divide the expenses of loading and unloading:

□ Liner Terms/Gross Terms or In and Out (I. & O.)

The ship-owner bears loading and unloading cost.

□Free In (F. I.)

The ship-owner is only responsible for unloading cost.

□ Free Out (F. O.)

The ship-owner is only responsible for loading cost.

□Free In and Out (F. I. O.)

The ship-owner does not bear loading and unloading cost.

□F. I. O. S. T. (free in and out, stowed and trimmed)

The ship-owner does not bear loading and unloading cost, not even bear the expenses of stowing and trimming.

If the charterer is responsible for the loading and unloading, he is obliged to complete them within the given period time. The charter party usually stipulates that if the charterer can not complete loading or unloading within the given period time, he will have to pay the shipowner a certain sum of fine, called demurrage. On the other hand, if he can finish loading or unloading before the given time expires, the shipowner will reward him with "dispatch money". Dispatch money is generally one half of the demurrage.

6.2 Other Modes of Transportation

Aside from ocean transportation, there are also various other modes of cargo transportation available for the delivery of goods from sellers to buyers, such as air transportation, rail (way) transportation, road transportation, and international multimodal transportation (IMT).

6.2.1 Air Transportation

Air transportation is one of the latest developed forms of distribution and one of the widely used forms of transportation in international trade. It simplifies documentation and provides quick and reliable service for the carriage of goods, thus minimizing the risk of damage and pilferage, the storage of goods and capital tie-up. However, the disadvantage of air transportation is also obvious: high operating cost, limited capacity and vulnerability to bad weather. These disadvantages make it only suitable for transporting small quantity of goods of high value and low weight ratio, or goods in urgent need.

(1) Types of Air Transportation

Air transportation services are divided into scheduled airlines, chartered carders, consolidated consignment and air express.

□Scheduled Airlines Scheduled airlines are operated on a regular service, over a fixed airline and between fixed airports. Thus regular schedule departures, specified routes with fixed base ports at fixed freight rate are the characteristics of scheduled airline. They are suitable for conveying fresh and perishable goods.

□ Chartered Carriers Chartered carriers are the hire of the entire or partial space of a craft by a total charter carrier or partial charter carriers to deliver cargoes. They are usually adopted by the air freight forwarders for carrying cargoes of large quantity or carrying cargoes of different shippers to the same destination.

□ Consolidated Consignment A consolidated consignment is adopted when air freight agents or forwarders assemble a number of individual shipments arriving at the same destination into one consignment and dispatch them on one air waybill.

□Air Express Air express offers the fastest and safest service to carry goods from desk to desk, but the freight rate is much higher than that of the other air transportation mode. In international trade practice, documents and samples needed urgently are usually dispatched by air express.

(2) Air Transportation Freight

Air freight varies greatly according to the types and nature of cargo, quantity of cargo, air flight distance and the types of service and so on. The types of rate available are general cargo rates, minimum charges, class rates, special commodity rates and so on. Air transportation freight rates are normally based on W, M and W/M. W, the actual gross weight (kilogram), is usually adopted for heavy cargoes, while M, the measurement weight (cubic centimeter), is often used for cargoes of large volume. For general cargoes, the usual basis is W/M, the actual gross weight or measurement weight, subject to the higher one.

As mentioned before, when W/M is adopted as the freight rate basis for liner freight obtainment, one needs to decide which basis is higher by making a comparison between W and M. In such a case, 1WT is considered to be equal to 1MT, that is, 1M/T = lm^3. However, for the comparison between W and M for air freight calculation, 1 unit of weight is 1 KG (gross weight) while 1 unit of measurement weight equals to 6 000cm^3, that is, 1kg =6 000cm^3.

6. 2. 2 Rail Transportation and Road Transportation

Rail transportation and road transportation are two modes of overland transportation commonly used in international trade.

(1) Rail Transportation

Rail transportation means transporting goods from a dispatching station to a destination station. Rail transportation is a major mode of transportation with large capacity and relatively high speed. Railway transportation is safe, punctual, and economical. Besides, it is less prone to bad weather. But it is confined to railroads and therefore is less flexible.

(2) Road Transportation

Road transportation is widely used for diverging goods from an inland point to the sea port, airport and railway station. Road transportation is limited in capacity and vulnerable to high risk of pilferage and damage in transit. Besides the operation cost for road transportation is relatively higher. Therefore it is not widely adopted in international trade transportation. However, its high flexibility, high distributive ability and door-to-door service make it still ideal for general merchandise and selective bulk cargoes in small quantities.

6. 2. 3 International Multimodal (Combined) Transportation

International multi-modal (combined) transportation is a brand new mode of transportation in the industry following the development of containerization of international transportation. International multi-modal (combined) transportation means the carriage of cargo from the place of sellers in one country to the site of the buyers in another country by at least two modes of transportation on the basis of a multi-modal transportation contract.

In the practice of multi-modal transportation, only one multi-modal transportation operator is responsible for taking the cargo from the consignor and delivering them to the consignee. Therefore, only one carriage contract and one freight rate for the whole journey are required in this case. All these advantages of multi-modal transportation make it possible to improve the operating efficiency, lower the operating cost and shorten the time period required for cargo movement. As a result, multi-modal transportation is becoming more and more popular in shipping practice.

6. 2. 4 Container Transportation

With the rapid development of containerization, containers as a very special form of transportation are widely used in different modes of transportation. Containerization is a method of distributing merchandise in a unitized form adopting an inter-modal system which provides a possible combination of sea, road and other modes of transportation.

To transport goods by container transportation, the carrier shall first stow large quantity of cargo into standard-sized and reusable vans at the manufacturer's plant inland, or at Container yard (CY) or the container freight station (CFS), and then ship them in unit loads to its destination. During transit, containers are loaded and unloaded by mechanical devices. From the moment a container is locked and sealed, the cargo inside is kept intact until it reaches the final destination.

(1) Features

Container transportation is highly efficient in terms of reliability, cost, quality of service and advanced technology. Features of container transportation are:

(2) Variety in service

Containerization permits door-to-door (DR-to-DR) service, services from door (DR) to container freight station (CFS) /container yard (CY), from CFS/CY to DR, and from CFS/CY to CFS/CY.

Involving one operator Containerization is usually used widely in different modes of transportation, especially multimodal transportation. When there is only one operator throughout the transportation, higher efficiency and security are achieved.

(3) Use of special equipment

Special equipment offers higher efficiency in loading and unloading (about 10 times as fast as that of a general cargo vessel) and enables quick transit and better quality. Thus goods usually arrive in better condition.

(4) Low risk of damage and pilferage

There is less or no need to reload or check the cargo during transit. The risk of damage and pilferage is greatly reduced.

(5) Substantial cost savings

Comparatively favorable premiums are offered by insurance companies due to low risks of damage or pilferage. Labor and handling expenses in loading and unloading are reduced by nearly 90% compared with those of a general cargo vessel. Less or no packing is required when goods are carried in containers.

Types of Container and Container Transportation Service

(6) There are many kinds of container to serve the different needs for cargo transportation. Containers can be classified into dry cargo container, refrigerated container, tanker container (it is designed for liquid cargo in bulk) and car container (designed for carriage of cars). Sizes of container also vary to a certain degree, but the most widely adopted sizes are twenty-foot equivalent unit (TEU) and forty-foot equivalent Unit (FEU).

Container transportation provides various services as well. According to the capacity needed, container transportation offers both FCL and LCL services. If the goods are of a container load, FCL service shall be adopted while if the goods are of small quantity, FCL is not suitable as freight for FCL is calculated based on container capacity and the origin and destination of the goods, not on the quantity of the goods involved. In such case, LCL service is preferred as it enables the shipper to have their goods shipped at reasonable freight rate. As far as cargo in small quantity is concerned, total freight under LCL is much less than that under FCL service because LCL allows the carrier to ship the goods at lower cost by consolidating them with consignments of different shippers, which are to be delivered to the same destination.

Bulk container

Tank container

Refrigerated container

Container transportation

Flat rack container

Figure 6 - 1　All kinds of Containers

According to the place of shipment and destination, container transportation service can be divided into CY to CY (Container Yard to Container Yard) service, CFS to CFS (Container Freight Station to Container Freight Station) service, DR to DR (Door to Door) service, DR to CFS (Door to Container Freight Station) service, CFS to DR (Container Freight Station to Door) service, etc.

The term CY and CFS are applied to the manner as well as the location of the cargo delivery and receipt in container transportation service. CY is the delivery (or receipt) of a whole container while CFS is the delivery (or receipt) of loose cargo.

FCL consignments are usually packed into the container either by the consignor himself or the carrier at the production side or the warehouse, and then sent to the container yard (CY) ready for shipment. After arrival at the port of destination, FCL consignments are accepted either directly by the consignee at container yard (CY) or forwarded by the carrier to the final place of destination.

LCL consignments are first sent to the container freight station (CFS) or inland container depot where the carrier can consolidate and pack the goods into containers according to the nature, destination, weight and so on and then send the containers to the container yard (CY) for shipment. At destination, LCL consignments are taken from the container yard (CY) by the carrier to the container freight station (CFS) or inland container depot. There consignments are taken out from the container and allocated to different consignees.

(7) Freight of Container Transportation

Two major freight rates are used for the calculation of container transportation freight: FCL and LCL. In the case of FCL service, freight rate is determined largely by the capacity of the container and the place of shipment and destination of the consignment, irrespective of the quantity of commodity carried. Under LCL service, however, freight rate criteria are similar to those of the ocean liner service, i. e. W, M, W/M, A. V., W/M or A. V., etc. In addition to the basic freight, various surcharges and additionals can be charged as well.

6.3 Transportation Documents

Transportation documents refer to the contract of carriage made between the shipper and the carrier. By the evidence of a transportation document, a shipper undertakes the payment of freight and the carrier undertakes the liability to carry the cargo to the place of destination as stipulated in the contract.

As bill of lading is the main transportation documents for ocean transportation, the focus of this section will be devoted to the introduction of its functions, contents and types. Documents concerning other transportation modes will also be briefly mentioned.

6.3.1 Bill of Lading

The most important transport document is the bill of lading. It is a document given by a shipping company, representing both a receipt for the goods shipped and a contract for shipment between the shipping company and the shipper. It is also a document of title to the goods, giving the holder or the assignee the right to possession of the goods.

6.3.1.1 Functions of Bill of Lading

A bill of lading has three major functions: first, it is a cargo receipt; second, it is evidence of a contract of carriage; and finally, it is a document of title to the goods.

(1) A Receipt of Cargo

A bill of lading is a cargo receipt. It is a receipt issued by a carrier evidencing that a consignment of goods has been received at his disposal for shipment, or actually loaded on board the ship. Thus a bill of lading will show the quantity and condition of the cargo loaded.

In international trade practice, the information about goods is normally provided by the shipper and confirmed by the carrier as the goods are transferred to him or loaded aboard the ship. However, the carrier is responsible only for the apparent compliance rather than the contents packed inside, that is, a carrier simply makes sure that the labels comply with the goods listed and that the packages are in good condition.

(2) An Evidence of Contract of Carriage

A bill of lading is an evidence of a contract of carriage. It states all the terms and conditions of the contract of carriage. Therefore, a bill of lading is the major evidence of duties and obligations of both parties.

(3) A Document Title to the Goods

A bill of lading is a document of title to the goods, that is, the legal owner of a bill of lading holds legal possession of the goods described in it. The legal holder of the bill of lading is given the right to obtain delivery of the goods at the port of destination. For this function, the goods still in transit can be transferred from one owner to another by means of selling and buying of a bill of lading.

6. 3. 1. 2 Contents of Bills of lading

A bill of lading is, firstly, a contract between the shipper and the shipping company, secondly, a receipt for the consignment, thirdly a document of title. A bill of lading does not only contain a full description of the consignment—numbers and weights and marks of packages but a lot of other information as well. It quotes the name of the consignee (unless the B/L is "to order", like a check), and the date of shipment, which is very important from a contractual point of view.

It may also contain a number of other clauses. Some bill of lading are marked "freight paid", when a shipper is selling CIF or CFR, others may allow transshipment, which means that the cargo may be transferred from one ship to another at some intermediate port. It is often important to a shipper that his bill of lading should be "clean" rather than "dirty", that is, that the shipping company should not have made any qualifications about the quantity or condition of the cargo actually shipped. This is because the shipper's letter of credit may insist on clean bills, just as it may insist on "on board" as opposed to "alongside" lading. Sometimes a mate's receipt is given to the shipper in advance of the B/L, which takes time to issue.

6. 3. 1. 3 Types of Bills of lading

Bills of lading can be classified into various forms according to different standards.

(1) Shipped B/L and Received for Shipment B/L

According to whether the goods have been loaded on board the carrying vessel, bills of lading can be classified into shipped (or on board) B/L and received for shipment (or received) B/L.

A shipped B/L refers to the one that shall be issued after the cargo has been actually hipped on board vessel. A shipped B/L is issued by the shipping company, on which both he loading date and the name of the vessel shall be indicated in detail. Since shipped bills of lading provide better guarantee for the arrival of goods at the destination, they are usually preferred by the importer.

A received B/L is the one that acknowledges that goods have been received for shipment but not been loaded on board the carrying vessel yet. A received for shipment bill is issued when the goods have been placed in the custody of the carrier awaiting shipment. Such a bill does not show the name of the carrying vessel and the date of shipment. The absence of date of shipment makes it difficult to anticipate the date of arrival of the goods; therefore a received B/L is usually not acceptable to buyers and banks.

A received B/L can become a shipped on board B/L by adding an on board notation, and signed by the carrier or agent on the received B/L. The notation may read: "Goods shipped on board vessel on May 10, 2007." or "Received from the shipper in apparent good order and condition for shipment on board S/S. Red Star on May 10, 2007."

(2) Clean B/L and Unclean B/L

According to the apparent condition of the received cargo, bills of lading can be classified into clean B/L and unclean B/L.

A clean B/L refers to the one that does not contain any notation declaring a defective condition of the exterior packing of goods. It is a proof that the goods have been "shipped in apparent good order and condition" or "clean on board" or the like.

A clean B/L is usually issued to the shipper when goods do not show any defects on their exteriors at the time of loading. By issuing a clean bill of lading, the carrier undertakes full liability for the goods in transit. A clean B/L is favored by buyers and banks for settlement, and therefore it is usually stipulated in the sales contract that the seller should obtain a clean bill of lading for presentation.

An unclean B/L (also named a dirty B/L, claused B/L or foul B/L) is the one that contains unfavorable notation about the apparent condition of the cargo. An unclean B/L is usually issued by the carrier when goods received for shipment are found in damaged condition. This is done by indicating the damage on the bill of lading, e. g. "2 cases missing"; "3 cartons wet"; "1 case broken"; or "cases inadequately packed". By issuing an unclean B/L, carrier's liability can be reduced if damages to the goods are due to these deficiencies. An unclean B/L is usually not acceptable to the buyer and banks because the inadequate packing may result in damages to the goods.

(3) Straight B/L, Order B/L and Bearer B/L

According to the address of the consignee, bills of lading can be divided into straight B/L, order B/L and open B/L.

A straight B/L refers to the one that is made out to a designated consignee. Under this bill, only the named consignee at the destination is entitled to take delivery of the goods under the bill. The consignee is usually designated by the shipper when he fills in the box of consignee with the words "Deliver to ... Co. Ltd" or the like. In this case, the carrier is obliged to hand over the cargo to that named consignee, not to any other party even if he is in possession of the bill. A straight B/L is not transferable.

An order B/L refers to the one that is made out in such a way that the goods are consigned or destined to the order of a named person instead of a definite consignee. Order bills are usually issued by carriers to the shipper/consignor by marking "To order", "To order of the shipper", or "To order of the consignor" in the box of consignee. This means that the carrier will deliver the goods to any consignee designated by the shipper/consignor at the port of destination. An order B/L is a negotiable and transferable document, but to transfer the title to the goods, the transferor, being the shipper in the case of "To order" or "To order of the shipper", should endorse the bill at the back of the B/L. If he does not endorse the bill, he then reserves the right to put the goods at the disposal of himself.

(4) Bearer B/L (Blank B/L or Open B/L)

A bearer B/L refers to the bill in which the name of a definite consignee is not mentioned and left blank or open. The wording "to Bearer" may appear in the box of consignee indicating that anyone who holds the open B/L is entitled to the goods the bill represents. An open B/L can be transferred without endorsement, i. e. ownership of the goods passes when the bill is handed over to anyone. Open Bs/L are not commonly used in international trade due to the high risk involved.

(5) Direct B/L and Transshipment B/L

According to whether transshipment is involved in transit, bills of lading can be classified into direct B/L and transshipment B/L.

A direct B/L is the one that states that the goods are shipped from the port of shipment directly to the port of destination without being transported during the voyage. Meanwhile, a transshipment B/L refers to one that states that the goods are transshipped at an intermediate port from one vessel to another before reaching the final destination. As transshipment involves additional unloading and loading operations in transit, a journey with transshipment usually last longer and the risk of damage and pilferage is higher. Thus a direct B/L is preferred by a buyer while a transshipment B/L is only acceptable when there is no direct service between the port of shipment and the port of destination or when the direct services are few and far between.

(6) Long Form B/L and Short Form B/L

According to the complexity or simplicity of the bill content, bills of lading can be classified into long form B/L and short form B/L.

A long form B/L is the one that, on the face and back of page, contains all the detailed clauses of the carriage contract, i. e. all terms and conditions about the rights and obligations of the carrier and shipper/consignor printed. And a short form B/L refers to one that contains only the basic terms and conditions on the face of the page and omits the general terms and conditions that otherwise appear on the back of a bill of lading. It is a simplified and abbreviated form of B/L.

(7) Freight Prepaid B/L and Freight to be Collected B/L

According to the payment condition of freight, bills of lading can be classified into freight prepaid B/L and freight to be collected B/L.

A freight prepaid B/L indicates that the freight has been paid by the consignor. This type of B/L is usually issued only after the freight has been paid. A freight to be collected B/L refers to the B/L on which "freight payable at destination" or "freight to collect (to be collected) at destination" is indicated.

Normally, freight is pre-paid at the port of shipment, especially when freight is born by the seller. Sometimes freight can be paid at the port of destination. For instance, under a FOB contract, the seller may arrange the contract of carriage on behalf of the buyer, but he bears no obligation to pay the freight. Thus, a freight to be collected B/L is adopted and the freight is paid by the buyer at the destination before he takes delivery of the goods.

(8) Original B/L and Copy B/L

According to the validity, bills of lading are classified into original B/L and copy B/L.

An original bill of lading refers to one that is signed and dated by either the shipping company or by a duly authorized agent. The bill of lading must show how many signed originals were issued. The originals are marked "Original" on their face and they become valid only after being signed by the carrier. The original B/L is a piece of evidence showing the ownership of goods, one of which must be presented to the carrier at the destination in exchange for the goods.

In some cases, a "full set" of rather than just one original bill of lading are required to be presented. In practice, bills of lading are normally made out in a set of three originals and if a full set is required, all three originals are to be delivered to the buyer or the consignee. When one of the originals is used, the others automatically become null and void.

A copy bill of lading is marked "Copy", "Duplicate" or "Non-negotiable" instead of "Original". For easy distinction, copy and original bill of lading are usually designed and printed in two different colors. Copy bills of lading are mainly used for reference or lot records.

(9) Other types of B/L

Other forms of bills of lading also exist according to different circumstances. They are stale B/L; ante-dated B/L; advanced B/L and on-deck B/L.

a. Stale B/L

A stale B/L is a B/L presented to the consignee or the bank later than the latest presentation date specified in the L/C or later than the goods' arrival at the destination. Sometimes, especially in the case of short voyages, it is a common occurrence that a bill of lading arrives late and in this case, it is necessary to add a clause that a "Stale B/L is acceptable" in the contract.

Without the bill of lading, the cargo normally cannot be released. Thus in order to facilitate the smooth claim of the goods, a bill of lading is usually required to be presented to the consignee or their bank within a specified time (i. e. presentation period). The late arrival of this important document may lead to additional costs, such as warehousing expenses and sometimes even loss or damage. Therefore, the buyer and the bank usually refuse to accept a stale B/L. According to UCP 600, the B/L shall be presented within 21 days after issuance, unless otherwise stipulated in the credit.

b. Ante-dated B/L

A B/L is antedated when the shipment date shown on the bill is earlier than the actual one. An ante-dated B/L is issued at the request of the shipper when the actual shipment date is later than that stipulated in the credit.

When the actual loading date is later than the date of shipment stipulated in the L/C, the bank would decline the bill because the bill fails to meet the L/C stipulation. Therefore, in order to negotiate payment, the seller sometimes may ask the carrier to issue an ante-dated B/L where the loading date is in line with the L/C stipulation.

c. Advanced B/L

An advanced B/L is the one that is issued before actual loading of the goods is completed or even before the commencement of the actual loading operation. An advanced B/L is usually issued when the time of shipment stipulated in the L/C is almost due but the actual loading of the goods is not yet completed or the goods are not ready for shipment. An advanced B/L is similar to an ante-dated B/L in that both of them are issued at the request of the seller, both carry false information as to the actual date of loading and finally both are for the avoidance of a non-acceptance for negotiation of payment at the bank. The difference between them is that an advanced B/L is issued before actual loading is finished while an ante-dated B/L is issued after it.

In both cases, the carrier is liable for all risks arising from the issuance of such B/L because the buyer will find out actual loading date in the sails log. Therefore, carrier normally will avoid these practices.

In practice, when the carrier agrees to issue an ante-dated B/L or an advanced B/L, the shipper should first submit to the carrier a letter of indemnity thereby undertaking all responsibilities for risks that may derive from the issuance of such a bill. However, since the letter is not considered to be a lawful document, the carrier usually finds it difficult to avoid liability for issuance of either an ante-dated B/L or an advanced B/L when disputes arises or when the consignee brings an arbitration or even a lawsuit against him for conducting a fraud.

d. On-deck B/L

An on-deck bill is the one indicating that the goods are stowed and shipped on deck. As the risks of the deck goods are great, the carrier shall not be responsible for the damage to and losses of the deck goods. So the buyer and the bank are usually unwilling to accept on deck B/L unless the credit stipulates otherwise.

However, some cargoes must be loaded on deck, such as livestock, plants, dangerous cargo, or awkwardly-shaped goods that cannot fit into the ship's hold. In these cases, "loading on deck to be allowed" is usually required in the sales contract and the relative L/C and specific insurance should be taken out by the shipper.

It must be noted that the above-mentioned types of bills of lading are not independent of each other. One bill may, at the same time, be in more than one form. For example, a received for shipment bill can be a clean order bill as well. In trade practice, the most common bill of lading is a clean, shipped direct bill of lading made out to order with a blank endorsement.

6.3.2 Other Types of Transportation Documents

Besides bills of lading, there are other types of transportation documents which are adopted in international trade. The following is a brief introduction to other documents such as sea waybill, air waybill, rail waybill, road consignment note and multimodal transportation document (or combined transportation document).

(1) Sea Waybill

Sea waybill is issued by the carrier or the agent evidencing that the goods have been received (taken over or loaded on board the vessel) and that the goods are to be delivered to the designated consignee at the port of destination.

Like a bill of lading, a sea waybill is a receipt for the goods as well as the evidence of contract of carriage. However, a sea waybill differs from a bill of lading in that it is not a document of title to goods. The consignee need not render the sea waybill to take delivery of the goods and the carrier will release the goods to the consignee against the proof that he is the consignee designated by the sea waybill. Thus the use of sea waybill is more convenient to the consignee when the goods are expected to arrive at the port of destination earlier than the documents, which is not impossible when the voyage is short and the time in handling documents on the part of the bank is comparatively long.

(2) Air Waybill

The air waybill, also called the air consignment note, is a document or consignment note used for the carriage of goods by air. It is basically a receipt of the goods for dispatch and evidence of the contract of carriage between the carrier and the consignor. Air waybills are supplied and issued by the carrier to the consignor.

An air waybill is evidence of a transportation contract signed between the consignor/shipper and the carrier/ airline. It is also a receipt of cargo from the airline acknowledging the receipt of the consignment from the shipper. It includes information concerning the flights and the conditions of transportation and consignment.

An air waybill is equivalent to a bill of lading with the notable difference that the air waybill is not a negotiable document because it is only a notice of arrival to release cargo, not a document of title to the consignment.

Normally, air waybills are made out in three originals and twelve copies. The exporter would retain the first original. The third would be retained by the airline and the second would travel with the consignment to the consignee at the destination. Copies of air waybill will go to the various parties involved, such as the shipper, consignee, issuing carrier, second carrier (if applicable), third carrier (if applicable), airport of destination, airport of departure, and will be used for other purposes.

(3) Consignment Note (Rail Waybill)

The most important document for rail transportation is the consignment note (also called rail waybill). Consignment notes for rail transportation serve as the contract of carriage between the railway and consignor, evidencing the receipt of the goods and the date of acceptance for carriage by the carrier.

The consignment note will be delivered with the cargo from the departure station to the consignee at the destination station after the freight and other charges have been paid. The duplicate of the consignment note is issued by the carrier to the consignor as the receipt of the goods and it is the main document for payment settlement as well.

As the goods are not delivered against the presentation of a consignment note, a consignment note is not a document of title and is not transferable or negotiable.

(4) Road Consignment Note

Road consignment note is similar to rail consignment note in form and contents. Like rail consignment note, it evidences the place and date of taking over carriage of the goods and the place designated for delivery. It is not a negotiable or transferable document or document of title.

The consignment note is made out in three copies and signed by the sender and the carrier. Usually the first one is an original kept by the seller, the third copy goes to the carrier and the second copy accompanies the consignment and is finally delivered to the consignee at the destination.

(5) Multi-modal Transportation Document (MTD)

The multimodal transportation document or combined transportation document, issued by a multi-modal transportation operator (MTO) or a combined transportation operator (CTO) under a multimodal/combined transportation contract, is a document which evidences the multimodal/combined transportation contract and indicates that the multimodal/combined transportation operator shall take over the goods and shall be responsible for carrying the goods to the destination according to the clauses in the contract.

When cargo is entrusted for multi-modal/combined transportation, a combined transportation bill of lading is issued by the MTO (CTO) or his agent. The bill covers the entire journey including sea, land or air transportations that are undertaken by different carriers. By evidence of a multimodal transportation document, the MTO (CTO) or his agent is responsible to the shipper for all losses and damages occurring during the whole journey except where he enjoys exemption from liability; carriers involved in multimodal transportation are responsible to the MTO for losses or damages that occur when the goods are in their respective custody.

6.4 Shipment Clause in the Sales Contract

The shipment clause in a sales contract usually include stipulations concerning time of delivery (time of shipment), port (place) of shipment and port (place) of destination, partial shipments, transshipment, or lay days, demurrage and dispatch money. The buyer and the seller should reach an agreement on these issues and specify them legibly in the contract. Clear stipulation of the shipment clause is an important condition for the smooth execution of the contract. The following is an example of shipment clause in the sales contract.

6.4.1 Time of Shipment and Time of Delivery

Time of shipment refers to the time limit for loading the goods on board the vessel at the port of shipment. Time of delivery refers to the time limit during which the seller shall deliver the goods to the buyer at the agreed place.

For all shipment contracts, time of shipment is time of delivery. They can be used interchangeably in the contract. According to Incoterms 2010, contracts concluded on the basis of terms like FOB, CFR, CIF, FCA, CFT, CIP are shipment contracts. Under shipment contract, the seller fulfills his obligation of delivery when the goods are shipped on board the vessel or delivered to the carrier and the seller only bears all risks prior to shipment. The delivery of goods under a shipment contract implies a symbolic delivery. Delivery is a symbolic one when the delivery of goods is symbolically made by means of the transfer of documents (among which B/L represents the title to goods) instead of the actual transfer of goods.

For all arrival contracts, time of shipment and time of delivery are two completely different concepts and time of delivery should be stipulated in contract. According to Incoterms 2010, contracts concluded on the basis of terms like DAF, DES, DEQ, DDU and DDP belongs to arrival contracts. Arrival contracts differ from shipment contract in that seller should be responsible for all risks of bringing the goods to the named destination. Arrival contracts usually suggest actual delivery. Actual delivery is made when the goods are actually delivered from the seller to the buyer.

(1) Stipulating "Time of Shipment" in the Sales Contract

Time of shipment is a very important clause in a contract as any delay or advance of delivery constitutes a violation of contract. There are basically two ways of stipulating time of delivery in the contract: one is clearly specifying a period of time or a deadline, the other is setting a time period between the shipment and the deadline by which the relevant L/C must reach the seller.

(2) Specifying a fixed period of time or a deadline

e. g. Shipment is to be made during January/February/March 2007

Shipment not later than 31 st July, 2007

(3) Setting a time period upon receipt of payment

Shipment is to be made within 30 days after receipt of the L/C. The relevant L/C must reach the seller not later than 30th June, 2008.

In case of payment by L/C, the seller should stipulate the time of delivery based on the time of receipt of L/C. By so doing, the seller is able to reduce his risks of losses resulted from the buyer's failure in opening the L/C required.

(4) Issues to Be Concerned

Sufficiency and clarity are two issues to be concerned when stipulating the time of shipment in a contract.

a. Sufficiency

The time of shipment stipulated in contract should be sufficient in terms of availability of goods and shipping space, and the payment. That is, the seller should consider whether he can get the goods ready before the latest shipment date and whether the ship or shipping space is available if the goods are ready. Normally, the seller favors a longer shipment time period so that it is easier for him to make the necessary shipping arrangements. In case of payment by L/C, long time of shipment also allows sufficient time for the seller to check the L/C and make necessary amendment. According to industry norm, the L/C should arrive at least 15 days before the time of shipment.

In case an L/C simply stipulates an expiry date and specify no time of shipment. This implies that the latest date of shipment should be the same as the expiry date of the L/C. For example, if the L/C stipulates that the expiry date is May 15th, but no time of shipment is indicated, then the deadline for shipment is also May 15th. In this case, the exporter should ship the goods much earlier or at least no later than May 15th so that time is left for him to get all the documents ready and present the documents to his bank within the validity of the L/C.

Stipulations like "shipment on May 15th" must be avoided because it leaves little flexibility of time to the seller. Time flexibility in arranging shipment is very important to the seller because it is extremely difficult for him as a shipper to guarantee that the shipment is to be made on that specified day. Even if a seller can manage to get the goods well prepared, shipment on that day is hardly guaranteed due to uncertainty of the weather conditions as well as the shipping space available. Thus the seller is more likely to breach the contract if the time of shipment is stipulated on one specific day.

b. Clarity

The time of shipment should be stipulated in a clear and explicit way. According to UCP600, unless required to be used in a document, expressions such as "prompt", "immediately", "as soon as possible", "shipment by first available vessel", "shipment by first opportunity", "shipment subject to shipping space available", and the like should be avoided as they may lead to future disputes.

6.4.2 Port of Shipment and Port of Destination

Port of shipment is the port where the goods are shipped and depart from, while port of destination is the port at which goods are ultimately discharged. In international trade, both of them should be clearly specified in the contract.

(1) Port of Shipment

The port/place of shipment is always stipulated in an export contract. In the case of shipment contracts based on FOB, CFR, CIF or FCA, CPT, CIP, the delivery of the goods is always at the port of shipment when the goods are loaded on board the vessel or at the named place when the goods are delivered to the carrier nominated by the buyer.

It is usual practice to designate only one port of shipment in one transaction. When large amounts of goods are involved and, in particular, the goods are manufactured or stored at different places, two or more ports of shipment are also specified, such as "Shanghai and/or Guangzhou" or "Dalian/ Qingdao/Shanghai".

(2) Port of Destination

The port/place of destination is usually determined by the buyer and confirmed by the seller. Normally, one specific port/place of destination is stipulated in the contract. However, sometimes the seller may accept two or more optional ports/places to meet the buyer's special requirements. When a buyer can not, at the time of contracting, make the decision as to which market should the goods be delivered to, optional ports are set forth in the contract such as "Liverpool, optional Hamburg/Rotterdam".

In case the "optional port" is adopted, it is advisable for the exporter to provide no more than 3 ports of destination for the importer to choose from. He also has to make sure that all the optional ports shall be the calling ports on the same sailing route of a liner service. Otherwise, it would be difficult or even impossible to book the shipping space and effect shipment. If possible, it is expected that a deadline is stipulated in the contract before which the buyer should designate one final specific port so that the seller will have sufficient time in making shipment arrangements.

(3) Issues to Be Concerned

When determining the port of shipment and the port of destination, sellers should pay attention to the following:

A shipment port should be close to the origin of the goods. For instance, when the goods are manufactured in Shandong Province, it is not a wise idea to stipulate "Guangzhou, China" as the port of shipment even though the trading company of the seller is located in Guangzhou, China.

Port facilities, regulations, specific transportation conditions, charges and possible sanctions should be taken into consideration. For example, if a consignment is intended to be shipped by a container liner, only a port with a container yard or container station can be considered as the port of shipment in the contract.

The stipulation of the port of destination should be definite and specific. Ambiguous terms, such as "European Main orts Japanese Ports" shall be avoided. Without a definite stipulation for the port of shipment, the seller will find it difficult to book shipping space and arrange shipment thus difficult to fulfill the contract.

In addition, name of the country and the place should be put in front of the name of the port for fear of the possibility of different ports having the same name. For example, there are 12 "Victoria" ports in the world. If only a "Victoria" port is defined as the port of shipment in the contract, the seller will find it difficult to book shipping space and arrange shipment thus unlikely to fulfill the contract.

6.4.3 Partial Shipment and Transshipment

Clauses concerning the issue of partial shipment and transshipment must also be clearly stipulated in the contract. Generally speaking, partial shipment or transshipment is favorable to the seller, as it puts the seller in a more flexible position to perform the contract.

(1) Partial Shipment

Partial shipment means the commodities under a contract are to be shipped in more than one lot. The reason for the involvement of partial shipment may include one of the following: the lack of means of conveyance or shipping space available; the limitation of loading or unloading facilities at the port of shipment or destination; the restriction of market capacity or production ability.

There are some disagreements about whether a shipment is considered partial or not in cargo transportation practice. In such cases, traders in international trade are suggested to refer to UCP600 Article 31 for resolution.

(2) Transshipment

Transshipment means unloading and reloading from one vessel to another during the course of ocean carriage from the port of loading to the port of discharge stipulated. Transshipment is allowed due to one or more of the following reasons: ships sailing direct to the port of destination are not available; direct sailings to the destination are few and far between; no suitable ships are available at the stipulated period; the port of destination does not tie along the sailing route of the liner service; the amount of cargo for a certain port of destination is so small that no ships will call at that port.

(3) Issues to Be Concerned

When it comes to the shipping clause concerning partial shipment and transshipment, sellers should pay attention to the following:

Contractual laws in some country stipulate that partial shipment and transshipment, if not stipulated in the contract, shall not be deemed to be allowed. This is contradictory to Article 31 of UCP600 where transshipment or partial shipment is allowed if they are not made out in the contract. Therefore it is essential for both parties concerned to make it clear in the contract whether partial shipments and/or transshipment are allowed with a view to avoiding unnecessary disputes in the future.

The time of delivery and quantity of each lot should also be stipulated in the contract. For instance, if the L/C stipulates "partial shipments are allowed in two monthly equal lots in May and June", it should be interpreted as shipment be made only in two equal lots, one in May and the other in June. In each lot, partial shipments are prohibited. It is unfavorable to the seller since he is considered to have breached the contract if he fails to ship goods of any lot. However, if a shipping clause in the contract allows partial shipment but without detailed stipulations, it is favorable to the seller. In that case, the seller can decide how many shipments as well as when and what quantities of each shipment are to be made, depending on the supplies of goods and the transportation conditions.

6.4.4 Lay time, Demurrage and Dispatch

As far as voyage charter is concerned, the time needed for loading and unloading is directly related to the interest of the ship-owner. If loading or unloading is delayed, the ship-owner has to bear additional costs such as port charges and freight loss resulted from the low turnover rate of the ship. If it is advanced, the ship-owner is benefited from less port charge and the high turnover rate of the ship. Therefore to safeguard his interest, the ship-owner will stipulate lay time and rate of loading and unloading together with the reward for dispatch and punishment for demurrage in the charter party.

However, in shipping practice, the party responsible for loading or unloading is sometimes not the charterer, but rather either the seller or the buyer in a sales contract. For example, under an FOB contract, the charterer is the buyer while the seller is responsible for loading at the port of shipment. Under a CIF contract, the charterer is the seller, however, it is the buyer who is held responsible for unloading at the port of destination. As a result, in order to expedite loading or unloading, the charterer will also stipulate lay time, demurrage and dispatch clause in the sales contract.

(1) Lay time

Lay time, also called lay day, is the period of time allowed without additional charge for the loading or unloading of goods. Lay time is normally counted as per days or hours. There are many methods used for the determination of lay time in shipping practice, of which the following three methods are more widely adopted:

Days or Running Days or Consecutive Days: A day here refers to a natural day consisting of 24 consecutive hours. Since no matter whether it is suitable for loading or unloading (e. g. bad weather, other force majeure events) or it is weekends or any other holidays, a day is counted as a day for lay time, this method is not favorable to the charterer in a charter party or the party responsible for loading or unloading in a sales contract.

Weather Working Days of 24 Hours: When the actual hours suitable for loading and unloading (excluding bad weather) amount to 24 hours, the 24 hours then is regarded as one weather working day. This method is more favorable to the ship-owner or the charter party in a sales contract since not only bad weather hour not suitable for loading or unloading can not be counted as the time used, but also un-working hour can be deducted.

Weather Working Days of 24 Consecutive Hours: A weather working day of 24 consecutive hours refers to 24 consecutive hours suitable for loading and unloading (excluding bad weather) irrespective of customary working hours for loading and unloading of a specific port. This is more suitable for ports where 24 consecutive hours can be used for loading and unloading of goods.

(2) Demurrage

Demurrage is the amount of money paid as a penalty at an agreed rate by the charterer to compensate the ship-owner for his losses in case the charterer fails to have loading and unloading completed within the lay time. In a sales contract, demurrage is paid to the charterer (buyer or seller) by the other party (seller or buyer) in case the loading or unloading is completed beyond the stipulated lay time.

(3) Dispatch

Dispatch is the amount of money paid as a bonus by the ship-owner to the charterer if they get loading and unloading done ahead of schedule. Normally dispatch money is half the demurrage as the benefit from the expedite loading or unloading is supposed to be shared by both the ship-owner and the charterer. In the case of a sales contract, dispatch is paid by the charterer (buyer or seller) to the other party (seller or buyer) in case the loading or unloading is completed ahead of the stipulated lay time.

6.5 Summary

The modes of international cargo transportation mainly include sea, land, air and multimodal. Containerization is widely used in different modes of international cargo transportation.

Ocean transportation is the most important mode of transportation in international trade thanks to its low freight and large capacity. There are mainly two types of ocean transportation, namely liner transportation and charter transportation.

Basic freight constitutes the main cost of liner service. The main criteria used in the tariff for basic liner freight are W, M, W/M, A. V., W/M or A. V., unit/head, minimum rate and open rate.

Transportation documents include bill of lading, sea waybill, air waybill, rail waybill, road consignment note and multimodal transportation document (or combined transportation document). Among them, bill of lading is the most important one that bears three functions: First, it is a cargo receipt. Second, it is evidence of a contract of carriage. Finally, it is a document of title to the goods.

There are a number of different types of bills of lading, such as on board B/L, received B/L, straight B/L, order B/L, clean B/L, unclean B/L, long form B/L, short form B/L, direct B/L, transshipment B/L, etc. Different types of bill of lading can be coexistent with each other.

Shipment clauses in a sales contract usually include stipulations concerning time of delivery (time of shipment), port (place) of shipment and port (place) of destination, partial shipments, transshipment, lay time, demurrage and dispatch.

Generally speaking, partial shipment or transshipment is favorable to the seller, which shall put the seller in a more flexible position to perform the relevant contract.

In case of charter, it is sometimes important for the charterer (buyer or seller) to reach an agreement concerning demurrage and dispatch and to stipulate the same in the sales contract.

Exercises

Ⅰ. Choices

1. For small emergency and valuable goods, the most favorable transportation is ________.

A. ocean transportation　　B. Parcel post

C. air service　　D. road transportation

2. In international business, transferable document by endorsement is ________.

A. waybill of railway　　B. ocean bill of lading

C. air waybill　　D. parcel post receipt

3. When carrier received consigned goods, but not to load, the carrier issued ________.

A. On board B/L　　B. Order B/L

C. receiving for shipment B/L　　D. On deck B/L

4. A ________ normally has regular scheduled departures, specified routes and comparatively fixed freight rates.

A. time charter　　B. voyage charter

C. conference liner　　D. non - conference liner

5. An order B/L with blank endorsement is a B/L showing ________.

A. neither the name of consignee nor the name of transferor

B. neither the name of consignee nor the name of transferee

C. both the name of consignee and the name of transferor

D. both the name of consignee nor the name of transferee

6. In liner freight list, "M" refers to ________.

A. Freight based on weight ton B. Freight based on measurement ton

C. Freight based on value D. freight based on per unit

7. ________ is not the specifying method of time of shipment.

A. Clear and specific time of shipment

B. Specifying some days shipment after receiving L/C

C. Generally specifying shipment in the near future

D. Specifying some days shipment before date of delivery

8. According to the classification of consignee in international trade, the most frequent using B/L is ________.

A. Straight B/L B. open B/L C. Order B/L D. Liner B/L

Ⅱ. Explain the following terms

1. liner term
2. Demurrage and dispatch money
3. time of delivery
4. Time of shipment

Ⅲ. Short questions

1. What are the functions of a bill of lading?
2. What are the ways of dividing charges of loading and unloading in a charter party?

Ⅳ. Case study

A Chinese exporter signed a CIF contract with a foreign importer. Payment was to be made by irrevocable sight L/C. Both the contract and the L/C prohibited transshipment. Within the validity of the Credit, the exporter shipped the cargo on board a liner sailing direct to the port of destination, and presented the direct B/L for negotiation. Later the foreign issuing bank also made payment against the direct B/L forwarded by the negotiation bank. However, in order to collect some other cargos, the carrying vessel unloaded the cargo at an intermediate port without authorization. The cargo was instead reloaded onto an old vessel, and thus arrived at the destination two months late. As a result, the buyer lodged a claim against the Chinese side for fraud, since the cargo was actually transshipped even though the direct B/L was issued. Finally the exporter accepted the claim and made compensation as requested, as he thought that he, as the person booking the vessel, should be liable for the carrier's unauthorized transshipment.

1. Do you think the settlement of this case appropriate?
2. Who should bear the loss? Why?
3. Who should be liable for the damage? Why?
4. What should the seller do?

Chapter 7 International Cargo Transportation Insurance

Learning Objectives

1. To master the fundamental principles of cargo insurance
2. To master the definition of total loss, actual total loss, constructive total loss and partial loss
3. To grasp the scope of the Ocean Marine Cargo Clauses of CIC
4. To understand and the reasons for the risks and losses in ocean transportation
5. To understand the frame the coverage of London Institute Cargo Clauses
6. To understand the procedure for lodging claims

Key Words

Perils of the sea; Natural calamity; Fortuitous accidents; Extraneous risks; Constructive total loss; General average; Particular average; Sue and labor expenses; Salvage charges; FPA; WPA; All risks; W/W Clause; General additional risk; Special additional risk; War risks; Strike risks; Aflatoxin; Failure to delivery; Insurance policy

For international trade, it is common for the goods to be transported for a long distance from the exporting country to the importing destination. Whatever mode of transport is used, there will always be risks around each stage of the transit. Accidents normally will result in losses of or damage to the goods. It is a natural desire for traders to avoid the potential losses. Based on the commercial expediency and need of the early merchants, marine insurance was pushed into rapid development, along with the growth of trade in Europe in the fourteenth century. This is evidenced by the earliest known marine insurance contract on ship "The Santa Clara" dated 1347 in Genoa. Since then marine insurance had been practically universal among the maritime nations of Europe.

Cargo insurance is defined in the Marine Insurance Act 1906 thus; 'a contact of marine insurance is a contract whereby the insurer undertakes to indemnify the assured in a manner and to the extent thereby agreed, against marine losses, that is to say, the loss incidental to marine adventure'. Hence this includes cargo insurance involving the maritime conveyance of merchandise form one country to another.

Cargo insurance is an extensive subject and it would be wrong not to include this chapter.

Nevertheless, in so doing the reader must be reconciles to the fact it is only possible to deal briefly with the salient parts on this subject. In international trade, cargo transportation insurance means that the insurant, referred to as either the exporter or importer, enters with an insurance company and/or an underwriter into a contract of insurance in which the insurant undertakes the payment of an insurance premium and the insurance company will, according to the terms indicated in the insurance contract, indemnify the insurant of any loss that occurs within the scope of coverage.

According to this chapter, there are two basic parties involved in a cargo insurance contract: one is the insurant and the other is the insurer. The party indemnified is called the insurant, also referred to as the insured or the assured. It refers to the one who buys insurance from the insurance company or the underwriter. In cargo insurance practice, the insurant can be either the seller or the buyer, depending largely on the Incoterms adopted for transaction and on which party is subject to main risks in transit.

On the contrary, the party undertaking to indemnify the insurant or the insured against losses or damages is known as the insurer, which usually refers to the insurance company. Another name for the insurer is the underwriter. This name comes from the practice that the insurer is always required to sign his name under the insurance policy as a party to the contract. In China, the People's Insurance Company of China (PICC) is usually chosen as the insurer.

For instance, while cargo insurance is arranged by the exporter under a CIF contract, it is the importer who bears the risk of the goods during the ocean journey since risk has been transferred once the goods get over the ship's rail at the port of shipment. If losses or damages occur after risk has been transferred, the importer will suffer and therefore be entitled to lodge the claim.

Cargo insurance must be seen as an indispensable adjunct to overseas trade. Adequate insurance is vital to protect the interests of those with goods in transit. The 1906 Act contains the basis of all cargo insurance affecting export consignments, while the 1909Act deals with the prohibition of gambling in maritime perils. Apart from the protection aspect, cargo insurance also plays a vital role in the financing of overseas trades by making it possible for banks to lend money against cargo in transit – proposition they will only consider if the cargo is protected by insurance.

In this case, the importer is the claimant. However, if losses or damages occur before the goods cross the ship's rail, it is often the exporter who shall lodge claims against the insurer after the incident because he still holds the insurable interest of the goods at the time of losses or damages. He would be the claimant as a result.

7.1 Fundamental Principles of Cargo Insurance

Cargo insurance is governed by the Marine Insurance Act 1906, which came into force on 1 January 1907. This Act did not create any new laws, but codified all the legal decisions which had been made during the preceding 300 years. Cargo transportation insurance is practiced subject to some general principles. According to Insurance Law of The People's Republic of China issued in 1995, there are basically four principles that shall be sought in such insurance. They are the insurable interest principle, the utmost good faith principle, the indemnity principle and the proximate cause principle. Aside from these four principles, there are other two principles also gain recognition in the insurance industry: the subrogation principle and the share principle.

7.1.1 Insurable Interest

Insurable interest is the interest on insurance subject matter (cargo or property accepted for insurance) held by the insurant and recognized by law, indicating that the insurant will be prejudiced by its loss, or by damage thereto, or by detention thereof, or incur liability in respect thereof. An individual ordinarily will have an insurable interest when he obtains some type of financial benefit from the preservation of the subject matter, or sustains pecuniary loss from its destruction or impairment. The most common forms of insurable interest in cargo insurance are as follows:

(1) Ownership of the Goods

There are two parties of ownership: the seller and the buyer, or we can call as the consignor and the consignee. The cargo owner has an insurable interest in the goods since he will benefit if the cargo arrives safely at the destination or suffer when it is lost or damaged. The insurance requirements of these parties will depend upon the terms of the contract of sale, which has been mentioned above.

(2) Charge of Insurance (Premium)

In cargo insurance the insurance amount reflects the cost of the goods plus the cost of insurance. The insured has an insurable interest in the premium paid in respect of any insurance he may affect. As premium will not be paid back no matter the cargo is subject to loss or damage or not, it is at the risk of the cargo owner.

(3) Freight

This is the cost of transporting the goods from the consignor's premises to the consignee's premises and is either pre-paid or payable at destination. In most cases, if the freight is advanced or pre-paid, it is not returnable even if the goods are lost and not delivered. In these instances, therefore, the freight pre-paid is at the risk of the cargo owner and, as in the case of premium, is merged with the value of the goods. Consequently, the insurance amount reflects the cost of the goods plus the cost of the insurance (premium) plus the cost of transportation (freight).

A policy effected without insurable interest is void, i. e. it has no legal value and is unenforceable at law. Therefore, almost in all kinds of insurance, there is a legal requirement that insurable interest exists at the time the insurance is effected. However, this rule doesn't apply in the case of cargo insurance. For example, under a CIF contract, the buyer acquires his interest when the title to the goods purchased is transferred to him sometime after the transit has commenced from the port of shipment. Therefore, in marine cargo insurance, proof of insurable interest is not required at the time of effecting insurance. But when making a claim, it is necessary for the insured to be able to show that he had an insurable interest at the time of loss.

7. 1. 2 Utmost Good Faith

The Marine Insurance Act 1906 provide that a contract of marine insurance is a contact based upon the 'Utmost Good Faith', and if the utmost good faith be not observed by either party, the other party may avoid the contract.

It would not be practical or, indeed, possible for underwriters to check the accuracy or completeness of information submitted to them in respect of a risk to be insured. They have to rely upon the other party—the proposer or the broker acting on his or her behalf—observing the principle of utmost good faith which means a full disclosure of all material circumstances relating to the risk before the contract is concluded. A material circumstance is one which would influence a prudent underwriter as to the desirability of the risk. Where there is a non-disclosure of a underwriter may also avoid the contract if the broker is guilty of misrepresenting the risk during the placing negotiations. It is important to understand that avoidance of the contract does not render the contract void. A void contract is one which has no legal value and, therefore, cannot serve as evidence in a court of law. However, if one party avoids the contract always provide that there is no fraud, the policy remains a valid document and the assured may contest the underwriter's action in a court of law. In practice, this situation usually arises where an underwriter refuses representation at the time of placing the insurance. If the assured does not accept this allegation, they may challenge the underwriter's right to avoid the contract.

7. 1. 3 Indemnity

The purpose of insurance is to protect the insurable interest of the assured whereby, in the event of loss of or damage to the subject matter insured resulting from an insured peril, he or she is placed in the same position that he or she enjoyed immediately before the loss occurred. This is "indemnity". In normal insurance practice, as it would not be practical for marine insurers to replace ships and cargoes lost or damaged, the damage or loss is almost always compensated by paying an amount of money equal to the value of the goods lost or damaged.

While replacement is the means of effecting indemnity in some types of insurance, it would not be practical for marine insurers to replace ships and cargos. The manner of indemnity is, therefore, a cash settlement. As explained above, the extent of this indemnity is the value of the insured property immediately before the loss occurs. However, there are limitations that shall be sought after: first, the total indemnification shall be limited to the insurance amount; second, the total indemnification shall be limited to the actual loss suffered by the insured; and finally, the amount of indemnification shall be limited to the insurable interest of the claimant.

7.1.4 Subrogation

Subrogation is the corollary of indemnity in so far as its application prevents the assured defeating the principle of indemnity by recovering his loss from more than one party. In practice the underwriter, upon payment of the claim for the damage, would automatically be subrogated to all rights and remedies the cargo owner had against the carrier and, accordingly, may exercise these rights either in his or her own name or that of the assured for a recovery against the amount paid by him or her under the insurance.

Pursuant to the contract law of PRC, it is regulated that where any third party is liable for the insured property, the insurer may indemnify the insured according to the insurance policy; but the insured shall transfer the right of recourse to the insurer and assist the insurer to recourse to the third party. This is subrogation. To put it technically, subrogation means that when the loss of the property insured is caused by a third party, the insurer is automatically entitled to seek compensation from the third party after indemnification has been made to the insurant.

The right of subrogation is exercised either in the name of the insurer or that of the insured for a recovery against the amount paid by the insurer under the insurance. Any indemnity the insurer makes in this respect is limited to the amount of the claim paid under the insurance. It is possible, for example, where the goods insured have been undervalued, that the insurer may recover more than the amount paid by him as a claim. In this event, he must pass the surplus proceeds to the insured.

7.1.5 The Proximate Cause Principle

In practice, sometimes it is difficult to determine the efficient cause of a loss. It is very easy to find out the initial event and the last event, but it' s difficult to decide whether there is a direct chain of causation between them or whether some new forces have intervened to supersede the initial cause as the event bringing about the ultimate loss.

There may be more than one cause that leads to the loss of or damage to the goods insured in transit Disputes concerning the causes and their relation to the loss or damage in question are likely to arise in such cases. The Proximate Cause Principle is therefore employed in the judgment of causation between accidents and losses. It refers to the major and/or effective reason that has caused the accident. The proximate cause is not necessarily the first cause or the last cause. Rather it is the dominant cause. According to this, the insurer shall only be responsible for the loss which has a direct link to the risks covered.

In the event that only one cause leads to the loss, this cause is obviously the efficient cause of the loss or the proximate cause. If this event is covered in the insurance policy, the insurer should answer the claim; otherwise the insurer should not be responsible for such a loss. Suppose the cargo suffers rain damage in the course of transit, the insurer should be held responsible for the loss only if the insurant applies for All Risks or Fresh Water and Rain Damage insurance on the basis of FPA or WPA (See Section 7. 3); if no additional risk is covered on the FPA or WPA, then the insurer is entitled to no payment.

If the loss of the subject matter insured is caused by two or more events, the following situations will exist:

If the former cause is within the exclusion of the coverage and there is a direct chain of causation between the former and latter cause, the proximate cause is considered out of the scope of insurance coverage and the insurer need not be held responsible for the loss or damage.

In the event that the loss is caused by several causes, and some are within the scope of insurance coverage but some are out of the insurance coverage, then the insurer should try to find out the dominant one. If the former cause is within the scope of insurance coverage and the latter one is out of the scope of insurance coverage, provided there is a direct chain of causation between them, the former cause is regarded as the proximate cause and the insurer shall be held responsible for the loss or damage.

If there are several causes operating, and all these causes are within the scope of insurance coverage, the insurer should pay the claim.

7. 1. 6 Share

Share means that under the circumstance of double insurance, all the insurers shall bear the loss on the subject matter jointly and share the loss according to their respective insurance proportion. It is stipulated that where a policy is subscribed by or on behalf of two or more insurers, each subscription, unless the contrary is expressed, constitutes a distinct contract with the insured.

When an individual has double insurance, he has the risks covered by two different insurance companies upon the identical interest in the identical subject matter. In this case, each insurer shall compensate a share in proportion to his respective insurance amount in the total amount of double insurance. Therefore, each insurer is, generally speaking, only liable, in case of total loss, to pay the insured to the extent of the sum written against his own name, that is, to the amount of his subscription or, in case of partial loss, some proportion of that sum.

7.2 Marine Risks and Losses

There are many types of risks in cargo transportation and even more in marine cargo transportation. These risks could result in the loss of or damage to the cargo in transit. This section will explain the major risks involved in the ocean transport, the possible losses resulted and the expenses incurred.

7.2.1 Marine Risks

The definition of marine risks is the dangers existing during the course of the ocean transport. It can be divided into two types of risks in the ocean transport: perils of the sea and extraneous or external risks.

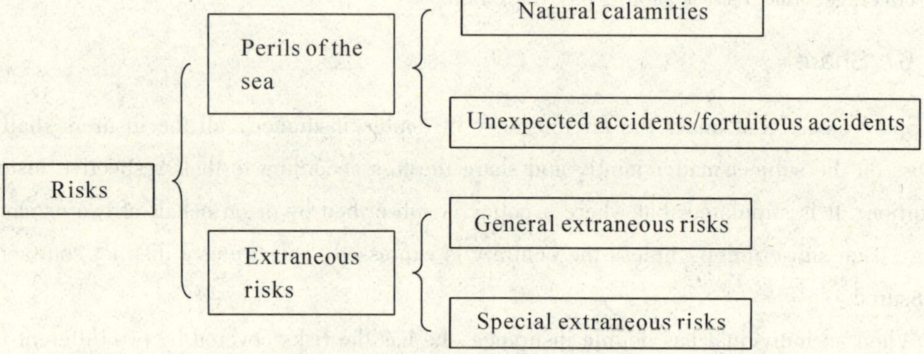

Figure 7 - 1 Types of Marine Risks

7.2.1.1 Perils of the Sea

Perils of the sea include both natural calamities and fortuitous or unexpected accidents. Natural calamities are disasters caused by force majeure events such as heavy weather, lightening, tsunami, earthquake, volcanic eruption, thunderbolt and so forth. It should be borne in mind that the natural calamities hereby referred to do not actually include all disasters due to natural forces. For instance, natural rusting shall not be included in the category of natural calamities.

Fortuitous or unexpected accidents, however, are understood as the accidents due to haphazard causes such as fire, explosion, vessel stranding, grounding, sinking or capsizing, collision, missing and so on.

7. 2. 1. 2 Extraneous Risks

Extraneous risks can be further divided into two categories: general extraneous risks and special extraneous risks.

General extraneous risks refer to the common risks such as theft, fresh water rain, shortage, leakage, clash and breakage, odor, heating and sweating, hook damage, rust, breakage of packing, etc.

Special extraneous risks are caused by military factors, political factors and government regulations such as war, striking, confiscation, and so forth.

7. 2. 2 Marine Losses

In cargo insurance practice, loss is generally known as average, which actually has nothing to do with its normal meaning. It refers to any loss or damage due to natural calamities and fortuitous accidents and the related costs incurred in the process of transit. Marine insurance defines its coverage in terms of the nature of the loss or damage, the extent of the loss or damage and the conditions under which it occur. Loss hence can be classified into two types according to the level of loss. One is total loss and the other is partial loss.

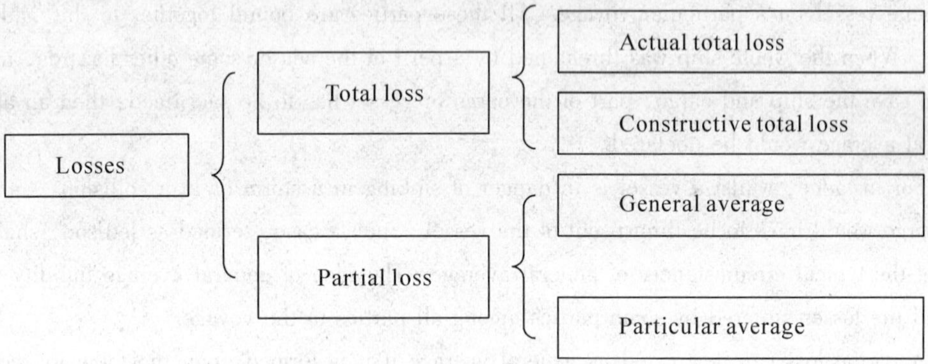

Figure 7 - 2 **Types of Marine Losses**

7. 2. 2. 1 Total Loss

Total loss refers to the loss of the entire value of the subject matter to the insured, normally involving the maximum amount for which a policy is liable. Most insurance policies provide for the payment of total loss up to the insurance amount. According to the situation of losses, total loss can be actual or constructive.

Actual total loss, also can be called as indicates, which means that the cargo has been totally lost or, has been damaged to the extent that it has lost its original usage.

Constructive total loss is not totally lost, but the actual total loss shall be unavoidable or the restoration fees together with other miscellaneous expenses will exceed the anticipated amount of profit when the cargo is delivered to the destination. In other words, when a ship or a cargo is so badly damaged that the cost of repair or the effort of rescue would be greater than the market value of the ship or cargo, they are treated as totally lost.

If a claim is made for total indemnity of the cargo lost or damaged under constructive total loss or actual total loss, the claimant must declare the abandonment of all the rights concerning the cargo. This is "notice of abandonment". If the abandonment is found to be valid, after indemnity has been made, the insurer is entitled to take over the interest of the insurant in whatever may remain of the insured subject matter and all proprietary rights thereto.

7.2.2.2 Partial Loss

Partial loss means a partial damage to or the total loss of part of the insured cargo. Partial loss can be further divided into general average and particular average.

General Average (GA) is defined as a partial and deliberate sacrifice of the ship, freight, cargo, or the additional expense incurred to rescue a ship and its cargo from impeding danger or for the common safety of the adventure under a peril of the sea or some other hazards.

According to marine law, those parties whose property was saved must contribute proportionally to cover the losses of those whose property was voluntarily sacrificed. General average is based upon a relationship between the ship-owner and all the shippers who have cargo aboard the same vessel on a particular voyage. All these parties are bound together in the "adventure". When the whole ship was threatened by a peril of the sea or some other hazards, in order to save the ship and cargo, part of the cargo or vessel has to be sacrificed, then an act of general average would be declared.

For instance, whilst a vessel is in danger of sinking in a storm or in a collision, some of the cargo would have to be thrown out of the vessel. Such a case, termed as jettison, shall be one of the typical circumstances of general average. The idea of general average liability is to spread the losses suffered by some parties among all parties to the voyage.

A partial loss can be treated as general average if it is formed upon the following conditions:

The danger that threats the common safety of cargo and/or vessel shall be materially existent and is not foreseen. If the measures are taken by the master due to his wrong judgment or a sacrifice occurs due to common accidents that can be foreseen according to commonsense, the loss shall not be considered that of a general average.

The measures taken by the master shall be aimed to remove the common danger of both vessel and cargo and shall be undertaken deliberately and reasonably for common safety. If a measure has been undertaken by the master merely for the interest of part of the cargo or the interest of the vessel only, the loss shall not be considered that of a general average.

The sacrifice shall be specialized and not caused by perils directly and the expense incurred shall be additional expense which is not within the operation budget. If an extra expense for common interest is acquired, only the surplus part which is out of the operation budget shall be counted as general average.

The actions of the ship's master shall be successful in saving the voyage. If the measures taken by the master fail to save the property, there would be no forthcoming contributions, because nobody has benefited from the general average act.

Generally speaking, general average loss is classified into two classes: the sacrifices of part of the vessel or cargo purposely made in order to save both vessel and cargo from perishing and the expenses incurred owing to extraordinary measures undertaken for the preservation of both vessel and cargo. Where there is a general average loss, the party on whom it falls is entitled, subject to the conditions imposed by maritime law, to a ratable contribution from the other parties interested, and such contribution is called a General Average Contribution (GA contribution). If the general average is covered by an insurance company, the insurance company shall consequently undertake full liability of all the losses and expenses. The loss of sacrifice as well as the expenses incurred in a general average shall be shared among all parties, including the carrier and all cargo owners, in proportion to their respective interested value benefited from the general average.

The calculation of the general average contribution is complicated, but it generally involves four stages.

First, it needs to identify the total general average contributory value. The contributory value refers to the value of property saved as the result of the general average act. Its calculation must cover two parts: the actual value of the property in question at the end of the voyage, including ship, cargo and freight; plus the respective general average loss, if applicable. The total of all parties' contributory value forms the basis for determining each party's share in contribution.

Second, it needs to identify the total general average loss. This is to calculate the sum of the costs of sacrifices and the extraordinary expenses defined as general average. The result will be the object of general average contribution.

Third, it needs to calculate the general average percentage. Since the general average contribution is conducted in proportion to the respective interested value benefited by the parties, it is important to establish a benchmark for the sake of calculation. The general average percentage is obtained by dividing the total general average loss by the total contributory value. The formula is illustrated below:

GA Percentage = Total GA Loss/ Total GA Contributory Value × 100%

At last, it needs to specify the individual general average contribution of all parties concerned. Once the general average percentage is available, the amount each party should contribute will be easily specified, by multiplying the respective individual contributory value with the general average percentage. GA Contribution = Contributory Value × GA percentage.

Example:

Suppose a cargo vessel loaded with cargo of Party A and Party B stranded in transit. To save the vessel as well as the goods on it, the master ordered to throw 1 000 cases of goods to the sea. The value of the goods thrown overboard for Party A is 20% of his goods (the total value of his goods is CNY20 000) and that for Party B is 10% of his goods (the total value of his goods is CNY60 000). Extra wages for the seamen to perform the act amounted to CNY 5 000. The value of the vessel is about CNY5 000 000. Based on the information above what is the GA contribution for each party involved?

Calculation:

Total GA loss = 20 000 × 20% + 60 000 × 10% + 5 000 = CNYI5 000

Total GA contributory value = 20 000 × 80% + 60 000 × 90% + 5 000 000

= CNY5 070 000

GA percentage = (Total GA loss / GA Total Benefit) × 100%

= (15000/5070000) × 100%

= 0. 295%

GA Contribution by Party A = 20 000 × 0. 295% = CNY59

GA Contribution by Party B = 60 000 × 0. 295% = CNYI77

GA Contribution by the Carrier = 5 000 000 × 0. 295% = CNYI4 750

The practice of general average is subject to the International General Average Rules, which was the result of two conferences, respectively held in York in 1864 and in Antwerp in 1877. It is therefore also referred to as the York-Antwerp Rules. The rules have been revised for several times thereafter and the latest edition which is now world-widely accepted is York-Antwerp Rules 2004.

Different from the general average which is contributed among parties who are interested in the adventure, the particular average falls entirely upon the particular owner of the property which has suffered the damage. Particular Average is a partial loss of the subject matter insured, caused by an event that has been insured against. Such loss or damage, if covered by an insurance policy, shall be reimbursed by the insurer.

Although both general average and particular average belong to the category of partial loss, there are still some differences between them:

Causes: Particular average is a kind of cargo loss usually caused directly by sea perils, while general average is caused by intentional measures taken to save the common interest.

Indemnification: Particular average is often borne by the party whose cargo is damaged, while general average should be proportionally contributed among all parties benefited from the intentional measures.

7. 2. 3 Expenses Incurred

Marine cargo insurance also covers the expenses incurred to avoid or reduce the damage to or loss of the subject matter insured. There are mainly two types of expenses. One issue and labor expenses, the other is salvage charges.

Sue and labor expenses are extraordinary expenses made in a time of peril by the insured to act to avert, or minimize any loss of or damage to the subject matter insured. Unlike general average, sue and labor expenses are not something carried out for the benefit of a common interest, but for the sole benefit of the subject matter insured. Expenses incurred for this purpose are recoverable under the insurance policy by the insured against the insurer.

Salvage Charges are expenses resulting from measures properly taken by a third party other than the insured, his agents, or any person employed by them to preserve maritime property from perils at sea. Such expenses, where properly and effectively incurred, can be recovered as particular charges or as a general average loss, according to the circumstances under which they were incurred.

7.3 Coverage of Marine Cargo Insurance of CIC

The most commonly used terms in cargo insurance in China is China Insurance Clauses, shortened as CIC. It was constituted in 1972 and revised in 1976 and 1981 respectively, according to which, marine cargo insurance scope falls into two general types: basic coverage and additional coverage. The purpose of identifying the different types of risks, losses and expenses is to arrange them under different insurance coverage so as to make it easier for the insured to effect insurance for his goods and for the insurer to indemnify in case of damage or loss.

7.3.1 Basic Marine Insurance Coverage

The risks under basic marine cargo insurance coverage refer to those that can be covered independently and not attached to any other particular coverage. Basic coverage can be further classified into three categories: FPA, WPA and All Risks.

7.3.1.1 FPA (Free from Particular Average)

FPA indicates non-liability of indemnification to a particular average. This coverage is the most limited form of cargo insurance coverage covering the following losses:

Actual total loss or constructive total loss of the consignment caused by natural calamities such as heavy weather, tsunami, earthquake, flood, etc.

Total loss or partial loss caused by fortuitous accidents such as stranding, striking upon the rocks, icebergs or other objects, collision, fire and explosion.

Partial loss attributable to heavy weather, lightening and/or tsunami, where the ship has been stranded, sunk, or burned, irrespective of whether the event took place after or before such accidents.

Partial or total loss consequent on falling of an entire package or packages into the sea during loading, unloading, and transshipment.

Reasonable expenses the insured makes for the salvage of the goods insured, and for averting or minimizing the losses, provided the expenses do not exceed the insured amount.

Expenses incurred by discharge of the insured cargoes at a port of distress following a sea peril as well as special charges arising from loading, warehousing at an intermediate port of call or refuge.

Sacrifice in and contribution to general average and salvage charges.

Losses reimbursed by the insured to the ship-owners is under the Contract of Affreightment "Both to Blame Collision" clause.

7.3.1.2 WPA (With Particular Average) / WA (With Average)

In addition to the liability scope of FPA, WPA (WA) also covers the partial loss of the insured goods caused directly by natural calamities such as heavy weather, lightning, tsunami, earthquake or flood. In other words, WPA provides a more extensive cover against all loss or damage due to marine perils throughout the duration of the policy.

7. 3. 1. 3 All Risks

The coverage of All Risks means that the insurer shall undertake, in addition to the liabilities under FPA and WPA, the liabilities to indemnify the insured the total or partial loss on the cargo insured either arising from perils of the sea or general extraneous risks during the course of transit. All Risks is the most comprehensive coverage among the three. However, even though the name of this coverage implies all risks, this coverage shall not cover against all risks of loss or damage. In other words, this insurance shall in no case be deemed to extend to cover loss, damage or expense caused by special extraneous risks of war, strike, etc. or exclusions such as delay, inherent vice, nature of the subject matter insured, etc.

7. 3. 2 Additional Insurance Coverage

To put it another way, any additional coverage should go with one of the three types of basic insurance coverage mentioned previously. While basic insurance coverage can be taken out independently, additional coverage, however, shall be made complementarily with the insurance company according to the actual situation. Additional insurance coverage includes general additional coverage and special additional coverage.

7. 3. 2. 1 General Additional Insurance Coverage

General additional insurance coverage mainly covers the general extraneous risks discussed above. There are normally 11 types of risks that are covered under general additional coverage.

Hook Damage covers the damage to the goods caused by hooks in the process of loading and unloading, such as the losses of cereals due to the damage of packing bags by hooks.

Risk of Clash and Breakage covers the risk of breakage of the fragile goods by vibration, clash or pressing during the course of transit.

Heating and Sweating Risk under this coverage is the risk of loss of or damage to the goods by sweating and heating as a result of the sudden change of temperature or the ventilation on the vessel being out of order.

Risk of Leakage covers the risk of seepage and leakage of the liquid goods caused by the damaged container during the course of transit.

Risk of Intermixture and Contamination covers the loss of or damage to the goods in the course of transit caused by its being intermixed or contaminated with each other.

Risk of Odor Edibles, herbal medicine, cosmetics or raw materials may sometimes be tainted by odor of their own. Such a risk is under this coverage.

TPND (Theft, Pilferage and Non-delivery) Risk of theft and pilferage refers to the risk against the possibility of the cargo being stolen in transit during the voyage. Risk of non-delivery refers to the risk against loss of complete packages (including boxes, cases, drums, etc.) due to improper unloading or for some other unknown reasons.

Fresh Water Rain Damage refers to the risk of loss of or damage to the goods directly caused by fresh water and/or rain, not sea water.

Risk of Shortage covers the shortage of weight for the goods during the course of transit due to the breakage of external packing. However, normal shortage of weight in transit is not covered.

Risk of Rust covers the risk of damage to the goods by rust caused by contamination with sea water during the course of transit. But goods getting rusty by itself or due to its own flaws are excluded.

Breakage of Packing Damage to the goods resulting from rough handling is covered by this risk.

But there is no need to apply for general additional coverage if All Risks is obtained since all the eleven types of general additional risks are covered under it. Sometimes it is necessary to apply for one or several of the above-mentioned types of coverage aside from FPA or WPA.

7. 3. 2. 2 Special additional insurance coverage

While general extraneous risks are covered by general additional insurance coverage, special extraneous risks however fall under special additional insurance coverage. There are eight types of special additional coverage:

War Risks. This covers loss of or damage to the insured goods caused directly by or in consequence of war, warlike operations, conventional weapons, etc. However, it does not cover loss, damage or expenses arising from any hostile use of atomic or nuclear weapons of war.

Strike, Riots & Commotions (SRCC). This covers loss of or damage to the goods insured directly caused by acts of strikers, locked-out workmen, etc.

Failure to Delivery Risk. This clause is to pay a total loss subject to full rights of subrogation in case the goods insured, once loaded on board the seagoing vessel, fail to be delivered at the destination within six months of scheduled date for arrival due to whatever cause it might be.

Import Duty Risk. This coverage covers Import Customs duty at the port of destination on the portion of the goods damaged by a peril insured against.

On Deck Risk. This clause covers the risks of jettison and/or washing overboard in case the insured goods are shipped on deck.

Rejection Risk. This clause is to indemnify the insured for rejection and/or condemnation at the port of entry by the government of the importing country.

Aflatoxin Risk. This clause is to cover loss of the insured goods when the cargo is rejected or confiscated by reason of the existence of aflatoxin, to an extent exceeding the limit sanctioned by the importing country.

Fire Risk Extension Clause (for Storage of Cargo at Destination Hong Kong, including Kowloon, or Macao). After being discharged at the final destination at Hong Kong, including Kowloon, or Macao from the carrying conveyance, if the insured cargo is directed to be stored in a warehouse specifically designated by the bank to whom the interests in the cargo are assigned, this insurance shall extend to cover fire risk at such warehouse from the time the marine coverage ceases until the termination of the said bank's interests in the cargo or the expiration of thirty days counted from the day the marine coverage ceases, whichever shall first occur.

7.3.3 Exclusions

Risks and losses not covered under either the basic coverage or the additional coverage by the insurer are referred to as exclusions in marine cargo insurance practice. After explaining all the risks, losses and expenses covered by the clauses of CIC, finally let's examine what are not covered by it. The exclusions of CIC include:

Loss or damage caused by the intentional act or fault of the insured.

Loss or damage falling under the liability of the consignor.

Loss or damage arising from the inferior quality or shortage of the insured goods prior to the attachment of this insurance.

Loss or damage arising from normal loss, inherent vice: or nature of the insured goods, loss of market and/or delay in transit and any expenses arising there from risks and liabilities excluded by the ocean marine cargo war risks clauses and strike, riot and civil commotion clauses of CIC.

7.3.4 Duration of Basic Insurance

According to the Warehouse to Warehouse Clause, the insurance company undertakes an insurance liability over the insured cargo from the warehouse or place of storage of the shipper named in the policy until the cargo has arrived at the warehouse or place of storage of the receiver named in the policy. There are different stipulations over this clause in the world; however, nearly all the cargo insurance business now includes what is called the Warehouse to Warehouse Clause (W/W Clause). Duration of insurance is the period throughout which the insurance company undertakes an insurance liability. However, this insurance shall be limited to sixty (60) days after completion of discharge of the insured goods from the seagoing vessel at the final port of discharge before they reach the above mentioned warehouse or place of storage.

The duration for War Risks commences from the time when the goods insured are loaded on board the vessel named in the policy until the insured goods are unloaded from the named vessel at the port of destination named in the policy. W/W Clause, however, is not suitable for War Risks. If the goods remain unloaded, the duration of insurance terminates on the expiry of 15 days after the midnight of the day when the vessel arrive at the port of destination.

7.4 Coverage of Marine Cargo Insurance of ICC

As Chinese companies usually follow CIC in insurance practice, insurance companies in other countries may also have their own insurance clauses to guide their insurance practice. Among them, the most important one is London Institute Cargo Clauses, shortened as ICC. It has exerted great influence on the development of international insurance. Many countries in the world have referred to them in devising their own insurance clauses.

ICC has undergone many revisions since their first publication in 1912. The latest revision came into effect on Jan. 1, 1982. The clauses of ICC are basically the same as the ocean marine cargo clauses of the People's Insurance Company of China. It is mainly composed of the following 6 clauses:

① Institute Cargo Clauses A, or ICC (A);

② Institute Cargo Clauses B, or ICC (B);

③ Institute Cargo Clauses C, or ICC (C);

④ Institute War Clauses—Cargo;

⑤ Institute Strike Clauses—Cargo;

⑥ Malicious Damage Clauses.

ICC (A), ICC (B) and ICC (C) have independent and complete structures and can be covered independently without being attached to any other particular coverage. Institute War Clause and Institute Strike Clause also have independent and complete structures, but can be covered independently only after agreement from the insurance company. However, Malicious Damage Clause is an additional coverage and can only be covered attached to other forms of basic coverage.

7.4.1 Institute Cargo Clause (C) —ICC (C)

The risks, losses and expenses covered by ICC (C) afford the minimum protection available and are suitable for goods which are customarily insured against major casualties only or which are shipped in bulk, or where the condition of the goods is not known by the insurer.

The loss of or damage to the subject matter insured covered by ICC (C) are attributable to fire or explosion; vessel of craft being stranded, grounded, sunk or capsized; over turning or derailment of land conveyance; collision or contact of vessel, craft or conveyance with any external object other than water; or discharge of cargo at a port of distress; general average sacrifice; or jettison.

7.4.2 Institute Cargo Clause (B) —ICC (B)

The scope of this insurance coverage is similar to that of WPA under CIC. Apart from those covered under ICC (C), Institute Cargo Clause B also covers loss of or damage to the subject matter insured attributable to earthquake, volcanic eruption or lightning; washing overboard; entry of sea, lake or river water into vessel, craft, conveyance, container, lift-van or place of storage; or total loss of any package lost overboard or dropped whilst loading onto or unloading from vessel or craft.

7.4.3 Institute Cargo Clause (A) —ICC (A)

The scope of this insurance is similar to that of All Risks under CIC. It represents the most extensive form of protection and provides all-risks cover against physical losses of and damages to the subject matter insured, including both total and partial losses. Aside from those covered under ICC (B), the risks, losses and expenses under ICC (A) may well extend to all risks of loss of or damage to the subject matter insured, general average and salvage charges and "Both to Blame Collision".

7.5 Other Types of Cargo Insurance

Marine Cargo Insurance is suitable for sea transportation mode, which is the most ancient and important means of transportation. However, cargo may also be carried from the seller to the buyer by other modes of transportation as mentioned in Chapter 5. Therefore, there also exist other types of cargo insurance such as Overland Transportation Insurance, Air Transportation Insurance and Parcel Post Insurance. This section is going to explain them in brief.

7.5.1 Overland Transportation Insurance

Insurance liability rests mainly on trains or trucks when cargo is delivered by surface transportation. A high volume of business is now conveyed by rail and road. It is essential that adequate cover be obtained for the land carriage. Insurance coverage for land transportation can be divided into two categories: Overland Transportation Risks and Overland Transportation All Risks.

The risks covered under Overland Transportation Risks are somewhat similar to those under WPA for marine cargo insurance. It covers total or partial loss of or damage to the insured goods caused in the course of transportation by natural calamities, accidents and reasonable costs incurred by the insured in salving the goods or minimizing a loss.

The risks covered under Overland Transportation All Risks are somewhat similar to those under All Risks for marine cargo insurance. Aside from the risks covered under Overland Transportation Risks, this insurance also covers all risks of loss of or damage to the insured goods, whether partial or total, arising from external causes in the course of transit.

Like that of WPA under Marine Cargo Insurance, the duration of Overland Transportation

Insurance also follows the W/W clause.

7. 5. 2 Air Transportation Insurance

Insurance liability rests mainly on aircrafts when cargo is delivered through air transportation. Due to the nature of air movements, for example, the shorter transit time, lighter packing required, quicker clearance at destination points and, in most places, stricter theft-pilferage control, a significant number of export dispatches are now sent by air. While an air disaster is spectacular and concentrates the public attention, it is true that air traffic is one of the safest methods of carrying goods. There are also two types of coverage: Air Transportation Risks and Air Transportation All Risks.

The scope of Air Transportation Risks coverage is almost as extensive as that of WPA in Marine Cargo Insurance. It covers total or partial loss of or damage to the insured goods caused in the course of transportation by lightning, fire, explosion, jettison due to the aircraft encountering bad weather or other perils, collision, overturning, crashing or missing the aircraft and other accidents.

In addition to what are covered under Air Transportation Risks, the coverage of Air Transportation All Risks also covers all risks of loss of or damage to the insured goods whether partial or total, arising from external causes in the course of transit.

The duration of Air Transportation Insurance also follows the W/W clause, but the insurance shall be limited to 30 days after completion of discharge of the insured goods from the aircraft at the final airport of discharge.

7. 5. 3 Parcel Post Insurance

The insurance liability of parcel post insurance does not depend on any special transportation vehicles because the parcel post may be conveyed either by ocean vessels, surface vehicles or by aircraft. It is classified into two conditions: Parcel Post Risks and Parcel Post All Risks.

Similarly, the risks covered under Parcel Post Risks are identical to those under WPA in Marine Cargo Insurance. It covers total or partial loss of or damage to the insured goods caused in the course of transportation by natural calamities, accidents and fire or explosion. Partial or total loss of the insured parcel, arising from external causes in the course of transit, however, is covered by Parcel Post All Risks. W/W Clause is also applicable to Parcel Post Insurance except in the case of failure of delivery, where the duration of insurance terminates on the expiry of 15 days counting from the midnight of the day when the notice of arrival of the parcel is issued by the post office at the destination.

It should be noted that the 11 types of general additional risks and 8 types of special additional risks under Ocean Marine Cargo Insurance can be applicable to Overland Transportation Insurance, Air Transportation Insurance and Parcel Post Insurance.

7.6 Procedures of Cargo Insurance

In international trade, who effects insurance depends on the particular trade terms adopted. For example, on CIF, CIP terms, it is the seller who arranges insurance with an insurance company. Under FOB, CFR contracts, it is usually the buyer who affects insurance, but he may ask the seller to arrange insurance on behalf of him. Whoever arranges insurance, he will undergo different steps in the completion of the insurance contract.

Normally, these steps are as follows:

① To calculate the insurance amount;

② To determine the insurance coverage;

③ To obtain the insurance premium rate;

④ To apply for marine insurance and pay the insurance premium;

⑤ To obtain an insurance policy;

⑥ To lodge an insurance claim at the time of loss or damage.

7.6.1 To Calculate the Insurance Amount

The insurance amount, also known as the Insured Amount or the Sum Insured, stands for the amount of insurance indicated in the insurance policy and agreed upon by the insurant and the insurer. It is the highest amount of indemnity given by the insurer when the subject matter is subject to a loss or damage and serves as the basis for the calculation of insurance premium. Generally speaking, the amount to be insured is based on the value of the commercial invoice. The recommended way of obtaining insurance amount is the total CIF or CIP invoice value plus a certain percentage (known as markup) coveting the expected profit and incidental costs incurred in the transaction. The formula for the calculation of insurance amount is:

Insurance amount = CIF (CIP) × (1 + markup rate)

7.6.2 To Determine the Insurance Coverage

After the insurance amount is obtained, the next consideration is to decide the scope of risks to be covered. Determining the tight coverage can be very easy, but sometimes it may also be difficult. According to Incoterms 2000, the insurance coverage for CIF or CIP is the minimum coverage, i. e. FPA coverage as per CIC. The decision on insurance coverage under contracts concluded on other Incoterms, however, can be more complicated. The factors that need to be taken into account are: the nature of product, packing considerations; the carriers of the transport; shipping route and ports considerations, etc. It is based on the above factors that the insured finally determines the insurance coverage to be effected.

7. 6. 3 To Obtain the Insurance Premium Rate

Insurance Premium is calculated on a basis of a percentage of the insured amount. The percentage is known as the premium rate. Once the insurance coverage is determined, it is easy to obtain the insurance premium rate. The premium rate may vary, for example, from 0. 5% to 2. 5% or more depending on factors such as the carrying vessel, nature of the packing used, type of coverage needed, previous experience with the insurer, the nature and volume of the goods insured and the modes of transportation adopted. Premium rate is important in the calculation of the premium the insurant needs to pay to the insurer.

7. 6. 4 To Apply for Marine Cargo Insurance and Pay the Insurance Premium

To apply for marine cargo insurance, the applicant needs to fill in a special form (the proposal form or application form), stating the name of the insured, quantity, packing, shipping marks, insurance amount, place of shipment and destination, name of the carrying conveyance, shipping date and coverage required under the terms of sales contract, etc. (See Specimen 7. 1)

Upon applying for marine cargo insurance, the applicant needs to pay the premium to the insurer. Insurance premium refers to the fees charged to the insured by the insurer for the indemnity liability undertaken. That the applicant pays the premium is the precondition for the insurance contract to become valid. Premium is not only the main income of the insure by way of operating insurance business but also the main source of insurance fun accumulated by the insurer.

Insurance premium is determined by the relationship between the insurance amount and insurance rate. The formula is shown as follows:

Insurance Premium (I) = insurance value × premium rate (R)

= CIF (CIP) × (1 + markup rate) × premium rate (R)

Illustration:

Suppose the CIF invoice value is USD 50 000 and goods are insured against All Risks and War Risk with premium rate to be 0. 5% and 0. 05% respectively. If markup rate is 10%, the insurance premium will be:

Insurance Premium (I) = 50 000 × (1 + 10%) × (0. 5% + 0. 05%)

= 55 000 × 0. 005 5 = USD 302. 5

7. 6. 5 To Obtain an Insurance Document

The payment of the insurance premium indicates that the insured and insurer enter into an insurance contract. An insurance document, although not an insurance contract itself, is the evidence of the insurance contract entered into by the insurer and the applicant or insurant. It serves as a document defining the obligations of the insurer and the insured. It is also the document according to which the insured lodges a claim and the insurer settles a claim when the loss or damage which is answerable under the terms of the coverage occurs. The most widely adopted insurance documents in cargo insurance practice are insurance policy, insurance certificate, open policy and combined certificate.

(1) Insurance Policy

Insurance policy is the most commonly used document that contains all the details concerning the goods, coverage, premium and the insured amount on the face and the detailed contract terms at the back. (See Specimen 6. 2) All the information must be sufficiently enough for the insured party to assess the risk and make insurance decision.

A complete insurance document includes the following details:

① The name, address and signature of the insurer and the insured;

② A description of the risks covered and the insurance duration;

③ A description of the consignment;

④ Details of the shipment such as means of transport, name of vessel, loading port and destination port;

⑤ The insurance amount and insurance premium.

Insurance Policy is always filled out by the insurer based the proposal form submitted by the insured. When the Insurance Policy is done, the insurer will normally return the duplicate to the insured with their rubber seal. The signed insurance policy will then become the legal document that serves as the shipping document evidencing insurance coverage.

(2) Insurance Certificate

Insurance certificate is the simplified form of the insurance policy certifying that insurance has been effected and that a policy has been issued. Unlike Insurance Policy, Insurance Certificate does not list all the terms of a formal insurance contract but it does clearly state the insurance conditions on which the shipment is covered. It is of the same legal validity as an Insurance Policy.

(3) Open Policy

Open Policy, also known as Open Cover, provides coverage for all goods shipped by the insured during a given period while the policy is in effect. Traders who do a large volume of business and have to effect shipment at frequent intervals always find it much more convenient to arrange an Open Policy with the insurer to hold all shipments there under covered during a given period. The duration of this policy may run from six to twelve months or may, sometimes, last indefinitely.

(4) Combined Certificate

Combined Certificate is the simplified form of Open Policy and is usually combined with the invoice in practice. It becomes effective when the insurer writes the specifications concerning the insurance on the invoice and signs it later.

Combined certificate is as effective as insurance policy and is mainly practiced in the trade concluded with overseas Chinese traders in Hong Kong and Macao of China, and in areas of Singapore and Malaysia. It can only be adopted when the letter of credit allows it to do so.

7.6.6 To Lodge a Claim at the Time of Loss or Damage

In the event of dangers, the insurant is obligated in the policy to do everything to minimize the loss or damage. Otherwise, he is not to be indemnified by the insurer. However, once damages or losses occur, the party who suffers should lodge a claim against the insurer and notify the insurer or claim agent immediately of the loss or damage.

(1) Prerequisites for a Claim

To lodge a claim against the insurer for compensation, the claimant should satisfy certain prerequisites. First, the risks exposed to the goods insured should fall within the insurance coverage stipulated in the insurance policy. The second prerequisite is that the claimant should be able to evidence the insurable interest he has in the goods insured. In other words, he needs to prove that he possesses the ownership of the goods lost or damaged. Finally, the risks covered should occur within the duration of the insurance liability.

(2) Advice of Losses

Most insurance policies require that immediate notice be given to the nearest branch or agency in the event of damage that gives rise to a claim under a policy. When notified of a damage or loss, the insurer or claim agent then appoints a marine surveyor (the adjuster) to inspect the subject matter insured and report on the cause of the loss or damage, the value of the cargo, and the extent of the damage. In some cases, the surveyor is named in the policy.

After investigation, the surveyor will issue a Certificate of Loss (Certificate of Survey), accompanied usually by the report of findings, to the consignee. The consignee may be required to pay a surveyor's fee, which may be refunded by the insurer or claim agent if the loss is recoverable under the policy.

(3) Presentation of Documents for a Claim

The presentation for a claim is made by negotiation on documents. When making an insurance claim, the claimant usually is required to submit the following documents:

① Original insurance policy or insurance certificate;

② Original bill of lading or other transport document;

③ Commercial invoice;

④ Packing list;

⑤ Certificate of Loss (Certificate of Survey);

⑥ The landing account or weight notes (notes on weight) at destination;

⑦ Any correspondence with the carder or any other party who could be responsible for the loss or damage;

⑧ Master's protest.

(4) Time Valid for a Claim

According to Ocean Marine Insurance Clauses of CIC, the time valid for a claim under the insurance shall not exceed a period of two years counting from the time of completion of discharge of the insured goods from the seagoing vessel at the final port or place of the final destination named in the policy. It's worth noting, however, that not all losses or damages incurred can be recoverable in the case of a valid claim.

(5) Payment of a Claim

In case of a valid claim, the insurer shall indemnify the claimant a certain amount of money as compensation. While the payment in a particular average claim usually is prompt, in a general average claim it may take many months because it takes time for the surveyor to carefully calculate the value of each shipment in proportion to the total value of the shipments and vessel.

In insurance practice, for goods that are insured against "Particular Average" or "Partial Loss" from perils of the sea and subject to breaking, leaking and lightening in transit, franchise is often adopted in an insurance practice. Franchise in insurance refers to the practice that the loss or damage below a certain specified percentage value is non-recoverable. In such a case, a franchise clause is usually specified in the insurance policy by the insurance company.

Franchise can be classified into two categories: deductible franchise and non-deductible franchise. Both categories indicate that the insurance company will not indemnify the loss or damage incurred on the cargo if such loss or damage is within the limit of specified percentages. Under a deductible franchise, where the loss or damage exceeds the percentage allowed, the insurance company needs merely indemnify the exceeding part to the insured whereas under a non-deductible franchise, as long as the loss or damage exceeds the franchise percentage, the insurance company shall indemnify full amount to the insured.

If the insurance is made with I. O. P. (irrespective of percentage), the insurance company is required to indemnify the loss or damage incurred regardless of the franchise rate, in other words, he is bound to pay in full for the loss or damage incurred.

Let's take the following case as an example to illustrate what is meant by the deductible franchise, non-deductible franchise and I. O. P.

7.7 Insurance Terms in the Sales Contract

The insurance term is one of the most important parts of the international sales contract. The contents of insurance terms may vary when different trade terms are chosen.

Under FOB, CFR, FCA or CPT term, insurance terms may simply be stipulated as: "Insurance to be covered by the buyer." In the event that the seller is entrusted by the buyer to arrange for insurance, besides the insurance amount, the risks covered and the insurance clause adopted, the name of the party who shall pay the insurance premium must also be specified in the contract.

In CIF or CIP contract, however, the insurance term should clearly stipulate the name of the party who shall arrange for insurance, the insurance amount, the risks covered and the name of the insurance clause applied (including the date on which the clause is to be attached).

It should be noted that insurance terms should be made in a clear and definite way and ambiguous clauses such as "usual risks" or "customary risks" should be avoided.

Example 1:

"Insurance is to be covered by the Sellers for 110% of invoice value against W. P. A. and War Risk as per Ocean Marine Cargo Clauses of the People's Insurance Company of China dated 1998. 1. 1."

Example 2:

"Insurance to be covered by the Seller on behalf of the Buyers for 110% of invoice value against Marine Risks as per Institute Cargo Clause (A) dated Jan. 1, 1982, premium to be for Buyer's account."

Example 3:

"Insurance to be covered by the Seller for 110% of total invoice value against Overland Transportation All Risks and All Risks as per Overland Transportation Cargo Insurance Clauses "Trains, Truck" and Ocean Marine Cargo Clauses of the People's Insurance Company of China dated 1998. 1. 1."

7.8 Summary

There are four widely accepted principles in cargo insurance: the insurable interest principle, the utmost good faith principle, the indemnity principle and the proximate cause principle. Insurable interest principle states that only when the insurant has an insurable interest in the goods insured can he be indemnified. Utmost Good Faith Principle stipulates that both parties shall be honest and faithful when entering into an insurance contract. Indemnity principle emphasizes that the insured will be placed in the same position that he enjoyed immediately before the loss occurred. Proximate cause principle helps seek the effective reason that has caused the loss incurred.

Insurance premium refers to the fees charged to the insured by the insurer for the indemnity liability undertaken. It is determined by the relationship between the insurance amount and the insurance premium rate. The formula is:

Insurance amount = CIF (CIP) × (1 + markup rate)

Insurance premium (I) = insurance value × premium rate (R)

= CIF (CIP) × (1 + markup rate) × Premium Rate (R)

There are many kinds of perils and risks in marine cargo transportation due to the long distance and uncertainty in the transit. Risks in marine cargo transportation can be classified into perils of the sea and extraneous risks. Losses in marine cargo transportation consist of two types: total loss and partial loss. The expenses incurred include sue and labor expenses and salvage charges.

General average includes the sacrifice of part of the vessel or cargo and the expenses incurred to save the vessel and cargo in danger. It differs from particular average in that it is not directly caused by sea perils and that it is proportionally contributed among all parties benefited from it. The way to calculate GA contribution is complicated:

GA contribution rate = Total loss of GA/Total value of GA

GA contribution of Party A = Party A' s GA benefit × GA contribution rate

China Insurance Clause includes three types of basic coverage that can be covered independently: FPA, WA and All Risks. It also has two types of additional coverage: general additional coverage and special additional coverage, which can only be taken out with FPA, WPA or All Risks. While general additional coverage is covered in All Risks, special additional coverage is not.

London Institute Cargo Clauses contain six clauses:

① Institute Cargo Clause (A): It is similar to China's All Risks;

② Institute Cargo Clause (B): It is similar to China's WPA;

③ Institute Cargo Clause (C): It is similar to China's FPA;

④ Institute War Clause;

⑤ Institute Strike Clause;

⑥ Malicious Damage Clause.

Warehouse to warehouse clause states that the insurance liability over the insured cargo commences from the warehouse of the shipper until the cargo has arrived at the warehouse of the receiver. However, the duration for War Risks commences from the time when the goods insured are loaded on board the vessel until the insured goods are unloaded from the named vessel at the port of destination.

While marine cargo insurance is the most widely adopted practice in international trade, one has to note that other forms of insurance such as overland transportation insurance, air transportation cargo insurance and parcel post insurance also play an important role in cargo transportation.

In international trade, the insurer will undergo different steps in the completion of the insurance contract: determining the insurance amount of the goods to be insured, the insurance coverage and insurance premium rate, applying for marine insurance, paying insurance premium, obtaining an insurance policy and lodging an insurance claim at the time of loss or damage.

In the sales contract, the insurance clause shall be expressly stipulated and shall include information such as the party who effects the insurance, the insurance amount, the risks covered and the name of the insurance clause applied, etc.

Exercises

Ⅰ. Choices

1. The main document adopted by the insured to make claims against the insurer is ________.

A. bill of lading　　B. transportation documents

C. insurance certificate　　D. insurance document

2. Perils of the sea, such as vessel being stranded or grounded covered in an insurance policy are one kind of ________.

A. natural calamities　　B. fortuitous accidents

C. general extraneous risks　　D. special extraneous risks

3. According to "Ocean Marine Cargo Clause of the People's Insurance Company of China", the coverage which cannot be effected independently is ________.

A. FPA　　B. WPA　　C. War Risk　　D. All Risks

4. Company A exported 5 metric tons of tea. The tea suffered heavy storm in transit. The sea water in the ship's hold led to the deterioration in the quality of part of the tea exported. This kind of loss is ________.

A. actual total loss　　B. constructive total loss

C. general average　　D. particular average

5. The insurance document that is acceptable mostly in Hong Kong of China, Singapore and Malaysia is ________.

A. insurance policy　　B. insurance certificate

C. combined certificate　　D. open policy

6. The coverage of ICC (A) is equivalent to that of ________ of CIC.

A. FPA　　B. WPA

C. All Risks　　D. Additional Risks

7. Risks such as "failure to delivery risk" or "rejection risk" fall within the category of ________.

A. general extraneous risks　　B. special extraneous risks

C. natural calamities　　D. fortuitous accidents

8. According to "Ocean Marine Cargo Clause of the People's Insurance Company of China", the basic coverage that is the least extensive is ________.

A. FPA　　B. WPA　　C. All Risks　　D. War Risk

9. In the case of air freight, if the subject matter insured failed to reach the warehouse at destination stipulated in the insurance policy, the expiration of the insurance is after completion

of discharge over side from the overseas vessel at the final port of ________ discharge.

A. 15 days B. 30 days C. 60 days D. 90 days

10. Under ________ coverage of London Institute Cargo Clause, only major casualties-are covered, but not natural calamities.

A. ICC (A) B. ICC (B)

C. ICC (C) D. Institute War Clause - Cargo

Ⅱ. Explain the following terms

1. insurable interest

2. cargo transportation insurance

Ⅲ. Short questions

1. Explain the two major types of ocean marine risks?

2. What are the fundamental principles of insurance of the firms must follow when they cover for goods?

3. What are the risks that are known as general additional coverage?

Ⅳ. Calculation

1. One of Japanese Company plans to transact with Chinese Company, that to export frozen food under CIF. The value of each canton is USD 100, and the amount of canton is 1000. The premium rate was 0.3% and the goods were insured for FPA with a markup of 10%. Please calculate the insurance amount and insurance premium respectively?

2. One exporting company plan to export light industrial products to a British importer at GBP20 000 per metric ton CIF London (insurance for All Risks with 10% markup and 2% premium rate). However, the importer intended to effect insurance by him, as a result, he counter - offered. CFR price. What is the CFR price? How much premium should the exporter need to deduct from the CIF price?

Ⅴ. Case studies

1. A cargo was insured for "all risks". On a night voyage, the ship had to sail without lights due to air attacks. As a result, it collided with another ship and sank. Was the loss covered by the insurance policy? Why or why not?

2. On a voyage the cargo ship had an accidental tire. To save the ship, the captain ordered to have water poured into the compartment. The fire was put out. For party X, her goods burnt amounted to 10% of USD0. 5 million cargo; For party Y, his goods damaged due to water poured accounted for 20% of USD1 million cargo; For the carder, engine damages due to the fire equaled 10% of USD50 million ship; Extra wages for the seamen totaled USD50 000. Based on the information above, indicate: Which is PA? Which is GA? What is the GA contribution for each party?

Chapter 8 International Payments

Learning Objectives

1. To master paying Instruments
2. To master paying ways: T/T, COLLECTION, L/C
3. To understand the Factoring and Forfeiting

Key Words

International settlement; Bill of exchange; Sight draft; Time bill; Drawer; Payee; Drawee; Endorsement; Acceptance; Telegraphic Transfer; Mail Transfer; Banker's Demand Draft; Financial Documents; Clean collection; Documentary collection; Documents against payment; Documents against acceptance; Sight payment credit; Acceptance credit; Transferable credit; Strict compliance

In international trade, how and when an exporter receives payment for the goods he sends abroad are problems that concern him the most. Payment in domestic trade is a fairly simple matter. It can be made either in advance or within a reasonably short period after delivery. However, these problems are magnified many times in international trade. Handling international payment can be complicated and risky. Different nations have different monetary units, and the currency of one country often cannot be used for making payments in another country. There are a number of different payment methods for foreign commerce. Some are riskier than others. Be very careful about what type of international payment method you will use or accept. Remember, it's difficult to assess long distance creditworthiness and even more difficult to collect payment if your buyer or shipper defaults across an international border.

8.1 Issues in Concern

Generally speaking, it is not very difficult for buyers and sellers in domestic trade to get to know each other's financial status and other information, and payment is likely to be made in a straightforward manner, say by remittance or by debiting the debtor's account. In international trade, however, things are far more complicated. Purchase and sale of goods and services are carried out beyond national boundaries, which makes it rather difficult for the parties concerned in the transaction to get adequate information about each other's financial standing and credit-worthiness. Therefore, mutual trust is hard to build. Both the exporter and the importer face risks as there is always the possibility that the other party may not fulfill the contract.

For the exporter there is the risk of buyer default. The importer might fail to pay in full for the goods. He might go bankrupt; his government might, for various reasons, ban trade with the exporting country or ban imports of certain commodities; the buyer might run into difficulties getting the foreign exchange to pay for the goods. It is even possible that the buyer is not reliable and simply refuses to pay the agreed amount on various excuses.

On the part of the importer, there is the risk that the shipment will be delayed, and he might only receive them long after payment. The delay may be caused by problems in production or transportation, and such delays may lead to loss of business. There is also a risk that wrong goods might be sent as a result of negligence of the exporter or simply because of his lack of integrity.

Political risks such as war, quotas, foreign exchange control; commercial risks like market change and exchange rate fluctuations; and even language barriers all add up to the problems in international trade. Because of these problems and risks, exporters are hesitant to release their goods before receiving payment, while importers prefer to have control over the goods before parting with their money.

Various methods of payment have been developed to cope with different situations in international trade. When the political and economic situation in the importing country makes payment uncertain or when the buyer's credit standing is dubious, the exporter may prefer cash in advance or partial cash in advance. In this case, the importer has no guarantee that the exporter will fulfill his obligations once he has made payment by cash. If the buyer and the seller know each other well, they may decide to trade on open account. This means that no documents are involved and that legally the buyer can pay anytime. The seller loses all control over the goods once they have been shipped. Sales on this basis are usually paid by periodic payments, and obviously the exporter must have sufficient financial strength to carry the cost of the goods until receiving payment. If the exporter wishes to retain title or ownership to the goods, he can enter into consignment transactions. This means the exporter has to send his goods abroad and will not get payment until the goods are sold. If not sold, the goods can be shipped back. Therefore, this arrangement should only be made with full understanding of the risks involved and is preferably to be limited to stable countries where the exporter has a trusted agent to look after his interest.

8.2 Paying Instruments

In international trade, the most frequently used means of payment include currencies and bills. The former is used for account, settlement and payment; the latter for settlement and payment. Due to the long distance between the parties concerned and the long time needed to handle the transaction, international payment depends heavily on the use of documents. There is a special category of financial documents which are called paying instruments. They have two characteristics in common. One is that they represent a unilateral promise to pay a fixed amount of money to the legitimate holder of the instrument. The other is that normally they are transferable or negotiable.

8.2.1 Bill of Exchange

A bill of exchange (draft) is a commercial instrument. It is an unconditional order to a bank or a customer to pay a sum of money to someone on demand or at a fixed time in the future. The person who draws the draft, usually the exporter, is called the drawer (出票人), and the person to whom the draft is drawn is called the drawee. There is yet another party the payee, i. e. the person receiving the payment, who and the drawer are generally but not necessarily the same person, as the drawer can instruct the drawee either to pay "to the order of ourselves" or to the order of someone else, for instance, the bank.

The meanings of the definition are as follows:

An unconditional order in writing;

Addressed by one person (the drawer)

To another (the drawee);

Singed by the person giving it;

Requiring the person to whom it is addressed to pay;

Time of payment or Tenor;

A certain sum in money;

To or to the order of a specified person or the bearer.

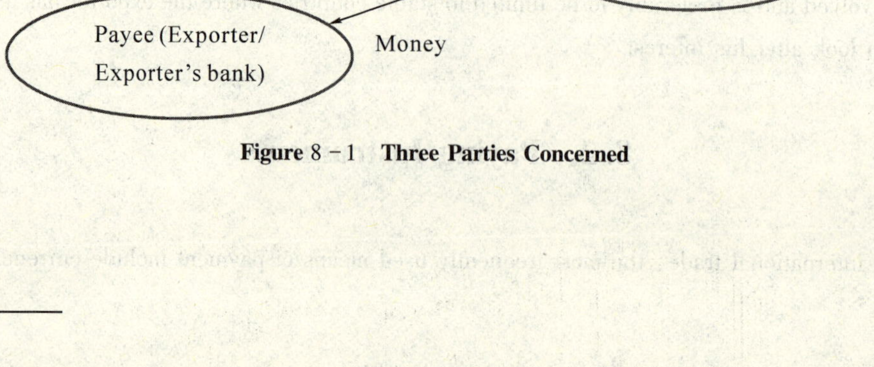

Figure 8-1 Three Parties Concerned

BILL OF EXCHANGE

No. 汇票编号 Date：出票日期

For 汇票金额

At 付款期限 sight of THIS FIRST BILL of EXCHANGE (second of the same tenor and date unpaid) pay to 受款人 or order the sum of Value received and charge the same to account of 大写金额

Drawn under 出票条款

L/C No. 编号 dated 签发日期

To. 付款人

出票人签章

BILL OF EXCHANGE

No. 汇票编号 Date： 出票日期

For：汇票金额

At 付款期限 sight of this second of exchange (first of the same tenor and date unpaid) pay to the order of 受款人 the sum of 大写金额

Drawn under 出票条款

L/C No. 编号 Dated 签发日期

To. 付款人

出票人签章

Procedure of Using a B/E

A bill of exchange is a three-party instrument. A drawer, a drawee and a payee are the three basic parties.

Issuance

When a party fills in the content of a bill of exchange and signs his name at the right side of the bottom of the paper, this party becomes the drawer of this B/E, the party to whom the B/E is addressed is the drawee. The third party who is supposed to receive the payment is the payee, or beneficiary. When the B/E is drawn, it will be sent to the drawee.

Presentation

This refers to a stage when the B/E is presented to the drawee. This may result in two different ways: being honored or dishonored.

Payment

A bill of exchange may be honored by payment. If the B/E issued requires the drawee to pay immediately, the drawee will make payment once the bill is presented.

Acceptance

If the B/E allows the drawee to pay in a later time, the drawee then will accept the bill by cross - signing on the face of the bill and promising to pay on a designated future date. The accepted B/E should be returned to the party presenting for acceptance. This is the scenario of a draft being honored by acceptance.

Discounting and Endorsement

An accepted draft, especially one accepted by reputable firms or banks, is negotiable in the financial market. In order to receive cash immediately, the holder can sell the draft at a discounted rate and transfer the title of the document to the buyer. For the purpose of transfer, the holder needs to make a signature on the back of the draft. This is called an "endorsement".

Dishonor

Dishonor happens when a bill of exchange is presented for payment but is not paid, or is presented for acceptance but is not accepted. If that is the case, the holder may need to, within a reasonable time, have such dishonor certified by a notary public so as to obtain his right of recourse.

Classification of Bill of Exchange

Clean Bill and Documentary Bill

A clean bill refers to the one which is used without the company of any commercial documents. A documentary bill on the other hand calls for the attachment of relevant commercial documents, especially the transportation document evidencing the title to cargoes.

Commercial Draft and Banker's Draft

If both the drawer and drawee of a draft are banks, the draft is a banker' s draft. A banker's draft can be viewed as a bank check which is a secured payment. A commercial draft is normally issued by a firm on another firm or a bank.

Sight Draft and Time Draft/Usance Draft

According to whether the drawer allows a period of credit, or as it is defined as tenor, there is the sight draft and the time draft or usance draft.

A sight draft is used when the exporter wishes to retain title to the shipment until it reaches its destination and payment is made. Before the original title document can be released to the buyer, payment must be properly received by the presenter of the draft. On a sight draft, there bears the wording as "at sight of this bill of exchange, pay to ... "

There is still some risk when a sight draft is used to control transferring the title of a shipment. The buyer's ability or willingness to pay might change from the time when the goods are shipped until the time when the drafts are presented for payment; there is no bank promise to pay standing behind the buyer's obligation. Additionally, the policies of the importing country could also change. If the buyer cannot or will not pay for and claim the goods, returning or disposing of the products becomes the problem of the exporter.

A time draft is used when the exporter extends a certain period of credit to the buyer. The draft states that payment is due by a specific time after the buyer accepts the draft and receives the goods. It normally reads as "at 30/60/90 days sight of this bill of exchange, pay to... ". By signing and writing "accepted" on the draft, the buyer is formally obligated to pay within the stated time. When this is done the time draft is then called a trade acceptance. It can be kept by the exporter until maturity or sold to a bank at a discount for immediate payment.

One important reason for using a draft is that, should the importer fail to pay for the goods purchased, the exporter, or more usually the foreign bank involved, can sue for the money on the basis of the documentary draft alone. It does not have to prove the terms of the export sales contract.

8.2.2 Promissory Note

The United Nations Convention on International Bills of Exchange and International Promissory Notes defines a promissory note as "a written instrument which contains an unconditional promise whereby the maker undertakes to pay a definite sum of money to the payee or to his order". A promissory note will normally identify the parties, the amount of the obligation, some form of recitation of the consideration for the obligation, that is, what the debtor received in return for signing the note and will usually include the terms of repayment, and the interest rate which will apply if any. It may also include an "acceleration clause" which will make the entire amount of the note due if a payment is missed. In international trade, the promissory note is drawn up by the importer in favour of the exporter. It contains an unconditional promise made by the importer to pay a definite sum of money on demand or on a specified future date.

Specimen:

Promissory Note for USD5000.00 HONG KONG,

10TH, JULY, 20 - -

At 30 DAYS AFTER Date we promise to pay to the order
of Hunan Provincial Imp. Exp. Corp. or order
the sum of FIVE THOUSAND US DOLLARS

For C Company
HONG KONG
SIGNATURE

Sharing most common features with bills of exchange, promissory notes differ significantly in one thing: it is a two-party instrument. In the usage of a promissory note, there are only two parties: the maker, or promisor as sometimes called, and the payee, or promisee. The maker of the note pays the exporter personally, rather than ordering a third party to do so. Another noteworthy feature of a promissory note is that it is typically an "unsecured" obligation. This means that in the event that the debtor declares bankruptcy, the debt secured by the note will only be repaid after all debts to the "secured creditors" have been paid. Thus when the amount involved is getting exceptionally large for the parties they are advised to choose another payment method or consult with a lawyer to make sure that the promissory note is bulletproof.

8.2.3 Check

Checks used in international trade are similar to those used in domestic trade, it is a direction in writing to a bank to pay a stated sum of money on demand to a named party, or to his order, or to the bearer. A check can be seen as a type of bill of exchange drawn on a bank, payable on demand.

To use a check properly, the drawer of the check must keep an account in the bank and be sure that the sum carried on the check will not exceed the amount he deposits in the account. Otherwise the check will not be honored. Apart from the possibility of dishonor, using a check in international trade has other disadvantages. At anytime before the check is paid, it can be cancelled. Furthermore, a check has to be sent back through banking channels to the local bank in the importer' s country for payment, which is costly and inconvenient for the exporter to handle. As a result checks are not a very satisfactory method from the exporter' s point of view, hence they are not frequently used.

Specimen:

EAST ASIA BANK

Hong Kong Branch Day Month Year

Pay ______________________ or bearer

US Dollars __________ $

"6534 8890 73934: 124756 236576" (signed)

8.3 Remittance

Sometimes it is easy to get confused by the payment instruments and the payment terms. Payment instruments refer to those financial documents which can be used in different manners, serving specific paying purpose. While payment terms are not documents. They are a series of activities or operations facilitating the movement of funds from one destination to the other. During the employment of different payment terms, the instruments discussed before can be used respectively under certain situation and requirement.

In the next section, three payment terms will be introduced. The choice of each one can depend on the relationship between the seller and the buyer, the trustworthiness of the two parties, the availability of working capital of each party and the bargaining power of the sides.

Remittance is the simplest one among the three methods of payment. It means that after the conclusion of a business transaction, the debtor, the importer in international trade, instructs his bank to send or "remit" the transaction amount to his creditor, the exporter in the exporting country. This operation purely depends on commercial credit, namely, the promise from the trading partner. Thus anyone who wants to use this approach should better conduct a credit check beforehand.

8.3.1 Procedure and Parties Involved

There are four parties involved in the remittance operation: remitter, remitting bank, paying bank and payee or beneficiary.

First, the importer, as a remitter, will approach his bank to submit a remittance application. To do so the importer needs to have sufficient funds in his account in the bank.

The bank, the remitting bank in this case, will either issue a remittance instruction to, or draw a draft on, one of its overseas branches or correspondent banks in the exporter's country.

When the overseas branch or correspondent bank receives the remittance instruction, it becomes the paying bank and will credit the exporter's account with the relevant amount accordingly.

In the event of using a demand draft, the remitting bank will give the draft to the importer and the importer will then provide the draft to the exporter by his own way. Once the exporter receives the draft, he can present it to the nominated paying bank for the withdrawal of payment.

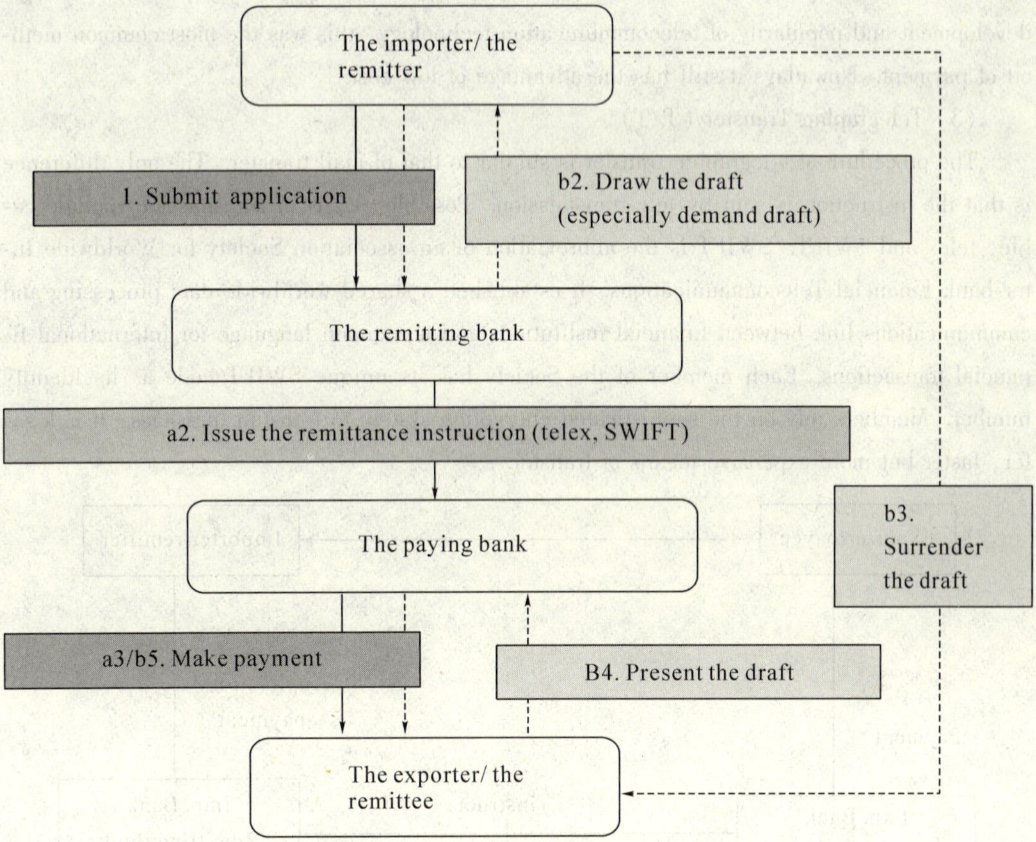

Figure 8-2 Procedure of Remittance

8.3.2 Types of Remittance

Depending on how the remittance instruction is delivered from the remitting bank to the paying bank, there exist three types of remittance.

(1) Remittance by Banker' s Demand Draft

As explained previously, the remittance instruction can be sent to the paying bank by using a demand draft which is drawn by the remitting bank on the paying bank in favor of the exporter. The importer can deliver the draft to the exporter by mail or by himself in person, especially when shipment inspection is required at the delivery of goods. The exporter can present the draft to the local bank for cash straight away. Apart from bills of exchange, promissory notes and checks can also serve the same purpose.

(2) Mail Transfer (M/T)

If the remitting bank puts the remittance instruction in a letter and sends it by ordinary mail or air mail, the practice is called mail transfer. After taking the remittance application from the remitter, the remitting bank debits its account and credits the account of its overseas branch or correspondent bank. The paying bank, on receipt of the remittance instruction, passes a reciprocal entry over its account with the remitting bank and pays the exporter. Before the development and popularity of telecommunication technology, this was the most common method of payment. Nowadays it still has the advantage of low cost.

(3) Telegraphic Transfer (T/T)

The procedure of telegraphic transfer is similar to that of mail transfer. The only difference is that the instruction is sent by tele-transmission. Possible means of transmission include cable, telex and SWIFT. SWIFT is the abbreviation of an association Society for Worldwide Inter-bank Financial Telecommunications. It established a shared worldwide data processing and communications link between financial institutions and a common language for international financial transactions. Each member of the Society has its unique SWIFT code as its identity number. Members rely on the sophisticated encryption system to transmit messages. It is a safer, faster but more expensive means of transfer.

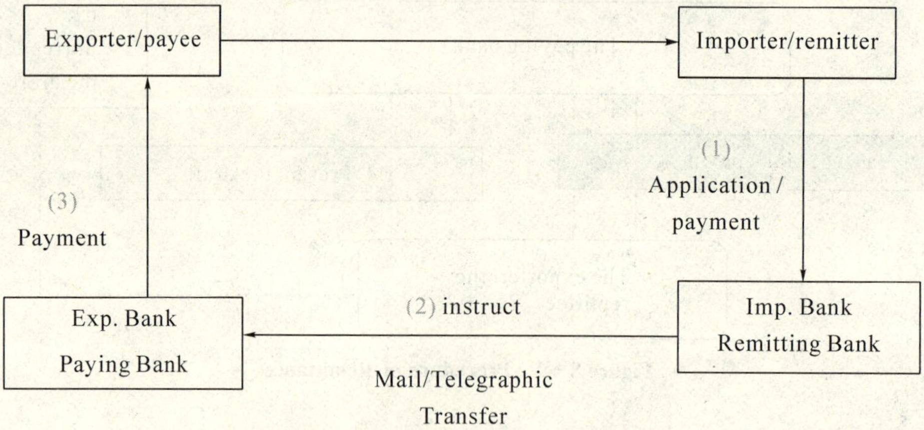

Figure 8 – 3 **M/T T/T**

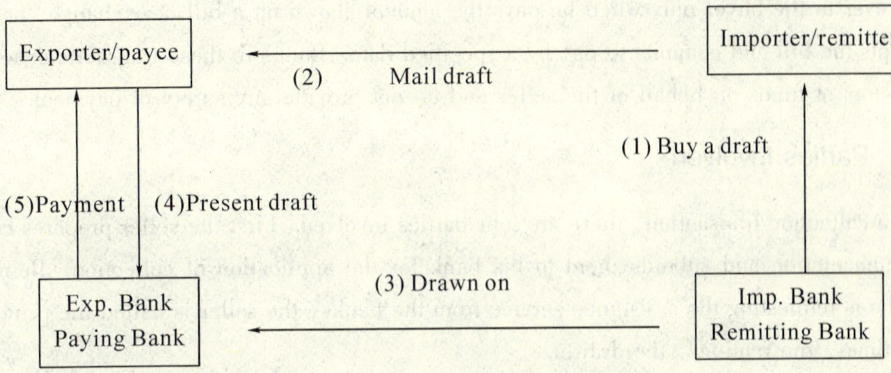

Figure 8 - 4 **D/D**

8.3.3 Remittance in Practice

Remittance in practice can have several applications.

(1) Payment in Advance

Receiving payment by cash in advance of the shipment might seem ideal. In this situation, the exporter is relieved of collection problems and has immediate use of the money. For the buyer, however, advance payment tends to create cash flow problems, as well as increase risks. Buyers are often concerned that the goods may not be sent if payment is made in advance. Exporters today seldom insist on this method of payment as their sole method because they may find themselves losing out to competitors who offer more flexible payment terms.

(2) Open Account

Open account payment is at the other extreme to payment in advance. It allows the importer to make payment after he receives the goods without providing any documents evidencing his commitment to payment. The buyer can pay immediately upon receipt of cargo or within a given period, usually from one to three months. It is sensible to view payment in advance and open account polar opposites. That is why it is more reasonable for traders to consider any alternatives in between the two terms which we will discuss in the following section.

8.4 Collection

When remittance is used, it is the debtor, the buyer who takes the initiative to arrange payment. The reality is that usually sellers take action first to collect the money by drawing a bill of exchange on the buyer and sending the bill with title documents to the buyer. If the seller chooses to use the banking channels to achieve the purpose, he can use a collection service.

By definition a collection means an arrangement whereby the seller draws a draft on the buyer and authorizes its bank to collect. It is a means of payment ensuring that the goods are handed over to the buyer only when he pays the amount shown on a bill of exchange, or when he accepts the bill and commits to pay by a specified date. Banks in these transactions act only as collectors of funds on behalf of the seller and do not provide any surety of payment.

8.4.1 Parties Involved

In a collection transaction, there are four parties involved. First the seller prepares collection documentation and submits them to his bank for the application of collection. Being the party who is requesting the assistance service from the banks, the seller is called the principal, or sometimes, the remitter, the drawer.

If the seller's local bank accepts his application for collection, the bank is then the remitting bank that receives the documents and is responsible for forwarding them to the buyer' s bank along with instructions for payment.

Normally for handling payment issues, the buyer will nominate one bank to the seller. If this bank is a correspondent bank of the remitting bank, it will receive the documents from the remitting bank and present them to the buyer for cash payment or a promise to pay in the future. It is called the presenting or collecting bank. In case the nominated bank of the buyer does not have a correspondent relationship with the remitting bank, the remitting bank will have to invite one of its correspondent banks to be the middle bank to facilitate the transaction.

The buyer is at the end of the collection flow. He is the one who owes the indicated amount and who is mentioned as drawee on the bill of exchange drawn by the seller. He is also known as the "drawee" in the collection practice. When notified by the collecting bank of the arrival of documents, the drawee has to make immediate cash payment or sign a draft according to the terms of collection order in exchange for the documents from the collecting bank.

8.4.2 Procedure of Documentary Collection

The main process of using documentary collection is described below:

◇The exporter collecting shipping documents

◇The exporter drawing a B/E on the importer

◇The exporter submitting all documents with complete instructions for collection to local bank (remitting bank) and instructing the bank to effect collection for him

◇The remitting bank forwarding B/E with other documents to its correspondent bank (collecting bank) in the importer' s country passing on exactly the instructions: received from exporter

◇The collecting bank/presenting bank presenting bill and documents to the importer

◇The collecting bank/presenting bank releasing documents to the importer upon receipt of payments or acceptance from the importer

◇The collecting bank remitting payments to the remitting bank

◇The remitting bank crediting payment to the principal (exporter)' s account

8.4.3 Types of Collection

The exporter' s arrangement for collecting payment through banks may lead to three primary means of collection.

(1) Clean Collection

When the transaction amount is small or when it is impossible or inconvenient to provide commercial documents, such as sending samples, high-tech product transaction, and seasonal commodity transaction, the exporter can conduct collection of a draft without the company of commercial documents.

(2) Documentary Collection

If the exporter can obtain relevant commercial documents, especially the transferable transport document, he will probably choose to effect documentary collection to use the title document in exchange for payment from the buyer. This is much more generally used in international commodity transactions.

There are two main types of documentary collection.

a. Documents against Payment (D/P)

In D/P terms, the Collecting bank releases the documents to the importer only upon full and immediate cash payment.

b. Documents against Acceptance (D/A)

If a period of credit to the importer has been agreed upon, then a usance bill will be used and instructions will require the documents to be released against acceptance by the importer. In this case, the importer signs his acceptance across the face of the draft, which is now due for payment on a future date, and obtains the documents of title to the cargo.

Documentary collection is in a sense beneficial to both the seller and the buyer. It is convenient for the buyer because there is no need for an advance payment; payment for goods can be made when shipping documents have been received. In case of D/A, the buyer has the possibility to sell the goods first and afterwards make payment to the seller. In the meantime, documentary collection assures the seller that the shipping documents will be released to the buyer only upon payment or acceptance of a bill of exchange.

It should also be noted that the exporter' s drawing a bill of exchange on the buyer and collecting the payment through banks does not guarantee payment and he has, to some extent, lost control of the goods when they are out of his own country.

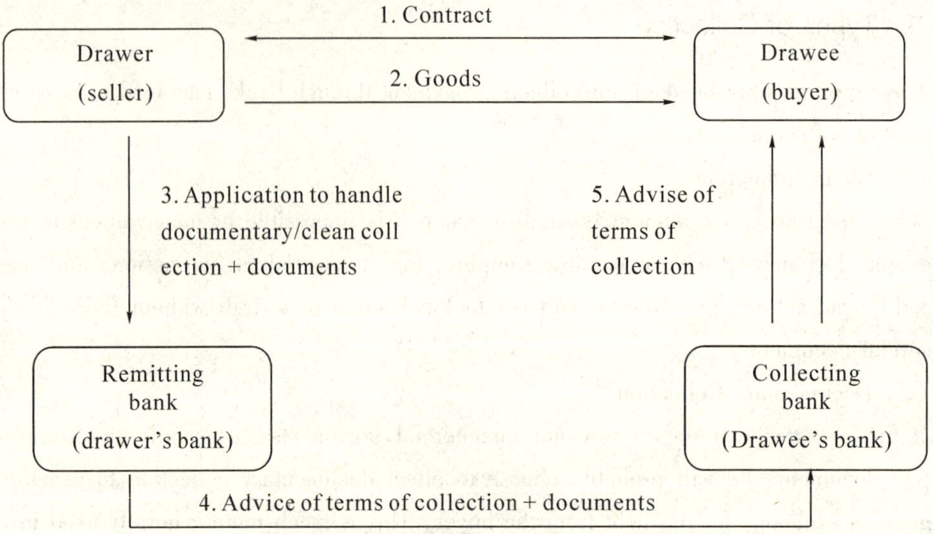

Figure 8 - 5 Procedure of Documentary Collection and Parties Involved

8.5 Basics of Letter of Credit

A classic dilemma exists in most trade situation. On the one hand exporters worry about their successful collection of payment if they ship the goods before receiving the money. On the other hand importers also feel reluctant to pay in advance for fear that goods purchased will never arrive or fail to meet requirements. The two terms of payment discussed before cannot solve this problem simply because they are built on commercial credit, if any party fails to carry out his obligation or promise, the other side may suffer.

The introduction of the use of letter of credit (L/C), especially documentary credit, in international trade has greatly improved the situation. As defined in the UCP 600, a letter of credit means "any arrangement, however named or described, whereby a bank acting at the request and on the instructions of a customer or on its own behalf, is to make a payment to or to the order of a third party, or is to accept and pay bills of exchange drawn by the third party." In other words, in an international trade context a letter of credit is the written promise of a bank, undertaken on behalf of a buyer, to pay a seller the amount specified in the credit provided the seller complies with the terms and conditions set forth in the credit.

What makes a letter of credit different from the other two approaches is that it is based on bank credit rather than commercial credit. Such method provides a high level of protection and security to both buyers and sellers engaged in international trade. The seller can be assured that payment will be made by a party independent of the buyer as far as the terms and conditions of the credit are well satisfied. The buyer gets the guarantee that his money will be released to the seller only if the bank receives the title documents required by the credit.

In spite of the advantages, a letter of credit does have its disadvantages. A major concern in using letter of credit is that in credit operations all parties only deal with documents, not with goods to which the documents may relate. The banks concerned hold no responsibility for verifying the effectiveness of documents presented at all. So far as the documents "appear on their face" to be consistent with the terms and conditions stipulated, banks will satisfy regardless what the actual situation of the goods or of the trade might be.

According to whether the usage of the credit requires the company of documents, letters of credit can be divided into two categories: clean credits and documentary credits. A clean credit does not require the presentation of documents. It is often used as a traveler' s check mainly for withdrawing cash abroad, or a bank guarantee for special purpose. In international trade the majority of credits are documentary ones as in a lot of cases concerned parties depend on the transfer of title documents for settling payment.

8.5.1 Opening an L/C

When the two parties of an international trade transaction finalize their deal a sales contract is established. This document is the basis for the importer to apply for a letter of credit. The content should directly or indirectly reflect the details of the sales contract. Upon its coming into force, however, the credit will become a completely separate document from the sales contract. The contractual relationship between the exporter and the importer has no impact on the credit operation what so ever. As a result, the exporter should pay special attention to examining the content of the credit so as to avoid any conflicting items.

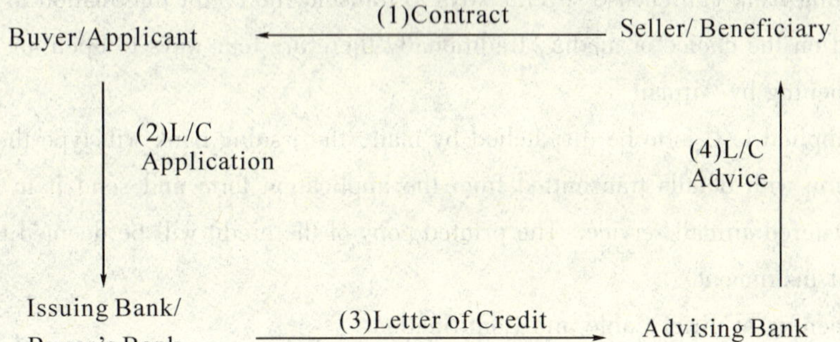

Figure 8 - 6 **Opening an L/C**

Typically a letter of credit contains the following contents:

① Name & address of the opening bank;

② Date of issuance of L/C;

③ Number of L/C;

④ Credit amount;

⑤ Description of goods;

⑥ Type of L/C;

⑦ Full name & address of the parties concerned;

⑧ Documents that shall be provided;

⑨ Details of shipment;

⑩ Validity period for L/C;

⑪ Settlement instructions;

⑫ Fee clauses;

⑬ Special clause, if any.

At the stage of issuance of a documentary credit, four parties are involved and their relationships are illustrated. The procedure may happen in the order as described.

After signing the sales contract with the seller, the buyer will present to his local bank the contract, an application letter and other documents required for the opening of an L/C. The importer is the applicant of the credit.

Depending on the buyer's credibility and relationship with the bank, the buyer may or may not be required to pledge a percentage of the value of the credit in cash funds or cash equivalents. The bank then issues the letter of credit to one of its branches or correspondent banks in the seller' s country. The importer' s local bank becomes the issuing bank of the credit and the overseas branch or correspondent bank is the advising bank.

The advising bank will notify the seller of the arrival of the credit. Once paying an advising fee, the seller receives the original of the documentary credit. He has to examine the credit closely before he accepts it.

An issuing bank can choose several ways to transmit the credit information to the advising bank. Based on the choice of media, traditionally there are four ways to open an L/C.

(1) Opening by Airmail

If the applied L/C is to be dispatched by mail, the issuing bank will type the credit on a re-printed form with details transmitted from the application form and send it to the advising bank by registered airmail service. The printed copy of the credit will be deemed to be the operative credit instrument.

(2) Opening by Brief Cable and Confirmation

If the applicant instructs to have the L/C pre-advised by telecommunication and confirmed by mail instrument, it is called opening by brief cable plus confirmation. The issuing bank will first send a brief advice of L/C by SWIFT or telex to the advising bank and then type the letter of credit with remarks to highlight that it is mail confirmation to the brief advice. Usually both the brief cable and the confirmation letter followed are integral parts of the credit.

(3) Opening by Full Cable or SWIFT

The most convenient way to open a credit is to transmit the full credit information through cable or SWIFT code. It is probably the most popular approach taken nowadays. Relying on an encryption technology, banks can transmit the financial information with high level of security, speeding up the process at the same time.

(4) Amendment

Due to its emphasis on the importance of documents, when the exporter receives a credit, it is crucial for him to inspect it thoroughly and carefully. If the beneficiary finds mistakes or terms and conditions which do not comply with the contract of sale, or he cannot fulfill in the future, he must contact the applicant and request for amendment of the credit without delay. If the applicant agrees to do so, a similar process as issuing a credit will be carried out again, until the beneficiary receives the amendment of credit from the same advising bank.

8.5.2 Methods of Settlement

Presumably the exporter will arrange production and shipment accordingly once the L/C is received. When he obtains the necessary documents among which the negotiable transport document is the most important one, he will present the package of documents to a local bank for collection of payment. The process of handling the payment is defined as L/C settlement, or sometimes availability.

Documentary credits are available in four different payment formats: sight payment, deferred payment, acceptance and negotiation.

(1) Settlement by sight payment

Under a sight payment credit, the issuing bank undertakes to pay at sight of documents which conform to the credit' s stipulations. The documents may but need not incorporate a bill of exchange drawn by the beneficiary on the issuing or nominated bank.

(2) Settlement by Deferred Payment

In a deferred payment credit, the issuing bank undertakes to give, in return for the documents, a further undertaking to make payment at the due date as stipulated in the credit, for example, 90 days after the date of the bill of lading.

(3) Settlement by Acceptance

In return for conforming documents under an acceptance credit, the issuing bank accepts liability on a draft drawn by the beneficiary. The accepting bank will then make payment to the holder of the draft on its maturity, for example, 90 days after "sight" (i. e. after the date of acceptance), if the beneficiary needs immediate funds, he may sell or discount the draft to a financial institution which will then present the draft in its own name for payment at maturity.

It is very much the same as the practice of settlement by deferred payment only that in a deferred payment credit there is no draft, but a draft is essential to the acceptance credit. In both deferred payment and acceptance credit, the applicant will not need to reimburse the issuing bank until the bank pays.

(4) Settlement by Negotiation

Unlike the other formats, under a negotiation credit, the issuing bank does not give a payment undertaking direct to the beneficiary but rather undertakes to reimburse a nominated bank if that bank "negotiates" the beneficiary' s documents in accordance with the credit' s terms. Although the beneficiary is still, in legal terms, relying on the issuing bank's undertaking, he is, in practical terms, dealing directly with the negotiating bank. As defined in UCP 600, negotiation means the purchase by the nominated bank of drafts and/or documents under a complying presentation. Upon submission of the document package, as far as the documents comply with the terms and conditions stipulated on the credit, the negotiating bank should advance or agree to advance funds to the beneficiary on or before the banking day on which reimbursement is due.

However, in some countries, notably on the India sub-continent and in South East Asia, even if it is under a negotiation credit, the negotiating bank agrees only to credit the beneficiary' s account if and when they receive the remittance from the issuing bank. This obviously is another example of international practice yielding to local context.

In all the above variants, the role of the issuing bank may be taken over by a confirming bank where one is used.

SPECIMEN:

363010 BOCSU CM

14027A LASD NL

100492 16. 35

MSG. : 001

TO: BANK OF CHINA, SHANGHAI, CHINA.

FM: F. VAN LANSCHOT BANKIERS N. V. , AMSTERDAM, THE NETHERLANDS.

DD: 9TH APRIL 1998

TEST: BETWEEN OUR HEAD - OFFICE SHFPIOGEMBOSCH AND YOURSHANGHAI (FOR USD. 91, 061. 90 DATED 10TH APRIL 1998).

WE HEREWITH OPAN OUR IRREVOCABLE DOCUMENTARY CREDIT NO. AM/VAO515ILC

BY ORDER OF: TIVOLI PRODUCTS PLCBERSTOFSGADE 48, AMSTERDAM, THE NETHERLANDS IN FAVOUR OF: UNIVERSAL TRADING CO. , LTD. RM. 1201 - 1216 MAYLING PLAZA. 131 DONGFANG RD. , SHANGHAI CHINA

FOR AN AMOUNT OF: USD91, 061. 90

EXPIRY - DATE: 15TH JUNE 1998 FOR NEGOTIATION IN CHINA.

THIS DOC. CREDIT IS AVAILABLE BY NEGOTIATION OF BENEFICIARY'S DRAFT (S) AT 45 DAYS AFTER SIGHT DRAWN ON F. VAN LANSCHOT BANKIERS N. V. , AMSTERDAM, THE NETHERLANDS,

ACCOMPANIED BY THE FOLLOWING DOCUMENTS:

+SIGNED COMMERCIAL INVOICE IN QUINTUPLICATE INDICATING BENEFICIA-

RY 'S CONTRACT NUMBER AND OUR ORDER NO. 98 – CS004

+ PACKINGLIST/WEIGHTMEMO IN TRIPLICATE MENTIONING TOTAL NUMBER OF CARTONS, GROSS WEIGHT AND MEASUREMENTS PER EXPORT CARTON.

+ 2/3 OF ORIGINAL CLEAN ON-BOARD MARINE BILLS OF LADING, PLUS 3 N. N. – COPIES, MADE OUT: "TO ORDER", AND BLANK ENDORSED MARKED: "FREIGHT PREPAID" SHOWING AS NOTIFY THE APPLICANT (GIVING FULL NAME, ADDRESS AND PHONE NUMBERS).

+ FULL SET 3/3 OF MARINE INSURANCE POLICY OR CERTIFICATE, ENDORSED IN BLANK FOR 110 PERCENT FULL CIF VALUE, COVERING INSTITUTE CARGO CLAUSES (A) AND WAR CLAUSES OF INSTITUTE CARGO CLAUSES.

+ G. S. P. CERTIFICATE OF ORIGIN FORM A IN DUPLICATE THAT THE GOODS ARE OF CHINESE ORIGIN.

+ BENEFICIARY'S CERTIFICATE STATING THAT ONE SET OF NON-NEGOTIABLE SHIPPING DOCUMENTS TOGETHER WITH THE 1/3 ORIGINAL B/L HAVE BEEN SENT TO THE APPLICANT BY DHL WITHIN 48 HOURS AFTER SHIPMENT.

+ COPY OF BENEFICIARY'S TELEX/FAX SENT TO APPLICANT (TELEX – NO. : 13174 + TIV NL OR FAX – NO. : + (31) 74 12 37 37) WITHIN TWO WORKING DAYS AFTER SHIPMENT INDICATING DATE OF DEPARTURE, SHIPPING MARKS, NUMBERS OF LC, B/L, CONTRACT AND ORDER AS WELL AS NUMBER OF CARTONS TOGETHER WITH THE TOTAL GROSS WEIGHT AND GOODS VALUE.

COVERING: 5 ITEMS OF TOTAL 2960 SETS AND 8498 PCS. OF PLUSH TOYS AS PER: APPLICANT'S ORDER NUMBER AND BENEFICIARY'S CONTRACT NUMBER HY98CS004.

LABEL: CE/IMP. 087 FOR ARTICLES KB7900, KP2273 AND KB0278 AND

LABEL: F – TOYS 2280 FOR ARTICLES KB0677 AND KC2048

PACKING IN NEUTRAL SEAWORTHY EXPORT CARTONS SUITABLE FOR LONG DISTANCE OCEAN TRANSPORTATION.

SHIPPING MARKS TO READ AS FOLLOWS: CE/IMP. 087

CHRISTIAENS

VIAAMSTERDAM

CARTON NO. 1 AND UP

FOLLOEED BY: ARTICIE NUMBER AND

F – TOYS 2280

GROBBENDONK

VIAAMSTERDAM

CARTON NO. 1 AND UP

FOLLOWED BY: ARTICLE NUMBER

TERMS OF DELIVERY：CIFAMSTERDAM

(INCOTERMS 1990).

ALL OF THE ABOVE MUST BE STATED ON THE INVOICE AND PACKING LIST.

PARTIAL SHIPMENTS：PROHIBITED.

TRANSHIPMENT：PROHIBITED.

LATEST DATE OF SHIPMENT：31ST MAY 1998.

SHIPMENT FROM：SHANGHAI

TO：AMSTERDAM

ALL (BANKING –) CHARGES OUTSIDE THENETHERLANDS ARE FOR BENEFICIARY'S ACCOUNT.

DOCUMENTS TO BE PRESENTED ULTIMATELY 15 DAYS AFTER THE DATE OF ISSUANCE OF THE RELATIVE TRANSPORT-DOCUMENT (S) BUT WITHIN THE VALIDITY OF THIS DOC. CREDIT.

DOCUMENTS TO BE SENT AS FOLLOWS (INSTRUCTION MARKED "X"):

( ) IN ONELOT BY REGISTERED IRMAIL

( ) IN TWO CONSECUTIVE REGISTERED AIRMAILS

( ) IN ONELOT BY INTERNATIONAL COURIER SERVICE

(X) 1 ST MAIL BY COURIER SERVICE AND 2 ND MAIL BY REGISTERED AIRMAIL

TO：F. VAN LANSCHOT BANKIERS N. V.,

STREET-ADDRESS：CONCERTGEBOUNPLTIN 20

1071 LNAMSTERDAM.

POSTAL-ADDRESS：P. O. BOX 75509,

1070 AMAMSTERDAM

THENETHERLANDS

UPON RECEIPT OF CORRECT DOCUMENTS BY US, WE SHALL COVER THE NEGOTIATING BANK (AS PER THEIR INSTRUCTIONS), IN THE CURRENCY OF THIS DOC. CREDIT ONLY.

PLEASE ADVISE BENEFICIARY, WITHOUT ADDING YOUR CONFIRMATION.

THIS DOC. CREDIT IS SUBJECT TO THE UNIFORM CUSTOMS AND PRACTICE FOR DOCUMENTARY CREDITS (REVISION 1993, I. C. C. PUBLICATION NO. 600)

THIS TELEX IS THE OPERATIVE CREDIT-INSTRUMENT AND NO MAIL-ADVICE WILL FOLLOW.

REGARDS,

F. VAN LANSCHOT BANKIERS N. V., AMSTERDAM

(TLX：14027 +LASD NL)

8.6 Types of Documentary Credit

Letters of credit are functionally flexible, as demonstrated by the variations in credit terms and credit features. A wide variety of credits by design serve different purposes. The next part will briefly introduce most of the credit types generally found in international trade, some of which are frequently used, and some of which are only employed with very special intentions. At the end of the discussion a sample letter of credit typically used for import and export is provided to draw together all the pieces about letter of credit hopefully being able to build up a full picture about the use of this payment method.

8.6.1 Revocable Credit vs. Irrevocable Credit

If an L/C can be amended or cancelled by the issuing bank at any time and without prior notice to the beneficiary, it is a revocable credit. Such a credit is unfavorable to the beneficiary who is the exporter. However, in the case of another bank having made payment, acceptance or negotiation to the beneficiary prior to receipt of notice of amendment or cancellation, the issuing bank is bound to reimburse the bank against documents appearing on their face to be in conformity with the terms and conditions of the credit.

In general, an exporter prefers an irrevocable credit because it can be amended or cancelled only if all parties concerned, i. e. the issuing bank, the beneficiary, and the confirming bank, if any, do agree. This type of credit gives the exporter greater assurance of payment, but offers the credit opener less flexibility to change credit terms.

8.6.2 Confirmed Credit vs. Unconfirmed Credit

Even though a letter of credit is based on bank credit, rather than commercial credit, occasionally the credibility or solvency of the issuing bank can be questionable. The exporter therefore may seek some other guarantors for his payment. A confirmed credit is one that a bank, other than the issuing bank, undertakes to honor the credit issued by adding its confirmation. On the credit, the confirming bank usually signs under the statement, "We hereby add our confirmation to this credit". This implies that the bank will be liable for payment in case of default by the issuing bank. By contrast, an unconfirmed credit does not indicate such an undertaking to effect payment by any other bank, except the issuing bank.

A confirmed letter of credit has to be an irrevocable one. The confirmation from the confirming bank must be authorized or requested by the issuing bank. Under a confirmed irrevocable credit both the issuing bank and the confirming bank undertake to honor a complying presentation, hence providing the beneficiary a double assurance of payment.

8. 6. 3 Sight Credit vs. Usance Credit

Under a sight credit, payment will be made immediately against the sight draft and required shipping documents. Under a term credit, or a usance credit as it is called sometimes, payment will not be made until the time bill, or usance bill, falls due on maturity date. By using a term credit the exporter allows the importer to have a credit period before he fulfills his obligation of payment.

8. 6. 4 Straight Credit vs. Open Credit

A straight L/C refers to one that is available to the beneficiary by presentation of documents to the issuing bank. The issuing bank's engagement to pay extends only to the beneficiary. This means that the beneficiary of the documentary credit is supposed to deal directly with the issuing bank in presenting documents under the credit. The issuing bank has no formal obligation to any other bank or financial institution who may purchases the documents from the beneficiary. The straight credit is of the greatest advantage to the buyer because he does not need to pay the seller until his own bank reviews the documents. Due to the inconvenience encountered by the beneficiary in his direct dealing with the issuing bank, which in most cases locates in another country, in practice a straight L/C normally nominates a local bank in the beneficiary' s country as the negotiating bank, handling the documents presented at the first place. The right to purchase or accept the documents is strictly limited to the nominated bank. As a result, the beneficiary will not be able to negotiate his documents under the credit with any other banks.

By contrast, an open credit is freely negotiable at any bank. It is also called free negotiable credit. The issuing bank commits to honoring drafts and documents held by third parties as far as the documents presented comply with the terms and condition stipulated on the credit. Open credits or negotiable credits are very common in international trade since exporters typically want to obtain payment immediately from their local bank once shipment is made.

8. 6. 5 Transferable Credit

Sometimes the buyer with whom the exporter is dealing is not the actual end buyer, but an agent or a middle-person. The intermediary may not like using his own fund in facilitating the transaction. In this case a transferable credit is of great help. Under a transferable credit the first beneficiary may make the credit available in whole or in part to one or more other parties who later become second beneficiaries. In the process, the intermediary requires the end buyer to open a documentary credit in favor of him. If this is a transferable credit, he then transfers both the obligation to supply the goods and part of the proceeds of the credit to the actual supplier. In such a way neither the middle-person needs to commit any funds to the transaction, nor would the identities of both the end buyer and end supplier be revealed to each other.

Table 8 - 1 Banks Possibly Involved in Use of L/C

Accepting bank	A bank which accepts a bill of exchange by endorsing it, and thus incurs the legal obligation of paying the bill's amount on its maturity date. It can be the opening bank itself or a nominated bank.
Advising bank	A correspondent bank in the exporter's country of the issuing bank that receives a letter of credit from the issuing bank for authenticating and informing the exporter about the issuance.
Confirming bank	A bank in the exporter's country which guarantees that the L/C established by the importer will be honored once the conditions therein are fully complied with. The confirming bank undertakes this responsibility on an arrangement with the issuing bank. The confirming bank normally will be the advising bank, but another bank may also fill this position.
Negotiating bank	The beneficiary's bank which agrees to pay the beneficiary by purchasing a negotiable instrument (bill of exchange).
Opening bank	The buyer's bank that opens a letter of credit at the request of the buyer, in favor of the seller. It is also called the issuing bank.
Paying bank	The bank nominated in the L/C to pay the drawings. It can be either the issuing or the advising Bank.
Presenting bank	A bank which receives the package of documents under an L/C and submits it to the paying bank for payment.
Reimbursing bank	A bank named in a documentary L/C from which the paying, accepting, or negotiating bank may request cover after receipt of the documents in compliance with the credit. It is often, but not always, the issuing bank.

According to UCP 600, a transferable credit must clearly state that it is "transferable". Terms, such as "divisible" "fractionally" "transmissible", do not make the credit transferable. Moreover, the credit can only be transferred once. A second beneficiary cannot transfer to a third beneficiary. If the first beneficiary transfers the credit to several parties, all these transferees are considered as second beneficiaries.

8.6.6 Revolving Credit

The application and opening of an L/C can be complicated and lengthy. If the exporter and the importer have an ongoing relationship and the transaction is done on an installment basis, the importer may choose to use a revolving credit. A revolving credit obliges the issuing bank to restore the credit to the original amount after it has been utilized, without the need for amendment. Such credits can be revocable or irrevocable, cumulative or noncumulative and can revolve by time or by amount.

In the case of a credit which revolves by time, a stated amount is available in a given period. When a new period starts, the full amount will then be automatically re-available. While a credit which revolves by amount will reinstate the fixed amount upon utilization within a given period.

8. 6. 7 Reciprocal Credit

A reciprocal credit is a counter credit under which the opener of a first credit becomes the beneficiary of the second reciprocal credit, while the beneficiary of the first credit becomes the opener of the second reciprocal credit.

Suppose A wants to sell raw materials to B and buy back the processed products. B will agree to purchase raw materials from A to make production only under the condition that A promises to buy the finished goods back. Under such a deal there are actually two transactions. B needs to open a letter of credit in favor of A to purchase the raw materials and A also needs to open a credit in favor of B to purchase the finished products. Since B wants A' s guarantee of buying back the goods, A will open the credit first and the issuance will be mentioned as a condition of effectiveness on the credit opened by B. The credit issued by B is then called a reciprocal credit.

Typically a reciprocal credit is a sight credit while the first one is a term credit. The design is to allow the applicant of the reciprocal credit to make production without paying for the materials first. Once finished goods are shipped, he can collect proceeds by presenting documents under the first credit and settle up his liability when the bill is mature.

Reciprocal credits are often used in barter transactions, trade of processing incoming materials, counter trade or compensation trade.

8. 6. 8 Back to Back Credit

Back-to-back credits are used in circumstances very similar to those of the transferable credit where a middle-person may be involved in the transaction. The difference is that back-to-back credit involves the issuing of a completely new credit. What happen is that when the intermediary receives a documentary credit from the end buyer in favor of him, he can use this credit as collateral or "backup" for issuing a new credit naming the actual supplier as the beneficiary and himself the applicant.

In a back-to-back credit situation, the first credit based on which the second one is opened must be irrevocable and non-transferable. Once the second credit is opened, the middle-person is responsible to the bank for payment regardless of whether or not he himself is paid under the first credit since he is the applicant for the second credit. When using such credit the end buyer is unaware of the existence of the actual supplier, therefore the intermediary keeps his business confidentiality well. The downside of this is that there is a lot more paperwork and more parties involved so mistakes and problems are easier to occur.

8. 6. 9 Red Clause Credit

An anticipatory credit is characterized by a special clause, known as "red clause," which is traditionally printed in red ink and authorizes the advising bank or confirming bank to make advances to the beneficiary before his presentation of documents required. It was originally used in the Australian wool trade to enable the seller to purchase raw materials or to pay other costs prior to receiving full payment. This arrangement allows the exporter to obtain funds prior to the shipment, easing his pressure of running out of working capital. On the other hand it increases the liability of the applicant who has to make repayment of the advances and all the costs such as interest or foreign exchange hedging incurred by any bank involved, if the beneficiary fails to present the required documents for settlement.

8. 6. 10 Standby Credit

A standby credit is a clean credit that guarantees the payment for a possible unfulfilled obligation on the part of the applicant. It is especially used as security for open account trading where the exporter requires some kind of "back up" in the event of the importer not paying for the goods. In case of default by the applicant, the beneficiary can demand payment from the guarantor, who is the issuing bank of the standby credit, by presenting a draft, along with a signed statement by the beneficiary about the applicant's failure to pay.

8. 7 Letter of Guarantee

To some extent a letter of guarantee shares many similarities with a standby letter of credit. It is an irrevocable undertaking by which the issuer holds itself financially liable for the consequences of non-performance of the obligations by a third party towards the beneficiary. A letter of guarantee can be used in a wider scope than a letter of credit: trade of commodity, labor and technology, contracting for construction project, undertaking of construction, customs declaration for material import and export, financing from financial institutions or on the financial market, leasing of complete sets of large equipment, litigation guarantee, performance of contractual obligations, etc.

It is distinctive that a L/G may allow the importer rather than the exporter as the beneficiary of this instrument. In an international trade situation, while using a L/C, the exporter has an advantage that as long as the documents on their face comply with the terms of credit, the exporter can receive the payment. As a result, the buyer may be defrauded or deceived. In many construction and financial transactions buyers often have a strong bargaining position, thus a L/G is used to protect their interest when the buyer becomes the beneficiary of the L/G. Sometimes an exporter may also demand an importer to provide a bank guarantee as the term of payment.

By the nature of guarantee responsibility, letter of guarantee can be divided into two kinds: credit L/G and payment L/G. Credit L/G includes tender guarantee, performance guarantee, advance payment guarantee, retention money guarantee, warranty guarantee, customs guarantee, etc. Payment L/G includes payment guarantee, financing guarantee, leasing guarantee, guarantee for compensation trade, etc. Generally speaking, letters of guarantee do not follow any specific format or wording; they tend to be constructed case by case. Meanwhile several essential requirements are common among most letters of guarantee. They are: irrevocable unconditional, fully transferable abstract (the guarantee must not be dependant on performance of the underlying supply contract) and divisible (each individual repayment amount and date must be specified).

The application of a L/G is subject to the Uniform Rules for Demand Guarantees (ICC Publication No. 458) and the Uniform Rules for Contract Guarantees (ICC Publication No. 325). However due to the regulations in some countries L/G are not generally acceptable. In this case, a standby L/C may be used.

8.8 Export Financing

A common problem faced by exporting companies, especially the SMEs is the shortage of cash, when several orders are being processed during a similar period of time, when a contract of an excessively large amount is signed or when long credit terms are granted to buyers. Typically exporters have two distinct cash-in-need periods that are differentiated by the shipment. The first one is the period required to prepare the goods for shipment that is known as pre-shipment. The second period is known as post-shipment and covers the period following shipment of the goods. To balance out the mismatch in cash flows exporters will use a mixture of two broad approaches. They can negotiate with suppliers and buyers for the trading conditions that will more closely match the timing of payments against expected receipts. Or they can seek extra sources of finance above the basic sources of capital and normal bank lending. This finance can best be found through channels relative to the export transactions themselves. Export financing, provided by various financial institutions allows exporters much greater choice of financial solutions.

Compared with conventional financing, financers enjoy some additional benefits from export financing. Besides the interest earned from the loan, there is also considerable revenue from the business of settlement of payment and foreign exchange dealing. In addition the transaction procedure for export financing is comparatively simpler and risk lower, provided that the export transactions in question do happen and sufficient precaution is taken. Taking into account the competition in the financial service market, a trader will not be surprised to find himself overwhelmed by the hospitable offering of a variety of confusing options from the international department of his bank.

Each export financing option has its pluses and minuses. Exporters should have a thorough understanding about the different alternatives before they decide on one. Normally the following factors are important to consider in making decision about financing:

① The need for financing;

② The length of time of financing;

③ The cost of the different financing methods;

④ The risks associated with the transaction for financing;

⑤ The occasion of financing: pre-shipment finance or post shipment finance.

8.8.1 L/C Related Financing

In addition to its original usage as a guaranteed payment term which replaces the solvency risk of the importer with the solvency risk of the bank issuing it, a letter of credit can make it possible for the exporter to receive money more quickly through certain channels of L/C financing.

(1) Packing Loan

Packing loan is a pre-shipment short-term financing provided by the local bank to enable the exporter to purchase and prepare the materials, and produce and ship the contracted goods without difficulty even when there is a shortage of self-owned capital.

Upon receipt of a L/C, the exporter may present the credit to a chosen bank for the application of the packing loan. Since the L/C is the only collateral of such a loan, and the guarantee of payment from a credit is conditional, the financing bank is exposed to considerable risk. Therefore it is necessary for the bank to conduct a thorough and careful examination of the content of the letter of credit, on the background of the exporter, if possible, on the reputation of the importer. Once the bank is satisfied, a loan contract will be signed between the bank and the exporter and the original L/C should be retained in the financing bank. In normal cases, 80% to 90% of the credit amount will be granted after deducting the predicted interest charge. It is assumed that the loan is only used for supporting the exporter to implement the export contract and once goods shipment is made and relevant documents under the L/C are obtained, the exporter should present the documents to the bank for negotiation as soon as possible. Furthermore, upon receipt of remittance of payment, it should be deemed as first resource to repay the packing loan.

Due to its high risk, financing banks takes great precautions and have less flexible conditions concerning loans, especially relating to the tenor. The term of the loan is normally from three to six months, and the maturity of the loan should not exceed fifteen days after the expiry date of the letter of credit.

(2) Negotiation under Documentary Credit

If the exporter didn' t take a packing loan at the early stage of his fulfillment of contract, he can choose another financing method after the shipment is made—negotiation under documentary credit. This approach shares one thing in common with a packing loan in that the loan is also based on a received documentary credit. After the exporter ships the goods and obtains all the documents under the credit, he can use the credit and the documents as the collateral for the application of the loan. If it is accepted, the financing bank will allow the loan to be 100% of the credit amount. Because the bank still has to deduct the predicted interest and commission charge, normally the proceeds received by the exporter must be less than the full value of the invoice.

It can be seen that this method of financing is exactly the same as the operation of settlement by negotiation. In countries where real settlement by negotiation cannot be realized, normally banks provide it as a different way of financing. If the local banking practice accepts settlement by negotiation as the normal settlement methods, this financing will not be applicable.

8.8.2 Factoring

Apart from using the letter of credit as an instrument for obtaining loans, exporters can also depend on other approaches for financing. Here we will only briefly introduce two approaches: factoring and forfeiting.

The origin of factoring can be traced back to the industrial revolution when the textile manufacturers from northern England appointed agencies in North America to sell their products and collected payment for them. The real development and prosperity of factoring business started in the late 1960s. In 1968 the Factors Chain International (FCI) was founded in Netherlands, headquartered in Amsterdam. As an umbrella organization for independent factoring companies around the world, FCI aimed to introduce the concept of factoring in countries where the service was not yet available and to develop a framework for international factoring that would allow factors in the country of both the exporter and the importer to work closely together. Today a standard communication system and a set of global code of conduct concerning factoring have become well established due to FCI's effort and international factoring has developed as a favorable alternative to traditional export finance such as letter of credit.

Factoring is a complete financial package that combines investigating the creditworthiness of buyers, assuming credit risk and giving one hundred percent protection against write-offs, collection and management of receivables and provision of finance through immediate cash advances against outstanding receivables. It is offered under an agreement between the factor and the seller. Under the agreement, the factor purchases the seller's accounts receivable, normally without recourse, and assumes the responsibility for the debtor's financial ability to pay. If the debtor goes bankrupt or is unable to pay its debts for credit reasons, the factor will pay the seller. Normally international factoring companies will work with partners abroad who will be responsible for the collection of payment in the country to which the export may go. The services of such local agents will prevent any problems that could arise because of differences in legal systems, customs and language.

The advantages for the exporter of using a factoring service are many. It allows the exporter to expand sales in overseas markets by offering foreign customers the same terms and conditions as local competitors. By providing a complete range of services which cover these aspects of exporting, factoring leaves the exporter free to concentrate on production and sales. In addition, through conducting a credit assessment on the importer and requiring purchasing credit protection, factoring protects the exporter against losses due to the insolvency of the importer. Moreover the efficient collection of outstanding invoices and remittance improve the exporter's cash flow and liquidity, enhancing his borrowing potential.

Factoring might not effectively meet the particular needs of every industry and the most suitable companies for a factoring service may be those who sell consumer goods and light industrial products on short-term open account credit in the developed countries. Products include textiles, clothing, food, consumer durables, engineering and electronic equipment. The parties in a factoring transaction are described below.

Exporter is the client of a factoring transaction. He needs to provide a business license or documents of a similar nature, report of his business operation and financial situation, if required, together with an application form to the local factoring company or bank chosen to initiate the service. Once accepted, the exporter then will sign a factoring agreement with the factor to sell all his receivables under agreed terms.

Importer also plays an important role in a factoring business. Normally how quickly or easily the exporter' s application for factoring service can be approved depends on the scale of business, performance and credibility of the importer.

Export factor in most cases must be an FCI member, it could be a local bank or a specialized factoring company in the exporter's country. Under the agreement with the exporter, the factor purchases the exporter' s receivables normally on a without-recourse basis and takes the responsibility for collecting payments and taking credit risk.

Import factor should also be an FCI member. It can be the overseas branch of the export factor or a nominated correspondent factor of the export factor. It is responsible for investigating the importer' s credit and handling all the related issues in the importer' s country locally.

The procedure of factoring usually includes the following steps:

The exporter signs a factoring contract assigning all agreed receivables to an export factor. The factor then becomes responsible for all aspects of the factoring operation.

The export factor chooses an FCI correspondent to serve as an import factor in the country where goods are to be shipped. The receivables are then reassigned to the import factor.

At the same time, the import factor investigates the credit standing of the buyer of the exporter's goods and establishes lines of credit. This allows the buyer to place an order on open account terms without opening letters of credit.

Once the goods have been shipped, the export factor may advance up to 80% of the invoice value to the exporter.

Once the sale has taken place, the import factor collects the full invoice value at maturity and is responsible for the swift transmission of funds to the export factor who then pays the exporter the outstanding balance.

If 90 days after the due date an approved invoice remains unpaid, the import factor will pay 100% of the invoice value under guarantee.

8. 8. 3 Forfeiting

Forfeiting is another payment technique an exporter can use to promote sales on a deferred payment basis. The term "forfeiting" has French origins, meaning "without recourse" and this financing method was initially devised to finance exports of capital goods from West German manufacturers to the growing markets of Eastern Europe, which were opening up in the late 1950s and early 1960s. In a forfeit transaction, the exporter or the borrower, after pledging acceptable notes or bills, forfeits his rights to future payments from the notes or bills and the funder by accepting the notes or bills forfeits his rights to recourse to the exporter/borrower in the event of non-payment from the guarantor of the notes or bills.

In the early stage of this practice, shortage of hard currency in the Eastern European countries meant importers requiring longer credit period than the traditionally acceptable three to six months. However, West German exporters were eager to settle their payment speedily so that they could have the resource of refinancing to operate in the new and vital market. But concerned about the uncertain political situation and financial risk in the Eastern European bloc, West German bankers were reluctant to extend the credit period to a longer extent. Consequently, the dilemma was solved by a group of financiers in Switzerland who were willing to discount the promissory notes or bills of exchange without recourse to the exporter. A financial commitment became known as forfeiting. This meant that if the importer or his bank failed to pay on the due dates, this would not be the problem of the exporter, but the forfeiting house, usually Swiss Banks, which had financed this transaction without recourse and therefore, had taken over the commercial venture. This resulted in the Swiss market being developed. Zurich became the center for such transactions in the 1960s.

Forfeiting finance now has become popular internationally. It is one of the most advantageous financing methods for the exporter as it bears several obvious benefits. First, it minimizes the political, physical and commercial risks and costs the exporter potentially has to endure due to long term settlement and collection of payment. It especially protects the exporter against the risk arising from the fluctuation of exchange rates. Second, the exporter can obtain 100% finance without resource. This significantly helps the exporter improving his financial condition. Third, the required documentation and handling procedures are comparatively simple, which would largely save the exporters' effort and time.

Forfeiting is typically used for transactions of high value, such as purchase of large scale machineries. Forfeiting houses normally would not expect transactions to be worth less than \$ 100 000. But the tenor of commercial papers accepted by the forfeiting house can range from one to ten years, depending on the country, the importer and the guarantor bank. Generally four parties get involved in the transaction: forfeiter, exporter, importer and guarantor.

Forfeiter is usually a major bank or financial institution in the exporter's country. Counting on the solvency of the importer and the guarantor, the forfeiter purchases the credit instruments from the exporter and is entitled to claim payment from the relevant parties. In case of dishonor of the instruments, however, the forfeiter has no right to recourse.

Exporter normally will have to clearly indicate the employment of forfeiting as the payment approach in the sales contract. And he also has to apply for the transaction from a local financial institution under certain conditions and terms. Once granted, the exporter needs to issue an usance instrument to the importer and have the instrument guaranteed by a financial institution in the importer's country. Upon presenting the document, the exporter may receive the net proceeds with deduction of the interest and commission.

Importer is the original drawee on the debt instrument issued by the exporter. Under the forfeiting arrangement, he may need to pay in a future time after enjoying a relatively long tenor without occurring any financing cost. The importer has to accept the usance instrument provided by the exporter in the first place and gets it guaranteed by his local financier before the forfeiting transaction comes into force.

Guarantor is preferably an internationally recognized bank, if not a state bank. The reputation and solvency of the guarantor greatly influence the granting decision of the forfeiter.

The major steps in a forfeiting transaction may be as follows:

① The exporter approaches the forfeiting house (or a local bank) and presents export-related documents for application of forfeiting.

② Once the usance debt instruments are accepted and guaranteed by the importer and the guarantor, the forfeiter will inform the exporter and confirm the forfeiting quotation.

③ The exporter will conclude a forfeiting agreement with the forfeiter.

④ The forfeiter will deposit proceeds to the exporter's account.

When time is due, the forfeiter will claim payment from the importer. The typical documents used in forfeiting are given below:

a note or bill purchase agreement executed between the forfeiting company and the exporter;

promissory notes or bills of exchange;

guarantee or aval (an unconditional and irrevocable guarantee written on the face of a promissory note or bill of exchange);

signature confirmations and authentications;

copies of necessary governmental approvals.

One way or the other, the development of modern financial services provides more and better alternatives to the exporters so that they can improve their operating capital while reducing the settlement risk from the purchasing side. In general, when making export financing decision, the exporter has to take all relevant factors such as risk, cost, availability and credit limit consideration.

8.9 Payment Problems

In international trade, problems involving bad debts are more easily avoided than rectified after they occur. Credit checks and the other methods that have been discussed in this chapter can limit the risks. Nonetheless, just as in companies' domestic business, exporters occasionally encounter problems with buyers who default on their payment. When these problems occur in international trade, obtaining payment can be both difficult and expensive. Even when the exporter has insurance to cover commercial credit risks, a default by a buyer still requires the time, effort, and cost of the exporter to collect a payment. The exporter must exercise normal business prudence in exporting and exhaust all reasonable means of obtaining payment before an insurance claim is honored. Even then there is often a significant delay before the insurance payment is made.

The simplest, and maybe the least costly solution to a payment problem is to contact and negotiate with the customer. With patience, understanding, and flexibility, an exporter can often resolve conflicts to the satisfaction of both sides.

This point is especially true when a simple misunderstanding or technical problem is to blame and there is no question of bad faith. Even though the exporter may be required to compromise on certain points—perhaps even on the price of the committed goods—the company may save a valuable customer and profit in the long run.

However, if negotiations fail and the sum involved is large enough to warrant the effort, a company should obtain the assistance and advice of its bank, legal counsel, and other qualified experts. Since arbitration is often faster and less costly, this step is preferable to legal action, if both parties can agree to take their dispute to an arbitration agency. The International Chamber of Commerce handles the majority of international arbitration and is usually acceptable to foreign companies because it is not affiliated with any single country. This will be fully discussed in Chapter 10.

8.10 Summary

Before a payment term is decided upon, a trader must consider several critical factors: the currency chosen for payment, the sharing of credit risk, the costs related to each payment method and the potential political and legal risks. There are three basic payment instruments used in international trade: bill of exchange, promissory note and check. Bill of exchange is the most commonly used one among the three in international transaction.

Among the three payment terms used in international trade, remittance is the simplest and least expensive one. Its application involves a remitter, a remitting bank, a paying bank and a payee. The transfer can be done by banker's draft, by mail, or by telegraphic transmission. Collection provides better protection to the exporter than remittance. Traditionally a letter of credit is the most secured payment method in international trade. It is a paying promise made by the importer's bank to pay to the exporter under the condition that the exporter fulfills all the terms and conditions listed on the credit. It is a payment term based on bank credit. Letter of credit has many variations. They are designed to serve different purposes.

A letter of guarantee is an irrevocable undertaking by which the issuer holds itself financially liable for the consequences of non-performance of the obligations by a third party towards the beneficiary. Factoring and forfeiting are the other channels through which the exporter can obtain funds.

Exercises

Ⅰ. Choices

1. If there is no specific provision, the draft under a letter of credit should draw on the ________.

   A. advising bank　　B. issuing bank

   C. negotiating bank　　D. applicant

2. The draft used in collection is ________.

   A. a banker's draft, based on bank credit

   B. a commercial draft, based on bank credit

   C. a banker's draft, based on commercial credit

   D. a commercial draft, based on commercial credit

3. A standby credit ________.

   A. is a documentary credit

   B. is a special clean credit

   C. can be a documentary credit as well as a clean credit

   D. is not a real letter of credit, but a letter of guarantee

4. Under collection once the importer refuses to pay, the ________ will be responsible for the cargo release, customs clearance, warehousing, and reselling in the importing country.

   A. drawee　　B. collecting bank　　C. principal　　D. presenting bank

5. The bill of exchange used in D/A must be a ________.

   A. sight bill　　B. bank bill　　C. bank accepted bill　　D. usance bill

6. If a bank other than the issuing bank guarantees the payment under an L/C, this L/C is ________.

   A. a confirmed credit　　B. an irrevocable credit

C. non - transferable credit D. a negotiable credit

7. Which of the following statements is NOT true about remittance? ________

A. It provides highest security to the buyer but not the seller.

B. It is cheaper to use than the other terms of payment.

C. It is based on commercial credit, not bank credit.

D. It may impose high risk either to the buyer or to the seller.

Ⅱ. Questions

1. After Bank X advised exporter Y of the L/C, the shipment was made. When the cargo was on the way, the importer filed for bankruptcy. Is Y out of luck of collecting the payment? Can the opening bank refuse to make reimbursement to the negotiating bank? Why or why not'?

2. Read the bill of exchange below and answer questions.

TWO COPIES

No. 80W5069 - 2 Date: 4th DEC. 2008

EXCHANGE FOR USD63, 162. 00

At 90 DAYS sight of this FIRST OF EXCHANGE (second of the same tenor and date unpaid) pay to the order of OURSELVES the sum of ________ Value received Draw under LC No. 314955B OF 1ST AUG. 1999 ISSUED BY YOURGOODSELVES

TO HORNER HENAN NATIVE PRODUCE & ANIMAL

TRUST CO. BY - PRODUCTS IMP. & EXP. CO.

PITTSBURG ____________________

MANAGER

1) Who is the drawer/drawee?

2) On which day was the draft drawn?

3) Is the Bill in sola (one copy) or two?

4) How much money is involved?

5) This bill only shows the sum of money is figures. Can you write out the same amount in words? Where do you write it .

6) In a bill of exchange, the places of the sender and the receiver are fixed. Where are they respectively?

7) How long is this bill valid?

8). According to the bill, what is the mode of payment used?

Ⅲ. Case studies

1. TESCO Company signed a contract to export goods to DH company in Africa. In September TESCO was notified of the L/C, but the money of account was different from that required by the sales contract. Besides, the goods were not ready for shipment. In November, DH urged TESCO to deliver the goods. TESCO requested an L/C amendment and an extension of the shipment date. The next day, DH cabled back, "L/C amended." TESCO shipped the

goods. However, the amended L/C never arrived, and the opening bank refused to pay against the shipping documents. The goods were stored in the warehouse at the port of destination. TESCO had to pay much rent and insurance. At this time, DH requested DP - TR. Should TESCO accept it? Is there any lesson to be learnt from this case'?

2. Some foreign trade company in China exported 2000 dozen textile to Canada by L/C. The buyer opened L/C timely and prohibited partial shipment stipulated in the L/C. When the seller arranged to ship, it was found that the quality of some goods was inferior to the requirements. So the seller just shipped 1900 dozen goods, and thought that the shortage of 100 dozen was allowed according to the stipulation of "allowed 5% less or more of quantity" in Uniform Customs and Practice for Commercial Documentary Credits (UCP). The negotiation bank ignored this during examining documents. But when these documents were posted to the issuing bank , they were dishonoured. The seller made representations to issuing bank repeatedly, and explained the case. Finally, the issuing bank accepted the documents. But seller suffered the loss of interest from late payment. Please explain it.

Chapter 9 Export Documentation

Learning Objectives

1. To understand the significance of documentation
2. To master the basic requirements for documentation
3. To master the prerequisites of documentation
4. To understand the types of export documents
5. To know clause concerning documents in the sales contract

Key Words

Commercial invoice; Transport documents; Insurance documents; Ocean bill of lading; Shipped B/L; Anti - dated B/L; Certificate of origin; Inspection certificate; Packing list

An important part of export practice and management is a good comprehension of the various documents involved in processing the export consignment. Moreover, the need to understand the role of such documents and their limitations together with likely problems which they may encounter is likewise important. If an exporter has any doubt over the role of, or query over, a particular document the best course to follow is to contact his or her bank or freight forwarder.

In processing an export consignment involving extensive documentation, which is an invisible part of international trade. It refers to the preparation and examination of documents involved in a transaction. The importance of documentation, in a sense, can be amplified by saying that in some international transactions the exchange of documents takes priority over the exchange of goods. For most transactions in international trade today, without documentation there will be no possibility of transactions. Considering its importance, this chapter is solely devoted to the introduction to the basic requirements and information source of export documentation, and the explanation of the major documents used in export trade.

9.1 Significance of Documentation

The major purpose of documentation is to provide a specific and complete description of the goods so that they can be correctly processed for transport, insurance, payment, customs clearance, etc. This is well illustrated in those contracts signed under the trade terms such as FOB/FCA, CFR/CPT and CIF/CIP, where the delivery of goods from the seller to the buyer is symbolized by the handover of title documents, rather than the actual delivery of physical goods. As these types of transactions take a large portion of the total volume of trade, the importance of documentation hence can not be underestimated.

It is crucial for both the seller and buyer to acquire sufficient documentation skills to be qualified practitioners. Without the proper documents, neither seller could send goods out of their countries and collect payments, nor could buyer release goods without problems. A smooth transaction heavily relies on the correct preparation and presentation of relevant documents at different stages. In the meantime, compared with importers, exporters are more susceptible to the impact of documentation. It is an essential condition for exportation in the first place. In order to get through the mandatory supervision and control of the customs, presentation of required documents is the prerequisite. This also applies to importers when they are handling the import customs formalities. In addition, documents serve as the proof of fulfillment of contract for the seller.

Most of the obligations listed on the sales contract could be reflected on the availability of certain documents or the certain contents of a document. A certificate of quality may be required to guarantee the quality of the product. A bill of lading, for example, indicates the details of sellers' performance of transportation. Sometimes the buyer requires some documents to ensure that the goods delivered are what he expects. As a result, by evidence of documents, exporters prove that they have delivered the right goods at the right time to the right place in the right manner. Furthermore, in most cases exporters have to use documents in their collection of payment.

9.2 Basic Requirements for Documentation

So far, there has been no well-established standard for documentation in international trade. In addition, documentary requirements may differ from transaction to transaction and from country to country. The differences mainly lie in areas such as the types needed, the forms, content and languages used, etc. Whatever differences there might be, generally speaking, documentation for every transaction should meet such basic requirements as correctness, completeness, conciseness, cleanness and promptness.

Documents are considered complete when all necessary documents (including the types and number of originals and duplicates) are prepared and presented in a complete set.

Documents are correct and accurate if the content (including the exact words used) conforms to that in the letter of credit and format of the documents is in line with the requirement. Aside from these, correctness is met when the right types of documents are prepared and the right number of the originals and duplicates are presented.

To be concise, the seller shall make sure that all documents should avoid redundant, unnecessary or ambiguous words or expressions. Meanwhile, to be clean, documents should bear no marks correction on the face. When the above "Cs" are all met, the seller should then prepare the documents in time and present them within the time for presentation stipulated in the letter of credit. This lives up to the requirement of promptness.

In brief, exporters should attach great importance to documentation and make sure all documents meet the above requirements in order to ensure the smoothness and success of every single transaction. To achieve this, the seller has to check very carefully so that all documents for a transaction should not only be in strict compliance with the stipulations in the relevant contract and letter of credit but also be in consistency with each other. A checklist is provided to serve this purpose:

A checklist for documentation errors:

Avoid redundant, unnecessary or ambiguous words or expressions in such terms as the name, quality, quantity, time or place of shipment, etc.

Avoid correction on the face of the documents.

Check typing errors in the name of commodity, figures such as quantity, package number, unit price and total amount, insurance amount, insurance premium, etc.

Check spelling errors in the names and addresses of the parties concerned.

Check the title of each document to make them the same as the stipulation of the L/C. For instance, an Insurance Certificate is not acceptable when the L/C requires an Insurance Policy.

Mark the date of each document clearly.

Make sure some documents' reference numbers required to be mentioned in other documents are correctly presented.

Prepare exactly the same numbers of originals and duplicates as required.

All documents must be properly issued, signed and sealed by the right party.

Arrange the documents according to the order of the issuing date on the documents.

9.3 Prerequisites of Documentation

Considering the significance of documentation, it is a must for the exporter to present documents correctly and completely. To avoid errors and inconsistency among documents, it is important for him to be aware of the source of information for producing relevant documents. Usually, documents for an export transaction are to be prepared and examined based on the information from the sales contract, any payment related documents.

The preparation of documents must refer to the relevant payment instructions as well, especially when a documentary letter of credit is used. If a transaction is made with payment by L/C, the credit will list all the documents demanded as the condition for the issuing bank to hold the liability of payment, independent of the importer. Though the issuance of a letter of credit is based on the sales contract, once issued the credit becomes a solely independent document and the guideline for settlement of payment. Beyond all questions, therefore, sellers have to make sure that all documents prepared strictly comply with the stipulations in L/C.

For instance, a packing list provided by the manufacturers usually indicates detailed information about the commodity including such details as quantity, specification, gross weight, net weight and measurement. Contents of documents should also be subject to original information obtained from the original documents provided by manufacturers.

It is also important to note that the above information bases for documentation are not independent of each other. In other words, documents should be made out based on all these criteria simultaneously.

9.4 Export Documents

Some documents are used for very specific reason and then only required at certain stage, others such as commercial invoice and packing list are of more general use, appearing at most of the stages throughout the performance of a transaction. The successful completion of a single transaction may involve many documents. They may include government granted documents such as export license and quota, commercial documents such as commercial invoice and packing list, transportation documents such as bill of lading and shipping advice, insurance documents such as insurance policy or insurance certificate and financial documents such as letter of credit.

To fully illustrate the sophistication of export documentation, the next part will develop an extensive discussion about the various kinds of documents, following the fulfillment of a CIF contract which requires payment by L/C. The reason to choose such a contract is two folded. It can provide a full picture of the documentation practice with considerable satisfaction. The flowchart of export procedure mentioned in chapter 1 can be viewed as a blueprint for the discussion here. On one hand, transactions of this type are very common in practice; on the other hand, such contract requires the use of documents of the greatest number and variety when comparing with others.

9.4.1 Documents Required before or at Contract Negotiation

Before the negotiation of the contract, the seller is expected to apply for Export License or at least make sure that he is able to obtain it if the commodity he is to sell falls under the export control. During the negotiation of the terms and conditions of a contract, sometimes offers are made on a Proforma Invoice, which in this case should only be seen as a form of quotation. After acceptance is made at the end of the negotiation, the seller and the buyer will draft a sales contract including all the necessary information for a transaction. Details about a sales contract can be referred back to chapter 1.

(1) Export License

The goods under export control normally include the main raw materials, machinery or equipment in short supply, military or other goods relating to national security, and works of art and antiques which are of national, cultural or historical importance. In some cases the licensing system is used to implement government policy such as economic sanctions against certain countries. Export licenses are issued by the government or its authorized institutions and required at the time of customs clearance. An export license is the first document a seller has to prepare when he intends to export commodities that are under export control of his country.

(2) Proforma Invoice

A proforma invoice is a document similar to a commercial invoice and it contains the same information as those in the commercial invoice. It is a statement of sales, issued before a transaction has been concluded rather than a record of sales already effected. It is usually issued by the seller as a response to an inquiry from the potential buyer.

If an irrevocable letter of credit is required by the exporter, the importer will use the pro forma invoice to substantiate the need for a letter of credit to his bank. A proforma invoice is needed in the following circumstances. Sometimes it is needed by the importer to apply for the import license and foreign exchange. A proforma invoice, in some other circumstances, may be required by the importer to help him apply for the relevant letter of credit. Therefore, a proforma invoice has no legal status and serves only as a means to facilitate the buyer to accomplish the above-mentioned tasks.

9. 4. 2 Documents Involved during Goods Preparation

After the seller has got the goods prepared and packed, he will then issue a commercial invoice and a packing list. Both documents are very important and required in all main stages of an export procedure. In many countries, especially in developing countries usually enforce an import license System or an Import Quota System. Importers must apply for the necessary import license or Foreign Exchange and they may not import any goods without the approval of an Import license or the allocation of foreign Exchange. And their application has to be supported by an informal invoice, a pro forma invoice, issued by the foreign exporter showing the name of the commodity, specifications, unit price.

(1) Commercial invoice

A commercial invoice is one of the most important documents used in international trade. It is the exporting firm's invoice, addressed to the foreign importer, describing key transaction details particularly the total value and claiming for payment. It is used as the foundation for keeping accounts and making declarations to the customs. It is often one of the documents required for payment settlement. The commercial invoice serves as a record of the essential details of a transaction. Usually, it includes the basic information:

A commercial invoice should include the following parts:

◇buyer's reference (order number/ indent number)

◇invoice number and date

◇export or import license number

◇method of dispatch

◇shipment terms

◇names and addresses of the seller and buyer

◇country from which the shipment is made

◇description of the goods: Quantity, weight or measurements of the goods; Unit price; Total amount payable, including price of goods, freight, insurance and so on

◇rebate incentives or similar incentives

◇signature of the exporter

Commercial invoices are usually required by all relevant parties involved in the transaction such as buyers, the paying bank, sellers and their bank, customs authorities in the exporting and importing countries, carriers and their agents at the port of shipment and discharge. At most cases, the buyer should check the each parts of the commercial invoice to whether the goods delivered to him conform to the terms and conditions stipulated in the contract. The bank also needs the commercial invoice together with other documents such as the bill of lading and the insurance certificate to effect payment. The customs needs the commercial invoice to calculate duties.

In the case of a transaction on L/C payment, it should be noted that according to UCP600, a commercial invoice must be issued by the beneficiary to the applicant in the L/C.

(2) Packing List

A packing list is one of the documents required for mandatory inspection, export and import customs formalities and negotiation of payment. It is a supplementary document to the commercial invoice used to make up the deficiency of an invoice by giving all the necessary particulars of the goods. A packing list is a document made out by the seller stating the detailed content of each individual shipment. It is also used to facilitate the general checking of goods before shipment by the seller. The buyer also needs the packing list to check the goods on their arrival at the destination. In addition, packing lists can facilitate insurance claims and claims settlements in case of loss or damage.

A packing list usually contains the following details:

A packing list should include

◇invoice number

◇buyer and consignee

◇country of origin

◇vessel or flight date

◇port or airport of loading and discharge

◇place of delivery

◇shipping marks

◇container number

◇weight and/or volume of the goods

◇full details of the goods

9.4.3 Documents Concerning Mandatory Inspection

If the goods need to go through mandatory inspection required by the stipulations of the government or the contract, the seller has to apply for it by filling out an inspection application form also known as Proposal Form. After inspection, if the goods are up to the required standard, the seller will receive the relevant inspection certificate from the inspection body.

(1) Export Commodity Inspection Application

The State Administration for Commodity Inspection, in the light of the needs in the development of foreign trade, makes, adjusts and publishes a List of Import and Export Commodities Subject to Inspection by the Commodity Inspection Authorities. Export commodity inspection application is one of the essential domestic documents for the export of many commodities in China. The export of commodities on this list is not allowed until they have been inspected. Therefore, if the goods of the seller are on this list, he is required to fill out an application form to apply for inspection.

Upon submission, he will also be asked to present other documents such as the sales contract, the letter of credit, the commercial invoice, and the packing list. In some cases, only the inspection report supplied by the manufacturer is required.

(2) Certificate of Inspection

An inspection certificate may be issued by a government institution, surveyors of chamber of commerce or an independent service company. Inspection certificates are required when the goods are cleared for export and import and when the seller negotiates payment at the bank. The inspection certificate is a document indicating the results of the inspection of the goods in terms of quality, quantity or any other element that has been specified. Its primary function is to ensure that the goods in question are meeting the relevant requirements stipulated by certain authorities.

The types of inspection certificates used in international trade vary greatly. They include certificates to cover such issues as quality, weight, quantity, veterinary standards, health, disinfection, fumigation and phytosanitary. Common types of inspection certificates include Inspection Certificate of Weight, Inspection Certificate of Quality, Inspection Certificate of Quantity, Inspection Certificate of Health, and Inspection Certificate of Quarantine, and Veterinary, and so on. The employment of certificates differs greatly among categories of products.

9.4.4 Documents Involved in Transportation

For booking shipping space or chartering vessel, the seller is required to fill out a booking note. In return, the seller will receive a shipping order from the carrier or the agent.

(1) Booking Note (B/N)

When shipping space is booked or a ship is chartered, the carrier or the agent will inform the exporter of the particulars by means of a shipping order (S/O). A booking note is a form which is to be filled out by the exporter providing the carrier or the shipping agent all the necessary particulars about the shipment when an exporter intends to book shipping space on a liner or charter a ship for the carriage of export goods.

(2) Shipping Order

This shipping order will be presented to the carrier at the time of loading. Without a shipping order, goods are not allowed to be loaded. A shipping order is a notice to the shipper (exporter) from the carrier or the agent, indicating that goods are received for loading. Thus a shipping order contains detailed information concerning the sailing, goods, place of loading, etc. When the carrier or the agents are in receipt of the goods, they will mark and sign the shipping order properly so that the goods can be ready for export clearance. After the customs clearance, the Customs will stencil on the face of the shipping order evidencing that goods are cleared for export.

9.4.5 Documents Needed for Export Customs Clearance

To clear goods for export, exporters should declare the export goods to the Customs by filling in the relevant customs forms such as the Customs Declaration for Export Commodity (used in China). The export goods can not be loaded for shipment until they are cleared for export. After customs clearance, the Customs or the authorized institution will either stencil on the face of the shipping order or issue a customs clearance for export commodity to the seller, evidencing that goods are cleared for export.

(1) Customs Declaration for Export Commodity

In addition, some supporting documents may need to be submitted as well such as a commercial invoice, a packing list, an export license (if required), a copy of the sales contract and an inspection certificate (in case of mandatory inspection) and a shipping order. To clear the export commodity for export customs, the seller should fill out a customs declaration, which will be submitted to the Customs or relative authorized institutions.

(2) Customs Clearance for Export Commodity

It usually shows customs clearance number, the information of the goods, the contract number, and the voyage. A customs clearance is issued by the Customs or the authorized institution evidencing the customs clearance for the export commodity. In some cases, a shipping order with the signature by the customs or their agent can serve the same purpose. A customs clearance is required when the goods are to be loaded.

9.4.6 Documents Received after Shipment

To ensure sufficient notice about the shipment, a shipping advice which is issued by the carrier or the shipping agent at the time of loading shall be forwarded to the importer by the seller without delay. After they are cleared for export and the customs clearance is obtained, the goods can be arranged to be loaded on the vessel. For his goods to be loaded, the seller shall produce the shipping order and/or the customs clearance to the carrier. Upon completion of the shipment, the exporter will get a bill of lading issued by the carrier.

(1) Mate's Receipt

A mate's receipt is a document issued and signed by the mate of the shipping vessel indicating that the goods have been received by the vessel for loading or that the goods have been loaded on board the vessel. The seller can exchange the mate's receipt for the on-board bill of lading at a later time.

(2) Shipping Advice

The purpose of the shipping advice is to notify the buyer that goods are loaded and that he can proceed to prepare for making payment and for receiving the goods at the destination. A shipping advice is a notice of the shipment details which is issued by the carrier when goods are loaded on board the vessel and given by the seller (shipper) to the buyer (consignee). If the contract is concluded under FOB, CFR or CPT, the seller also has to pass the shipping advice to the buyer so as to facilitate the buyer to arrange insurance.

A shipping advice should be delivered to the buyer with no delay, or within the period stipulated in the sales contract or letter of credit. Occasionally a copy of the shipping advice may be required for the purpose of payment.

A shipping advice should include:

◇the number of packages shipped

◇the total gross and net weight

◇the packing

◇the date and number of the B/L

◇the container number and seal number (if container is used)

◇ETD (estimated time of departure)

◇ETA (estimated time of arrival)

◇the name of the port of shipment and port of destination

(3) Bill of Lading

It evidences the receipt of goods by the carrier and serves as a contract of carriage between the shipper and the carrier at the same time. A bill of lading is a document which is issued by an ocean carrier to a shipper with whom the carrier has entered into a contract for the carriage of goods. Most importantly, a bill of lading is a property document representing title to the goods, thereupon the most needed document for the settlement of payment.

9.4.7 Insurance Documents

Insurance is normally obtained after the completion of the loading at the port of shipment. To take out insurance, an insurance application form, also known as the proposal form has to be filled out and submitted to an insurance company for the purchase of cargo insurance. When the application is accepted, an insurance policy or certificate will be issued by the insurer. Under a CIF contract, it is the exporter's obligation to cover insurance for the export goods.

(1) Insurance Application Form

After all necessary formalities concerning insurance is completed, insurance documents such as insurance policy are to be issued by the insurance company or their agent. An insurance application form, also known as insurance proposal form, is to be filled out by the insured, providing all information about the parties concerned and the shipment involved. The specific information may cover the name of the insured party, the description of the cargoes insured, the voyage insured, the insurance amount, the insurance coverage, etc. Documents needed for submission are the commercial invoice, the packing list, the port of shipment and destination, etc.

(2) Insurance Policy

An insurance policy is the contract made between the insurer and the insured, which is issued by the insurer and confirmed by the insured. In addition, in case of loss or damage, the insurance policy or certificate is the essential basis for claim and claim settlement. In an international trade transaction, an insurance policy or certificate forms part of the chief documents for transactions on a CIF or CIP basis.

9.4.8 Documents for Bank Negotiation

The documents needed for submission generally include the commercial invoice, the packing list, the bill of lading, the insurance policy, etc. Apart from these documents, there are also other types of documents required by the buyer and submitted to the bank for negotiation. Among them, the certificate of origin, consular invoice and customs invoice are worth mentioning. The last and the most important thing the seller has to do is to collect and check all documents specified in the L/C and present them within period required to the negotiating bank for payment settlement. While doing so, he should also fill out a bill of exchange (a draft).

(1) Bill of Exchange (B/E) or Draft

A bill of exchange (B/E) or draft is an unconditional order in writing signed by one party (drawer) requesting a second party (drawee/payer) to make payment in lawful money immediately or at a determined future time to a third party (payee).

It should be noted that a draft drawn under L/C is usually required to indicate the relevant L/C in the drawn clause and the B/E amount should in no case exceeds the L/C amount.

Usually, a draft is drawn and presented by the seller to the buyer or their banks as the payment instrument. Strictly speaking, a draft drawn under L/C is a payment instrument rather than a kind of the documents, though in practice it is accepted as one of the documents required for payment.

(2) Certificate of Origin

A certificate of origin should states the nature, quantity, value, and the place of manufacture. It is a document certifying the origin of the goods or the place/country of manufacturing. In China the certificate of origin is generally issued by two governmental authorities: one is the Entry – Exit Inspection and Quarantine of The People's Republic of China, the other is the China Chamber of International Commerce. In many countries the certificate of origin is usually prepared by the exporter, signed in the presence of a notary public institution and certified by a non-governmental commercial organization acceptable to the destination country.

There are normally two types of certificates of origin: one is the certificate of origin; the other is the generalized system of preferences certificate of origin (GSP Certificate of Origin). The GSP Certificate of Origin is a special type of certificate of origin used to obtain the preferential customs duty treatment imposed by some developed countries on import commodities from some developing countries.

In normal cases, the seller can start to prepare the certificate of origin when the commercial invoice is ready. Different types of certificate of origin may be made at different stage of the export procedure. However, in some cases, for example GSP Form E, the issuance of a certificate of origin is made based on the submission of both the commercial invoice and the bill of lading.

The main purpose of the certificate of origin is to prove the origin of the goods based on which the import Customs can set import duties and implement the applicable import controls such as sanctions, quotas, anti-dumping duties or favorable treatments.

(3) Consular Invoice

Such a form is required by certain countries in order to compile statistics, control imports, collect import duties and check the origin of goods and the credit of the exporter. A consular invoice is a form, usually only obtainable from the importing country's consulate in the exporting country, on which the seller or its agent must enter a detailed description of the goods being shipped.

Most of the consular invoices are in the language of the country to which the goods are shipped so it is usually considered as the most difficult document of all and must be filled in with special care. A consular invoice shall carry such information as the name of the goods, the number of the items, their weight, the value and origin of the goods and a declaration that the information given is correct.

(4) Customs Invoice

Generally, the invoice may include information required by the import Customs that is not stated on an ordinary commercial invoice. A customs invoice is one of the documents made out on a special form prescribed by the customs authorities of the importing country.

9.5 Clause Concerning Documents in the Sales Contract

In some cases, documents required are stipulated in the contract. In trade practice, stipulations concerning documents may not necessarily appear in every contract. They may constitute part or whole of the contents under the column "Remarks" or they may be mentioned in the attachment to a contract. It is not uncommon, however, that there are no such stipulations in the contract at all. In that case, the agreement concerning documents remains an oral one between the buyer and the seller and is binding upon the parties concerned. And it is advisable that the relevant stipulations be laid down in the contract in terms of the types, issuing authorities, number of originals or copies, and etc.

Under a L/C transaction, sellers are paid against documents presented; buyers pay and receive goods against documents released; and the banks deal in the documents instead of the goods. While it may not appear in a sales contract, the stipulation "Documents Required" is always an necessary part of a documentary L/C. Documents play such an essential role in L/C transaction that documents to be presented (or to be required) should be clearly stipulated in the relevant letter of credit.

Documents required:

◇Insurance Policy or Certificate in triplicate covering War Risk and All Risks irrespective of percentage for 110% of the invoice value

◇Signed commercial invoice in triplicate indicating the contract number made out to order of XXX company

◇Full set (3/3) plus two copies of clean "on board" marine bill of lading

◇Packing list in duplicate, indicating gross weight and net weight, measurements and quantity of the package

◇Weight and quality certificate in triplicate indicating the number of bags shipped, total gross and net weight, packing, actual quality analysis result issued by CIQ

◇GSP certificate of origin Form A in duplicate issued by CIQ

◇Fumigation/disinfection certificate in triplicate issued by CIQ

◇Health certificate in triplicate issued by CIQ for the importation

◇Phytosanitary certificate in triplicate issued by CIQ

◇One complete set of non-negotiable shipping documents has been sent to the applicant by fax (Fax No. XXXXXXXX) within 4 days of the shipment date

9.6 Summary

Documents for an export transaction are to be prepared and checked on all the bases such as contract, credit, and original information from the manufacturers.

From the perspective of sellers, documentation is not only one of his basic obligations under the contract, but also an important task concerning the collection of the export cargo proceeds.

Major export documents include the bill of exchange (draft), invoice, packing list, insurance policy, bill of lading, inspection certificate and certificate of origin, etc.

Generally speaking, the basic requirements for documentation are correctness, completeness, conciseness, cleanness and promptness.

Any negligence in documentation may hinder the fulfillment of the contract and might result in serious problems.

Exercises

Ⅰ. Choices

1. In an international trade transaction, an insurance policy or certificate forms part of the chief documents for transactions on a ________ basis.

A. FOB or CIF　　B. CIF or CIP　　C. CIF or CFR　　D. CIP or CPR

2. Under an ________ transaction, sellers are paid against documents presented; buyers pay and receive goods against documents released; and the banks deal in the documents in-

stead of the goods.

A. L/C B. D/P C. D/A D. T/T

3. The ________ is the basis of any other documents produced.

A. sales contract B. letter of credit

C. commercial invoice D. packing list

4. After ________ acceptance, which is made at the end of the negotiation, the seller and the buyer will draft a sales contract including all the necessary information for a transaction.

A. commercial invoice B. export license

C. pro forma invoice D. customs invoice

5. A ________ is the exporting firm's invoice, addressed to the foreign importer, describing key transaction details particularly the total value and claiming for payment.

A. commercial invoice B. export license

C. customs declaration D. customs invoice

6. A (An) ________ is a document indicating the results of the inspection of the goods in terms of the quality, quantity or any other element that has been specified.

A. inspection certificate B. inspection application

C. certificate of origin D. inspection certificate of quality

7. A (An) ________ is dispatched by the carrier or the agent to inform the exporter of the particulars of shipment arrangement after shipping space is booked.

A. booking note B. bill of lading

C. shipping advice D. shipping order

8. In international trade practice, stipulations concerning documents are an indispensable part of ________.

A. the sales contract

B. the documentary L/C

C. either the sales contract or the documentary L/C

D. both the sales contract and the documentary L/C

Ⅱ. True or false statements

1. Since stipulations concerning documents may not appear in every contract, documents are not so important in an international trade transaction. ( )

2. The inspection certificate is a document indicating the results of the inspection of the goods in terms of quality, quantity or any other element that has been specified. ( )

3. An export license is the only document a seller has to prepare when he intends to export commodities that are under export control of his country. ( )

4. Proforma invoice is a document the same as a commercial invoice and it contains the same information as those in the commercial invoice. ( )

5. There are no needs for documents that are correct and accurate if the content (inclu-

ding the exact words used) conforms to that in the letter of credit and format of the documents is in line with the requirement. ( )

6. If there is a discrepancy between the amount in a draft and that in the L/C, this draft is not acceptable to the issuing bank. ( )

7. A commercial invoice is the exporting firm's invoice, addressed to the foreign importer, describing key transaction details particularly the total value and claiming for payment. ( )

8. A packing list is a document made out by the seller stating the detailed content of each individual shipment. ( )

Ⅲ. Explain the following terms

1. Proforma Invoice

2. shipping order

3. certificate of origin

Ⅳ. Short questions

1. What document would be involved in transportation?

2. What documents should require after shipment?

3. What are the main documents required for the L/C transaction?

Ⅴ. Case study

Company A has contracted to export "Cider" to Italy on CIF terms with payment by irrevocable L/C at sight. The goods are prepared based on the contract and the name "Cider" is used. However, as the name in the coming L/C is "Apple Wine", "Apple Wine" is adopted in all the documents prepared by Company A so as to ensure that the documents strictly conform to the L/C stipulations. On arrival at the port of destination, the goods are detained by the Italian Customs due to the discrepancy between the documents presented and the covering goods. Consequently, the Italian buyer claims for compensation. Is Company A liable for the Buyer's loss? What should Company A have to do to avoid such a dispute?

Chapter 10 Inspection, Claim, Force Majeure and Arbitration

Learning Objectives

1. To master the definition of commodity inspection
2. To understand the type of commodity inspection
3. To understand the disputes and claims
4. To master Force Majeure
5. To master the definition of arbitration

Key Words

Force majeure; Material breach; Inspection; Claims; Arbitration; Litigation

In export trade, disputes between the buyers and the sellers may arise at anytime despite the fact that both parties of the sales contract work very carefully in the performance of the contract. In such cases, with a view to maintaining good relationship, the two parties of a dispute are normally recommended to rely on friendly negotiation and mediation. However, in case these means are not workable, the disputes may be submitted for arbitration or even litigation.

Inspection is an indispensable clause of a contract, and its aim is to protect the interests of both the buyer and the seller. Therefore, it is of great significance in international trade. Laws and regulations in various countries as well as international conventions have imposed inspection liabilities on both the sellers and the buyers. The failure in inspection and unfavorable inspection results may result in disputes between the buyers and the sellers and claims lodged by one party against the other.

10.1 Commodity Inspection

Commodity inspection is the inspection conducted by an authorized third party to testify whether the quality, quantity, weight, package, etc. are the same as those specified in the contract. In international trade, the quality and quantity of the goods delivered by the seller should be in conformity with the terms of the contract and should be packed in the manner required in the contract. After inspection, certain kinds of certificates can be issued and serve as evidence in the performance of the contract.

10.1.1 Time and Place of Inspection

The inspection of the goods can be conducted at various stages of the trade process. Before delivery, the manufacturers should make a precise and comprehensive inspection of the goods with regard to its quality, specifications, quantity or weight, and issue an inspection certificate certifying the technical data or the result of the inspection. Before shipment, the authorized department in the exporting country will conduct mandatory inspection as to the quality and quantity or weight of the goods and issue the relevant inspection certificates which serve as the basis for the negotiation of payments by the seller. After the arrival of the goods at the destination, the goods may be further inspected by relevant departments in the importing country, the unfavorable result of which serves as the basis for the claim made by the buyer.

Therefore, it is important to make clear when and where inspection should be conducted. CISG provides that except where the parties have agreed otherwise, the buyer has the right to inspect the goods and the time and place of inspection should be stipulated in detail in the contract.

There are generally three ways to stipulate the place and time of inspection in the sales contract: inspection at the factory or at the port of shipment, inspection at the port of destination, and inspection at the port of shipment and re-inspection at the port of destination.

(1) Inspection at the Factory or at the Port of Shipment

Inspection at the factory or at the port of shipment refers to the inspection conducted by an authorized party agreed upon by both parties of the sales contract to testify the quality, quantity, weight, package, etc. of the goods at the factory or at the port of shipment before the delivery of the goods. Another name for this is known as shipping quality and weight. The inspection certificate(s) thus issued will be considered final for the delivery of the goods by the seller, in other words, the seller will not be obliged to any change to the goods in transit after the goods has been inspected before delivery. Although the buyer can re-inspect the goods at the port of destination, normally he cannot claim for compensation based on the result of the re-inspection. Therefore, this method is more favorable to the seller.

(2) Inspection at the Port of Destination

Inspection at the port of destination is also referred to as landed quality and weight. It indicates the inspection conducted by an authorized party within the time period stipulated in the sales contract to testify the quality, quantity, weight, package, etc. of the goods at the port of destination. The inspection certificate (s) issued in the destination country is considered final for the delivery of the goods by the seller. Under this arrangement, if any discrepancies are found between the actual goods and terms described in the sales contract, the buyer can retain the fight of claim for compensation. Therefore, the buyer often prefers this method of inspection.

(3) Inspection at the Port of Shipment and Re-inspection at the Port of Destination

As discussed above, either way in stipulating time and place for inspection is satisfactory to both parties. To avoid further disputes, a third method has been created, stating that the inspection certificate (s) issued by the authorized party at the port of shipment can be used as one of the documents for the seller to settle payment after the delivery of the goods. However, the buyer retains the right to re-inspect the goods at the port of destination. If he obtains from an authorized party designated in the contract at the port of destination the inspection certificate (s) showing that the goods received are not as described in the contract, the buyer has the right to claim for compensation from the seller as long as there are evidences to show that the seller should be responsible for the discrepancies. Obviously, this method benefits both sides to a certain degree and therefore is widely adopted in international trade practice.

10.1.2 Inspection Bodies

In international trade, inspection certificates should be issued by authorized inspection bodies; otherwise, they will not be accepted as effective documents. Therefore before getting your goods inspected, you shall know something about the inspection bodies and their respective roles played in the inspection practice.

(1) Types of Inspection Body

There are normally two main types of inspection body: governmental and non-governmental inspection bodies. The former is owned or supervised by governments and specializes in inspection of particular commodities or commodities subject to mandatory inspection by governments. The Food and Drugs Administration (FDA) in USA is one such organization. A non-governmental inspection body is a private body that enjoys the same legal status as notary organizations and undertakes commodity inspections internationally. The most notable bodies of this type are Societe Generable De Surveillance S. A. (SGS) in Geneva Swiss, Lloyds Surveyors in Britain and Underwriters Laboratories (UL) in USA.

In China, it is SACI (the State Administration for Commodity Inspection) and its designated provincial divisions which are in charge of the inspection of Import and export commodities throughout the country. Inspections are carried out in accordance with the Law of the

People's Republic of China on Import and Export Commodity, Inspection (hereafter called the Law) and the Regulations for the Implementation of the Law of the People's Republic of China on Import and Export Inspection (hereafter called the Regulations).

(2) Tasks of Inspection Body

The basic task of the inspection authorities is to inspect goods for import and export. Import and export commodity inspections in China fall into two categories: statutory inspection and non-statutory inspection. Statutory inspection refers to the mandatory inspection carded out by the governmental bodies on imports and exports. While statutory inspection is a must, non-statutory inspection, on the other hand, is usually made on a random basis. SACI, in the light of the needs in developing foreign trade, makes, adjusts and publishes a List of Import and Export Commodities Subject to Inspection by the Commodity Inspection Authorities. As an exporter or importer, one should check the list of commodities in advance so as to ensure that he won't skip his obligation concerning commodity inspection.

Aside from inspecting the commodity for exports and imports, a second task falls upon SACI is to exercise supervision and control over the inspection conducted by the inspection agencies and personnel designated or accredited by the consignees, consignors, manufacturers, trading units, storage and transport units of the import and export commodities.

Finally, SACI and its designated or approved inspection agencies may accept the entrustment of the trading parties or by foreign inspection bodies for surveying services of import and export commodities within the specified scope and may issue certificates of survey.

10.1.3 Inspection Standard

Inspection certificates are issued only when they are proved to be up to certain standards. Then what standards should be followed as far as commodity inspection is concerned that inspection on import and export commodities performed in the commodity inspection authorities shall cover quality, specifications, quantity, weight, packing and the requirements for safety and hygiene. If the mandatory standards or other inspection standards which must be complied with are specified in the Law and the Regulations, the inspection, of course, shall be performed according to the standards as specified in the Law and the Regulation.

However, in the absence of the mandatory standards or other inspection standards, the inspection shall be performed according to the standards agreed upon in the international trade contracts. One thing that calls for attention is that if the trade is conducted against the sample, the inspection shall be performed simultaneously according to the sample provided.

In the process of inspection, it is likely that the standards specified in the Law and the Regulations are not consistent with those agreed upon by the sellers and buyers in the sales contract. In such cases, if the compulsory standards or other inspection standards specified in the Law and the Regulations are higher than the standards agreed upon in the contract, the inspection shall be conducted subject to the higher standard. If the standards specified in the

Law and the Regulations are lower than the standards agreed upon in the contract, the inspection shall be conducted according to the standards agreed upon in the contract.

Similarly, if the trade is conducted against the sample, the inspection shall be performed according to the sample provided.

Finally, in the case where there lack the inspection standards specified in the Law and the Regulations, and where the inspection standards are either not agreed upon or are unclear in the contract, the inspection shall be conducted according to the standards of the manufacturing country, or relevant international standards or the standards designated by the state inspection agency.

10.1.4 Inspection Certificate

After the commodities are inspected and proved up to the standard(s) recognized by the inspection authorities, the inspection authorities then will issue inspection statements. The inspection statement issued by the commodity inspection authorities after the commodities have undergone inspection is called the inspection certificate. The inspection certificates usually issued by the Chinese inspection authorities are as follows:

Inspection Certificate of Quality. This certifies that the quality and specifications of import and export commodities are in conformity with the contract stipulation.

Inspection Certificate of Weight or Quantity. This certifies that the weight or quantity of import and export commodities is in conformity with the contract stipulation.

Inspection Certificate of Value. This certifies that the price of import and export commodities in the invoice is a true reflection of the value of the goods transacted.

Inspection Certificate of Origin. This certifies that the name of the place is where the export commodity has been produced or manufactured.

Sanitary Inspection Certificate. This certifies that foods and animal products for eating are up to standards for export.

Veterinary inspection Certificate. This certifies that the animals to be exported are in a condition good enough for export.

Disinfection Inspection Certificate. This certifies that animal products to be exported have been disinfected.

Inspection Certificate on Damaged Cargo. This certifies the degree to which the goods imported have been damaged and the causes of the damage.

10.1.5 Inspection Clause in the Sales Contract

The inspection clauses in international trade contracts usually contain stipulations on the inspection right, the time and place of inspection or re-inspection, the inspection body, the inspection items and the inspection certificates. An example of inspection clause in the trade contract is as follows:

"It is mutually agreed that the Certificate of Quality and Quantity/Weight issued by the Manufacturer shall be part of the documents for payment under the relevant L/C. In case, the quality, quantity or weight of the goods are found not in conformity with those stipulated in this contract after re-inspection by the China Exit and Entry Inspection and Quarantine Bureau within. . . days after discharge of the goods at the port/place of destination, the Buyers shall return the goods to or lodge a claim against the Sellers for compensation of losses upon the strength of Inspection Certificate issued by the said Bureau, with the exception of those claims for which the insurers or the carriers are liable. All expenses (including inspection fees) and losses arising from the return of the goods or claims should be borne by the Sellers. In such case, the Buyers may, if so requested, send a sample of the goods in question to the Sellers, provided that the sampling is feasible."

10.2 Disputes and Claims

As has been shown in the first chapter, the last stage in the international trade procedure is settlement of disputes. Although it is not necessarily a stage for every trade transaction, as disputes from both the seller and buyer are sometimes unavoidable, it is important as well to deal with it here.

10.2.1 Disputes

In international trade, disputes arise from time to time for various reasons, for instance, a buyer may breach a contract by refusing to accept goods with improper reasons or failing to pay for the goods when payment is due; a seller may violate a contract by failing to make an agreed delivery, delivering goods that do not conform to the contract. Breach of contract means the refusal or failure by one party of a contract to fulfill an obligation imposed on him under that contract. In international trade practice, the main reasons for disputes can be concluded into three categories: breach of contract by the seller, breach of contract by the buyer and breach of contract by both the seller and the buyer.

(1) Breach of Contract by the Seller

A seller may be considered to have breached a contract if he:

① fails to make delivery of the goods within the shipment time stipulated in the contract;

② fails to deliver the goods;

③ fails to deliver the goods that are in conformity with the contract or the L/C in respect of quality, specifications, quantity and packing, etc.;

④ fails to present the shipping documents within the stipulated time period or the documents presented are incomplete and inadequate.

(2) Breach of Contract by the Buyer

Considering the different obligations undertaken by the buyer, a buyer may breach a contract if he:

① fails to open the relevant L/C within the stipulated period under an L/C payment;

② fails to accept the goods without sufficient reasons under an L/C payment;

③ fails to dispatch the vessel or notify the seller with sufficient information about the vessel according to the stipulations in the contract under FOB terms.

(3) Breach of Contract by Both Parties

Breach of contract by both parties is not rare to see in both export and import trade. For example, both parties may be held responsible due to misunderstanding or miscomprehension of a contract that is not clearly stipulated. Different interpretation or understanding of the terms may arise if vague expressions like "immediate shipment", "quantity about 300M/T", "destination: China Ports", etc. are used in the contract.

As the sales contract has a legal binding force upon both contracting parties, any party who has violated the contract shall be legally held responsible for the breach, and the injured party is entitled to remedies according to the stipulations of the contract or the relevant laws.

10.2.2 Claims

When disputes arise, the injured party usually will lodge a claim against the party concerned for compensation. Thus, claim can be defined as a demand made by one party upon another for a certain amount of payment on account of a loss sustained through its negligence. There are generally three types of claim related to international trade practice: claim regarding selling and buying, claim regarding transportation and claim concerning insurance. In this section, only the first type of claim will be covered as this is the only type of claim that is made between the two parties of the sales contract.

In import and export trade, claims regarding quality and quantity or weight are common, even though proper inspection of the goods has been conducted by designated surveyors or public inspection bureaus. The goods may have been damaged or lost during transit. Therefore, it is necessary to include a Discrepancy and Claim Clause in a contract. In case the goods delivered are inconsistent with the contract stipulations, the buyer should make a claim against the seller within the time limit of re-inspection under the support of an inspection certificate or survey report.

10.2.3 Claim Clause in the Sales Contract

As is well known, disputes are very common in international trade and are detrimental to the business relationship between the buyer and the seller. To avoid or to properly handle future disputes, it is necessary to include a claim clause in a contract. Normally, there are two ways to stipulate claim clause in the contract: Discrepancy and Claim Clause and Penalty

Clause.

Discrepancy and Claim Clause

In most trade contracts, it is only the Discrepancy and Claim Clause that is stipulated. The clause in this respect normally stipulates the relevant evidences or proofs to be presented and the relevant authoritative body for issuing the certificate. The evidence or proofs provided should be complete and clear, and the authority should be competent in issuing the relevant certificates. Otherwise, claims can be refused by the other party.

Besides the evidence to be presented, this clause shall also include a period within which a claim is lodged. Technically, the period for claim refers to the effective period in which the claimant can make a claim against a party for breach. Claims made after the agreed period can be refused by the party in breach. Generally speaking, a period that is too long may put the seller under a heavy responsibility and a period that is too short may make it impossible for the buyer to file a claim. Therefore, the period for a claim should be made as specific as possible in the clause.

Claim should be filed within XXX days,

① after the arrival of the goods at the port of destination;

② after the discharging of the goods at the port of destination;

③ after the arrival of the goods at the business place of the buyer;

④ after inspection.

If a claim is justified, prompt and well-supported, it can be settled in the following ways: making a refund, compensating for direct losses or expenses, selling the goods at lower prices or replacing the defective goods with good ones. As the discrepancy and claim clause is closely related to the inspection clause, they are combined as the inspection & claim clause in some contracts.

(2) Penalty Clause

For transactions where goods in substantial quantity or large mechanical equipment is concerned, a penalty clause will be stipulated in the contract together with a discrepancy and claim clause in case one party fails to implement the contract such as non-delivery, delayed delivery, delayed opening of L/C, etc. Under this clause, the party who has failed to carry out the contract must pay another party a fine, a certain percentage of total contract value. The provisions for the amount and the penalty ceiling should also be included in the clause.

Example of Discrepancy and Claim Clause in the sales contract

"Claim: Any claim by the Buyers regarding the goods shipped shall be filed within 30 days after arrival of the goods at the port of the destination specified in the relative Bill of Lading and supported by a survey report issued by a surveyor approved by the Sellers. Claims in respect of matters within responsibility of insurance company, shipping company/other transportation organization will not be considered or entertained by the Sellers."

Example of penalty Clauses in the Sales Contract penalty Clauses regarding sellers' delay in delivery:

"Should the Sellers fail to make delivery on time as stipulated in the contract, the Buyers shall agree to postpone the delivery on condition that the Sellers agree to pay a penalty which shall be deducted by the paying bank from the payment under negotiation, or by the Buyers direct at the time of payment. The rate of penalty is charged at 0.5% of the total value of the goods whose delivery has been delayed for every seven days, odd days less than seven days should be counted as seven days. But the total amount of penalty, however, shall not exceed 5% of the total value of the goods involved in the late delivery. In case the Sellers fail to make delivery ten weeks later than the time of shipment stipulated in the contract, the Buyers shall have the right to cancel the contract and the Sellers, in spite of the cancellation, shall still pay the aforesaid penalty to the Buyers without delay."

Example of penalty Clauses in the Sales Contract penalty Clauses regarding buyers' delay in opening of L/C:

"Should the Buyers for their own sake fail to open the Letter of Credit within the time stipulate in the contract, the Buyers shall pay a penalty to the Sellers? The penalty shall be charged at the rate of 0.5% of the amount of the letter of credit for every ten days of delay in opening the letter of credit, however, the total penalty shall not exceed 5% of the total value of the credit which the Buyers should have opened. Any fractional days less than ten days shall be deemed to be ten days for the calculation of penalty. The penalty shall be the sole compensation for the damage caused by such delay."

10.3 Force Majeure

After the conclusion of a contract, some events beyond the parties' control may occasionally take place, which makes it impossible for the parties concerned to fulfill the contract. In order to safeguard their interests, the parties of the contract usually stipulate a Force Majeure Clause in the Sales Contract.

10.3.1 Force Majeure Clause in the Sales Contract

Force majeure, also named Act of God, is a French word meaning "superior force". It refers to an event that can neither be anticipated nor be reduced to control. Force majeure events enable a seller to avoid his contractual obligations without paying a compensation or penalty. A force majeure clause in the sales contract should include the scope of force majeure events, time limit of notice to the other contractor, certificates and the agencies who issue them, and the relevant consequences.

(1) Scope of Force Majeure Events

Since there is still no definite agreement as to which events should be regarded as force majeure, the seller and the buyer usually stipulate in their contract the scope of force majeure events. Force majeure events include certain natural disasters such as fire, flood, storm, heavy snow, earthquake and social disturbances like war, strike and sanctions. However, with a view to clarifying what the term of force majeure covers under a particular contract, different methods of stipulation have been adopted.

△ Stipulation Made in a General Way

This means the force majeure events in the contract are not made specific but stated in a more general way by simply adopting the wording "force majeure events".

As this way of stipulation doesn't list the specific force majeure events, it is ambiguous and is likely to give rise to different interpretations from the perspectives of different parties, it is not suggested that this be adopted in practice.

△ Stipulation Made in a Specific Way

This way of stipulation lists the possible force majeure events in detail in the force majeure clause in the contract.

Example of Force Majeure Clause Made in a General Way:

"If tile shipment of the contracted goods is prevented or delayed in whole or in part due to Force Majeure events, the Seller shall not be liable for non-shipment or late shipment of the goods of this contract. However, the Seller shall notify the Buyer by cable or telex and furnish the latter within 15 days by registered airmail with a certificate issued by the China Council for the Promotion of International Trade attesting to such event or events."

Example of Force Majeure Clause Made in a Specific Way:

"If the shipment of the contracted goods is prevented or delayed in whole or in part by reason of war earthquake, flood, fire, storm, heavy snow, the Seller shall not be liable for non-shipment of the goods of this contract. However, the Seller shall notify the Buyer by cable or telex and furnish the latter within 15 days by registered airmail with a certificate issued by the China Council for the Promotion of International Trade attesting to such event or events."

Although this way of stipulation appears to be specific and clear in terms of force majeure events, the possibilities of leaving out details makes it far from satisfactory.

△ Stipulation Made in a Synthesized Way

Neither way being satisfactory, a synthesized way in stipulating force majeure clause in the contract is created.

This way of stipulation is specific and flexible. It avoids the problems in the first two ways of stipulation, and therefore, is widely adopted in Chinese international trade practice.

(2) Notification

As mentioned above, by stipulating a force majeure clause in a contract, a seller is able to avoid his contractual obligations without paying a compensation or penalty. However, this is possible only when he can promptly notify the buyer of the force majeure event and its effect on their ability of performing the contract right after the accident so that the latter is able to take necessary remedial measures. Otherwise, the seller will still be held responsible for the loss or extended loss caused.

Example 1 of Force Majeure Clause Made in a synthesized way:

"If the shipment of the contracted goods is prevented or delayed in whole or in part by reason of war, earthquake, flood, fire, storm, heavy snow or other causes of Force Majeure, the Seller shall not be liable for non-shipment of the goods of this contract. However, the Seller shall notify the Buyer by cable or telex and furnish the latter within 15 days by registered airmail with a certificate issued by the China Council for the Promotion of International Trade attesting such event or events."

Example 2 of Force Majeure Clause Made in a synthesized way:

"The Seller shall not be held responsible for failure or delay to perform all or part of this contract due to war, earthquake, flood, fire, storm, heavy snow or other cause of force majeure. However, the Seller shall immediately advise the Buyer of such occurrence, and within 15 days thereafter, shall send by registered airmail to the Buyer for their acceptance a certificate issued by the competent government authorities of the place where the accident occurs as evidence thereof; under such circumstance, the Seller however, is still under the obligation to take all necessary measures to hasten the delivery of the goods. In case the accident lasts for more than 3 weeks, the Buyer shall have the right to cancel the contract."

(3) Issuance of the Certificates

A force majeure event should be verified by a certificate that attests the occurrence of such an event. In other words, the party that failed to perform the contract should provide effective documents describing the frustrating events. Thus, the issuer of the certificate should also be mentioned in the clause.

If the party who failed to perform the contract fails to provide such effective certificates or the facts identified are not in conformity with his description, the liability of his failure to perform the contract will not be exempted or exempted totally.

10.3.2 Consequences of Force Majeure Events

There are usually two consequences resulting from force majeure events: postponement of the contract and/or termination of the contract. Whether terminating the contract or postponing the performance of the contract depends on the detailed stipulations in the contract or on the degree to which the force majeure event has affected the performance of the contract.

Example of Force Majeure Clause in a sales contract:

"Force Majeure: If the shipment of the contracted goods is prevented or delayed in whole or in part by reason of war, earthquake, flood, fire, storm, heavy snow or other causes of Force Majeure, the seller shall not be liable for non-shipment or late shipment of the goods or non-performance of this contract. However, the seller shall notify the buyer by cable or telex and furnish the latter by registered airmail with a certificate issued by the China Council for tile

Promotion of International Trade attesting to such event or events."

If the performance of a contract is delayed by a force majeure case on a temporary basis or for a short time, the contract may be postponed. After the force majeure accident finishes, the contract should resume. For example, if there is a delayed shipment because of industrial strike, the contract will be postponed. But when the strike is over, the contract should continue and the seller has to go on to ship the goods.

However, generally speaking, the contract can be avoided if the occurrence of the force majeure event makes it impossible to perform the contract. For example, if goods ready for shipment under the contract is damaged so seriously in an earthquake that it is impossible for the seller to recover within a short period of time. It this case, the seller can ask for the termination of the contract.

10.4 Arbitration

In Section 2 of this chapter, we have discussed disputes and claims. If one party is found to have breached the contract, the other party of the contract who suffers the damage or losses there from will lodge a claim against the former for refund or compensation. However, in most cases, the claim is not able to be settled smoothly as expected due to various reasons. Then what are the usual ways to settle disputes in international trade?

10.4.1 Methods of Dispute Settlement

In international trade practice, when disputes arise between exporters and importers, it can be settled through negotiation, mediation, arbitration or litigation.

Friendly negotiation is the best method of all and beneficial to both parties because the people concerned are most familiar with the problem and dealing with it personally can avoid damage to their friendship.

If the parties involved are not able to reach any agreement between them, they can then seek the help of a third party for mediation. This third party can be any impartial party or international chamber of commerce or a government trade authority. As these experts are skilled and experienced mediators, having a competent third party to speak as an intermediary is often more effective than speaking for oneself. A large portion of the disputes in international trade practice are settled this way because it helps maintain friendly business relations between exporters and importers. However, mediation only facilitates negotiation, no award or opinion on the merits of the disputes is given.

If the disputes cannot be settled through amicable negotiation or mediation, arbitration is the next best alternative. Arbitration differs from mediation in that the third party to whom the dispute is submitted decides the outcome. Arbitration is often provided for in a contract, parties who have not so provided can choose to have their dispute arbitrated alter it has arisen.

In case the three alternatives are not workable for the settlement, the parties involved can resort to the last one litigation. However, litigation is usually costly and time-consuming, and what's more, detrimental to the relationship between the parties concerned. Therefore, it is not suggested to use if other ways to settle the disputes are workable.

10.4.2 Differences among Mediation, Arbitration and Litigation

Except negotiation where settlement of a dispute is made between the parties involved in the dispute (the seller and the buyer), other three methods all rely on a third party to settle the disputes. Therefore, it may just as well know the differences among them.

(1) Differences between Arbitration and Mediation

Arbitration is the resolution of a dispute between two parties through a voluntary or contractually required hearing and determination by an impartial third party. The main difference between arbitration and mediation is that in arbitration the arbitrator hears evidence and makes a decision. Arbitration is more like court because parties still provide testimony and give evidence similar to a trial but is usually less formal. In mediation, the process is a negotiation with the assistance of a neutral third party. The parties do not reach a solution unless all sides agree.

(2) Differences between Arbitration and Litigation

The differences between arbitration and litigation are more significant:

□Arbitration is applied on the will of both parties concerned. In case no agreement can be reached, neither party can force the other to submit to arbitration. However while resorting to litigation, the plaintiff may take a unilateral action against the defendant without agreement between the two parties in advance.

□The arbitration organization is not an official one. The parties in question can appoint their own arbitrator respectively, however the third one will be appointed by the arbitration institution. By contrast, judges in litigation should be appointed by the government.

□The award made by arbitrators is final and binding on both parties, that is, neither party of the dispute shall bring an appeal for revision before a law court or any other organizations. An arbitral award once made has the force of law, but there is no need to register and keep it in a law court. While in the case of litigation, if the parties concerned refuse to obey the verdict, they can retain the right to appeal to a higher court.

As arbitration is simpler, less costly, time-consuming and more flexible in international trade practice, in case no settlement can be reached through amicable negotiations, the two parties would prefer to submit the dispute to arbitration rather than take it to the court for litigation. According to international trade practice, an arbitration agreement is to be made by the parties concerned before they decide to submit it to arbitration.

10.4.3 Arbitration Procedure

Internationally, the main arbitration body is the International Court of Arbitration. In China, the main arbitration body is the China International Economic and Trade Arbitration Commission (CIETAC). Pursuant to the current arbitration rules of CIETAC which took effect on May 1st, 2005, the general arbitration procedure is: applying for arbitration, forming arbitration tribunal, and hearing of an arbitration case, issuing an award, setting aside an award and enforcing an award.

(1) Applying for Arbitration

When applying for arbitration, the claimant must submit to the Secretariat of the Arbitration Commission an arbitration agreement, an application for arbitration in writing, and the facts and evidence on which his claim is based. At the same time, he also shall pay an arbitration fee in advance to the Arbitration Commission.

The application for arbitration shall include such information as the name and address of the claimant and those of the claimee, the arbitration agreement relied upon by the claimant, the facts of the case and the main points of dispute, and the claimant's claim and the facts and evidence on which his claim is based.

(2) Forming Arbitration Tribunal

After receipt of the notice of arbitration, an arbitration tribunal should be formed. There are normally two types of arbitration tribunal: sole-arbitrator tribunal composed of one arbitrator and collegiate tribunal with three arbitrators. An arbitrator (or arbiter) is the impartial third party chosen by a higher or neutral body or by the two parties in dispute to deal with a claim.

In the case of sole-arbitrator tribunal, both parties concerned may jointly appoint or jointly authorize the chairman of the arbitration body to appoint a sole arbitrator to hear the arbitration case alone.

A collegiate tribunal, on the other hand, normally consists of three arbitrators. The claimant and the claimee each should appoint an arbitrator from among the panel of arbitrators. The third arbitrator however shall be jointly appointed by both parties or appointed by the chairman of the arbitration body. The arbitration tribunal formed by the three arbitrators shall jointly hear the arbitration case. Most cases to which the normal procedure applies shall be examined and heard by a collegiate tribunal with three arbitrators unless otherwise agreed by the parties.

(3) Hearing an Arbitration Case

After an arbitration tribunal is formed, it is time to arrange the hearing of an arbitration case. However, if an oral hearing is needed, before hearing, the arbitration tribunal shall fix the date of the oral hearing after consultation with the Secretariat of the Arbitration Commission, and then communicate to the parties 30 days (in foreign-related economic cases and maritime cases) or 15 days (in domestic economic cases) before the date of the hearing so that the parties concerned may have sufficient time to make necessary arrangements.

However, at the request of the parties or with their consent, oral hearings may be omitted if the arbitration tribunal also deems that oral hearings are unnecessary. In this case, the arbitration tribunal may examine the case and make an award on the basis of documents only.

(1) Issuing an Award

As conclusion of the hearing, an award will be issued. For international arbitration cases, the time limit of the issuing of such award is within 9 months from the date on which the arbitration tribunal is formed. In case of oral hearing, the arbitration tribunal shall make an award within 30 days from the date of the oral hearing.

The date on which the arbitral award is made is the date on which the arbitral award is final and the award comes into effect. The arbitration award is final and binding upon both parties. Neither party may bring a suit before a law court, or make a request to any other organization to revise the arbitral award.

(2) Setting Aside an Award

Although the arbitration award is final and binding upon both parties, if one party deems that there are matters not in conformity with the statutory procedure in the award, after receipt of the arbitral award, he can apply for setting aside the arbitral award. For example, the parties have neither included an arbitration clause in their contract nor subsequently concluded a written arbitration agreement or the formation of an arbitrator or arbitration tribunal is not in conformity with arbitration rules.

(3) Enforcing an Award

If no award is set aside, the parties must execute the arbitral award within the time limit specified. In case one party fails to execute the arbitral award, the other party may apply to the competent court for enforcement. If the residence or the properties of the losing party is located within the territory of China, the other party may apply to the Intermediate People's Court for enforcement of the award; if the residence of the losing party or the property of the losing party is located outside China, the other party may apply to the competent court in that country for enforcement. Whenever one party applies for enforcement to the competent court, he shall submit a written application for enforcement together with the arbitration agreement and the original copy of arbitral award.

10.4.4 Arbitration Costs

Arbitration cost consists of two parts: arbitration fee and actual cost. As mentioned above, the arbitration fee shall be paid in advance by the claimant when applying for arbitration.

The actual costs include the costs of making investigations and collecting evidence, costs of engaging expert to make appraisals, etc. The arbitration tribunal shall decide in the arbitral award which party shall bear the actual fees and expenses, and how much each party should bear. For example, the arbitration tribunal has the power to decide that the losing party shall pay the winning party as compensation a proportion of the expenses reasonably incurred by the winning party in dealing with the case. The amount of such compensation shall not in any case exceed 10% of the total amount awarded to the winning party.

10.4.5 Arbitration Clause in the Sales Contract

Different from other clauses in the sales contract, an arbitration clause shall be regarded as existing independently and separately from the other clauses of the contract. Similarly, an arbitration agreement attached to a contract shall be treated as a part of the contract, but existing independently and separately from the other parts of the contract. An arbitration clause or agreement expresses the willingness of the parties to submit the disputes to arbitration.

An eligible, effective, complete and accurate arbitration agreement or arbitration clause should have the following elements: place of arbitration, arbitration body, applicable arbitration rules, arbitration award, etc. The following is an example of arbitration clause in a sales contract.

Example of Arbitration clause in a sales contract

"Any disputes arising from or in connection with this contract, shall be settled amicably through negotiation. In case no settlement can be reached through negotiation, the case shall then be submitted to the China International Economic and Trade Arbitration Commission of the China Council for the Promotion of International Trade, Beijing for arbitration which shall be conducted in accordance with the Commission's Arbitration Rules in effect at the time of applying for arbitration. The arbitral award is final and binding upon both partiers."

10.5 Summary

Commodity inspection is the inspection conducted by a third, authorized party to testify whether the quality, quantity, weight, package, etc., which would be the same as those specified in the contract. Inspection in international trade can be made at the factory or at the port of shipment, at the port of destination or at the port of shipment and re-inspection at the port of destination. After inspection, certain kinds of certificate can be issued and serves as evidence in the performance of the contract.

Breach of contract means the refusal or failure by one party to a contract to fulfill an obligation imposed on him under that contract. In international trade, most disputes arise from breach of contract by either the seller or the buyer or by both.

Claim refers to the demand made by one party upon another for a certain amount of payment on account of a loss sustained through its negligence. When disputes arise, claims sometimes are unavoidable. Therefore, it is necessary to include a discrepancy and claim clause or a penalty clause in a contract. It is of great importance that the time period for the claim should be clearly stipulated in the clause and claims be filed strictly within that period.

Force majeure refers to an event that can neither be anticipated nor be reduced to control. Force majeure events enable a seller to avoid his contractual obligations without paying a compensation or penalty. However, as the definition for the scope of force majeure events varies from country to country, it is necessary to define them clearly in the contract. The best way suggested is to stipulate them in a synthesized way.

When disputes arise, it is suggested that both parties concerned settle the disputes first through amicable and friendly negotiation. If negotiation is not workable, they then can resort to a third party for mediation. In case neither ways are proved workable, they may submit them to arbitration. Litigation is always the last choice to make as it is usually costly, time - consuming and detrimental to the relationship between the parties concerned.

Arbitration is the resolution of a dispute between two parties through a voluntary or contractually required heating and determination by an impartial third party. The general arbitration procedures are: applying for arbitration, forming arbitration tribunal, hearing an arbitration case, issuing an award, setting aside an award and enforcing an award.

In case of arbitration, it is common for both parties to make an arbitration agreement before they decide to submit it to arbitration. The agreement may include such items as the name of arbitration body, the place of arbitration, the number of arbitrators, the method of selection of arbitrators, the applicable law, the application of ordinary procedure or summary procedure, etc. The award made by arbitrators is final and binding on both parties.

Exercises

Ⅰ. Choices

1. In export trade, __________ between the buyers and the sellers may arise at anytime despite the fact that both parties of the sales contract work very carefully in the performance of the contract.

A. claim　　B. dispute

C. breach of contract　　D. settlement of disputes

2. Which of the following may possibly result in disputes? __________

A. breakage of the package　　B. rising of price

C. fluctuation of exchange rate　　D. quota

3. __________ is a clause in a contract and meanwhile a law itself?

A. arbitration　　B. Claim

C. dispute　　D. force majeure

4. According to usual practice, the penalty of a contract shall not exceed of the total value of the goods __________.

A. 3%　　B. 4%　　C. 5%　　D. 5. 5%

5. Force majeure clause is a clause that __________.

A. protects the fight of the seller

B. protects the fight of the buyer

C. enables the seller to avoid his contractual obligations

D. enables the buyer to avoid his contractual obligations

6. After a dispute, in case that the parties concerned are unable to reach an agreement, they can ask a third party to help settle the dispute. This action is called ________.

A. negotiation B. mediation C. arbitration D. litigation

7. Before going for arbitration, both parties involved in a dispute needs to make an arbitration agreement in written form, in which they agree to refer the subject in dispute to a third party. This indicates the ________ nature of arbitration.

A. flexible B. simplified C. compulsory D. voluntary

8. The best way to stipulate the place and time of inspection is ________.

A. inspection at the factory

B. inspection at the port of shipment

C. inspection at the port of destination

D. inspection at the port of shipment

Ⅱ. True or false statements

1. It is mutually agreed that the Certificate of Quality and Quantity/Weight issued by the Manufacturer shall be part of the documents for payment under the relevant L/C. ( )

2. A force majeure event should be verified by a certificate that attests the occurrence of such an event. ( )

3. If the disputes cannot be settled through amicable negotiation or mediation, arbitration is only one of the next best alternatives. ( )

4. According to international trade practice, an arbitration agreement is to be made by the parties concerned before they decide to submit it to arbitration. ( )

5. The arbitration tribunal shall decide in the arbitral award which party shall bear the actual fees and expenses, and how much each party should bear. ( )

6. When disputes arise, claims sometimes are unavoidable. ( )

7. The main ways to settle disputes in international trade are negotiation, mediation, arbitration and litigation. ( )

8. The arbitration tribunal has the power to decide that the losing party shall pay the winning party the arbitration fee incurred in dealing with the case. ( )

Ⅲ. Explain the following terms

1. arbitration

2. claimant

3. statutory inspection

4. penalty clause

Ⅳ. Short questions

1. What information should be included in a commercial invoice?

2. What is proforma invoice? What is the different between a commercial invoice and a proforma invoice?

3. What is the function of documentation in international trade?

Ⅴ. Case study

In May, a China export company of signed a contract with a foreign company for the export of agricultural products with the time of delivery in December. However, in July and August of the same year, the producing area suffered great draught and the exporter was unable to make delivery within the time stipulated in the contract. As a result, the exporter asked for the termination of the contract on the basis of force majeure event. Is the exporter appropriate in asking for the termination? Why or why not?

Appendix

1. International Trade Terms 2010

INCOTERMS AND THE EXPORTER

International Commercial Terms, known as "Incoterms", are internationally accepted terms defining the responsibilities of exporters and importers in the arrangement of shipments and the transfer of liability involved at various stages of the transaction. Incoterms do not cover ownership or the transfer of title of goods. It is crucial to agree on an Incoterm at the start of a negotiation/quotation of a sale, as it will affect the costs and responsibilities involved in shipping, insurance and tariffs. The new Incoterms 2010 rules were revised by the International Chamber of Commerce and will become effective from January 1, 2011. Four terms were eliminated (DAF, DEQ, DES, DDU) and two were added: Delivered at Place (DAP) and Delivered at Terminal (DAT).

The modifications affect obligations, risk transfer, and cost sharing for the seller and buyer, resulting in better clarification and application of the eleven (11) Incoterms, and consistent with the way global trade is actually conducted since the last update in 2000.

In any sales transaction, it is important for the seller and buyer to agree on the terms of sale and know precisely what is included in the sale price. Exporters should choose the Incoterm that works best for their company, but also be prepared to quote on other terms.

See VEDP Fast Facts – Responding to Inquiries

Inexperienced exporters may want to use the Incoterm "Ex Works" (EXW), because this term carries the least burden for them. Under EXW, an exporter's responsibility ends at their facility's loading dock, which includes making the goods available for pick up and providing any product information needed for filing the Electronic Export Information (EEI). The importer's agent (i. e. their designated U. S. freight forwarder) will arrange and pay for the pre-carriage, shipping, insurance and any additional costs from the exporter's door. A sale based on the Incoterm "CIF", on the other hand, requires the exporter to arrange and pay for the pre-carriage, shipping, and insurance to a named port. In this case, the sale price (invoice) includes not only the cost of goods, but also insurance and freight costs that the importing buyer pays the exporting seller.

When designating the Incoterm on a commercial invoice or a quotation to the buyer, the term should be followed by the city or port of load/discharge, such as "EXW Factory, Richmond, VA" or "CIF Rotterdam". Using the actual address is better to avoid any confusion or misinterpretation. Communication throughout the entire process is crucial. For example, under Ex Works, the shipper should notify the importer when the goods are ready and after they have been picked up by the importer's selected carrier. The exporter's freight forwarder often provides the vessel and sail date, or air cargo service used, and any ocean bill of lading or airway bill number to keep the parties informed of the arrangements and status of the shipment (even though technically under Ex Works the exporter's responsibility ends at their loading dock).

The most burdensome Incoterm for the exporter is Delivered Duty Paid (DDP), because all arrangements and costs are borne by the exporter, usually with the assistance of agents (freight forwarders and customs house brokers). With DDP, the exporter bears all risks and costs of transportation, including duties and tariffs, until the goods are received by the importer, usually at the importer's factory or warehouse. Since DDP represents the maximum obligation to the seller, it is not recommended for companies that are new-to-export.

DDP Example: Four palletized drums of chemicals at US $ 40,000, DDP 123 Main St., Santiago, Chile.

In the DDP example, for $ 40,000 total, the exporter arranges and pays for all transit costs, including delivery to a designated facility at123 Main Street, Santiago, including any insurance coverage and duties/tariff charges. While these costs are added to the product's price and are sometimes itemized on the commercial invoice, the exporter takes full responsibility for the added logistics costs and potential headaches, such as delays at customs, demurrage or detention, or changes in inland or ocean transportation costs. Shipping DDP should only be used by the most experienced exporters. Many details must be considered, such as trade barriers, duties, currency exchange, reputability of service providers, and delivery to the final destination. For example, if your product is a large, custom-made piece of machinery for a factory:

Are there local out-of-gauge, heavy lift service providers?

Does the road to the factory allow access by an oversized truck?

What are the dimensions and capability of the buyer's receiving dock?

How will you repair any damage that may occur during transit?

INCOTERM DEFINITIONS/CHANGES

The 11 Incoterms consist of two groups and are listed below in order of increasing risk/liability to the exporter. Under the revised terms, buyers and sellers are being urged to contract precisely where delivery is made and what charges are covered. This should avoid double-billing of terminal handling charges at the port of discharge. References to "ship's rail" were taken out to clarify that delivery means "on-board" the vessel. Insurance, electronic documentation, and supply chain security are addressed in more detail, and gender-neutral language is now used.

Rules for Sea and Inland Waterway Transport

FAS—Free Alongside Ship: Risk passes to buyer, including payment of all transportation and insurance costs, once delivered alongside the ship (realistically at named port terminal) by the seller. The export clearance obligation rests with the seller.

FOB—Free On Board: Risk passes to buyer, including payment of all transportation and insurance costs, once delivered on board the ship by the seller. A step further than FAS.

CFR—Cost and Freight: Seller delivers goods and risk passes to buyer when on board the vessel. Seller arranges and pays cost and freight to the named destination port. A step further than FOB.

CIF—Cost, Insurance and Freight: Risk passes to buyer when delivered on board the ship. Seller arranges and pays cost, freight and insurance to destination port. Adds insurance costs to CFR.

Rules for Any Mode or Modes of Transportation:

EXW—Ex Works: Seller delivers (without loading) the goods at disposal of buyer at seller's premises. Long held as the most preferable term for those new-to-export because it represents the minimum liability to the seller. On these routed transactions, the buyer has limited obligation to provide export information to the seller.

FCA—Free Carrier: Seller delivers the goods to the carrier and may be responsible for clearing the goods for export (filing the EEI). More realistic than EXW because it includes loading at pick-up, which is commonly expected, and sellers are more concerned about export violations.

CPT—Carriage Paid To: Seller delivers goods to the carrier at an agreed place, shifting risk to the buyer, but seller must pay cost of carriage to the named place of destination.

CIP—Carriage and Insurance Paid To: Seller delivers goods to the carrier at an agreed place, shifting risk to the buyer, but seller pays carriage and insurance to the named place of destination.

DAT—Delivered at Terminal: Seller bears cost, risk and responsibility until goods are unloaded (delivered) at named quay, warehouse, yard, or terminal at destination. Demurrage or detention charges may apply to seller. Seller clears goods for export, not import. DAT replaces DEQ, DES.

DAP—Delivered at Place: Seller bears cost, risk and responsibility for goods until made available to buyer at named place of destination. Seller clears goods for export, not import. DAP replaces DAF, DDU.

DDP—Delivered Duty Paid: Seller bears cost, risk and responsibility for cleared goods at named place of destination at buyers disposal. Buyer is responsible for unloading. Seller is responsible for import clearance, duties and taxes so buyer is not "importer of record".

INCOTERMS DO NOT...

Determine ownership or transfer title to the goods, nor evoke payment terms.

Apply to service contracts, nor define contractual rights or obligations (except for delivery) or breach of contract remedies.

Protect parties from their own risk or loss, nor cover the goods before or after delivery.

Specify details of the transfer, transport, and delivery of the goods. Container loading is not considered packaging, and must be addressed in the sales contract.

Remember, Incoterms are not law and there is NO default Incoterm!

Incoterms—Seller/Buyer Risks, Costs and Obligations Transfer

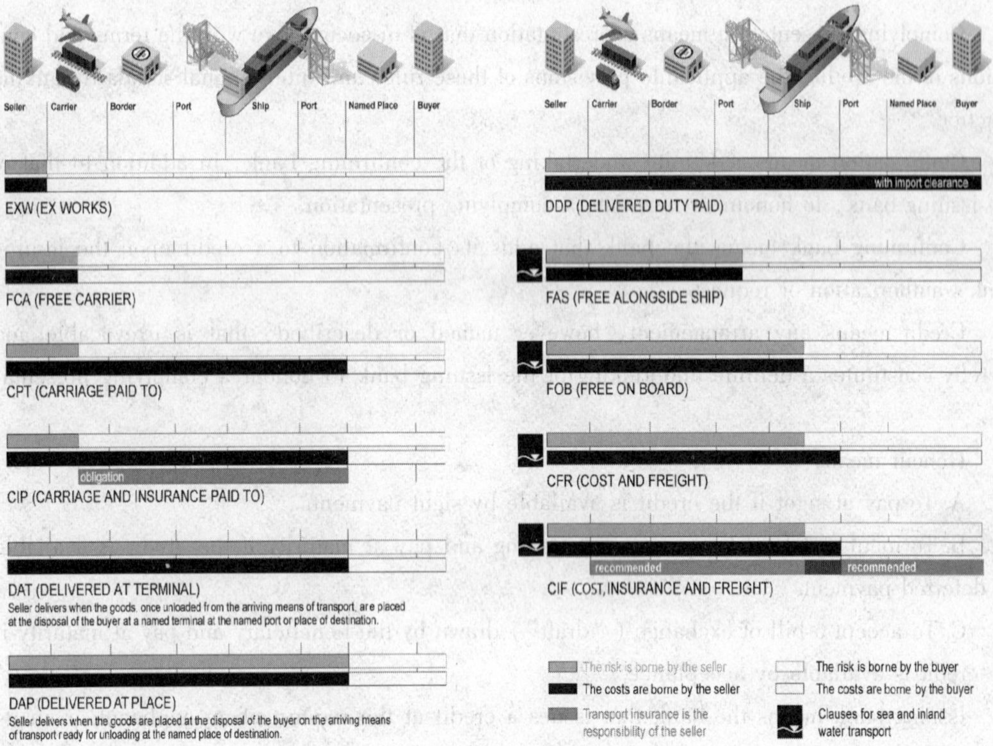

Figure 1 Two Different Groups of Incoterms® 2010

2. UCP 600

Article 1 Application of UCP

The Uniform Customs and Practice for Documentary Credits, 2007 Revision, ICC Publication no. 600 ("UCP") are rules that apply to any documentary credit ("credit") (including, to the extent to which they may be applicable, any standby letter of credit) when the text of the credit expressly indicates that it is subject to these rules. They are binding on all parties thereto unless expressly modified or excluded by the credit.

Article 2 Definitions

For the purpose of these rules:

Advising bank means the bank that advises the credit at the request of the issuing bank.

Applicant means the party on whose request the credit is issued.

Banking day means a day on which a bank is regularly open at the place at which an act subject to these rules is to be performed.

Beneficiary means the party in whose favor a credit is issued.

Complying presentation means a presentation that is in accordance with the terms and conditions of the credit, the applicable provisions of these rules and international standard banking practice.

Confirmation means a definite undertaking of the confirming bank, in addition to that of the issuing bank, to honour or negotiate a complying presentation.

Confirming bank means the bank that adds its confirmation to a credit upon the issuing bank's authorization or request.

Credit means any arrangement, however named or described, that is irrevocable and thereby constitutes a definite undertaking of the issuing bank to honour a complying presentation.

Honour means:

A. To pay at sight if the credit is available by sight payment.

B. To incur a deferred payment undertaking and pay at maturity if the credit is available by deferred payment.

C. To accept a bill of exchange ("draft") drawn by the beneficiary and pay at maturity if the credit is available by acceptance.

Issuing bank means the bank that issues a credit at the request of an applicant or on its own behalf.

Negotiation means the purchase by the nominated bank of drafts (drawn on a bank other than the nominated bank) and/or documents under a complying presentation, by advancing or agreeing to advance funds to the beneficiary on or before the banking day on which reimbursement is due to (to be paid the nominated bank).

Nominated bank means the bank with which the credit is available or any bank in the case of a credit available with any bank.

Presentation means either the delivery of documents under a credit to the issuing bank or nominated bank or the documents so delivered.

Presenter means a beneficiary, bank or other party that makes a presentation.

Article 3 Interpretations

For the purpose of these rules:

Where applicable, words in the singular include the plural and in the plural include the singular.

A credit is irrevocable even if there is no indication to that effect.

A document may be signed by handwriting, facsimile signature, perforated signature, stamp, symbol or any other mechanical or electronic method of authentication.

A requirement for a document to be legalized, visaed, certified or similar will be satisfied by any signature, mark, stamp or label on the document which appears to satisfy that requirement.

Branches of a bank in different countries are considered to be separate banks.

Terms such as "first class", "well known", "qualified", "independent", "official", "competent" or "local" used to describe the issuer of a document allow any issuer except the beneficiary to issue that document.

Unless required to be used in a document, words such as "prompt", "immediately" or "as soon as possible" will be disregarded.

The expression "on or about" or similar will be interpreted as a stipulation that an event is to occur during a period of five calendar days before until five calendar days after the specified date, both start and end dates included.

The words "to", "until", "till", "from" and "between" when used to determine a period of shipment include the date or dates mentioned, and the words "before" and "after" exclude the date mentioned.

The words "from" and "after" when used to determine a maturity date exclude the date mentioned.

The terms "first half" and "second half" of a month shall be construed respectively as the 1st to the 15th and the 16th to the last day of the month, all dates inclusive.

The terms "beginning", "middle" and "end" of a month shall be construed respectively as the 1st to the 10th, the 11th to the 20th and the 21st to the last day of the month, all dates inclusive.

Article 4 Credits vs. Contracts

a. A credit by its nature is a separate transaction from the sale or other contract on which it may be based. Banks are in no way concerned with or bound by such contract, even if any reference whatsoever to it is included in the credit. Consequently, the undertaking of a bank to honour, to negotiate or to fulfil any other obligation under the credit is not subject to claims or defences by the applicant resulting from its relationships with the issuing bank or the beneficiary.

A beneficiary can in no case avail itself of the contractual relationships existing between banks or between the applicant and the issuing bank.

b. An issuing bank should discourage any attempt by the applicant to include, as an integral part of the credit, copies of the underlying contract, proforma invoice and the like.

Article 5 Documents vs. Goods, Services or Performance

Banks deal with documents and not with goods, services or performance to which the documents may relate.

Article 6 Availability, Expiry Date and Place for Presentation

a. A credit must state the bank with which it is available or whether it is available with any bank. A credit available with a nominated bank is also available with the issuing bank.

b. A credit must state whether it is available by sight payment, deferred payment, acceptance or negotiation.

c. A credit must not be issued available by a draft drawn on the applicant.

d. i. A credit must state an expiry date for presentation. An expiry date stated for honour or negotiation will be deemed to be an expiry date for presentation.

ii. The place of the bank with which the credit is available is the place for presentation. The place for presentation under a credit available with any bank is that of any bank. A place for presentation other than that of the issuing bank is in addition to the place of the issuing bank.

e. Except as provided in sub-article 29 (a), a presentation by or on behalf of the beneficiary must be made on or before the expiry date.

Article 7 Issuing Bank Undertaking

a. Provided that the stipulated documents are presented to the nominated bank or to the issuing bank and that they constitute a complying presentation, the issuing bank must honour if the credit is available by:

i. sight payment, deferred payment or acceptance with the issuing bank;

ii. sight payment with a nominated bank and that nominated bank does not pay;

iii. deferred payment with a nominated bank and that nominated bank does not incur its deferred payment undertaking or, having incurred its deferred payment undertaking, does not pay at maturity;

iv. acceptance with a nominated bank and that nominated bank does not accept a draft drawn on it or, having accepted a draft drawn on it, does not pay at maturity;

v. negotiation with a nominated bank and that nominated bank does not negotiate.

b. An issuing bank is irrevocably bound to honour as of the time it issues the credit.

c. An issuing bank undertakes to reimburse a nominated bank that has honoured or negotiated a complying presentation and forwarded the documents to the issuing bank. Reimbursement for the amount of a complying presentation under a credit available by acceptance or deferred payment is due at maturity, whether or not the nominated bank prepaid or purchased before maturity. An issuing bank's undertaking to reimburse a nominated bank is independent of the issuing bank's undertaking to the beneficiary.

Article 8 Confirming Bank Undertaking

a. Provided that the stipulated documents are presented to the confirming bank or to any other nominated bank and that they constitute a complying presentation, the confirming bank must:

i. honour, if the credit is available by:

a) sight payment, deferred payment or acceptance with the confirming bank;

b) sight payment with another nominated bank and that nominated bank does not pay;

c) deferred payment with another nominated bank and that nominated bank does not incur its deferred payment undertaking or, having incurred its deferred payment undertaking, does not pay at maturity;

d) acceptance with another nominated bank and that nominated bank does not accept a draft drawn on it or, having accepted a draft drawn on it, does not pay at maturity;

e) negotiation with another nominated bank and that nominated bank does not negotiate.

ii. negotiate, without recourse, if the credit is available by negotiation with the confirming bank.

b. A confirming bank is irrevocably bound to honour or negotiate as of the time it adds its confirmation to the credit.

c. A confirming bank undertakes to reimburse another nominated bank that has honoured or negotiated a complying presentation and forwarded the documents to the confirming bank. Reimbursement for the amount of a complying presentation under a credit available by acceptance or deferred payment is due at maturity, whether or not another nominated bank prepaid or purchased before maturity. A confirming bank's undertaking to reimburse another nominated bank is independent of the confirming bank's undertaking to the beneficiary.

d. If a bank is authorized or requested by the issuing bank to confirm a credit but is not prepared to do so, it must inform the issuing bank without delay and may advise the credit without confirmation.

Article 9 Advising of Credits and Amendments

a. A credit and any amendment may be advised to a beneficiary through an advising bank. An advising bank that is not a confirming bank advises the credit and any amendment without any undertaking to honour or negotiate.

b. By advising the credit or amendment, the advising bank signifies that it has satisfied itself as to the apparent authenticity of the credit or amendment and that the advice accurately reflects the terms and conditions of the credit or amendment received.

c. An advising bank may utilize the services of another bank ("second advising bank") to advise the credit and any amendment to the beneficiary. By advising the credit or amendment, the second advising bank signifies that it has satisfied itself as to the apparent authenticity of the advice it has received and that the advice accurately reflects the terms and conditions of the credit or amendment received.

d. A bank utilizing the services of an advising bank or second advising bank to advise a credit must use the same bank to advise any amendment thereto.

e. If a bank is requested to advise a credit or amendment but elects not to do so, it must so inform, without delay, the bank from which the credit, amendment or advice has been received.

f. If a bank is requested to advise a credit or amendment but cannot satisfy itself as to the apparent authenticity of the credit, the amendment or the advice, it must so inform, without delay, the bank from which the instructions appear to have been received. If the advising bank or second advising bank elects nonetheless to advise the credit or amendment, it must inform the beneficiary or second advising bank that it has not been able to satisfy itself as to the apparent authenticity of the credit, the amendment or the advice.

Article 10 Amendments

a. Except as otherwise provided by article 38, a credit can neither be amended nor cancelled without the agreement of the issuing bank, the confirming bank, if any, and the beneficiary.

b. An issuing bank is irrevocably bound by an amendment as of the time it issues the amendment. A confirming bank may extend its confirmation to an amendment and will be irrevocably bound as of the time it advises the amendment. A confirming bank may, however, choose to advise an amendment without extending its confirmation and, if so, it must inform the issuing bank without delay and inform the beneficiary in its advice.

c. The terms and conditions of the original credit (or a credit incorporating previously accepted amendments) will remain in force for the beneficiary until the beneficiary communicates its acceptance of the amendment to the bank that advised such amendment. The beneficiary should give notification of acceptance or rejection of an amendment. If the beneficiary fails to give such notification, a presentation that complies with the credit and to any not yet accepted amendment will be deemed to be notification of acceptance by the beneficiary of such amendment. As of that moment the credit will be amended.

Article 11 Teletransmitted and Pre-Advised Credits and Amendments

a. An authenticated teletransmission of a credit or amendment will be deemed to be the operative credit or amendment, and any subsequent mail confirmation shall be disregarded.

If a teletransmission states "full details to follow" (or words of similar effect), or states that the mail confirmation is to be the operative credit or amendment, then the teletransmission will not be deemed to be the operative credit or amendment. The issuing bank must then issue the operative credit or amendment without delay in terms not inconsistent with the teletransmission.

b. A preliminary advice of the issuance of a credit or amendment ("pre-advice") shall only be sent if the issuing bank is prepared to issue the operative credit or amendment. An issuing bank that sends a pre-advice is irrevocably committed to issue the operative credit or amendment, without delay, in terms not inconsistent with the pre-advice.

Article 12 Nomination

a. Unless a nominated bank is the confirming bank, an authorization to honour or negotiate does not impose any obligation on that nominated bank to honour or negotiate, except when expressly agreed to by that nominated bank and so communicated to the beneficiary.

b. By nominating a bank to accept a draft or incur a deferred payment undertaking, an issuing bank authorizes that nominated bank to prepay or purchase a draft accepted or a deferred payment undertaking incurred by that nominated bank.

c. Receipt or examination and forwarding of documents by a nominated bank that is not a confirming bank does not make that nominated bank liable to honour or negotiate, nor does it constitute honour or negotiation.

Article 13 Bank-to-Bank Reimbursement Arrangements

a. If a credit states that reimbursement is to be obtained by a nominated bank ("claiming bank") claiming on another party ("reimbursing bank"), the credit must state if the reimbursement is subject to the ICC rules for bank-to-bank reimbursements in effect on the date of issuance of the credit.

b. If a credit does not state that reimbursement is subject to the ICC rules for bank-to-bank reimbursements, the following apply:

i. An issuing bank must provide a reimbursing bank with a reimbursement authorization that conforms with the availability stated in the credit. The reimbursement authorization should not be subject to an expiry date.

ii. A claiming bank shall not be required to supply a reimbursing bank with a certificate of compliance with the terms and conditions of the credit.

iii. An issuing bank will be responsible for any loss of interest, together with any expenses incurred, if reimbursement is not provided on first demand by a reimbursing bank in accordance with the terms and conditions of the credit.

iv. A reimbursing bank's charges are for the account of the issuing bank. However, if the charges are for the account of the beneficiary, it is the responsibility of an issuing bank to so indicate in the credit and in the reimbursement authorization. If a reimbursing bank's charges are for the account of the beneficiary, they shall be deducted from the amount due to a claiming bank when reimbursement is made. If no reimbursement is made, the reimbursing bank's charges remain the obligation of the issuing bank.

c. An issuing bank is not relieved of any of its obligations to provide reimbursement if reimbursement is not made by a reimbursing bank on first demand.

Article 14 Standard for Examination of Documents

a. A nominated bank acting on its nomination, a confirming bank, if any, and the issuing bank must examine a presentation to determine, on the basis of the documents alone, whether or not the documents appear on their face to constitute a complying presentation.

b. A nominated bank acting on its nomination, a confirming bank, if any, and the issuing bank shall each have a maximum of five banking days following the day of presentation to determine if a presentation is complying. This period is not curtailed or otherwise affected by the occurrence on or after the date of presentation of any expiry date or last day for presentation.

c. A presentation including one or more original transport documents subject to articles 19, 20, 21, 22, 23, 24 or 25 must be made by or on behalf of the beneficiary not later than 21 calendar days after the date of shipment as described in these rules, but in any event not later than the expiry date of the credit.

d. Data in a document, when read in context with the credit, the document itself and international standard banking practice, need not be identical to, but must not conflict with, data in that document, any other stipulated document or the credit.

e. In documents other than the commercial invoice, the description of the goods, services or performance, if stated, may be in general terms not conflicting with their description in the credit.

f. If a credit requires presentation of a document other than a transport document, insurance document or commercial invoice, without stipulating by whom the document is to be issued or its data content, banks will accept the document as presented if its content appears to fulfil the function of the required document and otherwise complies with sub-article 14 (d).

g. A document presented but not required by the credit will be disregarded and may be returned to the presenter.

h. If a credit contains a condition without stipulating the document to indicate compliance with the condition, banks will deem such condition as not stated and will disregard it.

i. A document may be dated prior to the issuance date of the credit, but must not be dated later than its date of presentation.

j. When the addresses of the beneficiary and the applicant appear in any stipulated document, they need not be the same as those stated in the credit or in any other stipulated document, but must be within the same country as the respective addresses mentioned in the credit.

Contact details (telefax, telephone, email and the like) stated as part of the beneficiary's and the applicant's address will be disregarded. However, when the address and contact details of the applicant appear as part of the consignee or notify party details on a transport document subject to articles 19, 20, 21, 22, 23, 24 or 25, they must be as stated in the credit.

k. The shipper or consignor of the goods indicated on any document need not be the beneficiary of the credit.

l. A transport document may be issued by any party other than a carrier, owner, master or charterer provided that the transport document meets the requirements of articles 19, 20, 21, 22, 23 or 24 of these rules.

Article 15 Complying Presentation

a. When an issuing bank determines that a presentation is complying, it must honour.

b. When a confirming bank determines that a presentation is complying, it must honour or negotiate and forward the documents to the issuing bank.

c. When a nominated bank determines that a presentation is complying and honours or negotiates, it must forward the documents to the confirming bank or issuing bank.

Article 16 Discrepant Documents, Waiver and Notice

a. When a nominated bank acting on its nomination, a confirming bank, if any, or the issuing bank determines that a presentation does not comply, it may refuse to honour or negotiate.

b. When an issuing bank determines that a presentation does not comply, it may in its sole judgement approach the applicant for a waiver of the discrepancies. This does not, however, extend the period mentioned in sub-article 14 (b).

c. When a nominated bank acting on its nomination, a confirming bank, if any, or the issuing bank decides to refuse to honour or negotiate, it must give a single notice to that effect to the presenter.

The notice must state:

i. that the bank is refusing to honour or negotiate; and

ii. each discrepancy in respect of which the bank refuses to honour or negotiate; and

iii. a) that the bank is holding the documents pending further instructions from the presenter; or

b) that the issuing bank is holding the documents until it receives a waiver from the applicant and agrees to accept it, or receives further instructions from the presenter prior to agreeing to accept a waiver; or

c) that the bank is returning the documents; or

d) that the bank is acting in accordance with instructions previously received from the presenter.

d. The notice required in sub-article 16 (c) must be given by telecommunication or, if that is not possible, by other expeditious means no later than the close of the fifth banking day following the day of presentation.

e. A nominated bank acting on its nomination, a confirming bank, if any, or the issuing bank may, after providing notice required by sub-article 16 (c) (iii) (a) or (b), return the documents to the presenter at any time.

f. If an issuing bank or a confirming bank fails to act in accordance with the provisions of this article, it shall be precluded from claiming that the documents do not constitute a complying presentation.

g. When an issuing bank refuses to honour or a confirming bank refuses to honour or negotiate and has given notice to that effect in accordance with this article, it shall then be entitled to claim a refund, with interest, of any reimbursement made.

Article 17 Original Documents and Copies

a. At least one original of each document stipulated in the credit must be presented.

b. A bank shall treat as an original any document bearing an apparently original signature, mark, stamp, or label of the issuer of the document, unless the document itself indicates that it is not an original.

c. Unless a document indicates otherwise, a bank will also accept a document as original if it:

i. appears to be written, typed, perforated or stamped by the document issuer's hand; or

ii. appears to be on the document issuer's original stationery; or

iii. states that it is original, unless the statement appears not to apply to the document presented.

d. If a credit requires presentation of copies of documents, presentation of either originals or copies is permitted.

e. If a credit requires presentation of multiple documents by using terms such as "in duplicate", "in two fold" or "in two copies", this will be satisfied by the presentation of at least one original and the remaining number in copies, except when the document itself indicates otherwise.

Article 18 Commercial Invoice

a. A commercial invoice:

i. must appear to have been issued by the beneficiary (except as provided in article 38);

ii. must be made out in the name of the applicant (except as provided in sub-article 38 (g));

iii. must be made out in the same currency as the credit; and

iv. need not be signed.

b. A nominated bank acting on its nomination, a confirming bank, if any, or the issuing bank may accept a commercial invoice issued for an amount in excess of the amount permitted by the credit, and its decision will be binding upon all parties, provided the bank in question has not honoured or negotiated for an amount in excess of that permitted by the credit.

c. The description of the goods, services or performance in a commercial invoice must correspond with that appearing in the credit.

Article 19 Transport Document Covering at Least Two Different Modes of Transport

a. A transport document covering at least two different modes of transport (multimodal or combined transport document), however named, must appear to:

i. indicate the name of the carrier and be signed by:

☐ the carrier or a named agent for or on behalf of the carrier, or

☐ the master or a named agent for or on behalf of the master.

Any signature by the carrier, master or agent must be identified as that of the carrier, master or agent.

Any signature by an agent must indicate whether the agent has signed for or on behalf of the carrier or for or on behalf of the master.

ii. indicate that the goods have been dispatched, taken in charge or shipped on board at the place stated in the credit, by:

☐ pre-printed wording, or

☐ a stamp or notation indicating the date on which the goods have been dispatched, taken in charge or shipped on board.

The date of issuance of the transport document will be deemed to be the date of dispatch, taking in charge or shipped on board, and the date of shipment. However, if the transport document indicates, by stamp or notation, a date of dispatch, taking in charge or shipped on board, this date will be deemed to be the date of shipment.

iii. indicate the place of dispatch, taking in charge or shipment and the place of final destination stated in the credit, even if:

a. the transport document states, in addition, a different place of dispatch, taking in charge or shipment or place of final destination, or

b. the transport document contains the indication "intended" or similar qualification in relation to the vessel, port of loading or port of discharge.

iv. be the sole original transport document or, if issued in more than one original, be the full set as indicated on the transport document.

v. contain terms and conditions of carriage or make reference to another source containing the terms and conditions of carriage (short form or blank back transport document). Contents of terms and conditions of carriage will not be examined.

vi. contain no indication that it is subject to a charter party.

b. For the purpose of this article, transhipment means unloading from one means of conveyance and reloading to another means of conveyance (whether or not in different modes of transport) during the carriage from the place of dispatch, taking in charge or shipment to the place of final destination stated in the credit.

c. i. A transport document may indicate that the goods will or may be transhipped provided that the entire carriage is covered by one and the same transport document.

ii. A transport document indicating that transhipment will or may take place is acceptable, even if the credit prohibits transhipment.

Article 20 Bill of Lading

a. A bill of lading, however named, must appear to:

i. indicate the name of the carrier and be signed by:

□ the carrier or a named agent for or on behalf of the carrier, or

□ the master or a named agent for or on behalf of the master.

Any signature by the carrier, master or agent must be identified as that of the carrier, master or agent.

Any signature by an agent must indicate whether the agent has signed for or on behalf of the carrier or for or on behalf of the master.

ii. indicate that the goods have been shipped on board a named vessel at the port of loading stated in the credit by:

□ pre-printed wording, or

□ an on board notation indicating the date on which the goods have been shipped on board.

The date of issuance of the bill of lading will be deemed to be the date of shipment unless the bill of lading contains an on board notation indicating the date of shipment, in which case the date stated in the on board notation will be deemed to be the date of shipment.

If the bill of lading contains the indication "intended vessel" or similar qualification in relation to the name of the vessel, an on board notation indicating the date of shipment and the name of the actual vessel is required.

iii. indicate shipment from the port of loading to the port of discharge stated in the credit.

If the bill of lading does not indicate the port of loading stated in the credit as the port of loading, or if it contains the indication "intended" or similar qualification in relation to the port of loading, an on board notation indicating the port of loading as stated in the credit, the date of shipment and the name of the vessel is required. This provision applies even when loading on board or shipment on a named vessel is indicated by pre-printed wording on the bill of lading.

iv. be the sole original bill of lading or, if issued in more than one original, be the full set as indicated on the bill of lading.

iv. contain terms and conditions of carriage or make reference to another source containing the terms and conditions of carriage (short form or blank back bill of lading). Contents of terms and conditions of carriage will not be examined.

vi. contain no indication that it is subject to a charter party.

b. For the purpose of this article, transhipment means unloading from one vessel and reloading to another vessel during the carriage from the port of loading to the port of discharge stated in the credit.

c. i. A bill of lading may indicate that the goods will or may be transhipped provided that the entire carriage is covered by one and the same bill of lading.

ii. A bill of lading indicating that transhipment will or may take place is acceptable, even if the credit prohibits transhipment, if the goods have been shipped in a container, trailer or LASH barge as evidenced by the bill of lading.

d. Clauses in a bill of lading stating that the carrier reserves the right to tranship will be disregarded.

Article 21 Non-Negotiable Sea Waybill

a. A non-negotiable sea waybill, however named, must appear to:

i. indicate the name of the carrier and be signed by:

· the carrier or a named agent for or on behalf of the carrier, or

· the master or a named agent for or on behalf of the master.

Any signature by the carrier, master or agent must be identified as that of the carrier, master or agent.

Any signature by an agent must indicate whether the agent has signed for or on behalf of the carrier or for or on behalf of the master.

ii. indicate that the goods have been shipped on board a named vessel at the port of loading stated in the credit by:

· pre-printed wording, or

· an on board notation indicating the date on which the goods have been shipped on board.

The date of issuance of the non-negotiable sea waybill will be deemed to be the date of shipment unless the non-negotiable sea waybill contains an on board notation indicating the date of shipment, in which case the date stated in the on board notation will be deemed to be the date of shipment.

If the non-negotiable sea waybill contains the indication "intended vessel" or similar qualification in relation to the name of the vessel, an on board notation indicating the date of shipment and the name of the actual vessel is required.

iii. indicate shipment from the port of loading to the port of discharge stated in the credit.

If the non-negotiable sea waybill does not indicate the port of loading stated in the credit as the port of loading, or if it contains the indication "intended" or similar qualification in relation to the port of loading, an on board notation indicating the port of loading as stated in the credit, the date of shipment and the name of the vessel is required. This provision applies even when loading on board or shipment on a named vessel is indicated by pre-printed wording on the non-negotiable sea waybill.

iv. be the sole original non-negotiable sea waybill or, if issued in more than one original, be the full set as indicated on the non-negotiable sea waybill.

v. contain terms and conditions of carriage or make reference to another source containing the terms and conditions of carriage (short form or blank back non-negotiable sea waybill). Contents of terms and conditions of carriage will not be examined.

vi. contain no indication that it is subject to a charter party.

b. For the purpose of this article, transhipment means unloading from one vessel and reloading to another vessel during the carriage from the port of loading to the port of discharge stated in the credit.

c. i. A non-negotiable sea waybill may indicate that the goods will or may be transhipped provided that the entire carriage is covered by one and the same non-negotiable sea waybill.

ii. A non-negotiable sea waybill indicating that transhipment will or may take place is acceptable, even if the credit prohibits transhipment, if the goods have been shipped in a container, trailer or LASH barge as evidenced by the non-negotiable sea waybill.

d. Clauses in a non-negotiable sea waybill stating that the carrier reserves the right to tranship will be disregarded.

Article 22 Charter Party Bill of Lading

a. A bill of lading, however named, containing an indication that it is subject to a charter party (charter party bill of lading), must appear to:

i. be signed by:

- the master or a named agent for or on behalf of the master, or
- the owner or a named agent for or on behalf of the owner, or
- the charterer or a named agent for or on behalf of the charterer.

Any signature by the master, owner, charterer or agent must be identified as that of the master, owner, charterer or agent.

Any signature by an agent must indicate whether the agent has signed for or on behalf of the master, owner or charterer.

An agent signing for or on behalf of the owner or charterer must indicate the name of the owner or charterer.

ii. indicate that the goods have been shipped on board a named vessel at the port of loading stated in the credit by:

· pre-printed wording, or

· an on board notation indicating the date on which the goods have been shipped on board.

The date of issuance of the charter party bill of lading will be deemed to be the date of shipment unless the charter party bill of lading contains an on board notation indicating the date of shipment, in which case the date stated in the on board notation will be deemed to be the date of shipment.

iii. indicate shipment from the port of loading to the port of discharge stated in the credit. The port of discharge may also be shown as a range of ports or a geographical area, as stated in the credit.

iv. be the sole original charter party bill of lading or, if issued in more than one original, be the full set as indicated on the charter party bill of lading.

b. A bank will not examine charter party contracts, even if they are required to be presented by the terms of the credit.

Article 23 Air Transport Document

a. An air transport document, however named, must appear to:

i. indicate the name of the carrier and be signed by:

· the carrier, or

· a named agent for or on behalf of the carrier.

Any signature by the carrier or agent must be identified as that of the carrier or agent.

Any signature by an agent must indicate that the agent has signed for or on behalf of the carrier.

ii. indicate that the goods have been accepted for carriage.

iii. indicate the date of issuance. This date will be deemed to be the date of shipment unless the air transport document contains a specific notation of the actual date of shipment, in which case the date stated in the notation will be deemed to be the date of shipment.

Any other information appearing on the air transport document relative to the flight number and date will not be considered in determining the date of shipment.

iv. indicate the airport of departure and the airport of destination stated in the credit.

v. be the original for consignor or shipper, even if the credit stipulates a full set of originals.

vi. contain terms and conditions of carriage or make reference to another source containing the terms and conditions of carriage. Contents of terms and conditions of carriage will not be examined.

b. For the purpose of this article, transhipment means unloading from one aircraft and reloading to another aircraft during the carriage from the airport of departure to the airport of destination stated in the credit.

c. i. An air transport document may indicate that the goods will or may be transhipped, provided that the entire carriage is covered by one and the same air transport document.

ii. An air transport document indicating that transhipment will or may take place is acceptable, even if the credit prohibits transhipment.

Article 24 Road, Rail or Inland Waterway Transport Documents

a. A road, rail or inland waterway transport document, however named, must appear to:

i. indicate the name of the carrier and:

· be signed by the carrier or a named agent for or on behalf of the carrier, or

· indicate receipt of the goods by signature, stamp or notation by the carrier or a named agent for or on behalf of the carrier.

Any signature, stamp or notation of receipt of the goods by the carrier or agent must be identified as that of the carrier or agent.

Any signature, stamp or notation of receipt of the goods by the agent must indicate that the agent has signed or acted for or on behalf of the carrier.

If a rail transport document does not identify the carrier, any signature or stamp of the railway company will be accepted as evidence of the document being signed by the carrier.

ii. indicate the date of shipment or the date the goods have been received for shipment, dispatch or carriage at the place stated in the credit. Unless the transport document contains a dated reception, stamp, an indication of the date of receipt or a date of shipment, the date of issuance of the transport document will be deemed to be the date of shipment.

iii. indicate the place of shipment and the place of destination stated in the credit.

b. i. A road transport document must appear to be the original for consignor or shipper or bear no marking indicating for whom the document has been prepared.

ii. A rail transport document marked "duplicate" will be accepted as an original.

iii. A rail or inland waterway transport document will be accepted as an original whether marked as an original or not.

c. In the absence of an indication on the transport document as to the number of originals issued, the number presented will be deemed to constitute a full set.

d. For the purpose of this article, transhipment means unloading from one means of conveyance and reloading to another means of conveyance, within the same mode of transport, during the carriage from the place of shipment, dispatch or carriage to the place of destination stated in the credit.

e. i. A road, rail or inland waterway transport document may indicate that the goods will or may be transhipped provided that the entire carriage is covered by one and the same transport document.

ii. A road, rail or inland waterway transport document indicating that transhipment will or may take place is acceptable, even if the credit prohibits transhipment.

Article 25 Courier Receipt, Post Receipt or Certificate of Posting

a. A courier receipt, however named, evidencing receipt of goods for transport, must appear to:

i. indicate the name of the courier service and be stamped or signed by the named courier service at the place from which the credit states the goods are to be shipped; and

ii. indicate a date of pick-up or of receipt or wording to this effect. This date will be deemed to be the date of shipment.

b. A requirement that courier charges are to be paid or prepaid may be satisfied by a transport document issued by a courier service evidencing that courier charges are for the account of a party other than the consignee.

c. A post receipt or certificate of posting, however named, evidencing receipt of goods for transport, must appear to be stamped or signed and dated at the place from which the credit states the goods are to be shipped. This date will be deemed to be the date of shipment.

Article 26 "On Deck", "Shipper's Load and Count", "Said by Shipper to Contain" and Charges Additional to Freight

a. A transport document must not indicate that the goods are or will be loaded on deck. A clause on a transport document stating that the goods may be loaded on deck is acceptable.

b. A transport document bearing a clause such as "shipper's load and count" and "said by shipper to contain" is acceptable.

c. A transport document may bear a reference, by stamp or otherwise, to charges additional to the freight.

Article 27 Clean Transport Document

A bank will only accept a clean transport document. A clean transport document is one bearing no clause or notation expressly declaring a defective condition of the goods or their packaging. The word "clean" need not appear on a transport document, even if a credit has a requirement for that transport document to be "clean on board".

Article 28 Insurance Document and Coverage

a. An insurance document, such as an insurance policy, an insurance certificate or a declaration under an open cover, must appear to be issued and signed by an insurance company, an underwriter or their agents or their proxies.

Any signature by an agent or proxy must indicate whether the agent or proxy has signed for or on behalf of the insurance company or underwriter.

b. When the insurance document indicates that it has been issued in more than one original, all originals must be presented.

c. Cover notes will not be accepted.

d. An insurance policy is acceptable in lieu of an insurance certificate or a declaration under an open cover.

e. The date of the insurance document must be no later than the date of shipment, unless it appears from the insurance document that the cover is effective from a date not later than the date of shipment.

f. i. The insurance document must indicate the amount of insurance coverage and be in the same currency as the credit.

ii. A requirement in the credit for insurance coverage to be for a percentage of the value of the goods, of the invoice value or similar is deemed to be the minimum amount of coverage required.

If there is no indication in the credit of the insurance coverage required, the amount of insurance coverage must be at least 110% of the CIF or CIP value of the goods.

When the CIF or CIP value cannot be determined from the documents, the amount of insurance coverage must be calculated on the basis of the amount for which honour or negotiation is requested or the gross value of the goods as shown on the invoice, whichever is greater.

iii. The insurance document must indicate that risks are covered at least between the place of taking in charge or shipment and the place of discharge or final destination as stated in the credit.

g. A credit should state the type of insurance required and, if any, the additional risks to be covered. An insurance document will be accepted without regard to any risks that are not covered if the credit uses imprecise terms such as "usual risks" or "customary risks".

h. When a credit requires insurance against "all risks" and an insurance document is presented containing any "all risks" notation or clause, whether or not bearing the heading "all risks", the insurance document will be accepted without regard to any risks stated to be excluded.

i. An insurance document may contain reference to any exclusion clause.

j. An insurance document may indicate that the cover is subject to a franchise or excess (deductible).

Article 29 Extension of Expiry Date or Last Day for Presentation

a. If the expiry date of a credit or the last day for presentation falls on a day when the bank to which presentation is to be made is closed for reasons other than those referred to in article 36, the expiry date or the last day for presentation, as the case may be, will be extended to the first following banking day.

b. If presentation is made on the first following banking day, a nominated bank must provide the issuing bank or confirming bank with a statement on its covering schedule that the presentation was made within the time limits extended in accordance with sub-article 29 (a).

c. The latest date for shipment will not be extended as a result of sub - article 29 (a).

Article 30 Tolerance in Credit Amount, Quantity and Unit Prices

a. The words "about" or "approximately" used in connection with the amount of the credit or the quantity or the unit price stated in the credit are to be construed as allowing a tolerance not to exceed 10% more or 10% less than the amount, the quantity or the unit price to which they refer.

b. A tolerance not to exceed 5% more or 5% less than the quantity of the goods is allowed, provided the credit does not state the quantity in terms of a stipulated number of packing units or individual items and the total amount of the drawings does not exceed the amount of the credit.

c. Even when partial shipments are not allowed, a tolerance not to exceed 5% less than the amount of the credit is allowed, provided that the quantity of the goods, if stated in the credit, is shipped in full and a unit price, if stated in the credit, is not reduced or that sub - article 30 (b) is not applicable. This tolerance does not apply when the credit stipulates a specific tolerance or uses the expressions referred to in sub - article 30 (a).

Article 31 Partial Drawings or Shipments

a. Partial drawings or shipments are allowed.

b. A presentation consisting of more than one set of transport documents evidencing shipment commencing on the same means of conveyance and for the same journey, provided they indicate the same destination, will not be regarded as covering a partial shipment, even if they indicate different dates of shipment or different ports of loading, places of taking in charge or dispatch. If the presentation consists of more than one set of transport documents, the latest date of shipment as evidenced on any of the sets of transport documents will be regarded as the date of shipment.

A presentation consisting of one or more sets of transport documents evidencing shipment on more than one means of conveyance within the same mode of transport will be regarded as covering a partial shipment, even if the means of conveyance leave on the same day for the same destination.

c. A presentation consisting of more than one courier receipt, post receipt or certificate of posting will not be regarded as a partial shipment if the courier receipts, post receipts or certificates of posting appear to have been stamped or signed by the same courier or postal service at the same place and date and for the same destination.

Article 32 Instalment Drawings or Shipments

If a drawing or shipment by instalments within given periods is stipulated in the credit and any instalment is not drawn or shipped within the period allowed for that instalment, the credit ceases to be available for that and any subsequent instalment.

Article 33 Hours of Presentation

A bank has no obligation to accept a presentation outside of its banking hours.

Article 34 Disclaimer on Effectiveness of Documents

A bank assumes no liability or responsibility for the form, sufficiency, accuracy, genuineness, falsification or legal effect of any document, or for the general or particular conditions stipulated in a document or superimposed thereon; nor does it assume any liability or responsibility for the description, quantity, weight, quality, condition, packing, delivery, value or existence of the goods, services or other performance represented by any document, or for the good faith or acts or omissions, solvency, performance or standing of the consignor, the carrier, the forwarder, the consignee or the insurer of the goods or any other person.

Article 35 Disclaimer on Transmission and Translation

A bank assumes no liability or responsibility for the consequences arising out of delay, loss in transit, mutilation or other errors arising in the transmission of any messages or delivery of letters or documents, when such messages, letters or documents are transmitted or sent according to the requirements stated in the credit, or when the bank may have taken the initiative in the choice of the delivery service in the absence of such instructions in the credit.

If a nominated bank determines that a presentation is complying and forwards the documents to the issuing bank or confirming bank, whether or not the nominated bank has honoured or negotiated, an issuing bank or confirming bank must honour or negotiate, or reimburse that nominated bank, even when the documents have been lost in transit between the nominated bank and the issuing bank or confirming bank, or between the confirming bank and the issuing bank.

A bank assumes no liability or responsibility for errors in translation or interpretation of technical terms and may transmit credit terms without translating them.

Article 36 Force Majeure

A bank assumes no liability or responsibility for the consequences arising out of the interruption of its business by Acts of God, riots, civil commotions, insurrections, wars, acts of terrorism, or by any strikes or lockouts or any other causes beyond its control.

A bank will not, upon resumption of its business, honour or negotiate under a credit that expired during such interruption of its business.

Article 37 Disclaimer for Acts of an Instructed Party

a. A bank utilizing the services of another bank for the purpose of giving effect to the instructions of the applicant does so for the account and at the risk of the applicant.

b. An issuing bank or advising bank assumes no liability or responsibility should the instructions it transmits to another bank not be carried out, even if it has taken the initiative in the choice of that other bank.

c. A bank instructing another bank to perform services is liable for any commissions, fees, costs or expenses ("charges") incurred by that bank in connection with its instructions.

If a credit states that charges are for the account of the beneficiary and charges cannot be collected or deducted from proceeds, the issuing bank remains liable for payment of charges.

A credit or amendment should not stipulate that the advising to a beneficiary is conditional upon the receipt by the advising bank or second advising bank of its charges.

d. The applicant shall be bound by and liable to indemnify a bank against all obligations and responsibilities imposed by foreign laws and usages.

Article 38 Transferable Credits

a. A bank is under no obligation to transfer a credit except to the extent and in the manner expressly consented to by that bank.

b. For the purpose of this article:

Transferable credit means a credit that specifically states it is "transferable". A transferable credit may be made available in whole or in part to another beneficiary ("second beneficiary") at the request of the beneficiary ("first beneficiary").

Transferring bank means a nominated bank that transfers the credit or, in a credit available with any bank, a bank that is specifically authorized by the issuing bank to transfer and that transfers the credit. An issuing bank may be a transferring bank.

Transferred credit means a credit that has been made available by the transferring bank to a second beneficiary.

c. Unless otherwise agreed at the time of transfer, all charges (such as commissions, fees, costs or expenses) incurred in respect of a transfer must be paid by the first beneficiary.

d. A credit may be transferred in part to more than one second beneficiary provided partial drawings or shipments are allowed.

A transferred credit cannot be transferred at the request of a second beneficiary to any subsequent beneficiary. The first beneficiary is not considered to be a subsequent beneficiary.

e. Any request for transfer must indicate if and under what conditions amendments may be advised to the second beneficiary. The transferred credit must clearly indicate those conditions.

f. If a credit is transferred to more than one second beneficiary, rejection of an amendment by one or more second beneficiary does not invalidate the acceptance by any other second beneficiary, with respect to which the transferred credit will be amended accordingly. For any second beneficiary that rejected the amendment, the transferred credit will remain unamended.

g. The transferred credit must accurately reflect the terms and conditions of the credit, including confirmation, if any, with the exception of:

- the amount of the credit,
- any unit price stated therein,
- the expiry date,
- the period for presentation, or
- the latest shipment date or given period for shipment,

any or all of which may be reduced or curtailed.

The percentage for which insurance cover must be effected may be increased to provide the amount of cover stipulated in the credit or these articles.

The name of the first beneficiary may be substituted for that of the applicant in the credit.

If the name of the applicant is specifically required by the credit to appear in any document other than the invoice, such requirement must be reflected in the transferred credit.

h. The first beneficiary has the right to substitute its own invoice and draft, if any, for those of a second beneficiary for an amount not in excess of that stipulated in the credit, and upon such substitution the first beneficiary can draw under the credit for the difference, if any, between its invoice and the invoice of a second beneficiary.

i. If the first beneficiary is to present its own invoice and draft, if any, but fails to do so on first demand, or if the invoices presented by the first beneficiary create discrepancies that did not exist in the presentation made by the second beneficiary and the first beneficiary fails to correct them on first demand, the transferring bank has the right to present the documents as received from the second beneficiary to the issuing bank, without further responsibility to the first beneficiary.

j. The first beneficiary may, in its request for transfer, indicate that honour or negotiation is to be effected to a second beneficiary at the place to which the credit has been transferred, up to and including the expiry date of the credit. This is without prejudice to the right of the first beneficiary in accordance with sub-article 38 (h).

k. Presentation of documents by or on behalf of a second beneficiary must be made to the transferring bank.

Article 39 Assignment of Proceeds

The fact that a credit is not stated to be transferable shall not affect the right of the beneficiary to assign any proceeds to which it may be or may become entitled under the credit, in accordance with the provisions of applicable law. This article relates only to the assignment of proceeds and not to the assignment of the right to perform under the credit.

3. Business Negotiation

Enquiry

CRYSTAL KOBE LTD

1410 BROADWAY, ROOM 300 NEW YORK, NY10018 U. S. A.

TEL: 599 - 525 - 7000 FAX: 73423 FNCB HX

TO: SHANGHAI TEXTILES IMPORT &EXPORT CORPORATION

(FAX: 8621 - 65124743)

FM: CRYSTAL KOBE LTD. (FAX: 73423 FNCB HX)

DT: August 8, 2013

Dear Sirs:

We are importers of textiles and manufactured cotton goods. We have recently conclude some satisfactory business with CHINA TEX KNITWEAR AND MANUFACTURED GOODS IMPORT & EXPORT CORPORATION. We now have a good demand for ladies' blouse 400 DOZ and therefore write to you in the hope of establishing business relations.

From your recently published catalogue, we notice that you are able to supply ladies' blouse, and we should be grateful if you would kindly send us some samples of the goods which you can supply together with a comprehensive price list giving details of packing and specification the time of shipment so as to enable us to go fully into the possibilities of business.

We look forward to your early news and trust that through our mutual cooperation we shall be able to conclude some transactions with you in the near feature.

Yours Faithfully

CRYSTAL KOBE LTD.

Purchasing Manager

Offer:

SHANGHAI TEXTILES IMPORT & EXPORT CORPORATION

27. CHUNGSHAN ROAD E. 1.
SHANGHAI CHINA
TEL: 8621 - 65342517 FAX: 8621 - 65724743

TO: CRYSTAL KOBE LTE. (FAX: 73423 FNCB HX)
FM: SHANGHAI TEXTILES IMPORT & EXPORT CORPORATION
DT: August 12, 2013

Dear Sirs:

We are very pleased to receive your enquiry of 8th August and enclose our price list giving the details you ask for. Also by separate post we are sending you some samples and feel confident that when you have examined you will agree that the goods are both excellent in quality and reasonable in price.

Because of their softness and durability, our all ladies' blouse are rapidly becoming popular and after studying our prices you will learn that we are finding it difficult to meet the demand.

We look forward very much to the pleasure of receiving an order from you.

Yours Sincerely
SHANGHAI TEXTILES IMPORT & EXPORT CORP.
× × ×

Quotation:

中国纺织品进出口公司上海市分公司

CHINA NATIONAL TEXTILE IMPORT & EXPORT CORPORATION

SHANGHAI BRANCH

27 Chungshan Road E. 1 SHANGHAI CHINA

TEL: 8621 - 65342517 FAX: 8621 - 65124743

报价单

QUOTATION

致

Messrs. …CRYSTAL KOBE LTD. 日期

Dated…AUG. 8, 2013.

兹报供下列商品，均以我最后确认为准

The following articles are quoted subject to our final confirmation:

货号 ART. NO.	品名 COMMODITY	规格 SPECIFICATIONS	包装 PACKING	单价 UNIT PRICE	装船期 SHIPMENT
H32331SE	LADIES'BLOUSE	55% ACRYLIC 45% COTTON KNITTED	IN CORTON	USD 50 PER DOZ CIF NY	ON OR BEFORE DEC. 20, 2013

付款方式

PAYMENT: BY SIGHT L/C

保险

INSURANCE: For 110% INVOICE VALUE COVERING ALL RISKS

Counter－offer：

CRYSTAL KOBE LTD.

1410 BROADWAY, ROOM 300 NEW YORK, NY10018 U. S. A.

TEL：599－525－7000　FAX：73423 FNCB HX

TO：SHANGHAI TEXTILES IMPORT &EXPORT CORPORATION
(FAX：8621－65124743)

FM：CRYSTAL KOBE LTD. (FAX：73423 FNCB HX)

DT：August 20, 2013

Dear Sirs：

Thank you for your letter dated August 12, 2013 and attached quotation.

After careful examining and comparison with other brands of similar products, we found that your price is higher than the average in the market. In order to allow us a better competing position, we shall be grateful if you could reduce the price to USD 45 per DOZ CIF LESS 3% DISCOUNT. Moreover, we advise you to make some adjustment of your terms of payment L/C to D/P at sight and that the time of shipment should be on or before NOV 20, 2013.

We hope we can enter a lasting business relationship with you and look forward to receiving your reply.

Yours Faithfully,
CRYSTAL KOBE LTD.
Purchasing Manager

SHANGHAI TEXTILES IMPORT & EXPORT CORPORATION

27. CHUNGSHAN ROAD E. 1.

SHANGHAI CHINA

TEL: 8621 - 65342517 **FAX**: 8621 - 65724743

TO: CRYSTAL KOBE LTE. (FAX: 73423 FNCB HX)

FM: SHANGHAI TEXTILES IMPORT & EXPORT CORPORATION

DT: August 23, 2013

Dear Sirs:

We have received your fax of August 20, 2013. We are sorry to tell you that your prices are not appropriate to us. As you know, wages and materials have risen considerably theses days.

We are compelled to adjust our prices to cover the increasing cost. USD 48. 5 per DOZ is our lowest level, which leaves us with only the smallest profit.

Although we have confidence in your integrity, our usual terms of payment by sight L/C remain unchanged in all cases with new clients. So for the time being, we regret our inability to accept your D/P terms. Maybe after several smooth and satisfactory transactions, we can consider other flexible ways.

The time of shipment should be effected within 2 months from receipt of the relevant L/C.

For your information, the demand for our products has been extremely great recently. This offer is valid for 5 days and we looking forward to receiving your order at the earliest date.

Yours Sincerely

SHANGHAI TEXTILES IMPORT & EXPORT CORP.

× × ×

Acceptance：

SHANGHAI TEXTILES IMPORT & EXPORT CORPORATION

27. CHUNGSHAN ROAD E. 1.

SHANGHAI CHINA

TEL：8621 – 65342517 FAX：8621 – 65724743

TO：CRYSTAL KOBE LTE. （FAX：73423 FNCB HX）

FM：SHANGHAI TEXTILES IMPORT & EXPORT CORPORATION

DT：August 26，2013

Dear Sirs：

Thank you for your fax of August 24，2013.

Enclosed are two copies of your Sales Confirmation No 21SSG – 017. Please sign and return one copy for our file.

We can assure you of the high quality as well as the punctuate delivery so long as the relative L/C reaches our end in time. We suppose the conclusion of this transaction will lead to more business in future.

We appreciate your co – operation and look forward to receiving your further orders.

Yours Truly

SHANGHAI TEXTILES IMPORT & EXPORT CORP.

× × ×

SALES CONFIRMATION：

中国纺织品进出口公司上海市分公司
CHINA NA TIONAL TEXTILES IMPORT & EXPORT CORPORATION
SHANGHAI BRANCH
27 Chungshan Road E. 1 SHANGHAI CHINA
TEL：8621 - 65342517 FAX：8621 - 65124743

编号
TO：CRYSTAL KOBE LTD. No. 21SSG - 017

售货确认书
日期
SALES CONFIRMATION
Date：AUG. 26，2013

货号 ART. NO.	品名及规格 COMMODITY AND SPECIFICATION	数量 QUANTITY	单价及价格条款 UNIT PRICE&TERMS	金额 AMOUNT
H32331SE	LADIES' 55% ACRYLIC 45% COTTON KNITTED BLOUSE	120 CARTON	USD 48. 5 PER DOZ CIFC3% NEW YORK	USD24 250

总金额
TOTAL AMOUNT USD24，250

装运条款
SHIPMENT：SHIPMENT ON OR BEFOR NOV. 20，2013 WITH PARTIAL SHIPMENTS ARE NOT ALLOWED TRANSSHIPMENT IS ALLOWED FROM SHANGHAI TO NEW YORK

付款方式
PAYMENT：THE BUYER SHALL OPEN THOUGH A BANK ACCEPTABLE TO THE SELLER AN IRREVOCABLE L/C AT SIGHT TO REACH THE SELLER 30 DAYS BEFORE THE MONTH OF SHIPMENT REMAINED VALID FOR NEGOTIATION IN CHINA UNTIL THE 15TH DAY AFTER THE DATE OF SHIPMENT。

保险
INSURANCE：THE SELLER SHALL COVER INSUREANCE AGAINST ALL RISKS FOR 110 % OF THE TLTAL INVOICE VALLUE AS PER THE RELEVANT OCEAN MARINE CARGO CLAUSE OF P. I. C. C. DATED JAN. 1ST，1981。

注意：请完全按本售货确认书开证并在证内注明本售货确认书号码。
IMPORTANT：PLEASE ESTABLISH L/C EXACTLY ACCORDING TO THE TERMS AND CONDITIONS OF THIS S/C AND WITH THIS S/C NUMBER INDICATED.

______________________	SHANGHAI TEXTILES I/E CORPORATION
买方（The Buyers）	卖方（The Sellers）

CONTRACT:

上海市纺织品进出口公司
SHANGHAI TEXTILES
IMPORT&EXPORT CORPORATION

正本
(ORIGINAL)

中国上海中山东一路27号
27 **Zhong Shan Road (E. 1.) Shanghai, China**

合 同 号 码
Contract No.

买　方：
The Buyers:

合　同
CONTRACT

日　期：
Date:
传　真：
FAX: 021-291730
电 传 号：
Telex number: TEXTILE

兹经买卖双方同意，由买方购进，卖方出售下列货物，并按下列条款签订本合同：

This CONTRACT is made by and between the Buyers and the Sellers; whereby the Buyers agree to buy and the Sellers agree to sell the undermentioned goods on the terms and conditions stated below:

(1) 货物名称、规格、包装及唛头 Name of Commodity, Specifications, Packing Terms and Shipping Marks	(2) 数量 Quantity	(3) 单价 Unit Price	(4) 总值 Total Amount	(5) 装运期限 Time of Shipment

(6) 装 运 口 岸：
Port of Loading:
(7) 目 的 口 岸：
Port of Destination :

(8) 付 款 条 件：买方在收到卖方关于预计装船日期及准备装船的数量的通知后，应于装运前20天，通过上海中国银行开立以卖方为受益人的不可撤销的信用证。该信用证凭即期汇票及本合同第(9)条规定的单据在开证行付款。

Terms of Payment: Upon receipt from the Sellers of the advice as to the time and quantify expected ready for shipment, the Buyers shall open, 20days before shipment, with the Bank of China , Shanghai, an irrevocable Letter of Credit in favour of the Sellers payable by the opening bank against sight draft accompanied by the documents as stipulated in Clause (9) of this Contract.

(9) 单据：各项单据均须使用与本合同相一致的文字，以便买方审核查对。

Documents: To facilitate the Buyers to cheek up, all documents should be made in a version identical to that used in this contract.

A. 填写通知目的口岸对外贸易运输公司的空白抬头、空白背书的全套已装船的清洁提单。（如本合同为FOB价格条件时，提单应注明“运费到付”或“运费按租船合同办理”字样；如本合同为CFR价格条件时，提单应注明“运费已付”字样。）

Complete set of Clean On Board Shipped Bill of Lading made out to order, blank endorsed, notifying the China National Foreign Trade Transportation Corporation ZHONGWAIYUN at the port of destination. (if the prise in this Contract is Based on FOB, marked “freight to collect” or “freight as per charter party”; if the price in this Contract is Based on CFR, marked “freight prepaid”.)

B. 发票：注明合同号、唛头、载货船名及信用证号，如果分批装运，须注明分批号。

Invoice: indicating contract number, shipping marks, name of carrying vessel, number of the Letter of Credit and shipment number in case of partial shipments.

C. 装箱单及（或）重量单：注明合同号及唛头，并逐件列明毛重、净重。

Packing List and/or Weight Memo: indicating contract number, shipping marks, gross and net weights of each package.

D. 制造工厂的品质及数量、重量证明书。

Certificates of Quality and Quantity/Weight of the contracted goods issued by the manufactures.

品质证明书内应列入根据合同规定的标准进行化学成分、机械性能及其他各种试验结果。

Quality Certificate to show actual results of tests to be made, on chemical compositions, mechanical properties and all other tests called for by the Standard stipulated heron.

E. 按本合同第（11）条规定的装运通知电报抄本。

Copy of telegram advising shipment according to Clause (11) of this Contract.

F. 按本合同第（10）条规定的航行证明书。（如本合同为CFR价格条件时，需要此项证明书，如本合同为FOB价格条件时，则不需此项证明书。）

Vessel's itinerary certificate as per Clause (10) of this Contract, (required if the price in this Contract is based on CFR; not required if the price in this Contract is based on FOB.)

寄送 To be distributed 份数 Number of copies 单证 Documents required	A	B	C	E	E	F
送交付银行（正本） To be negotiationg bank (original)	3	4	3	3	1	1
送交付银行（副本） To be negotiating bank (duplicate)	1					
空邮目的口岸外运公司（副本） to ZHONGWAIYUN at the port of destination by airmail (duplicate)	2	3	2	2		

（10）装运条件

Terms of Shipment：

A. 离岸价条款 Terms of FOB Delivery：

a. 装运本合同货物的船只，由买方或买方运输代理人中国租船公司租订舱位。卖方负担货物的一切费用风险到货物装到船面为止。

For the goods ordered in this Contract, the carrying vessel shall be arranged by the Buyers or the Buyers' Shipping Agent China National Chartering Corporation. The Sellers shall bear all the charges and risks until the goods are effectively loaded on board the carrying vessel.

b. 卖方必须在合同规定的交货期限三十天前，将合同号码、货物名称、数量、装运口岸及预计货物运达装运口岸日期，以电报通知买方以便买方安排舱位。并同时通知买方在装港的船代理。倘在规定期内买方未接到前述通知，即作为卖方同意在合同规定期内任何日期交货，并由买方主动租订舱位。

The Sellers shall advise the Buyers by cable, and simultaneously advise the Buyers' shipping agent at the loading port, 30 days before the contracted time of shipment, of the contract number, name of commodity, quantity, loading port and expected date of arrival of the goods at the loading port, enabling the Buyers to arrange for shipping space. Absence of such advice within the time specified above shall be considered as Sellers' readiness to deliver the goods during the time of shipment contracted and the Buyers shall arrange for shipping space accordingly.

c. 买方应在船只受载期 12 天前将船名、预计受载日期、装载数量、合同号码、船舶代理人，以电报通知卖方。卖方应联系船舶代理人配合船期备货装船。如买方因故需要变更船只或更改船期时，买方或船舶代理人应及时通知卖方。

The Buyers shall advise the Sellers by cable, 12 days before the expected loading date, of the estimated laydays, contract number, name of vessel, quantity, to be loaded and shipping agent. The Sellers shall then arrange with the shipping agent for loading accordingly. In case of necessity for substitution of vessel or alteration of shipping schedule, the Buyers or the shipping agent shall duly advise the Sellers to the same effect.

d. 买方所租船只按期到达装运口岸后，如卖方不能按时备货装船，买方因而遭受的一切损失包括空舱费、延期费及/或罚款等由卖方负担。如船只不能于船舶代理人所确定的受载期内到达，在港口免费堆存期满后第 16 天起发生的仓库租费，保险费由买方负担，但卖方仍负有载货船只到达装运口岸后立即将货物装船之义务并负担费用及风险。前述各种损失均凭原始单据核实支付。

In the event of the Sellers' failure in effecting shipment upon arrival of the vessel at the loading port, all losses, including dead freight, demurrage fines etc. thus incurred shall be for Sellers' account. If the vessel fails to arrive at the loading port within the laydays. previously declared by the shipping agent, the storage charges and insurance premium from the 16th day after expiration of the free storage time at the port shall be borne by the Buyers. However, the Sellers shall be still under the obligation to load the goods on board the carrying vessel immediately after her arrival at the loading port, at their own expenses and risks. The expenses and losses mentioned above shall be reimbursed against original receipts or invoices.

B. 成本加运费价条款 Terms of CFR Delivery：

卖方负责将本合同所列货物由装运口岸装直达班轮到目的口岸，中途不得转船。货物不得用悬挂买方不能接受的国家的旗帜的船只装运。

The Sellers undertake to ship the contracted goods from the port of loading to the port of destination on adirect liner, with no transhipment allowed. The contracted goods shall not be carried by a vessel flying the flag of the countries which the Buyers can not accept.

(11) 装运通知：卖方在货物装船后，立即将合同号、品名、件数、毛重、净重、发票金额、载货船名及装船日期以电报通知买方。

Advice of Shipment: The Sellers shall upon competition of loading, advise immediately the Buyers by cable of the contract number, name of commodity, number of packages, gross and net weights, invoice value, name of vessel and loading date.

(12) 保 险：自装船起由买方自理，但卖方应按本合同第（11）条通知买方。如卖方未能按此办理，买方因而遭受的一切损失全由卖方负担。

Insurance: To be covered by the Buyers from shipment, for this purpose the Sellers shall advise the Buyers by cable of the particulars as called for in Clause (11) of this Contract, In the event of the Buyers being unable to arrange for insurance in consequence of the Sellers' failure to send the above advice, the Sellers shall be held responsible for all the losses thus sustained by the Buyers.

(13) 检验和索赔：货卸目的口岸，买方有权申请中华人民共和国国家质量监督检验检疫总局进行检验。如发现货物的品质及/或数量/重量与合同或发票不符：除属于保险公司及/或船公司的责任外，买方有权在货卸目的口岸后 90 天内，根据中华人民共和国国家质量监督检验检疫总局出具的证明书向卖方提出索赔，因索赔所发生的一切费用（包括检验费用）均由卖方负担。FOB 价格条件时，如重量短缺，买方有权同时索赔短重部分的运费。

Inspection and Claim: The Buyers shall have the right to apply to the General Administration of Quanlity Supervision, Inspection and Quarantine of the People's Republic of China (AQSIQ) for inspection after discharge of the goods at the port of destination. Should the quality and/or quantity/weight be found not in conformity with the contract or invoice the Buyers shall be entitled to lodge claims with the Sellers on the basis of AQSIQ ' s Survey Report, within 90 days after discharge of the goods at the port of destination , with the exception, however, of those claims for which the shipping company and/or the insurance company are to be held responsible. All expenses incurred on the claim including the inspection fee as per the AQSIQ inspection certificate are to be borne by the Sellers. In case of FOB terms, the buyers shall also be entitled to claim freight for short weight if any.

(14) 不可抗力：由于人力不可抗拒事故，使卖方不能在合同规定期限内交货或者不能交货，卖方不负责任。但卖方必须立即通知买方，并以挂号函向买方提出有关政府机关或者商会所出具的证明，以证明事故的存在。由于人力不可抗拒事故致使交货期限延期一个月以上时，买方有权撤销合同。卖方不能取得出口许可证不得作为不可抗力。

Force Majeure: In case of Force Majeure the Sellers shall not held responsible for delay in delivery or non-delivery of the goods but shall notify immediately the Buyers and deliver to the Buyers by registered mail a certificate issued by government authorities or Chamber of Commerce as evidence thereof. If the shipment is delayed over one month as the consequence of the said Force Majeure, the Buyers shall have the right to cancel this Contract. Sellers' inability in obtaining export licence shall not be considered as Force Majeure.

(15) 延期交货及罚款：除本合同第（14）条人力不可抗拒原因外，如卖方不能如期交货，买方有权撤销该部分的合同，或经买方同意在卖方缴纳罚款的条件下延期交货。买方可同意给予卖方 15 天优惠期。罚款率为每 10 天按货款总额的 1%。不足 10 天者按 10 天计算。罚款自第 16 天起计算。最多不超过延期货款总额的 5%。

Delayed Delivery and Penalty: Should the Sellers fail to effect delivery on time as stipulated in this Contract owing to causes other than Force Majeure as provided for in Clause (14) of this Contract, the Buyers shall have the right to cancel the relative quantity of the contract, Or altenatively, the Sellers may, with the Buyers' consent, postpone delivery on payment of penalty to the Buyers. The Buyers may agree to grant the Sellers a grace period of 15 days. Penalty shall be calculated from the 16th day and shall not exceed 5% of the total value of the goods involved.

(16) 仲裁：一切因执行本合同或与本合同有关的争执，应由双方通过友好方式协商解决。如经协商不能得到解决时，应提交北京中国国际贸易促进委员会对外经济贸易仲裁委员会。按照中国国际贸易促进委员会对外经济贸易仲裁委员会仲裁程序暂行规定进行仲裁。仲裁委员会的裁决为终局裁决，对双方均有约束力。仲裁费用除非仲裁委员会另有决定，由败诉一方负担。

Arbitration: All disputes in connection with this Contract or the execution thereof shall be friendly negotiation. If no settlement can be reached, the case in dispute shall then be submitted for arbitration to the Foreign Economic and Trade Arbitration Commission of the China Council for the Promotion of International Trade in accordance with the Provisional Rules of Procedure of the Foreign Economic and Trade Arbitration Commission of the China Council for the Promotion of International Trade. The Award made by the Commission shall be accepted as final and binding upon both parties. The fees for arbitration shall be borne by the losing party unless otherwise awarded by the Commission.

(17) 附加条款：以上任何条款如与以下附加条款有抵触，以以下附加条款为准。

Additional Clause : If any of the above - mentioned Clauses is inconsistent with the following Additional Clause (s), the latter to be taken as authentic.

买　方	卖　方
The Buyers:	The Sellers:

D/R:

Shipper （发货人）	D/R No.（编号）
Consignee （收货人）	场站收据 Received by the Carrier the Total number of containers or other packages or units stated below to be transported subject to the terms and conditions of the carrier's regular form of Bill of Loading (for Combined Transport or port to Port Shipment) which shall be deemed to be incorporated herein. Date（日期）:
Notify Party （通知人）	
Pre carriage by（前程运输）Place of Receipt（收货地点）	
Ocean vessel（船名）Voy. No.（航次）Port of Loading(装货港)	场站章

Port of Discharge（卸货港）Place of delivery（交货地点）	Final Destination for Merchant's References（目的地）

— Particulars Furnished by Merchants —	Container No.（集装箱号）	Seal No.（封志号）Mark & Nos.（标记与号码）	No. of Containers or P'kgs.（箱数或件数）	Kind op Packages; Description of Goods（包装种类与货名）	Gross Weight 毛重(公斤)	Measurement 呎码(立方米)
	TOTAL NUMBER OF CONTAINERS OR PACKAGES(IN WORDS) 集装箱数或件数合计（大写）					

Container No.（箱号）Seal No.（封志号）Pkgs.（件数）Container No.（箱号）Seal No.（封志号）Pkgs.（件数）

Received（实收）	By Terminal clerk（场站员签字）

FREIGHT & CHARGES	Prepaid at(预付地点)	Payable at(到付地点)	Place of Issue(签发地点)	
	Total Prepaid(预付总额)	No. of Original B(s)/L（正本提单份数）	BOOKING(订舱确认) APPROVED BY	

Service Type on Receiving □-CY, □-CFS, □-DOOR	Service Type on delivery □-CY, □-CFS, □-DOOR	Reefer Temperature Required.（冷藏温度）		°F	°C
TYPE OF GOODS（种类）	□Ordinary, □Reefer □Dangerous, □Auto. （普通） （冷藏） （危险品） （裸装车辆）		危险品	Glass: Property: IMDG Code Page: UN NO.	
	□Liquid, □Live Animal, □Bulk, □______ （液体） （活动物） （散货）				

BOOKING NOTE：

THE NAME AND ADDRESS OF BENEFICARY
托运单 BOOKING NOTE

收货人：Consignee
通知人：Notify

(17) 提单号：B/L No.
(18) 船名 VSL.
(19) 编号 NO.：
(20) 日期 Date：
(21) 起运地 Loading Port：
(22) 装运地 Destination：

(3) 标记 Shipping Marks：	(4) 件数 Quantity：	(5) 货名 Description of Goods：	(6) 净重 毛重 N/W G/W	(7) 尺码 Measurement：

(23) 特殊条款 Special Conditions：

(8) 可否分批
(9) 可否转船
(10) 装船期限
(11) 结汇期限

(13) 正本
(14) 副本
(15) 存货地点
(16) 运费缴付方式

(12) 运费吨：　　运费率：　　运费金额：

SHIPPING ORDER:

NAME OF BENEFICIARY AND SIGNATURE

中国外轮代理公司 (货)

CHINA OCEAN SHIPPING AGENCY

装货单

SHIPPING ORDER

托运人
Shipper

编号 船名
No. S/S

目的港
For

兹将下列完好状况之货物装船后希签署收货单

Receive on board the undermentioned goods apparent in good order and condition and sign the accompanying receipt for the same

标记及号码 Marks & Nos	件数 Quantity	货名 Description of Goods	重量(公斤) Weight Kilos	
			净重	毛重
			Net	Gross

共计件数(大写)
Total Number of Package in Writing

日期 时间
Date Time

装入何舱
Stowed

实 收
Received

理货员签名 经办员
Tallied by Approved b

MATE'S RECEIPT:

中国外轮代理公司 货

CHINA OCEAN SHIPPING AGENCY

装货单

MATE'S RECEIPT

托运人

Shipper

编号 船名

No. S/S

目的港

For

兹将下列完好状况之货物装船后希签署收货单

Receive on board the undermentioned goods apparent in good order and condition and sign the accompanying receipt for the same

标记及号码 Marks & Nos	件数 Quantity	货名 Description of Goods	重量（公斤）Weight Kilos	
			净重 Net	毛重 Gross

共计件数（大写）

Total Number of Package in Writing

日期 时间

Date Time

装入何舱

Stowed

实收

Received

理货员签名 大副

Tallied by Chief Officer

B/L:

托运人 Shipper	B/L No.
收货人或指示 Consignee or order	SINOTRANS 中国对外贸易运输总公司 北 京 BEIJING **联 运 提 单** **COMBINED TRANSPORT BILL OF LADING**
通知地址 Notify address	RECEIVED the foods in apparent good order and condition as specified below unless otherwise stated herein. THE Carrier, in accordance with the provisions contained in this document, 1) undertakes to perform or to procure the performance of the entire transport form the place at which the goods are taken in charge to the place designated for delivery in this document, and 2) assumes liability as prescribed in this document for such transport One of the bills of Lading must be surrendered duty indorsed in exchange for the goods or delivery order

前段运输 Pre - carriage by	收货地点 Place of Receipt		
海运船只 Ocean Vessel	装货港 Port of Loading		
卸货港 Port of Discharge	交货地点 Place of Delivery	运费支付地 Freight payable at	正本提单份数 Number of original Bs/L

标志和号码 Marks and Nos.	件数和包装种类 Number and kind of packages	货 名 Description of goods	毛重（公斤） Gross weight(kgs.)	尺 码（立方米） Measurement(m^3)

以上细目由托运人提供

ABOVE PARTICULARS FURNISHED BY SHIPPER

运费和费用 Freight and charges	IN WITNESS whereof the number of original bills of Lading stated above have been signed, one of which being accomplished, the other (s) to be void.
	签单地点和日期 Place and date of issue
	代表承运人签字 Signed for or on behalf of the carrier
	代 理 as Agents

B/L（背面）

1. DEFINIYIONW herever the term "Shipper" occurs hereinafter. It shall be deemed to include also Receiver, Consignee. Holder of this Bill of Lading and Owner of the goods.

2. JURISDICTION All disputes arising under and in connection with this Bill of Lading shall be determined by the court in the People's Republic of China.

3. DEMISE CLAUSE If the ship is not owned by or chartered by demise to the corporation by whom this Bill of Lading is issued (as may be the case notwithstanding anything that appears to the contrary) this Bill of Lading shall take effect only as a contract with the Owner or demise charterer as the case may be as principal made through the agency of the said corporation who act as agents only and shall be under no personal liability whatsoever in respect thereof

4. HAGUE RULES This Bill of Lading shall have effect in respect of Carrier's liabilities, responsibilities, rights and immunities subject to the Hague Rules contained in the International Convention for the Unification of Certain Rules Relating to Bills of Lading 1924.

5. PACKING AND MARKS The Shipper shall have the goods properly packed accurately and clearly marked before shipment. The port of destination of the goods should be marked in letters of 5 cm high, in such a way as will remain legible until their delivery.

6. OPTIONAL STOWAGE (1) The goods may be stowed by the Carrier in containers or similar articles of transport used to consolidate goods (2) Goods stowed in containers other than flats, pallets, trailers, transportable tanks or similar articles of transport whether by the Carrier or the Shipper, may be carried on or under deck without notice to the Shipper. Such goods whether carried on or under deck shall participate in general average.

7. DECK CARGO. PLANTS AND LIVE ANIMALS Cargo on deck, plants and live animal are received, handled, carried, kept and discharged at Shipper's or Receiver's risk and the Carrier shall not be liable for loss thereof or damage thereto.

8. FREIGHT (1) Freight and charges shall be deemed earned on receipt of the goods by the Carrier and shall be paid by the Shipper and non - returnable and non - deductible in any event. Freight payable at destination together with other charges is due on arrival of the goods at the place of destination and shall be paid before delivery of the goods. (2) For the purpose of verifying the freight basis, the Carrier reserves the right to have the goods and the contents of containers, trailers or similar articles of transport inspected in order to ascertain the weight,

measurement, value or nature of the goods. In case the particulars of the goods furnished by the Shipper are incorrect, the Shipper shall be liable and bound to pay to the Carrier a sum either five times the difference between the correct freight and the freight charged or to double the correct less the freight charged, whichever sum is the smaller, as liquidated damages to the Carrier.

9. LIEN The Carrier shall have a lien on the goods and any documents relating thereto for all sums payable to the Carrier under this Bill of Lading and for general average contributions to whomsoever due and for the cost of recovering the same, and for that purpose shall have the right to sell the goods by public auction or private treaty without notice to the Shipper. If on sale of the goods, the proceeds fail to cover the amount due and the cost incurred, the Carrier shall be entitled to recover the deficit from the Shipper.

10. TIME BAR, NOTICE OF LOSS In any event the Carrier shall be discharged from all liabilities un-

der this Bill of Lading unless suit is brought within one year after the delivery of the goods or the date when the goods should have been delivered. Unless notice of loss of or damage to the goods and the general nature of it be given in writing to the Carrier at the place of delivery before or at the time of the removal of the goods into the custody of the person entitled to delivery thereof under this Bill of Lading, or, if the loss or damage such removal shall be prima facie evidence of the delivery by the Carrier of the goods as described in this Bill of Lading. In the case of any actual or apprehended loss or damage the Carrier and the Shipper shall give all reasonable facilities to each other for inspecting and tallying the goods.

11. THE AMOUNT OF COMPENSATION (1) When the Carrier is liable for compensation in respect of loss of or damage to the goods, such compensation shall be calculated by reference to the invoice value of the goods plus freight and insurance premium of paid. (2) Notwithstanding clause 4 of this Bill of Lading the limitation of liability under the Hague Rules shall be deemed to be RMB. ¥700 per package or unit. (3) Higher compensation may be claimed only when, with the consent of the Carrier, the value for the goods declared by the Shipper which exceeds the limits laid down in this clause has been stated in this Bill of Lading and extra freight has been paid as required. In that case the amount of the declared value shall be substituted for that limit. Any partial loss or damage shall be adjusted pro rata on the basis of such declared value.

12. LOADING, DISCHARGING AND DELIVERYT he goods shall be supplied and taken delivery of by the owner of the goods as fast as the ship can take and discharge them, without

interruption, by day and night. Sundays and Holidays included, notwithstanding any custom of the port to the contrary and the owner of the goods shall be liable for all losses or damages incurred in default thereof. Discharge may commence without previous notice. If the goods are not taken delivery of by the Receiver in due time from alongside the vessel, or if the Receiver refuses to take delivery of the goods, or in case there are unclaimed goods, the Carrier shall be at liberty to land such goods on shore or any other proper places at the sole risk and expense of the Shipper or Receiver, and the Carrier's responsibility of delivery of goods shall be deemed to have been fulfilled. If the goods are unclaimed during a reasonable time, or wherever the goods will become deteriorated, decayed or worthless, the Carrier may, at his discretion and subject to his lien and without any responsibility attaching to him, sell, abandon or otherwise dispose of such goods solely at the risk and expense of the Shipper.

13. LIGHTERAGE Any lighterage in or off ports of loading or ports of discharge shall be for the account of the Shipper or Receiver.

14. FORWARDING, SUBSTITUTE OF VESSEL, THROUGH CARGO AND TRANSHIPMENT If necessary, the Carrier may carry the goods to their port of destination by other persons or by rail or other means of transport proceeding either directly or indirectly to such port, and to carry the goods or part of them beyond their port of destination, and to transship and forward same at Carrier's expense but at Shipper's or Receiver's risk. The responsibility of the Carrier shall be limited to the part of the transport performed by him on the vessel under his management.

15. DANGEROUS GOODS, CONTRABAND (1) The Shipper undertakes not to tender for transportation any goods which are of a dangerous, inflammable, radio - active, and/or any harmful mature without previously giving written notice of their nature to the Carrier and marking the goods and the container or other covering on the outside as required by any laws or regulations which may be applicable during the carriage. (2) Whenever the goods are discovered to have been shipped without complying with the subclause (1) above or the goods are found to be contraband or prohibited by any laws or regulations of the port of loading, dis-

charge or call or any place or waters during the carriage, the Carrier shall be entitled to have such goods rendered innocuous, thrown overboard or discharged or otherwise disposed of at the carrier's discretion without compensation and the Shipper shall be liable for and indemnify the Carrier against any kind of loss, damage or liability including loss of freight, and any expenses directly or indirectly arising out of or resulting from such shipment. (3) If any goods shipped complying with the subclause (1) above become a danger to the ship or cargo, they may in like manner be rendered innocuous, thrown overboard or discharged or otherwise disposed of at the Carrier's discretion without compensation except to general average, of any.

16. REFRIGERATED CARGO (1) The Shipper undertakes not to tender for transportation any goods which require refrigeration without previously giving written notice of their nature and particular temperature range to be maintained. If the above requirements are not complied with, the Carrier shall not be liable for any loss of or damage to the goods howsoever arising. (2) Before loading goods in any insulated space, the Carrier shall, in addition to the Class Certificate, obtain the certificate of the Classification Society's Surveyor or other competent person, stating that such insulated space veyor or other competent person fit and safe for the carriage and preservation of refrigerated goods. The aforesaid certificate shall be conclusive evidence against the Shipper, Receiver and/or any Holder of Bill of Lading. (3) Receivers have to take delivery of refrigerated goods as soon as the ship is ready to deliver, otherwise the Carrier shall land the goods at the wharf at Receiver's or Shipper's risk and expense.

17. TIMBER Any statement in this Bill of Lading to the effect that timber has been shipped "in apparent good order and condition" does not involve any admission by the Carrier as to the absence of stains, shakes, splits, holes or broken pieces, for which the Carrier accepts no responsibility.

18. BULK CARGO As the Carrier has no reasonable means of checking the weight of bulk cargo, any reference to such weight in this Bill of Lading shall be deemed to be for reference only, but shall constitute in no way evidence against the Carrier.

19. COTTON Description of the apparent condition of cotton or cotton products does not relate to the insufficiency of or torn condition of the covering, nor to any damage resulting therefrom, and Carrier shall not be responsible for damage of such nature.

20. OPTIONAL CARGE The port of discharge for optional cargo must be declared to the vessel's agents at the first of the optional ports not late than 48 hours before the vessel's arrival there. In the absence of such declaration the Carrier may elect to discharge at the contract of carriage shall then be considered as having been fulfilled, Any option must be for the total quantity of goods under this Bill of Lading.

21. GOODS TO MORE THAN ONE CONSIGNEE Where bulk goods or goods without marks or goods with the same marks are shipped to more than one Consignee, the Consignees or

Owners of the goods shall jointly and severally bear any expense or loss in dividing the goods or parcels into pro rata quantities and any deficiency shall fall upon them in such proportion as the Carriers, his servants or agents shall decide.

22. HEAVY LIFTS AND OVER LENGTH CARGO Any one piece or package of cargo which exceeding 2000 kilos or 9 meters must be declared by the Shipper in writing before receipt by the Carrier and/or length Clearly and durably on the outside of the piece or package in letters and figures not less than 2 inches high by the Shipper. In case of the Shipper's failure in his obligations aforesaid, the Shipper shall be liable for loss of or damage to any property or for personal injury arising as a result of the Shipper's said failure and shall indemnify the Carrier against any kind of loss or liability suffered or incurred by the Carrier as a result of such failure.

23. SHIPPER－PACKED CONTAINERS. ETC. (1) If a container has not been filled, packed or stowed by the Carrier, the Carrier shall not be liable for any loss of or damage to its contents and the Shipper shall cover any loss or expense incurred by the Carrier, of such loss, damage or expense has been cause by negligent filling, packing or stowing of the container; or the contents being unsuitable for carriage in container; or the unsuitability or defective condition of the container unless the container has been supplied by the Carrier and the unsuitability or defective condition would not have been apparent upon reasonable inspection at or prior to the time when the container was filled, packed or stowed. (2) The provisions of the sub－clause (1) above also apply with respect to trailers, transportable tanks, flats and pallets which have not been filled, packed or stowed by the Carrier.

24. WAR, QUARANTINE, ICE, STRIKES, CONGESTION, ETC. Should it appear that war, blockade, pirate, epidemics, quarantine, ice, strikes, congestion and other causes beyond the Carrier's control would prevent the vessel from safely reaching the port of destination and discharging the goods thereat, the Carrier is entitled to discharge the goods at the port and the contract of carriage shall be deemed to have been fulfilled. Any extra expenses incurred under the aforesaid circumstances shall be borne by the Shipper or Receiver.

25. GENERAL AVERAGE General average shall be adjusted in Beijing in accordance with the Beijing Adjustment Rules 1975.

26. BOTH TO BLAME COLLISION If the carrying ship comes into collision with another ship as a result of the negligence of the other ship and any act, neglect or default in the navigation or the management of the carrying ship, the Shipper undertakes to pay the Carrier, or, where the Carrier is not the Owner and in possession of the carrying ship, to pay to the Carrier as trustee for the Owner and/or demise charterer of the carrying ship, a sum sufficient to indemnify the Carrier and/or the Owner and/or demise charterer of the carrying ship against all loss or liability to the other or non－carrying ship or her Owners insofar as such loss or liability represents loss of or damage to his goods or any claim whatsoever of the Shipper, paid or payable by the other or non－carrying ship or her Owners to the Shipper and set－off, recouped or recovered by the other or non－carrying ship or her Owners as part of their claim against the carrying ship or her Owner or demise charterer or the Carrier. The foregoing provisions shall also apply where the Owners, operations, or those in charge of any ship or ships or objects, other than, or in addition to, the colliding ships or objects, are at fault in respect to a collision, contact, stranding or other accident.

27. U. S. A. CLAUSE Notwithstanding any other term hereof the Carriage of Goods by Sea Act 1936 of the United States of America shall have been affect subject to in respect to carriage of goods to and from the United States of America. If any provision of this Bill of Lading be invalid under the Carriage of Goods by Sea Act 1936, such provision shall, to the extent of such invalidity, but no further, be null and void.

INSURANCE POLICY：

中国人民保险公司
THE PEOPLE'S INSURANCE COMPANY OF CHINA

Head Office：BEIJING　　Established in 1949

保 险 单　　号次

INSURANCE POLICY　　No. SH02/304246

中 国 人 民 保 险 公 司 （以下简称本公司）

This Policy of Insurance witnesses that The People's Insurance Company of China (hereinafter called
根 据
"the Company"), at the request of ____________________
（以下简称被保险人）的要求，由被保险人向本公司缴付约定
(hereinafter called "the Insured") and in consideration of the agreed premium paid to the Company by the
的保险费，按照本保险单承保险别和背面所载条款与下列
Insured, undertakes to insure the undermentioned goods in transportation subject to the conditions of this Policy
条款承保下述货物运输保险，特立本保险单。
as per the Clause printed overleaf and other special clauses attached hereon.

标　　记 Marks & Nos.	包装及数量 Quantity	保险货物项目 Description of Goods	保险金额 Amount Insured
As per Invoice No.			

总保险金额：
Total Amount Insured：____________________

保费　　费率　　装载运输工具
Premium：as arranged　Rate　as arranged　Per conveyance S. S. __________

开行日期　　自　　至
Slg. on or abt.　As Per B/L From ________ to __________

承保险别
Conditions

所保货物，如遇出险，本公司凭本保险单及其他有关证件给付赔款。
Claims, if any, payable on surrender of this Policy together with other relevant documents.
所保货物，如发生本保险单项下负责赔偿的损失或事故，
In the event of accident whereby loss or damage may result in a claim under this Policy immediate notice applying
应立即通知本公司下述代理人查勘。
For survey must be given to the Company's Agent as mentioned hereunder：

赔款偿付地点
Claim payable at ____________

日期　　上海
Date __________ Shanghai

地址：中国上海中山东一路23号。
Address：23 Zhongshan Dong Yi Lu Shanghai，China.
Cables：42001 Shanghai.
Telex：33128 PICCS CN

中国人民保险公司上海分公司
THE PEOPLE'S INSURANCE CO. OF CHINA
SHANGHAI BRANCH

____
General Manager

(1/1/1981)　　THE PEOPLE'S INSURANCE COMPANY OF CHINA

ENDORSEMENT：

中国人民保险公司

THE PEOPLE'S INSURANCE COMPANY OF CHINA

日期　年　月　日

Date

保险批单

ENDORSEMENT

保险金额：

Insured Amount ____________

船名：

Conveyance（s）____________

批单号次：

End. No. ____________

保险单或凭证号次

Policy/Certificate

开航日期：

No. ______ Slg. Date ______

被保险人：

Name of Insured ____________

保险费率：

Rate as arranged ____________

INSURANCE DECLARATION：

中国纺织品进出口公司上海市分公司

CHINA NATIONAL TEXTILES IMPORT & EXPORT CORPORATION

SHANGHAI BRANCH

27. ZHONGSHAN ROAD E. 1

SHANGHAI, CHINA

TEL：8621 -65342517　FAX：8621 -65724743

INSURANCE DECLARATION

(SHIPPING ADVICE)

Shanghai,

Messrs.

Dear Sir,

L/C No. --

Cover Note (or Open Policy)

No. --

Under the captioned Credit and Cover Note (or Open Policy), please insure the goods as detailed in our Invoice No.

Enclosed, other particulars being given below：

Carrying Vessel's Name：

Shipment Date：

Covering risks：

Kindly forward directly to the insured your Insurance Acknowledgement.

中国纺织品进出口公司上海市分公司

China National Textiles Import & Export Corporation

Shanghai Branch

SHANGHAI, CHINA

Manager

Bill of exchange under documentary credit:

BILL OF EXCHANGE

凭　　　　　　　　　　　　信用证

Drawn under·· L/C NO. ···············

日期

Dated······························支取　Payable with interest @····. . %······按······息······付款

号码　　　　汇票金额　　　　　　　　　　　　上海

NO·········　Exchange for　　　　　　Shanghai ······················20············

见票······················日后（本汇票之正本未付）付交

At ··············· sight of this SECOND of Exchange (First of Exchange being unpaid) Pay to the order of

金额

the sum of

此致:

To···

···

Bill for collection:

BILL OF EXCHANGE

号码　　　　汇票金额　　　　　　　　　　　　上海

No. ________ Exchange for　　　　　　Shanghai···········20············

见票　　　　日后（本汇票之副本未付）付交

At ____________ sight of this FIRST of Exchange (Second of Exchange being unpaid) pay to the order of ____

金额

the sum of

此致

To ________________________________

____

COLLECTION ORDER

Sender:
SHANGHAI GARMENT CORP.
No. 567 MAOTAI RD.
SHANGHAI CHINA

Documentary Collection
Place/Date
SHANGHAI, 12th, September 201

Registered

Our Reference AK/88
We send you here with the following documents for collection

BANK OF CHINA SHANGHAI BRANCH
documentary collection
P. O. Box 6006 SHANGHAI

<table>
<tr><td rowspan="2">Amount
USD 15 000</td><td rowspan="2">Maturity
D/P at sight</td><td>Drawee
MAXWELL HAMMERTON INC.
12, BROADWAY
NEW YORK. N. Y. 10014</td></tr>
<tr><td>Drawee Bank
COMMERCIAL CREDIT BANK
NEW YORK</td></tr>
</table>

Draft	INN.	CUST. INV.	INS POL.	CERT. ORIG	PKG. LIST	B/L	AWB	W/M CERT.	OTHER DOCUMENTS
3		4	2	4	2	3			

Goods: 11 700 SETS GIRL'S T/R VEST SUITS
By: S/S GLORIAFrom: SHANGHAITo: N. Y. On: 31th, Aug. 2013

Please follow the instructions marked "x"

<table>
<tr><td colspan="6">Documents goods to be delivered against</td><td colspan="2">Draft</td><td></td><td colspan="3">state the exact due - date</td></tr>
<tr><td>×</td><td colspan="2">payment</td><td></td><td colspan="2">Acceptance</td><td></td><td>to be sent back after acceptance</td><td></td><td colspan="3">to be collected on due - date</td></tr>
<tr><td>×</td><td colspan="5">Your charges for drawee's account, if refused</td><td>×</td><td>waive charges</td><td></td><td colspan="3">do not deliver documents</td></tr>
<tr><td>×</td><td colspan="5">Your correspondent's charges are for Account; if refused</td><td></td><td>waive charges</td><td>×</td><td colspan="3">do not deliver documents</td></tr>
<tr><td>×</td><td>Protest in case of</td><td>×</td><td>non - payment</td><td></td><td>non - acceptance</td><td>×</td><td>do not protestin case of</td><td>×</td><td>non - payment</td><td></td><td>non - acceptance</td></tr>
<tr><td>×</td><td>Advise</td><td>×</td><td>non - Payment</td><td></td><td>non - acceptance</td><td></td><td>by airmail</td><td>×</td><td>by cable</td><td>×</td><td>givin-greason</td></tr>
</table>

Please credit the proceeds as follows:

- to our SFr. Account No. 298 - 5678HL - M88
- Remit

Remarks:

In case of difficulties, the collecting bank is requested to inform our representatives: Messrs. Beach & Co. Inc., Broad Street 485, New York 34, who will be of assistance but who are not allowed to alter the above instructions.

Signature SHANGHAI GARMENT CORP.

The execution of this order is subject to the《Uniform rules for collections》 issued by the international chamber of Commerce Publication No. 522

IRREVOCABLE DOCUMENTARY CREDIT APPLICATION:

IRREVOCABLE DOCUMENTARY CREDIT APPLICATION

TO: L/C No. Date:

<table>
<tr><td colspan="2">Applicant</td><td>Beneficiary (full neame, address and tel etc.)</td></tr>
<tr><td>Partial shipments
( ) allowed
( ) not allowed</td><td>Transhipment
( ) llowed
( ) not allowed</td><td>issued by
( ) teletransmission
( ) express delivery</td></tr>
<tr><td colspan="2">Loading on board/dispatch/ taking in charge at/from</td><td>Contract No.:
Credit Amount (both in figures and words):

Trade Term: ( ) FOB ( ) CFR ( ) CIF
( ) Others:</td></tr>
<tr><td colspan="2">Description of goods:</td><td>Date and place of expiry: Aug. 30., 2004 CHINA

Credit available with
( ) by sight payment ( ) by acceptance
( ) by negotiation ( ) by deferred payment at

against the documents detailed herein
( ) and beneficiary's draft for of invoice value

On issuing bank</td></tr>
</table>

Documents required: (marked with X)

1. (X) Signed commercial invoice in 3 copies indicating L/ C No. and Contract No. SMST/24116
2. (X) Full set of clean on board Bills of Lading made out [X] to order/ [ ] to the order of and blank endorsed, marked " freight [X] prepaid/ [ ] to collect showing freight amount" notifying [ ] the applicant/ [ ]
3. ( ) Air Waybills showing "freight [ ] prepaid/ [ ] to collect indicating freight amount" and consigned to
4. ( ) Insurance Policy/Certificate in 3 copies for 110 % of the invoice value showing claims payable in China in currency of the draft, blank endorsed, covering ([ ] Ocean Marine Transportation / [ ] Air Transportation / [ ] Over Land Transportation) All Risks, War Risks. / [ ]
5. (X) Packing list / Weight Memo in 3 copies indicating
6. (X) Certificate of Quantity/ Weight in 3 copies issued by [X] manufacturer / [ ] Seller / [ ] independent surveyor at the loading port, indicating the actual surveyed quantity / weight of shipped goods as well as the packing condition.
7. (X) Certificate of Quality in 3 copies issued by [X] manufacturer / [ ] public recognized surveyor / [ ]
8. (X) Beneficiary's Certified copy of fax dispatched to the applicant within 2 days after shipment advising the contract number, name of commodity, quantity, invoice value, bill of loading, bill of loading date, the ETA date and shipping Co.
9. ( ) Beneficiary's Certificate certifying that extra copies of the documents have been dispatched to the [ ] applicant/ [ ]
10. ( ) Certificate of Origin in copies certifying.
11. ( ) Other documents, if any:

Addition instruction: (marked with X)

1. (X) All banking charges outside the opening bank are for beneficiary's account.
2. (X) Documents must be presented within 21 days after the date of issuance of the transport documents but within the validity of this credit.
3. ( ) Third party as shipper is not acceptable, Short Form / Blank B/l is not acceptable.
4. ( ) Both quantity and amount % more or less are allowed.
5. (X) All documents to be forwarded in one lot by express unless otherwise stated above.
6. ( ) Other terms, if any:

<table>
<tr><td>For banks use only</td><td rowspan="2">我公司承担本申请书背面所列
责任及承诺，并保证按照办理。

（申请人
名称及
印鉴章）

RMB A/C No.
USD or ( ) A/C No.
联系人： 电话：</td></tr>
<tr><td>Seal and / or Signature checked by ( )
L/C Margin % checked by ( )
Credit Facility checked by ( )

Ent ( ) Ver ( ) App ( )
Date:</td></tr>
</table>

This L/C is subject to the Uniform Customs and Practice for Documentary Credit (1993 Revision) ICC Publication No. 500.

L/C:

纽约银行

BANK OF NEW YORK

PAGE 1

48 WALL STREET	IRREVOCABLE DOCUMENTARY
P. O. BOX 11000	CREDIT NO. L - 02 - I - 03437
NEW YORK, N. Y. 10249, U. S. A.	DATE AND PLACE OF EXPIRY:
DATE AND PLACE OF ISSUE:	Dec. 5th, 2001
Sept. 30th, 2001 NEW YORK	IN THE COUNTRY OF THE BENEFICIARY
APPLICANT	BENEFICEARY:
CRYSTAL KOBE LTD.,	SHANGHAI TEXTILES I/E. CORP.
1410 BROADWAY, ROOM 3000	27. CHUANGSHAN ROAD E. 1
NEW YORK, N. Y. 10018 U. S. A.	SHANGHAI, CHINA
ADVISING BANK:	AMOUNT: USD23, 522. 50
BANK OF CHINA,	(SAY UNITED STATES DOLLARS TWENTY
SHANGHAI BRANCH	THREE THOUSAND FIVE HUNDRED TWENTY
CHINA.	TWO AND 50/100 ONLY)
PARTIAL SHIPMENTS ARE NOT ALLOWED	CREDIT AVAILABLE BY NEGOTIATION
TRANSHIPMENT IS ALLOWED	AGAINST PRESENTATION OF THE DOC
SHIPMENT FROM SHANGHAI	DETAILED HEREIN AND OF YOUR DRAFT (S)
TO NEW YORK	AT SIGHT DRAWN ON US
LATEST Nov. 20th, 2001	FOR FULL INVOICE VALUE

LIST OF DOCUMENTS TO BE PRESENTED:

--- SIGNED COMMERCIAL INVOICE QUADRUPLICATE INDICATING S/C NO. 21SSG - 017 OF SHANGHAI TEXTILE IMPORT & EXPORT CORP.

--- PACKING LIST AND WEIGHT NOTE IN TRIPLICATE.

--- INSURANCE POLICY OR CERTIFICATE IN 2/2 AND ENDORSED IN BLANK FOR 110 PCT OF FULL TOTAL INVOICE VALUE COVERING ALL RISKS, WAR RISKS AS PER THE RELEVANT OCEAN MARINE CARGO CLAUSE OF P. I. C. C. DATED JAN. 1ST, 1981. WITH CLAMS, IF ANY, PAYABLE AT DESTINATION

--- FULL SET OF AT LEAST IN 3/3 CLEAN ON BOARD MARINE BILL OF LADING MADE OUT CRYSTAL KOBE LTD., 1410 BROADWAY, ROOM 300 NEW YORK, NY10018 U. S. A. NOTIFY ABOVE MENTIONED APPLICANT WITH FULL ADRESS AND TEL. NO. 559 - 525 - 70000 AND MARKED "FREIGHT PREPAID".

--- COPY OF BENEFICIARY'S CABLE/TELEX DESPATCHED TO APPLICANT (CABLE ADDRESS 5665NY TELEX NO. 62361 THK OK NY) ADVISING SHIPMENT DETAILS INCLUDING CREDIT NO., VESSEL'S NAME, SHIPMENT DATE, PACKAGES, AMOUNT, QUANTITY AND SHIPPING MARK ON OR BEFORE SHIPMENT DFFECTED.

CONTINUE TO NEXT PAGE

纽约银行
BANK OF NEW YORK

48 WALL STREET PAGE 2

P. O. BOX 11000

NEW YORK , N. Y. 10249 , U. S. A.

CONTINUATION OF IRREVOCABLE DOCUMENTARY CREDIT NUMBER L－02－I－03437

--- BENEFICIARY'S CERTIFICATE UNDERTAKING THAT IN CASE UNUSAL QUALITY PROBLEMS OCCUR UNDER THIS L/C, THE BUYER HOLDS THE RIGHT OF RETURNING, EXCHANGING OF GOODS OR CLAIMS UPON PRESENTING EFFECTIVE INSPECTION CERTIFICATE ISSUED BY CHINA EXIT AND ENTRY INSPECION AND QUARANTINE BUREAU WITHIN 90 DAYS OF ARRIVAL OF GOODS IN DESTINATION.

COVERING SHIPMENT' OF

LADIE'S 55% ACRYLIC 45% COTTON KNITED BLOUSE STYLE NO. H32331SE

ORDER NO. 21SSG－017

QUANTITY：

500 DOZ AT USD48. 50 PER DOZ CIF NEW YORK LESS 3 PCT

SHIPPING MARK：

CRYSTAL KOBE LTD. ,
NEW YORK
ORDER NO. 21SSG－017
STYLE NO. H32331SE
L－02－I－03437
CARTON/NO. 1－－120
MADE IN CHINA

SPECIAL INSRUCTION（S）：

--- ALL BANKING CHARGES OUTSIDE NEW YORK ARE FOR ACCOUNT OF BENEFICIARY

--- A FEE OF USD25. 00 WILL BE DEDUCTED FROM THE REIMBURSEMENT CLAIM FOR EACH PRESENTATION OF DISCREPANT DOCUMENTS UNDER THIS CREDIT.

--- PACKING LISTS TO SHOW QUANTITY OF PIECES AND EACH PIECE PER CARTON.

--- DOCUMENTS ISSUED IN COMBINED FORM NOT ACCEPTABLE.

--- NEGOTIATION OF THIS CREDIT IS RESTERICTED TO BANK OF CHINA.

CONTINUE TO NEXT PAGE

纽约银行

BANK OF NEW YORK

48 WALL STREET PAGE 3

P. O. BOX 11000

NEW YORK , N. Y. 10249, U. S. A.

CONTINUATION OF IRREVOCABLE DOCUMENTARY CREDIT NUMBER L-02-I-03437

INSTRUCTIONS TO THE NEGOTIATING BANK:

--- THE NEGOTIATING BANK IS KINDLY REQUESTED TO FORWARD ALL DOCUMENTS TO US (48 WALL STREET P. O. BOX 11000 NEW YORK, N. Y. 10249, U. S. A.) IN ONE LOT BY REGISTERED AIRMAIL.

--- IN REIMBURSEMENT FOR YOUR NEGOTIATION (S), WE SHALL CREDIT YOUR ACCOUNT WITH US UPON MATURITY AFTER RECEIVING OF DOCUMENTS PROVIDED THAT ALL TERMES CONDITIONS OF THIS CREDIT HAVE BEEN FULLY COMPLIED WITH.

* * * END OF L/C * * *

WE HEREBY ISSUE THIS DOCUMENTARY CREDIT IN YOUR FAVOUR . IT IS SUBJECT TO THE UNIFORM CUSTOMS AND PRACTICE FOR DOCUMENTARY CREDITS (1993 REVISION INTERNATIONAL CHAMBER OF COMMERDE, PARIS. FRANCE, PUBLICATION NO. 500) AND ENGAGES US IN ACCORDANCE WITH THE TERMS THEREOF, AND ESPECIALLY IN ACCORDANCE WITH THE TERMS OF ARTICLE 10 THEREOF. THE NUMBER AND THE DATE OF THE CREDIT AND THE NAME OF OUR BANK MUST BE QUOTED ON ALL DRAFTS REQUIRED, IF THE CREDIT IS AVAILABLE BY NEGOTIATION, EACH PRESENTATION MUST BE NOTED ON THE REVERSE OF THIS ADVICE BY THE BANK WHERE THE CREDIT IS AVAILABLE.

YOURS FAITHFULLY

FOR BANK OF NEW YORK

NEW YORK

AUTHORIZED SIGNATURES

REIMBURSEMENT CLAIM
BANK OF CHINA

Date ______________

To: Reimbursement Unit

LETTER OF CREDIT NO. ______________
ISSUING BANK ______________
OUR REFERENCE NO. ______________

Gentlemen:

We have negotiated documents under this Letter of Credit. Please reimburse us in accordance with the instructions checked.

( ) Credit our account (number) ______________ with you for ______________

( ) Remit $ to

(Address) ______________ (Accepted Number) ______________ for

credit to our account ______________ with them.

( ) Accept draft and (discount/ hold until maturity)

( ) The amount of our claim represents negotiation amounting to

$ ______________ plus our charges (if any) of $ ______________

( ) Advise payment via ( ) Airmail ( ) Cable/ Wire

( ) Advise non – payment via ( ) Airmail ( ) Cable/ Wire

Yours truly

____

(Authorized Signature)

偿付授权书

REIMBURSEMENT AUTHORIZATION ON LETTERS OF CREDIT

(LETTER HEAD OF NEGOTIATING BANK)

Date ________________

TO: Reimbursement Unit

LETTER OF CREDIT NO. ____________
FOR $ ____________________________
VALID UNTILL ______________________

Gentlemen:

We have advised the above Sight/ Usance through ______________designating you as the reimbursing bank.

Please honor reimbursement requested by debiting our account with you as follows:

(   ) All charges are for our account

(   ) All charges for beneficiary's account

(   ) Accept drafts at __________ days, date ________or sight.

Acceptance commission and discount charges (if any) are for our/ beneficiary's account.

(   ) Special instructions

Yours truly

____

(Authorized Signature)

COMMERCIAL INVOICE：

上海市纺织品进出口公司

SHANGHAI TEXTILES IMPORT & EXPORT CORPORATION

27 CHUNGSHAN ROAD E. 1.

SHANGHAI, CHINA

TEL：8621－65342517　FAX：8621－65724743

COMMERCIAL INVOICE

TO：M/S.

号码

No：__________

订单或合约号码

Sales Confirmation No. __________

日 期

Date __________

装船口岸

From __________

目的地

To __________

信用证号数

Letter of Credit No. __________

开证银行

Issued by __________

唛号 Marks & Nos.	货名数量 Quantities and Descriptions	总 值 Amount

上海市纺织品进出口公司

We certify that the goods are of Chinese origin.

Shanghai Textiles Import & Export Corporation

SHANGHAI, CHINA

CANADA CUSTOMS INVOICE:

Revenue Canada　Revenue Canada　**CANADA CUSTOMS INVOICE**

Customs and Excise　Douanes et Accise　FACTURE DES DOU ANES CANADIENNE

1 Vendor (Name and Address)　2 Date of Direct Shipment to Canada / Date d'expedition directe

/ Vendeur (Name et adresse).　vers le Canada

3 Other References (Include Purchaser's Order No)

Autres references (Inclure le n de commande de l' acheteur)

4 Consignee (Name and Address)　5 Purchaser's Name and Address (if other than Consignee)

/ Destinataire (Nom et adresse)　Nom et adresse de l' acheteur (S' il differe du destinataire)

6 Country of Transhipment / Pays de transbordement

7 Country of Origin of Goods　IF SHIPMENT INCLUDS

Pays d' origine des marchandises　GOODS OF DIFFERENT

ORIGINS ENTER ORIGINS

AGAINST ITEMS IN 12.

8TransportationGiveModeandPlaceofDirectShipmentto　9 Conditions of Sale and Terms of Payment

Canada Transport Preciser mode et point d' expedition directe (i. e. Sale, Consignment Shipment. Leased Goods, etc.)

Vers le Canada　Conditions de vente et modalites de paiement

(p. ex. vente, expedition en consignation, location de marchan - dises. etc.)

10 Currency of Settlement / Devises du paiement

11 No of　12 Specification of Commodities (Kind of Packages, 13 Quantity (State Unit) Selling Price / Prix de vente

Pkgs ND'e Marks and Numbers, General Description and Char - (Preciser l' unite)　14 Unit Price　15 Total

De colis　acteristics, i. e. Grade, Quality　Prix unitaire

18 If any of fields 1 to 17 are included on an attached commercial -　16 Total Weight / Poids Total　17 Invoice Total

invoice. Check this box

Commercial Invoice No. ______________ Net Gross / Bru

19 Exporter's Name and Address (If other than Vendor)
Nom et adresse de l' exportatur (S' il deffere du vendeur)

20 Originator (Name and Address) / Expediteur d' origine
(Nom et adresse)

21 Departmental Ruling (If applicable) / Decision du Ministere
(S' il y a lieu)

22 If fields 23 to 25 are not applicable, check this box
Si les zones 23 a 25 sont sans object, cocher cette boite

23 If included in field 17 indicate amount
Si compris dans le total a la zone 17. Preciser
(i) Transportation charges, expenses and insurance from the place of direct shipment to Canada.

$ __________

(ii) Costs for construction, erection and assembly incurred afer importation into Canada.

$ __________

(iii) Export packing

$ __________

24 If not included in field 17 indicate amount
Si non copris dans le total a la zone 17 preciser
(i) Transportation charges. Expenses and insurance to the place of direct shipment to Canada.

$ __________

(ii) Amounts for commissions other than buying commissions.

$ __________

(iii) Export packing

$ __________

25 Check (If applicable):
Cocher (S' il y a lieu):
(i) Royalty payments or subsequent proceeds are paid or payable by the purchaser.
(ii) The purchaser has supplied goods or services for use in the production of these goods.

DEPARTMENT OF NATIONAL REVENUE CUSTOMS AND EXCISE　MINISTERE DU REVENU NATIONAL DOUANES ET ACCISE

XXXXXX 有限公司
XXXXXX CO. , LTD. Room 2901, HuaRong Mansion, GuanJiaQiao 85#, Shanghai 200005, P. R. China TEL: 021 - 4711363　FAX: 021 - 4691619

PROFORMA INVOICE

TO:	SAMAN AL - ABDUL KARIM AND PARTNERS CO. POB 13552, RIYADH 44166, KSA TEL: 4577301/4577312/4577313　FAX: 4577461	INVOICE NO. :	DS2001INV205
		INVOICE DATE:	Sep. 09, 2001
		S/C NO. :	DS2001SC205
		S/C DATE:	Mar. 23, 2001

TERM OF PAYMENT:	By Irrevocable Letter of Credit to be opened by full amount of S/C, Payment at Sight document to presented within 21 days after date of B/L at beneficiary's account.
PORT TO LOADING:	SHANGHAI PORT, P. R. CHINA
PORT OF DESTINATION:	DAMMAM PORT, SAUDI ARABIA
TIME OF DELIVERY:	Before Jun. 05, 2001
INSURANCE:	TO BE COVERED BY THE BUYER.
VALIDITY:	

Marks and Numbers	Number and kind of package / Description of goods	Quantity	Unit Price	Amount
			USD	
				CFR DAMMAM PORT, SAUDI ARABIA
N/M	CANNED APPLE JAM 24 TINS X 340 GMS	2200CARTONS	USD6. 80	USD14960. 00
	CANNED STRAWBERRY JAM 24 TINS X 340 GMS	2200CARTONS	USD6. 80	USD14960. 00
	Total Amount:	4400CARTONS		USD29920. 00

SAY TOTAL:	U. S. DOLLAR TWENTY NINE THOUSAND NINE HUNDRED AND TWENTY ONLY.

BENEFICIARY:	XXXXXX CO. , LTD. Room 2901, HuaRong Mansion, GuanJiaQiao 85#, Shanghai 200005, P. R. China TEL: 021 - 4711363　FAX: 021 - 4691619
ADVISING BANK:	BANK OF CHINA SHANGHAI BRANCH
NEGOTIATING BANK:	BANK OF CHINA SHANGHAI BRANCH

上海纺织品进出口有限公司

SHANGHAI TEXTILES I/E CORP.

PACKING LIST

ADD：27，CHUNGSHAN ROAS E1.

TEL：8621－65342517　FAX：8621－65724743

MESSR：

CRYSTAL KOBE LTD.，　　INVOICE NO：STP015088

1410 BROADWAY，ROOM 3000　　S/C NO：21SSG－017

NEW YORK，N. Y. 10018 U. S. A　Date：NOV. 8th，2013

DESCRIPTION OF GOODS	SHINPPING MARKS：
55% ACRYLIC 45% COTTON LADIES' KNITTED BLOUSE STYLE NO. H32331SE： PAYMENT BY L/C NO. L－02－I－03437 SHIPPING S/C NO.	CRYSTAL KOBE LTD.， NEW YORK ORDER NO. 21SSG－017 STYLE NO. H32331SE L－02－I－03437 CARTON/NO. 1－120 MADE IN CHINA

COLOUR BREAKDOWN：　SIZE

COLOR		PACK	S	M	L	XL	XXL	XXXL	TOTAL（PCS)
IVORY			120	360	240				720
BLACK			320	360	440				1120
NAVYBLUE			180	180	100				460
RED			432	580	440				1452
WHITE			78	234	156				468
BROWN			160	280	220				660
TAWNY			320	360	440				1120
TOTAL（PCS)：									6000

SIZE ASSORTMENT								QUANTITY	
CTN NO.	COLOR	CTNS	S	M	L	XL	XXL	XXXL	(PCS)
1－20	IVORY	20	6	18	12				720
21－40	BLACK	20	16	18	22				1120
41－50	NAVYBLUE	10	18	18	10				460
51－66	RED	16	16	28	22				1056
67－79	WHITE	13	6	18	12				468
80－89	BROWN	10	16	28	22				660
90－109	TAWNY	20	16	18	22				1120
110－120	RED	11	16	12	8				396

TOTAL：　6000 PCS IN 120 CARTONS ONLY.

GROSS WT：	2584KGS	NET WT：	2326KGS
MEASUREMENT：	60×40×40CBCM		11.58CBM

For and on behalf of

上海纺织品进出口有限公司
SHANGHAI TEXTILES I/E CORP.

Authorized Signature（s）

中国纺织品进出口公司上海市分公司

CHINA NATIONAL TEXTILES IMPORT&EXPORT CORPORATION

SHANGHAI BRANCH

27. CHUNGSHAN ROAD E. 1.
SHANGHAI, CHINA
TEL：8621－65342517　FAX：8621－65724743

To：M/S

装船通知

SHIPPING ADVICE

发票号码　　　　　　　　日　期
No. ______　　　　　　　　Date ______

装船口岸　　　　　目的地
From ______　　　　To ______

信用证号数　　　　　　开证银行
Letter of Credit No. ______　　Issued by ______

唛号 Marks & Nos.　　货 名 数 量 Quantities and Description　　总　值 Amount

上列货物装运船名
The above goods shipped per s. s. ______
开 航 日 期
Sailing on or about ______

中国纺织品进出口公司上海市分公司
China National Textiles Imp. & Exp. Corporation

SHANGHAI BRANCH
SHANGHAI CHINA

______

SHANGHAI TEXTILES IMPORT & EXPORT CORPORATION

27. CHUNGSHAN ROAD E. 1.

SHANGHAI CHINA

TEL: 8621 - 65342517 FAX: 8621 - 65724743

SHIPPING ADVICE

Nov. 20th, 2013

Messre: CRYSTAL KOBE LTD.,

Dear Sirs:

Re: Invoice No.: STP015088 L/C No.: L-02-I-03437

We hereby inform you that the goods under the above mentioned credit have been shipped. The details of the shipment ae stated below.

Commodity:	LADIE'S 55% ACRYLIC 45% COTTON KNITED BLOUSE
Quantity:	120 CARTONS
Amount:	USD 23 522γ50
Ocean Vessel:	ZHELU V. 031118SE
Bill of lading No.:	CSA1505
E. T. D.:	On / or about Nov. 25th, 2001
Port of Loading:	SHANGHAI
Destination:	NEW YORK

We hereby certify that the above content is true and correct.

SHANGHAI TEXTILES IMPORT & EXPORT CORP.

× × ×

Export license：

1. 申领许可证单位 编码 Exporter			3. 出口许可证编号 License No.		
2. 发货单位 Consignee			4. 许可证有效期 Validity		
5. 贸易方式 Terms of trade			8. 输往国家（地区） Country of destination		
6. 合同号 Contract No.			9. 收款方式 Terms of payment		
7. 启运口岸 Port of shipment			10. 运输方式 Means of transport		
11. 唛头—包装件数 Marks & numbers - number of packages					
12. 商品名称 商品编码 Description of commodity Commodity No.					
13. 商品规格、型号 Specification	单位 Unit	14. 数量 Quantity	15. 单价 Unit price	16. 总值 Amount	17. 总值折美元 Amount in USD
18. 总计 Total					
19. 备注 Supplementary			20. 发证机关盖章 Issuing Authority's Stamp 发证日期 Signature Date		

中华人民共和国出口许可证申请表

<table>
<tr><td colspan="3">1. 出口商： 代码：

领证人姓名： 电话：</td><td colspan="3">3. 出口许可证号：</td></tr>
<tr><td colspan="3">2. 发货人： 代码：</td><td colspan="3">4. 出口许可证有效截止日期：
年 月 日</td></tr>
<tr><td colspan="3">5. 贸易方式：</td><td colspan="3">8. 进口国（地区）：</td></tr>
<tr><td colspan="3">6. 合同号：</td><td colspan="3">9. 付款方式：</td></tr>
<tr><td colspan="3">7. 报关口岸：</td><td colspan="3">10. 运输方式：</td></tr>
<tr><td colspan="6">11. 商品名称： 商品编码：</td></tr>
<tr><td>12. 规格、等级</td><td>13. 单位</td><td>14. 数量</td><td>15. 单价(币别)</td><td>16. 总值(币别)</td><td>17. 总值折美元</td></tr>
<tr><td></td><td></td><td></td><td></td><td></td><td></td></tr>
<tr><td></td><td></td><td></td><td></td><td></td><td></td></tr>
<tr><td></td><td></td><td></td><td></td><td></td><td></td></tr>
<tr><td></td><td></td><td></td><td></td><td></td><td></td></tr>
<tr><td>18. 总 计</td><td></td><td></td><td></td><td></td><td></td></tr>
<tr><td colspan="3" rowspan="2">19. 备 注

申请单位盖章

申领日期：</td><td colspan="3">20. 发证机构审批（初审）：

经办人：</td></tr>
<tr><td colspan="3">终审：</td></tr>
</table>

填表说明：1. 本表应用正楷逐项填写清楚，不得涂改、遗漏，否则无效。

2. 本表内容需打印多份许可证的，请在备注栏内注明。

3. 本表填写一式二份。

一般原产地证书
ORIGINAL

1. Exporter (full name and address)

2. Consignee (full name, address, country)

CERTIFICATE NO

CERTIFICATE OF ORIGIN
OF
THE PEOPLE'S REPUBLIC OF CHINA

3. Means of transport and route

4. Country / region of destination

5. For certifying authority use only

6. Marks and numbers	7. Number and kind of packages description of goods;	8. H. S. Code	9. Quantity	10. Number and date of invoices

11. Declaration by the exporter

The undersigned hereby declares that the above details and statement are correct; that all the goods were produced in China and that they comply with the Rules of Origin of the People's Republic of China.

Place and date, signature and stamp of authorized signatory

12. Certification

it is hereby certified that the declaration by the exporter is correct.

Place and date, signature and stamp of certifying authority

普惠制产地证明书申请书

申请人单位（盖章）：　　　　　　　　　　　证书号：________

申请人郑重声明：　　　　　　　　　　　　　注册号：________

本人是被正式授权代表出口单位办理和签署本申请书的。

本申请书及普惠制产地证格式 A 所列内容正确无误，如发现弄虚作假，冒充格式 A 所列货物，擅改证书，自愿接收签证机关的处罚及负法律责任。现将有关情况申报如下：

生产单位		生产单位联系人电话	
商品名称（中英文）		H. S税目号（以六位数码计）	

商品（FOB）总值（以美元计）		发票号	
最终销售国	证书种类划“√”	加急证书	普通证书
货物拟出运日期			

贸易方式和企业性质（请在适用处划“√”）

正常贸易 C	来进	料加工 L	补偿贸易 B	中外合资 H	中外合作 Z	外商独资 D	零售 Y	展卖 M

包装数量或毛重或其他数量	

原产地标准：

本项商品系在中国生产，完全符合该给惠国给惠方案规定，其原产地情况符合以下第　条；

（1）“P”（完全国产，未使用任何进口原材料）；

（2）“W”其 H. S税目号为……………………（含进口成分）；

（3）“F”（对加拿大出口产品，其进口成分不超过产品出厂价值的 40%）。

本批产品系：　1. 直接运输从………………到……………………；　2. 转口运输从………………中转国（地区）……………到…………；

申请人说明　　　　　　　领证人（签名）

电　话：

日期　　　　年　　月　　日

现提交中国出口商业发票副本一份，普惠制产地证明书格式 A（FORM A）一正二副，以及其他附件　　份，请予审核签证。

注：凡含有进口成分的商品，必须按要求提交《含进口成分受惠商品成本明细单》。

商 检 局 联 系 记 录	

普惠制原产地证书

ORIGINAL

<table>
<tr>
<td colspan="3">1. Goods consigned from (Exporter's business name, address, country)</td>
<td colspan="3" rowspan="2">Reference No:
GENERALIZED SYSTEM OF PREFERENCES
CERTIFICATE OF ORIGIN
(Combined declaration and certificate)
FORM A
Issued in THE PEOPLE'S REPUBLIC OF CHINA
(country)
See Notes, overleaf</td>
</tr>
<tr>
<td colspan="3">2. Goods consigned to (Consignee's name, address, country)</td>
</tr>
<tr>
<td colspan="3">3. Means of transport and route (as far as known)</td>
<td colspan="3">4. For official use</td>
</tr>
<tr>
<td>5. Item number</td>
<td>6. Marks and numbers of packages</td>
<td>7. Nunber and kind of packages; description of goods</td>
<td>8. Orign criterion (see Notes Overleaf)</td>
<td>9. Gross weight or other quantity</td>
<td>10. Number and date of invoices</td>
</tr>
<tr>
<td colspan="3">11. Certification
It is hereby certified, on the basis of control carried out, that the declaration by the exporter is correct.

Place and date, signature and stamp of certifying authority</td>
<td colspan="3">12. Declaration by the exporter
The undersigned hereby declares that the above details and statements are correct; that all the goods were produced in CHINA
(country)
and that they comply with the origin requirements specified for those goods in the Generalized System of Preferences for goods exported to

(importing country)

Place and date, signature of authorized signatory</td>
</tr>
</table>

中华人民共和国出入境检验检疫
出境货物报检单

报检单位（加盖公章）：　　　　　　　　＊编　号________

报检单位登记号：　　联系人：　电话：　　报检日期：　年　月　日

发货人	（中文）				
	（外文）				
收货人	（中文）				
	（外文）				
货物名称（中/外文）	H.S.编码	产地	数/重量	货物总值	包装种类及数量

运输工具名称号码		贸易方式		货物存放地点	
合同号		信用证号		用途	
发货日期		输往国家（地区）		许可证/审批号	
启运地		到达口岸		生产单位注册号	
集装箱规格、数量及号码					

合同、信用证订立的检验检疫条款或特殊要求	标记及号码	随附单据（划“√”或补填）	
		• 合同 • 信用证 • 发票 • 换证凭单 • 装箱单 • 厂检单	• 包装性能结果单 • 许可/审批文件

需要证单名称（划“√”或补填）		＊检验检疫费	
• 品质证书　_正_副 • 重量证书　_正_副 • 数量证书　_正_副 • 兽医卫生证书　_正_副 • 健康证书　_正_副 • 卫生证书　_正_副 • 动物卫生证书　_正_副	• 植物检疫证书　_正_副 • 熏蒸/消毒证书　_正_副 • 出境货物换证凭单 • 出境货物通关单	总金额（人民币元）	
		计费人	
		收费人	

报检人郑重声明：	领取证单	
1. 本人被授权报检。 2. 上列填写内容正确属实，货物无伪造或冒用他人的厂名、标志、认证标志，并承担货物质量责任。	日期	
签名：________	签名	

注：有“＊”号栏由出入境检验检疫机关填写　　◆国家出入境检验检疫局制［1-1(2000.1.1)］

入境货物报检单

中华人民共和国出入境检验检疫
入境货物报检单

报检单位（加盖公章）：　　　　　　　＊编　号

报检单位登记号：　联系人：　电话：　报检日期：年　月　日

收货人	（中文）		企业性质（划"√"）	□合资□合作□外资	
	（外文）				
发货人	（中文）				
	（外文）				
货物名称 （中/外）	H. S. 编码	原产国（地区）	数/重量	货物总值	包装种类及数量
运输工具 名称号码			合同号		
贸易方式		贸易国别 （地区）		提单/运单号	
到货日期		启运国家 （地区）		许可证/审批号	
卸毕日期		启运口岸		入境口岸	
索赔 有效期至		经停口岸		目的地	
集装箱规格、数量 及号码					
合同订立特殊条款 以及其他要求			货物存放地点		
			用　途		
随附单据（划"√"或补填）		标记及记号	＊外商投资财产（划"√"）	□是□否	
□合同 □发票 □提/运单 □兽医卫生证书 □植物检疫证书 □动物检疫证书 □卫生证书 □原产地证书 □许可/审批文件	□到货通知 □装箱单 □质保书 □理货清单 □磅码单 □验收报告 □ □ □		＊检验检疫费		
			总金额 （人民币元）		
			计费人		
			收费人		
报检人郑重声明： 1. 本人被授权报检。 2. 上列填写内容正确属实。 签名：＿＿＿＿			领取单证		
			日期		
			签名		

注：有"＊"号栏由出入境检验检疫机关填写　　◆国家出入境检验检疫局制[1－1(2000.1.1)]

出境货物换证凭单

中华人民共和国出入境检验检疫

出境货物换证凭单

类别：　　预检　　　　　　　　　　　　编号 320800202016597

发货人	安徽省安庆市＊＊＊公司	标记及号码 暂　无	
收货人	＊＊＊		
品名	经编晴纶毯		
H. S. 编码	63019000. 10		
报检数/重量	3000 条		
包装种类及数量	纸箱 100 箱		
申报总值	美元： 9300 元		
产地	江 苏　　无 锡	生产单位（注册号）	无锡 *** 家用纺织品有限公司
生产日期	2012 年 7 月	生产批号	02AQXH0405
包装性能检验结果单号	320800301003705	合同/信用证号	02AQXH0405/ ***
		运输工具名称及编号	***　***
输往国家或地区	＊ ＊ ＊	集装箱规格及数量	***　***
发货日期	***	检验依据	FZ61002－90 标准及合同
检验检疫结果	本批产品共 100 箱/3000 条，经按 FZ61002－91 标准，在仓库随机抽取代表性样品 150 条，根据检验依据要求进行检验，结果如下： 成　　　份：　腈纶 规　　　格：　100cm × 140cm 重　　　量：　0. 7kg/pc 外观检验评定：　合格 评　　　定：　上述货物符合检验依据要求。 ＊＊＊＊＊＊＊＊＊ 签字：　　　　日期：　2012 年　7　月　8　日		
本单有效期	截止于 2013 年 7 月 7 日		
备注	＊＊＊		

分批出境核销栏	日期	出境数/重量	结存数/重量	核销人	日期	出境数/重量	结存数/重量	核销人

说明：1. 货物出境时，经口岸检验检疫机关查验货证相符，且符合检验检疫要求的予以签发通关单或换发检验检疫证书；2. 本单不作为国内贸易的品质或其他证明；3. 涂改无效。

A 5432818　　　　①办理换证　　　　[5－3(2001. 1. 1) ＊1]

出入境货物代理报检委托书

出入境货物代理报检委托书

委托单位		十位编码	
地址		联系电话/经办人	

我单位将于__________年__ 月进口 □ 出口 □ 以下货物

货物名称		H. S. 编码		件数/重量	
货值		贸易性质		包装性质	
货物起运国		货物产地		合同号或发票号	
企业性质		运单号		信用证号	
经营范围					

随附单据名称、份数及编号：

1. 合同____ 份；编号：____
2. 发票____ 份；编号：____
3. 装箱清单____ 份；编号：____
4. 登记手册____ 本；编号：____
5. 许可证____ 份；编号：____
6. 不办、免办证明____份；编号：____
7. 机电证明______份；编号：____
8. 海关免表______份；编号：____
9. 换证凭单或电子转单______份；编号：____
10. ________________________

我单位郑重声明，保证遵守中华人民共和国出入境检验检疫有关法律、法规的规定和检验检疫机构的各项规章制度。如有违反行为，自愿接受检验检疫机构的处罚并负法律责任。

我单位所委托受委托人向出入境检验检疫局提交的“报检单”和随附各种单据所列内容是真实无讹的。

（以上内容由委托单位填写）

被委托单位		报检单位注册号	
地址		联系电话	
经办人		报检证号	

（以上内容由被委托单位填写）

代理报检企业章		委托单位章及其法人代表章	

QUALITY CERTIFICATE

中华人民共和国出入境检验检疫

ENTRY - EXIT INSPECTION AND QUQRANTINE

OF THE PEOPLE'S REPUBLIC OF CHINA

品质检验证书

QUALITY CERTIFICATE

编号

No.:

发货人:

Consignor

收货人:

Consignee

品名:

Description of Goods

标记及号码

Mark & No.

报验数量/重量:

Quantity/Weight Declared

包装种类及数量:

Number and Type of Packages

运输工具:

Means of Conveyance

检验结果:

Results of Inspection

我们已尽所知和最大能力实施上述检验，不能因我们签发本证书而免除买方或其他方面根据合同和法律所承担的产品质量责任和其他责任。

All inspections are carried out conscientiously to the best of our knowledge and ability. This certificate does not in any respect absolve the seller and other related parties from his contractual and legal obligations especially when product quality is concerned.

进口商品检验证书

中华人民共和国上海进出口商品检验局
SHANGHAI IMPORT & EXPORT COMMODITY INSPECTION BUREAU
OF THE PEOPLE'S REPUBLIC OF CHINA

地址：上海市中山东一路 13 号　　　　No.
Address：13，Zhongshan Road
(E. 1), Shanghai

检　验　证　书
INSPECTION CERTIFICATE

日期
Date

电话：
Tel：8621 - 32155296

受 货 人：
Consignee：
发 货 人：
Consignor：
品　名：
Commodity：
报验数量/重量：
Quantity/Weight
Declared：
运　输：
Transportation：
进口日期：
Date of Arrival：
卸毕日期：
Date of Completion
of Discharge：
发 票 号：
Invoice No.：
合 同 号：
Contract No.：
标记及号码：
Mark & No.：

注意：本证书译文如有任何异点，概以中文为主。
(N. B. In case if divergence, the Chinese text shall be regarded as authentic)

兽医检验证书

中华人民共和国上海进出口商品检验局

SHANGHAI IMPORT & EXPORT COMMODITY INSPECTION BUREAU

OF THE PEOPLE'S REPUBLIC OF CHINA

地址：上海市中山东一路13号 No.

Addressa：13，Zhongshan Road

(E.1)，Shanghai

检 验 证 书

INSPECTION CERTIFICATE

日期

Date

电话：

Tel：8621－32155296

发 货 人：

Consignor：______________________________

受 货 人：

Consignee：______________________________

品 名：

Commodity ____________

标记及号码：

Mark & No.

报验数量/重量：

Quantity/Weight

Declared ________________

官方兽医证明如下：

1．the undersigned Official Veterinarian，certify that：

主 任 兽 医

Chief Veterinarian

中华人民共和国海关进口货物报关单

中华人民共和国海关进口货物报关单

预录入编号：　　　　　　　　　　海关编号：

进口口岸	备案号	进口日期		申报日期
经管单位	运输方式	运输工具名称		提运单号
收货单位	贸易方式	征免性质		征税比例
许可证号	起运国（地区）	装货港		境内目的地
批准文号	成交方式	运费	保费	杂费
合同协议号	件数	包装种类	毛重（公斤）	净重（公斤）
集装箱号	随附单据			用途
标记唛码及备注				

项号	商品编号	商品名称、规格型号	数量及单位	原产国(地区)	单价	总价	币制	征免

税费征收情况

兹声明以上申报无讹并承担法律责任 录入员　录入单位 报关员	海关审单批注及放行日期（签章） 审单　　审价
	征税　　统计
单位地址　　申报单位（签章） 邮编　　电话　　填制日期	查验　　放行

中华人民共和国海关出口货物报关单

中华人民共和国海关出口货物报关单

预录入编号：　　　　　　　　　　　　海关编号：

<table>
<tr><td>出口口岸</td><td>备案号</td><td colspan="2">出口日期</td><td>申报日期</td></tr>
<tr><td>经管单位</td><td>运输方式</td><td colspan="2">运输工具名称</td><td>提运单号</td></tr>
<tr><td>发货单位</td><td>贸易方式</td><td colspan="2">征免性质</td><td>结汇方式</td></tr>
<tr><td>许可证号</td><td>运抵国（地区）</td><td colspan="2">指运港</td><td>境内货源地</td></tr>
<tr><td>批准文号</td><td>成交方式</td><td>运费</td><td>保费</td><td>杂费</td></tr>
<tr><td>合同协议号</td><td>件数</td><td>包装种类</td><td>毛重（公斤）</td><td>净重（公斤）</td></tr>
<tr><td>集装箱号</td><td colspan="3">随附单据</td><td>生产厂家</td></tr>
<tr><td colspan="5">标记唛码及备注</td></tr>
<tr><td colspan="5">项号　商品编号　商品名称、规格型号　数量及单位　最终目的国(地区)单价　总价　币制　征免</td></tr>
<tr><td colspan="5"></td></tr>
<tr><td colspan="5"></td></tr>
<tr><td colspan="5"></td></tr>
<tr><td colspan="5"></td></tr>
<tr><td colspan="5"></td></tr>
<tr><td colspan="5">税费征收情况</td></tr>
<tr><td colspan="3" rowspan="3">兹声明以上申报无讹并承担法律责任

录入员　录入单位
报关员

单位地址　　　　　　　　申报单位（签章）

邮编　　　电话　　　填制日期</td><td colspan="2">海关审单批注及放行日期（签章）
审单　　　　审价</td></tr>
<tr><td colspan="2">征税　　　　统计</td></tr>
<tr><td colspan="2">查验　　　　放行</td></tr>
</table>

中华人民共和国海关专用缴款书格式

海关　　专用缴款书

收入系统　　　　填发日期：　　年　月　日　　　　号码 No.

收款单位	收入机关			缴款单位	名称	
	科目		预算级次		账号	
	收款国库				开户银行	

税号	货物名称	数量	单位	完税价格（¥）	税率（%）	税款金额（¥）
金额人民币（大写）					合计（¥）	

申请单位编号		报关单编号		填制单位	收款国库（银行）
合同（批文）号		运输工具（号）			
缴款期限		提/装货单号		制单人________ 复核人________	
备注					

从填发缴款书之日起限 15 日内缴款（期末遇法定节假日顺延），逾期按日征收税款总额千分之一的滞纳金。

海关　　专用缴款书

收入系统　　　　填发日期：　　年　月　日　　　　号码 No.

收款单位	收入机关			缴款单位	名称	
	科目		预算级次		账号	
	收款国库				开户银行	

税号	货物名称	数量	单位	完税价格（¥）	税率（%）	税款金额（¥）
金额人民币（大写）					合计（¥）	

申请单位编号		报关单编号		填制单位	收款国库（银行）
合同（批文）号		运输工具（号）			
缴款期限		提/装货单号		制单人________ 复核人________	
备注					

从填发缴款书之日起限 15 日内缴款（期末遇法定节假日顺延），逾期按日征收税款总额千分之一的滞纳金。

进出口货物代理报关委托书

进出口货物代理报关委托书

编号：

委托单位		十位编码	
地　　址		联系电话	
经 办 人		身份证号	

我单位委托__________________公司代理以下进出口货物的报关手续，保证提供的报关资料真实、合法，与实际货物相符，并愿承担由此产生的法律责任。

货物名称		商品编号		件　数	
重　　量		价　　值		币　制	
贸易性质		货物产地		合同号	
是否退税		船名/航次			

委托单位 开户银行		账　号	

随附单证名称、份数及编号：

1. 合同	份：	6. 机电证明	份、编号：
2. 发票	份：	7. 商检证	份：
3. 装箱清单	份：	8.	
4. 登记手册	本、编号：　　　　；	9.	
5. 许可证	份、编号：　　　　；	10.	

（以上内容由委托单位填写）

被委托单位		十位编码	
地　　址		联系电话	
经 办 人		身份证号	

（以上内容由被委托单位填写）

代理（专业） 报关企业章及 法人代表章		委托单位章及法人代表章：	

年　　月　　日

Glossary

abandonment	弃船，弃货	7
acceleration clause	加速条款，提前条款	8
acceptance	接受（报盘）	2
acceptance	承兑	8
actual/real tare	实际皮重	4
actual delivery (physical delivery)	实际交货	3
actual total loss	实际全损	7
ad valorem	从价运费	6
additional for alternation of destination	变更卸港附属费	6
additional on direct	直航附属费	6
additional on optional discharging port	选择港附属费	6
additionals	附属费	6
advanced B/L	预签提单	6
advising bank	通知行	8
aflatoxin risk	黄曲霉素险	7
air express	航空急件运送	6
air transport	航空运输	6
air waybill	空运单	6
airway bill	航空运单	9
All Risks	一切险	7
Antedated B/L	倒签提单	6
anticipatory credit	预支信用证	8
appeal	上诉	10
applicant	开证申请人	8
appreciation	（货币）升值	8
appropriation	划拨，分拨	3
arbitral/arbitration award	仲裁裁决	10
arbitral/arbitration tribunal	仲裁法庭	10
arbitration	仲裁，公断	10
arbitration agreement	仲裁协议	10

arbitration body	仲裁机构	10
arbitration clause	仲裁条款	10
arbitration fee	仲裁费	10
arbitration hearing	仲裁审理	10
arbitration law	仲裁法	10
arbitration panel/panel of arbitration	仲裁委员会	10
arbitrator/arbiter	仲裁员	10
arrival contract	到货合同	3
auction	拍卖	4
authentication	认证，证明	8
aval	票据保证，付款保证	8
average tare	平均皮重	4
award	裁决	10
banker's acceptance draft	银行承兑汇票	8
banker's draft	银行汇票	8
barcode	条形码	4
barter trade	易货贸易	1
base ports	基本港	6
basic freight	基本运费	6
basic rate	基本费率	6
bearer B/L	不记名提单	6
beneficiary	受益人	8
bid	递盘	2
bill of exchange	汇票	8
bill of exchange（draft）	汇票	9
blank endorsement	空白背书	6
breach	违反，中断，中止	10
breach of contract	违反合同，违约	10
Breakage of Packing Damage	包装破裂险	7
British system	英制	4
Bulk cargo	散装货	6
Bulky cargo additional	超大附属费	6
Bunker surcharge	燃油附加费	6
Buying offer	买方询盘	2
carriage	运费，运输	3
carrier	承运人	3
case number	箱号	3
certificate of Loss/certificate of survey	海损证书	9

certificate of origin	原产地证明书	9
CFS (container freight station)	集装箱货运站	6
charter (tramp)	不定期货船	6
charter party	租船契约	6
charter party B/L	租船提单	6
charter transport	租船运输	6
chartered carriers	包机运输	6
cheque	支票	8
claim	索赔	10
claim for compensation	要求赔偿	10
claim letter	索赔书	10
claim settlement	理赔	10
claimant	索赔人	10
Claimee	被索赔人	10
Claims document	索赔文件，索赔单据	10
Claims expenses	索赔费用	10
clean B/L	清洁提单	6
clean bill	光票	8
clean collection	光票托收	8
clean credit	光票信用证	8
collecting bank	代收行	8
collection	托收	8
collective packing	集合运输包装	4
combined certificate	联合凭证	7
combined certificate	联合凭证	9
commercial documents	商业单据	9
commercial draft	商业汇票	8
commercial invoice	商业发票	9
commission	佣金	5
comparative advantage	比较优势	1
competent court	主管法院	10
computed tare	约定皮重	4
concluded price	成交价	5
condemnation	没收，充公	7
conditioned weight	公量	4
conference liner vessel	同盟/工会定期	6
confirmed L/C	保兑信用证	8
confirming bank	保兑行	8

confirming sample	确认样	4
confiscate	没收，充公	7
consideration	对价	8
consignment	寄售	4
consignment note	货物承运收据	9
consolidated consignment	集中托运	6
constructive total loss	推定全损	7
consular invoice	领事发票	9
container B/L	集装箱提单	6
container transport (containerization)	集装箱（货柜）运输	6
containerization	集装箱运输	6
contract of carriage	运输合同	3
contract of insurance	保险合同	3
copy B/L	副本提单	6
correspondent bank	关系行	8
corrosive goods	腐蚀性物品	4
counter - offer	还盘	2
counter sample	回样/对等样	4
country of origin	原产国	4
credit check	资信调查	8
credit L/G	信用保函	8
credit reference	资信证明	1
credit risk	信用风险	8
currency risk	货币风险	8
currency surcharge	货币贬值附加费	6
Customary practice	惯例	3
customary tare	习惯皮重	4
customs clearance	清关	3
customs declaration for export commodity	出口货物报关单	9
customs invoice	海关发票	9
CY (container yard)	集装箱堆场	6
D/P after sight	远期付款交单	8
D/P at sight	即期付款交单	8
days/running days/consecutive days	连续日	6
dead freight	空仓费	6
deductible franchise	绝对免赔率	7
default	违约，拖欠	8
defendant	被告	10

deferred payment	延期付款	8
delivery	交货	3
demand draft （D/D）	即期汇票	8
demise/bareboat charter	光租船	6
demurrage	滞期费	6
depreciation	（货币）贬值	8
deviation surcharge	绕道附加费	6
direct B/L	直航提单	6
direct trade	直接贸易	1
direct transit trade	直接过境贸易	1
discount	折扣，贴现	5
dishonor	拒付，拒兑	8
dispatch （money）	速遣费	6
dispute	争议，纠纷	10
disputing parties	争议当事人	10
division of responsibilities, risks and costs	责任、风险和费用的划分	3
Do not stow on deck.	勿装甲板上	5
Documentary bill	跟单汇票	8
Documentary collection	跟单托收	8
documentary letter of credit	跟单信用证	8
documents against acceptance （D/A）	承兑交单	8
documents against payment （D/P）	付款交单	8
documents for payment settlement	结汇单据	9
domestic cost	国内成本	5
domestic documents	国内单据	9
domestic trade	国内贸易	1
draw on sb.	向某人开立汇票	8
drawee	受票人	8
drawer	出票人	8
economies of scale	规模经济	1
endorsement	背书	8
endorsement	保险更改批单	9
enquiry	询盘	2
entrepot trade	转口贸易	1
Entry · Exit Inspection and Quarantine of the People's Republic of China 中华人民共和国出入境检验检疫		9
exclusions	除外责任	7
exhibition sale	展卖	4

explosive goods	爆炸品	4
Export Commodity inspection Application	出境货物报检单	9
Export Commodity Statement	出口货物清单	9
Export cost for foreign exchange（ECFE）	出口换汇成本	5
Export factor	出口保理商	8
Export financing	出口融资	8
Export license	出口许可证	9
Export profit margin	出口盈亏率	5
Export trade	出口贸易	1
external/extraneous risks	外来风险	7
F. I. （free in）	船方管卸不管装	6
F. I. O. （free in and out）	船方不管装卸	6
F. I. O. S. T. （free in and out，stowed and trimmed） 船方不管装卸、理舱和平舱		6
F. O. （free out）	船方管装不管卸	6
Failure to Delivery Risk	交货不到险	7
FAQ（fair average quality）	良好平均品质	5
FCL（full container load）	整装箱	6
FEU（forty-foot equivalent unit）	40 英尺标准箱	6
Final price	最终价格	5
Finance documents	金融单据	9
Fire Risk Extension Clause	火险责任扩张险	7
firm/definite offer	实盘	2
fixed price	固定价格	5
flexible container	集装袋	4
fluctuation of exchange rate	汇率波动	8
force majeure	不可抗力	10
foreign document	外贸单据	9
forfeiter	包买商	8
forfeiting	福费庭，包买票据	8
formalities	手续	3
FPA（Free from Particular Average）	平安险	7
fragile	易碎	4
franchise	免赔率	7
free－liquidation trade	自由结算贸易	1
freight	海运费	3
freight prepaid B/L	运费预付提单	6
freight rates	运费率	6

freight to collect B/L	运费到付提单	6
freight ton	运费吨	6
Fresh Water Rain Damage	淡水雨淋险	7
GA contribution	共同海损分摊	7
General average	共同海损	7
General export trade	一般出口贸易	1
general import trade	一般进口贸易	1
general risks	一般外来风险	7
general trade	一般贸易	1
Generalized System of Preferences Certificate of Origin 普惠制原产地证明书		9
GMQ（good merchantable quality）	上好可销品质	4
Gross for Net	以毛作净	4
Gross weight	毛重	4
guarantor	担保人	8
Handle with care.	小心轻放。	4
Hard currency	硬通货（币）	8
Heating and Sweating Risk	受热受潮险	7
Heavy lift additional	超重附属费	6
hedge	对冲，套期保值	8
honor the draft	支付（承兑）汇票	8
Hook Damage	钩损险	7
ICC（Institute Cargo Clauses）	协会货物保险条款	7
Import Duty Risk	进口关税险	7
Import factor	进口保理商	8
Import trade	进口贸易	1
Incoterms 2010	2010 年国际贸易术语解释通则	3
Indicative mark	指示性标志	4
Indirect trade	间接贸易	1
Indirect transit trade	间接过境贸易	1
Industry norms	行业惯例	8
Inherent vice	内在缺陷	7
initial price	最初价格	5
inland water transport	内河运输	6
inner package	内包装	4
insolvency	无偿付能力	8
inspection	检查，检验	10
inspection bureau	检验局	10

inspection certificate	检验证书	10
inspection certificate of disinfection	消毒检验证书	9
inspection certificate of fumigation	熏蒸证书	9
inspection certificate of health	卫生检验证书	9
inspection certificate of quality	品质检验证书	9
inspection certificate of quantity	数量检验证书	9
inspection certificate of weight	重量检验证书	7
insurable interest principle	可保利益原则	7
insurance application form	投保单	9
Insurance certificate	保险凭证	7
Insurance claim	保险索赔	7
Insurance cover （age）	保险险别	7
Insurance documents	保险单据	9
Insurance policy	保险单	7
Insurance premium	保险费	7
Insurance rate	保险费率	7
Insured amount/insurance amount	保险金额	7
insurer	保险人	7
International Chamber of Commerce （1CC）	国际商会	3
International Combined Transport （1CT）	国际联合运输	6
International Multimodal Transport （1MT）	国际多式联运	6
International System of Units	国际单位制	4
International trade	国际贸易	1
Invisible trade/intangible goods trade	无形贸易	1
10P （inspective of percentage）	不计免赔率	7
Irrevocable L/C	不可撤销信用证	8
irrevocable offer	不可撤销发盘	2
issuance of a letter of credit	开信用证	8
issuing bank	开证行	8
Keep away from heat.	远离热源。	5
L/C amendment	信用证改证	8
L/C negotiation	信用证议付	8
L/C settlement	信用证结算	8
Land bridge transport	大陆桥运输	6
Lay day	装卸天数	6
Lay time	装卸时间	6
LCL （less than container load）	拼装箱	6
legal weight	法定重量	4

lengthy cargo additional	超长附属费	6
letter of guarantee（L/G）	保函	8
liner B/L	班轮提单	6
liner transport	班轮运输	6
liner/gross terms	班轮条件（船方管装卸费）	
liquidity	流动性，清偿能力	8
litigant	诉讼当事人	10
litigation	诉讼	10
litigation cost	诉讼费	10
loading & unloading charge	装卸费	6
long form B/L	全式提单	6
lot number/batch number	批号	5
mail transfer（M/T）	信汇	8
marine surveyor/adjuster	海损理算师	7
master's protest	船长海事报告	7
material price index	原材料价格指数	5
Mate's Receipt	大副收据	9
Means of transport	运输工具	3
Measurement（T）on	尺码吨	6
mediation	调停，调解	10
mediation board	调解委员会	10
mediator	调解员	10
metric system	公制	4
minimum cover/coverage	最低限度的险别	7
Ministry of Commerce（MOFCOM）	商务部	3
Mode of transport	运输方式	3
Money of account	计价货币	5
Money of payment	支付货币	5
More or less clause	溢短装条款	5
MTD（multimodal transport document）/CTD（combined transport document）多式联运提单		6
MTO（multimodal transport operator）/CTO（combined transport operator）多式联运经营人		6
multimodal transport/combined transport	多式联运	3
natural calamity	自然灾害	7
negotiating bank	议付行	8
negotiation	谈判	10
net weight	实物净重	4

net price	净价	5
net weight	净重	4
neutral packing	中性包装	4
non-transferable L/C	不可转让信用证	8
non-conference liner vessel	非同盟/工会定期船	6
non-deductible franchise	相对免赔率	7
non-firm offer	虚盘	2
non-statutory inspection	非法定检验	10
nude cargo	裸装货	4
obligation	义务	3
ocean（sea）transport	海洋运输	6
ocean bill of lading（B/L）	海运提单	6
offer	发盘，报盘	2
offeree	受盘者	2
offerer	发盘者	2
on board bill of lading（shipped B/L）	已装船提单	6
on deck B/L	舱面提单	6
On Deck Risk	舱面险	7
Open account	赊账交易	8
Open credit	自由议付信用	8
Open policy	预约保单	7
Open rate	议价运费	6
Optional port	选择港	6
Order B/L	指示提单	6
Original B/L	正本提单	6
Outer package	外包装	4
Packed cargo	包装货	4
Packing list	装箱单	9
Packing loan	打包放款	8
pallet	托盘	4
parcel post receipt	邮包收据	9
parcel post transport	邮包运输	6
partial loss	部分损失	7
partial shipments	分批装运	6
particular average	单独海损	7
payee	收款人	8
payer	付款人	8
payment by installments	分期付款	8

payment in advance	预付	8
payment instrument	支付工具	8
payment L/G	付款保函	8
payment terms	支付方式	8
penalty clause	罚金条款	10
per B/L/minimum rate	按提单计收运费/最低运费	6
perils of the sea	海上风险	7
perishable goods	易腐烂商品	5
Phytosanitary Certificate	植物检疫证书	9
plaintiff	原告	10
poisonous goods	有毒物品	5
port congestion surcharge	港口拥挤附加费	6
port of destination	目的港	6
port of shipment	装运港	6
Port Surcharge	港口附加费	6
premises	场所	3
presentation	提示	8
presenting / collecting bank	代收行	8
price adjustment clause	价格调整条款	5
price including commission	含佣价	5
principal	委托人	8
Principle of indemnity	赔偿原则	7
Proforma invoice	形式发票	9
Promissory note	本票	8
Proposal form	投保单	7
Proximate cause principle	近因原则	7
Purchase price	购买价	5
Quality certificate	质检证	9
Quality control（Q. C.）	质检	3
Quality latitude	品质机动幅度	4
Quality tolerance	品质公差	4
Quantity discount	数量折扣	5
Quantity latitude	数量机动幅度	4
quotation	报价	5
radioactive substances	放射性物质	4
rail（way）transport	铁路运输	6
rebate	回扣	5
receivables	应收账款	8

received for shipment B/L	备运提单	6
reciprocal credit	对开信用证	8
recourse	追索权	8
red clause credit/anticipatory credit	红条款信用证	8
reference sample	参考样	4
regain	回潮率	4
reimbursing bank	偿付行	8
Rejection Risk	拒收险	7
remittance	汇付	8
remitter	汇款人	8
remitting bank	托收行	8
revocable L/C	可撤销信用证	8
revocation of an offer	撤销发盘	2
revolving credit	循环信用证	8
right of recourse	追索权	7
Risk of clash and breakage	破碎碰损险	7
Risk of intermixture and contamination 沾	污混杂险	7
Risk of breakage	渗漏险	7
Risk of odor	串味险	7
Risk of rust	生锈险	7
Risk of shortage	短量险	7
Road transport	陆路运输	6
SRCC（strikes，riots and civil commotions）	罢工、暴动、民变险	7
sale by actual commodity	凭实际货物买卖	4
sale by actual quality	凭实际品质买卖	4
sale by descriptions or illustrations	凭说明书或图样买卖	4
sale by grade	凭等级买卖	4
sale by origin	凭产地名称买卖	4
sale by sample	凭样品买卖	4
sale by specifications	凭规格买卖	4
sale by standard	凭标准买卖	4
sale by trade mark or brand name	凭商标或品牌买卖	4
sales contract	销售合同	2
sales package	销售包装	4
scheduled airlines	班机运输	6
sea way transport	海洋运输	3
sea waybill	海运单	6
selling offer	卖方询盘	2

Share Principle	分摊原则	7
Shipment contract	装运合同	3
Shipment notice	装船通知	3
Shipping advice	装船（运）通知	9
Shipping mark	运输标志	5
Shipping note	订舱单	9
Shipping package	运输包装	4
Shipping sample	装船样	4
Short form B/L	简式提单	6
Sight draft	即期汇票	8
Sight L/C	即期信用证	8
Single unit packing	单件运输包装	4
special discount	特别折扣	5
special endorsement	记名背书	6
special export trade	特殊出口贸易	1
special import trade	特殊进口贸易	1
special risks	特殊外来风险	7
stale B/L	过期提单	6
standby L/C	备用信用	8
statutory inspection	法定检验	10
stow	理舱	3
straight B/L	记名提单	6
straight credit	限制议付信用证	8
subject matter insured	保险标的	7
Subrogation Principle	代位求偿权原则	7
subscription	订金	7
summary procedure	简易程序	10
surcharge	附加费	6
symbolic delivery	象征性交货	3
TPND（theft, pilferage and non-delivery）	偷窃、提货不着险	7
tare	皮重	4
telegraphic transfer（T/T）	电汇	8
tenor	汇票期限	8
TEU（twenty-foot equivalent unit）	20 英尺标准箱	6
The China International Economic and Trade Arbitration Commission（CIETAC） 中国国际经济贸易仲裁委员会		10
The insured/insurant/assured	被保险人	7
The Revised American Foreign Trade Definitions 1951（RAFD）		

	1951 年美国对外贸易定义修订本	3
theoretical weight	理论重量	4
This side up	此面向上	4
Through B/L	联运提单	6
Time charter	期租船	6
Time Of delivery	交货期	6
Time of shipment	装运期	6
time/usance draft	远期汇票	8
title document/document of title	物权凭证	8
total loss	全部损失	7
total price	总价	5
trader's acceptance draft	商业承兑汇票	8
transfer of risk	风险转移	3
transferable L/C	可转让信用证	8
transit trade	过境贸易	1
transportation documents	运输单据	9
transshipment	转船	6
transshipment B/L	转船提单	6
transshipment surcharge	转船附加费	6
tribunal	法庭	10
trim	平舱	3
U. S. system	美制	4
Unclean B/L (foul B/L, dirty B/L)	不洁提单	6
Use no hook.	勿用手钩	4
Utmost Good Faith Principle	最大诚信原则	7
Valued policy	定值保险单	7
variant	变形	3
verdict	裁决	10
veterinary inspection certificate	兽医证明	9
visible trade/tangible goods trade	有形贸易	1
voyage charter	程租船	6
W/W clause (warehouse to warehouse clause)	仓至仓条款	7
Wage index	工资指数	5
War Risks	战争险	7
Warning mark	警告性标志	4
Weather working days of 24 consecutive hours	连续 24 小时好天气工作日	6
Weather working days of 24 hours	累计 24 小时好天气工作日	6
Weight memo	重量单	9

Weight ton (WT/W)	重量吨	6
With Particular Average (WPA)	水渍险	7
Withdrawal of an offer	撤回	2

References

[1] Alan E. Branch. Export Practice and Management [M]. Fifth Edition. 北京：清华大学出版社, 2008.

[2] Dennis R. Appleyard, Alfred J. field, Jr. , Steven L. Cobb. International Trade [M]. 2nd Edition. Mc Graw - hill Education, 2008.

[3] James Gerber. World Economics [M]. Fourth Edition. Pearson Education, 2008.

[4] Kitty O. Locker, Donna S. Kienzler. Business and Administrative Communication [M]. Eighth Edition. Mc Graw - hill Education, 2008.

[5] Michael R. Czinkota, Ilkka A. Ronkainen, Michael H. Moffett. International Business [M]. Sixth Edition. South - western Thomson Learning, 2002.

[6] 程铭. 国际贸易实务 [M]. 上海：上海大学出版社, 2006.

[7] 高运胜. 国际贸易实务 [M]. 上海：华东师范大学出版社, 2011.

[8] 惠丰廷. 国际贸易实务 [M]. 北京：经济科学出版社, 2011.

[9] 胡丽华. 国际贸易实务 [M]. 长沙：中南大学出版社, 2011.

[10] 冷柏军. 国际贸易实务 [M]. 北京：北京大学出版社, 2009.

[11] 黎孝先, 石玉川. 国际贸易实务 [M]. 北京：对外经济贸易大学出版社, 2008.

[12] 齐俊妍, 唐丽. 简明国际国际贸易实务（英文版）[M]. 北京：清华大学出版社, 2010.

[13] 阮绩智. 国际贸易实务 [M]. 杭州：浙江大学出版社, 2008.

[14] 帅建林. 国际贸易实务（英文版）[M]. 北京：对外经济贸易大学出版社, 2007.

[15] 帅建林. 国际贸易惯例案例解析 [M]. 北京：对外经济贸易大学出版社, 2006.

[16] 许葵花. 国际贸易英语教程（第二版）[M]. 西安：西安交通大学出版社, 2009.

[17] 薛荣久. 国际贸易 [M]. 北京：对外经济贸易大学出版社, 2008.

[18] 吴百福, 徐小薇. 进出口贸易实务 [M]. 上海：上海人民出版社, 2007.

[19] 周瑞琪. 国际贸易实务（英文版）[M]. 北京：对外经济贸易大学出版, 2008.

[20] 周瑞琪. 国际贸易实务（英文版）辅导用书 [M]. 北京：对外经济贸易大学

出版社，2008.

[21] 周维家，葛萍．国际贸易专业英语（双语）[M]．上海：复旦大学出版社，2008.

[22] 周丽霞．国际贸易理论与实务 [M]．武汉：武汉理工大学出版社，2010.

[23] 赵宏，杨春梅．国际贸易实务（英文）[M]．北京：中国铁道出版社，2009.

[24] 张琦生，马朝阳．国际贸易实务 [M]．北京：中国商务出版社，2009.